PRODUCT DESIGN

Resistant Materials Technology

2nd Edition

Lesley Cresswell
Barry Lambert
Alan Goodier

Edexcel
Success through qualifications

Heinemann

Heinemann Educational Publishers
Halley Court, Jordan Hill, Oxford OX2 8EJ
Part of Harcourt Education

Heinemann is a registered trademark of Harcourt
Education Limited

© Lesley Cresswell, Barry Lambert, Alan Goodier,
2003

First published in 2000
Second edition 2003

08 07 06
10 9 8 7 6 5 4

British Library Cataloguing in Publication Data is
available from the British Library on request.

10-digit ISBN: 0 435757 69 5
13-digit ISBN: 978 0 435757 69 4

Copyright notice

Edited by Rebecca Harman
Designed by Wendi Watson
Typeset by 𝍐 Tek-Art, Croydon, Surrey
Printed and bound in Great Britain by Scotprint

Original illustrations © Harcourt Education Limited
2003

Illustrated by 𝍐 Tek-Art, Croydon, Surrey
Picture research by Peter Morris

Acknowledgements

The authors would like to thank Parul Patel and
Peter Neale at Edexcel for their valuable guidance
and support. For their kind assistance in providing
artwork and coursework in the making of this
publication, a special thanks to students L. Arnold,
L. Byat, C. Crossley, R. Door, A. Hodson, A. Hunt,
J. McCraith, A. Malloy, J. Manington, C. Romenuik
and C. Travis.

The authors would like to thank the following for
permission to reproduce copyright material:

British Standards Institute (BSI) for the BSI
kitemark and CE marking on p.36, and BSI
anthropometric data on p.119 from the
Compendium of Essential Design and Technology
Standards for Schools and Colleges. Envirowise for
photos and logo from the Environmental
Technology Best Practice Programme Publication
CH115 (February 1998) appearing on pp.226, 229;
Penguin Books Ltd for diagrams adapted from
Metals in the Service of Man, 11th edition, by Arthur
Street and William Alexander (Penguin Science)
©1995 appearing on pp.194; HarperCollins for dia-
grams adapted from *GCSE D&T Technology* by P.
Fowler and M. Horsley (Collins Educational) ©
1998 appearing on pp.272, 281.

The authors would like to thank the following for
permission to reproduce photographs:
Alamy p.103 (right); Alessi Modus p.29; Apple
Macintosh p.96; Art Archive p.180 (top left); Art
Directors & Trip/H Rogers p.38, 89 (left), 186 (2nd
from bottom); Art Directors & Trip/J Wender p.66;
AVAD p.227; Baygen p.108; Beauleau Motor
Museum p.218; Bettman/Corbis p.105 (bottom);
Black & Decker p.110; BOSCH p.221; Boxford Ltd
p.145 (all), 147; Bridgeman Art Library p.105 (top
left); Chris Honeywell p.186 (middle); Christies
p.104, 106 (bottom), 115 (top), 180 (right), 181
(bottom); Cooper-Hewitt Museum p.106 (top);
Corbis p.85 (left), 90 (top), 97 (left), 102, 103
(left), 116 (bottom left), 207, 222, 225, 242 (top),
246, 248, 295; Craft Space Touring p.208;
Crocodile Clips p.131; Denford Ltd p.126, 136,
238, 259; Design Council/Manchester
Metropolitan University p.182; Dorling Kindersley
p.105 (top right); Envirowise p.226 (top); Fenichi
p.23; Ford p.120; Getty/Taxi p.27; Gareth Boden
p.43, p.48, p.90 (bottom left), 91 (both), 193, 291
(all); Giles Chapman p.89 (left), 128; Hemera
Photo Objects p.40; Henry Moore Foundation
p.116 (bottom); Hulton Archive p.97 (right); John
Walmsley p.85 (right); Mitutoyo p.242 (top), 263;
Olivetti p.114 (bottom); Peter Morris p.13, 28, 184
(both) 186 (top); PhotoDisc p.90 (bottom right),
186 (2nd from top), 188; Prima p.18, 26, 36;
PSION p.98 (top); Robert Bircher p.25, 127; Rex
Features p.98 (bottom); SABA p.117; Science
Photo Library p.112, 191; Peter Menzel p.304;
Science & Society Picture Library p.99; Techsoft
p.139 (top), 140, 142 (both), 143 (both); The Croc
p.130, 138, 139 (bottom), 261; Thomas Dobbie
p.107; Tudor Photography p.44, 46, 49 (both), 50,
51, 53, 54, 55, 58, 61, 62, 296, 299, 300, 302, 203,
306, 307, 308, 310, 312, 313; V&A Picture Library
p.114 (top right), 115 (bottom), 116 (top), 186
(bottom); VK&C Enterprises p.17; Which p.211.

Cover photographs by Powerstock.

Every effort has been made to contact copyright
holders of material reproduced in this book. Any
omissions will be rectified in subsequent printings if
notice is given to the publishers.

Tel: 01865 888058 www.heinemann.co.uk

Contents

Unit 5 Product development II (R5)

Unit 6 Design and technology capability (R6)

Part 1

Introduction

This Advanced Design and Technology book is designed to support the Edexcel Advanced Subsidiary (AS) and Advanced GCE Specification for Product Design: Resistant Materials Technology.

The book follows the structure of the Specification and is intended to support you through the course. The content of the book will provide you with a great deal of knowledge and understanding and will help you prepare for assessment. As with any Advanced Level course you are advised to read around the subject to broaden your knowledge and understanding.

How to use this book

Part 1

Part 1 provides advice on how to use the book, explains how the course is structured and offers guidance on how to manage your own learning during the course. This includes advice on planning, organising and managing your work. You should read this section before starting your course.

Parts 2 and 3

Parts 2 and 3 provide unit-by-unit guidance on each of the AS Units 1–3 (Part 2) and the Advanced GCE Units 4–6 (Part 3). These sections will provide you with knowledge and understanding to help you through your course. They will also help you prepare for internal and external assessment and increase your chances of success. You should therefore refer to these sections of the book for guidance on the subject content and to help you understand how each unit is assessed.

Parts 2 and 3 also look at the structure, subject content and assessment requirements of the Edexcel Specification. Each of the three AS and three A2 units use similar headings and subheadings to those found in the Specification, so you know that you are covering the content of the course. Each unit is structured as shown in Table 1.1.

Tasks, questions and information appear throughout the text as follows:
- The tasks:
  - help you to understand issues such as industrial practices
  - give you practice in some aspect of designing or manufacturing
  - or help you practise specific skills, such as how to do market research or test the suitability of materials.
- 'Factfile' boxes contain information which may explain:
  - technical terms
  - or illustrate points in the text.
- 'Think about this!' boxes explain different issues, such as industrial practices, or 'values issues' which may influence your design decisions.
- 'To be successful you will …' boxes appear at the end of each section in the coursework units. They contain the assessment criteria that you will need to meet, in order to be successful.
- In A2 Units 4–6 you may find 'Signposts' to the AS units. These refer you back to information or topics that have been discussed in the AS course.

Table 1.1 Structure of book's AS/A2 units

Summary of expectations for the unit	Unit content	Student checklist/practice exam questions
The first page of the unit summarises: • what you are required to do • what you will learn • how the unit is assessed.	This covers the subject content in detail. It: • explains what you will learn in each unit • helps you understand the assessment requirements • provides tasks, questions and information to guide you through the unit.	The last page of the unit provides checklists and practice exam questions to help you: • check the progress of your coursework • revise for and prepare for the exams • be as successful as possible.

- The coursework Units 2 and 5 will provide many opportunities for you to generate evidence for your Key Skills portfolio. You may find it helpful to check out Key Skills requirements for Communication, Application of Number and Information Technology at Level 3.

- Technical terms are in bold when they first occur and are explained in context in the text. They also appear in a glossary on pages 333–43.

How the course is structured

There are three units at Advanced Subsidiary (AS) and three units at Advanced GCE (A2).

The AS units

The three AS units combine to make the AS course. The AS units:

- build on the knowledge, understanding and skills you developed through the study of GCSE Design and Technology
- provide a discrete course leading to an AS qualification, *or*
- provide the first half of the Advanced GCE course. The AS units contribute 50 per cent of the Specification content. You must follow the AS course before progressing to A2.

The A2 units

The A2 units combine with the three AS units to make the Advanced GCE course. The A2 units:

- build on the knowledge, understanding and skills developed in the AS course, to achieve the full Advanced GCE standard

- provide the other 50 per cent of the Specification content
- enable you to achieve a greater level of sophistication and more in-depth knowledge and understanding.

A summary of the AS and A2 units is provided in Table 1.2

How the AS units are assessed

Units 1 and 3 are externally assessed by examination. Unit 2 is the coursework unit. This is assessed by internal marking and external moderation by the Edexcel Moderator (see the summary in Table 1.3).

How the A2 units are assessed

Units 4 and 6 are externally assessed by examination. Unit 5 is the coursework unit. This is assessed by internal marking and external moderation by the Edexcel Moderator (see the summary in Table 1.4).

Table 1.2 *Summary of the AS and A2 units*

AS 50% of the Specification content		A2 50% of the Specification content	
Unit 1	Industrial and commercial products and and practices	Unit 4	Further study of materials, components and systems with options
Unit 2	Product development I	Unit 5	Product development II
Unit 3	Materials, components and systems with options	Unit 6	Design and technology capability

Table 1.3 *Assessment of Units 1–3*

AS 50% of the Specification content		Assessed by:	% of AS course	% of A2 course
Unit 1	Industrial and commercial products and practices	External assessment 1½-hour examination	30%	15%
Unit 2	Product development I	Internal assessment Coursework project	40%	20%
Unit 3	Materials, components and systems with options	External assessment 1½-hour examination	30%	15%

Table 1.4 Assessment of Units 4–6

A2 50% of the Specification content		Assessed by:	% of A2 course
Unit 4	Further study of materials, components and systems with options	External assessment 1½-hour examination	15%
Unit 5	Product development II	Internal assessment Coursework project	20%
Unit 6	Design and technology capability	External assessment 3-hour examination	15%

Unit guidance

The following section guides you through the three AS units and the three A2 units.

Unit 1 Industrial and commercial products and practices

This unit enables you to develop an understanding of industrial and commercial practices through product analysis. Throughout the unit you should investigate the design, manufacture, use and disposal of a range of products. The areas of study for Unit 1 include:

a Basic product specification: develop a product specification for a range of products
b Working characteristics of a range of materials and components
c Scale of production
d Manufacturing processes
e Quality
f Health and safety
g Product appeal

Throughout the unit you should undertake a variety of tasks to enable you to understand the subject content. For example, you could:

- work collaboratively with others on some investigative activities, e.g. when analysing a range of products
- work individually on some tasks, e.g. when developing creative communications skills to record the investigation of products (communications skills can include writing, drawing, sketching, graphics, charts, flow diagrams, systems diagrams, computer-aided design (CAD), modelling, etc.)
- work individually on the detailed analysis of products, to gain a personal understanding of product development and manufacture.

Assessment (written exam)

Unit 1 is assessed through a 1½-hour product analysis exam, which assesses your understanding of the unit subject content. The style of assessment remains the same each time the unit is assessed, but the product to be analysed will be different.

Unit 2 Product development I

Product development I is a full coursework project. Unit 2 builds on the knowledge, understanding and skills you gained during your GCSE coursework. At AS level you are expected to take a more commercial approach to designing and making a product, to meet needs that are wider than your own. This could mean designing and making a one-off product for a specified user or client, or designing and making a product that could be batch or mass-produced for users in a target market group.

When choosing an AS coursework project you should ensure that the project enables you to meet all the assessment criteria. Before you start your coursework you should refer to the section on Unit 2, which explains the assessment criteria in detail. As you work through your AS coursework project, refer to this section as and when you need.

Assessment (coursework project)

Your AS project should comprise a product and a coursework project folder. The project will be marked by your teacher or tutor and moderated by the Edexcel Moderator.

Unit 3 Materials, components and systems with options

This unit has two sections, both of which must be studied. Section A includes subject content related to resistant materials, components and systems.

Section B has three options, each with subject content. You must study one option from Section B. A summary of Unit 3 is given in Table 1.5.

Table 1.5 Unit 3 areas of study

Unit	Level	Components	Areas of study
3	AS	Section A: Materials, components and systems	• Classification of materials and components • Working properties and processes • Testing materials
		Section B: Options	• Design and technology in society • CAD/CAM • Mechanisms, energy and electronics

During the unit you should undertake a variety of tasks to enable you to understand the subject content. For example, you could:

- work individually on some activities, e.g. when using a database to research materials and components
- work individually on some tasks, e.g. when undertaking practical tasks to develop understanding of working properties and processes
- work collaboratively with others on some activities, e.g. when testing materials.

Assessment (written exam)

Unit 3 is assessed through a 1½-hour written exam which assesses your understanding of the unit subject content. You are required to answer two sections:

- Section A: Materials, components and systems
  Section A consists of short-answer, knowledge-based questions, worth a total of 30 marks. Examiners will look for a description, explanation or annotated sketch which show your understanding of the topic or process. You are advised to spend approximately 45 minutes on Section A.
- Section B: Options
  Section B consists of two compulsory questions, each worth 15 marks. You are expected to demonstrate understanding of the technology associated with the option studied. You are advised to spend approximately 45 minutes on Section B.

Unit 4 Further study of materials, components and systems with options

Unit 4 has two sections, both of which must be studied. Section A includes further subject content related to resistant materials, components and systems. Section B has three options, each with subject content. You must study the same option from Section B that you studied in Unit 3. A summary of Unit 4 is given in Table 1.6.

During the unit you should undertake a variety of tasks to enable you to understand the subject content. For example, you could:

- work individually on some tasks, e.g. when undertaking practical tasks to develop understanding of the relationship between properties and the selection of materials
- work individually on some activities, e.g. when using the Internet to research information about new technologies and new materials
- work collaboratively with others on some activities, e.g. when developing understanding of the impact that 'values issues' have on the design, development, use and disposal of a range of products.

Assessment (written exam)

Unit 4 is assessed through a 1½-hour written exam which assesses your understanding of the unit subject content. You are required to answer two sections:

Table 1.6 Unit 4 areas of study

Unit	Level	Components	Areas of study
4	A2	Section A: Further study of materials, components and systems	• Selection of materials • New technologies and the creation of new materials • Values issues
		Section B: Options	• Design and technology in society • CAD/CAM • Mechanisms, energy and electronics

- Section A: Materials, components and systems
  Section A is similar in style to Unit 3, consisting of short-answer knowledge-based questions, worth 30 marks. Examiners will look for a more in-depth response when describing or explaining topics or processes. You are advised to spend approximately 45 minutes on Section A.
- Section B: Options
  Section B is similar in style to Unit 3, consisting of two compulsory questions, each worth 15 marks. You are expected to demonstrate understanding of the technology associated with the option studied. You are advised to spend approximately 45 minutes on Section B.

Unit 5 Product development II

Product development II is a full coursework project. Unit 5 builds on the knowledge, understanding and skills that you gained during your AS coursework. At A2, you will need to work more independently, which may involve using a wider range of people to support you in your work.

At A2 you should take a commercial approach to designing and manufacturing, to meet needs that are wider than your own. This could mean designing and making a one-off product for a specified user or client, or designing and manufacturing a product that could be batch or mass-produced for users in a target market group. You will need to develop your A2 project in collaboration with potential users or with a client (such as a local business or organisation). You should make use of feedback from your user, client or target market group in order to access the full range of marks.

Your A2 project should demonstrate clear progression from the standard achieved at AS level. This can be achieved through demonstrating a higher level of 'design thinking':

- undertake research that targets more closely the problem/design brief
- select and use relevant research information
- make closer connections between research and the development of ideas
- use a higher level of understanding about materials, processes and manufacturing techniques

- demonstrate greater understanding of relevant technical terminology
- use higher level communication and presentation skills
- demonstrate appropriate use of ICT; including finding a balance between computer-generated images and those that are hand drawn.

Assessment (coursework project)

Your A2 project should comprise a product and a coursework project folder. The project will be marked by your teacher or tutor and moderated by the Edexcel Moderator, using the same assessment criteria as the AS project. Before you start your coursework you should refer to Unit 5, which explains the assessment criteria in detail. As you work through your A2 coursework project, refer to this section as and when you need.

Unit 6 Design and technology capability

This unit is called Design and technology capability because it assesses the knowledge, understanding and skills you have gained during your Advanced GCE course.

Unit 6 focuses on the designing and making process including knowledge and understanding of product development and manufacture. Since this knowledge and understanding is taught throughout the whole Advanced GCE course, no new learning is expected during Unit 6. However, it is essential that you review and revise what you have already learned and undertake exam practice in order to prepare fully for this exam.

Assessment (Design Paper)

- Your centre will be sent a Design Research Paper in March of the year of the exam. This will give you a context for design, together with bullet points that give you direction about what to research.
- In the three-hour Design Exam there will be one compulsory design question that is based on the research context. You will be asked to produce a design solution and describe how your solution can be manufactured.
- You may take all your research materials into the exam and use them as reference throughout, but the research material is not submitted for assessment.

Managing your own learning during the course

The purpose of this section is to help you take more responsibility for planning and managing your own work. This is an essential feature of any course that you will be undertaking at AS and Advanced GCE level. The ability to manage your own learning is an essential skill in higher education and is highly valued by employers.

In order that you may take responsibility for your work, you need to be very clear about what is expected of you during the course. This book aims to provide you with such information.

- Read the whole of Part 1 before you start the course, so you understand the course structure and the assessment requirements. It will also give you an overview of the requirements of each unit.
- Get to grips with the coursework projects that you need to produce and with the deadlines that you are required to meet. Investigate the coursework assessment and mark scheme.
- Before you start a unit, read the relevant 'Summary of expectations' in Parts 2 or 3. This will give you an understanding of the unit requirements and provide information about how each unit is assessed.

Taking responsibility for your own learning

Once you have a clear understanding of the course requirements, you can plan your time and your work. Taking responsibility for this will enable you to be more independent and take more responsibility for your own decisions. Being independent will require you to manage your own learning, develop project management skills and use a wide range of support beyond your teacher or tutor.

Project management

Learning to manage your work is called project management. This is an essential skill in higher education and in employment. Project management means knowing:

- what is required
- planning and setting targets
- managing time, resources, budgets and people
- monitoring progress and 'getting it right'.

In order that you manage your own projects successfully, you will need to develop the following:

- research skills
- communication skills

- an understanding of industrial and commercial practice
- ICT skills.

Research skills

You will need to use both primary and secondary research to help you design, develop and manufacture your product.

You can use primary research to identify:

- user preferences – such as buying behaviour, taste and lifestyle of target market groups
- market trends – such as style, design and colour trends
- existing products – using product analysis to investigate product design and manufacture.

You can use secondary research, including information from books, magazines, catalogues, databases, CD-ROMs or the Internet, to identify:

- existing products and price ranges
- information about materials, components, systems, processes, technology, production, quality and safety issues
- the work of other designers.

Communications skills

During your Design and Technology course you will need to apply a range of communications skills, such as the following:

- talking and listening to others
- reading, analysing and recording research information
- developing an understanding of form, function and design language
- drawing and sketching
- using professional practice – such as writing reports and presenting ideas to peers or clients.

Understanding industrial and commercial practice

You will be expected to develop an understanding of industrial approaches to design and manufacture during your course and to evidence them in your coursework. You will learn about industrial practices in Unit 1, but there are other approaches you could use to enhance this understanding. For example, you could:

- investigate work-related materials produced by a business
- use the expertise of visitors from business
- make an off-site visit to see a business at work
- use work experience to inform your understanding of how organisations work

- use modern contexts to develop products for real/imaginary companies, e.g. that project a brand image appropriate to a specific company or retailer
- use ICT to research information about products, e.g. finding out about materials, components, systems, processes, the way products are marketed, about company values.

You should evidence your understanding of industrial practices in AS and A2 coursework through the designing and manufacturing activities that you use to develop products. These may include:

- developing design briefs and specifications
- undertaking market research and product analysis
- generating, developing and evaluating ideas
- modelling and prototyping prior to manufacture
- producing a production plan
- testing against specifications.

In order to evidence industrial practices you should also use industrial-type terminology. To learn about this you should investigate the glossary on pages 333–43 and refer to the two coursework units in Part 2.

ICT skills

You should investigate how you could use ICT in your coursework projects and use it *where appropriate and available*. The use of ICT is assessed in the AS and A2 coursework projects, when developing and communicating design proposals; in planning manufacture and in product manufacture.

Currently, you will not be penalised for non-use of ICT. Where CAD is available, however, you should aim to find a balance between computer-generated images and those that are hand drawn. It will be essential to make use of your drawing skills in some of the exams, in particular in Unit 1 and Unit 6.

In order to enhance your Design and Technology capability you could investigate how you could use:

- ICT for research and communications – such as using the Internet, e-mail, video conferencing, digital cameras or scanners
- word processing, databases or spreadsheets for planning, recording, handling and analysing data
- CAD software to model, prototype, test and modify design proposals in 2D/3D
- computer-aided manufacture (CAM) for computer control, using CNC machines.

Part 2

Industrial and commercial products and practices (R1)

Summary of expectations

1. What to expect

This unit will develop your understanding of industrial and commercial practices through the investigation of a range of manufactured products. This will help you develop your understanding of product design, development and manufacture.

2. How will it be assessed?

The work that you do in this unit will be externally assessed through a 1½-hour Product Analysis examination. In the exam you will be given photographs and details of a resistant materials product. You will be required to analyse this product and answer seven specific questions about it. The style of questions will remain the same in each exam, so you will know what to expect. The product will be different in each exam, either a one-off, batch or mass produced product. The assessment criteria are set out in Table 1.1.

Table 1.1 Assessment criteria for Unit 1

Assessment criteria	Marks
A Outline the product design specification for this product.	7
B Justify the use of:	
i) material or component	3
ii) material or component.	3
C Give four reasons why this product is one-off, batch or mass produced.	4
D Describe the stages of production for the product. Include references to industrial manufacturing methods in your answer.	16
E Discuss quality issues for the product.	8
F Discuss the health and safety issues for this product.	8
G Discuss the appeal of the product.	8
H Quality of written communication	3
Total marks	60

3. What will be assessed?

a The following list summarises the topics covered in Unit 1 and what will be examined:

- Basic product specification: develop product design specifications for a range of products, under the following headings:
- purpose/function
- performance
- market
- aesthetics/characteristics
- quality standards
- safety.

b Working characteristics of a range of materials and components: understand that properties and working characteristics influence the choice of materials and components used in a range of products.

c Scale of production: understand that products are manufactured by different manufacturing systems.

d Manufacturing processes: understand how one-off, batch and high volume manufacture of products is achieved using:
- preparation
- processing
- assembly
- finish.

e Quality: understand the importance of quality of design and manufacture.
- quality control in production
- quality standards.

f Health and safety: understand the principles of health and safety legislation and good manufacturing practice.
- safe use of product
- safe procedures in production.

g Product appeal: influences on the design, production and sale of products:
- artistic, cultural, economic, environmental, ethical, moral, political and social influences
- influences of target market, market trends, style, colour, lifestyle, demographics
- aesthetics, performance and after-sales
- cost, i.e. value for money.

4. How to be successful in this unit

To be successful in this unit you will need to:

- analyse a range of manufactured products using the Assessment criteria in Table 1.1

- apply your knowledge and understanding to a given product in the exam
- give clear and concise answers, using bullet points with explanatory sentences
- use clear annotated diagrams where they make the answers clearer
- use specialist vocabulary, correct spelling and grammar.

5. How much is the unit worth?

This unit is worth a total of 30 per cent of your AS qualification. If you go on to complete the whole course, then this unit accounts for 15 per cent of the full Advanced GCE.

Unit 1	Weighting
AS level	30%
A2 level (full GCE)	15%

Understanding commercial products and industrial practices

This unit will help develop your understanding of products and the industrial and commercial practices by which they are manufactured. It will provide you with useful information about resistant materials, manufacturing processes, product assembly, quality and safety. In industry, product analysis includes the collection of data from catalogues and trade literature and the practical analysis of existing products, which may be own company products or those of a commercial rival. You will find product analysis very useful when you develop your own coursework product, because it is a good starting point for design. Product analysis enables designers to:

- evaluate the properties of the materials used in a product
- assess the product's fitness-for-purpose for a specific end-use
- see how well the product's characteristics and price meet user requirements
- evaluate the processes used to manufacture the product
- work out how the product was assembled
- examine the product's quality of design and manufacture
- find out why an own company product is selling or not selling as predicted
- see how and why a competitor's product is successful
- develop a product design specification and design ideas for a new product.

Developing a strategy for undertaking product analysis

Think about the last time you bought a new mobile phone or a portable CD player. When you shop for products such as these, you evaluate the function, style and value for money that such products provide. What you also do is to make value judgements about the product's quality of design and manufacture. This means that you are already well practised in judging the worth of a product from a user's point of view. You will now need to apply your product analysis skills in a more formal and objective way. This is best achieved by practice.

Developing product analysis skills

The key to developing product analysis skills is to look, examine and question. Looking at products will enable you to examine them by eye and by taking them apart. Asking questions about products should target what you need to

find out. It is important to investigate different types of products that have been manufactured by a range of production processes, different levels of production and from a variety of materials. This will involve analysing a selection of one-off, batch produced and high volume products. Remember to include actual physical products that you can handle as well as products from catalogues. It is important to undertake the following exam practice:

- practice developing design specifications for different types of products
- undertake short tasks and timed tasks based on each of the assessment criteria
- practice doing timed product analysis encompassing all of the assessment criteria.

Using the product analysis assessment criteria

The sections of this unit are organised around the structure of the assessment criteria (see Table 1.1). The sections will take you through each criterion, explaining what each involves, what you are expected to do and how many marks are awarded, so you know what to expect in the exam. Each section provides knowledge and understanding, so you can be sure that you are covering the required material about commercial products and industrial practices. It is worth remembering that in the exam, the assessment criteria (the questions you are asked) remain the same each time and it is only the product that is different. Your responses to all the assessment criteria will depend on the scale of production of the product.

Figure 1.1 In the Product Analysis exam you will be given photographs and details of a resistant materials product.

a) Outline the product design specification for the product (7 marks)

In the exam you will be asked to address at least four of the following:

* purpose/function
* performance
* market
* aesthetics/characteristics
* quality standards
* safety.

When you undertake product analysis during your course it is important to address all of the above specification headings. This will give you practice in developing meaningful product specification criteria. When you undertake product analysis during the end-of-unit exam you should use the given headings to help structure your answers. You will have the option of addressing all the specification criteria or concentrating on just four of them. The key to achieving all seven marks is to provide seven appropriate points, even if you are addressing only four of the headings. Each of your specification points needs to be justified, which means providing a fully explained answer. For example, for the purpose/function 'The hand blender should work as intended' needs more explanation, such as 'The hand blender should mix and blend food efficiently into small pieces.'

Factfile

In industry, a product design specification is an essential document that sets out the criteria for the development of a product. It is also used as a checklist against which the performance of the product can be measured. All product design specifications vary according to the type of product and its end-use. For example, the specification for a low cost hand blender would be different from that of an upmarket multifunctional food processor.

Purpose/function

In the exam paper you will be given photographs and details of a resistant materials product. You will need to take a few minutes to carefully study this information so you are clear about what you are being asked to respond to in the assessment questions.

The first product specification criteria asks you to define the purpose and function of the product by explaining:

* the aim or end-use of the product, e.g. 'A domestic iron with an electrically heated base, that converts water into steam. It can be used as a dry or steam iron to remove creases from clothes'
* how the product will be used or what it should do, e.g. 'A wind-up radio designed for use in less economically developed countries, to enable access to the media where there is no mains electricity and where batteries are too expensive.'

It is important that you fully explain (justify) the purpose and function of the product in order to gain the available marks.

Task

Choose a product with which you are familiar, such as a product that you use at home. Use the following questions to develop a specification for its purpose/function:

* What is the aim of this product?
* What is the need it provides for?
* What is the end-use of this product?
* Where, when and how will it be used?
* What benefits will it bring to the users?
* How does it fulfil its purpose?

Performance

In the product specification criteria you are asked to explain the performance requirements of the product, materials and components. Make sure that you read again the information given in the exam paper about the product and the materials and components it is made from. This will enable you to explain:

* how the product should perform, e.g. 'The computer desk should hold a computer screen and peripherals on the desktop'
* how the materials/components should perform, e.g. 'The laminated board should be durable and robust to support the weight of the computer hardware.'

Market

In this next product specification criteria you need to think about two different aspects of the term 'market'; the retail market for the product and the target market group. The size of the market usually determines the level of production for a product.

The retail market for the product has a considerable influence on how it is designed and manufactured. For example, a tubular steel garden chair, with an 'engineered' design style might be batch produced for sale in an upmarket designer garden shop. On the other hand, a basic cheap and cheerful plastic biro, with a style little changed since its development in 1938, will be produced in high volume for sale in every High Street shop or supermarket world-wide. When you analyse a product it is therefore important to look for design clues that can help you decide the product retail market and therefore the kind of user who might buy it. For example, the retail market for a hand blender is likely to be kitchen accessory outlets and the target market will be domestic users or chefs.

The second aspect of the term 'market' is the target market group (TMG), i.e. the users of the product. All products are designed with users in mind. Many manufacturers use extensive market research to establish their TMG, without which it would be almost impossible to design a product. Establishing the TMG means knowing who you are designing for and what their needs are; are the users male or female, young or old, able-bodied or disabled, expert or novice users of the product? The type of end-user will help determine the characteristics of a product to enable it to meet user needs and therefore have a good sales potential. When you think about the TMG you may need to make references to ergonomics. This is the science of designing products for human use, matching the product to the user. An ergonomically designed hand blender, for example, will be designed for comfortable use, to give a good speed of performance and to improve the user's satisfaction when using

it. When you analyse a product you will need to decide if the product is made in a specific size to meet the needs of children, women or men, if it needs to be made in specific dimensions to make the product more usable or to improve the users' interaction with it.

Aesthetics/characteristics

Aesthetics play a very important role in the design and marketing of products as the main reason for buying a product is often how it looks and the image it can give the user. For many products appearance and design characteristics are based on the manufacturer's perception of user needs. When you address the aesthetics/ characteristics of the product in the exam, you need to focus on the aesthetic properties and characteristics that the product *should* have in order to meet the TMG requirements. You will gain few marks for simply describing the product. For example, the aesthetics and characteristics of a flat pack self-assembly computer desk include:

- it should be easy to assemble with basic tools
- it should be easy to transport in flat pack form
- it should be eye-catching with a contrasting colour scheme in line with design trends
- it should have ergonomically designed handles so the drawers are easy to open
- it should have wheels so its easy to move from room to room
- it should have a laminated surface that is easy to wipe clean
- it should have a pull-out keyboard desk at an ergonomic height
- it should have a work area suitable for a range of computer peripherals.

In the Product Analysis exam you would not be expected to produce a long list of points about the aesthetics/characteristics of a product, because the maximum marks available for any of the specification headings is four. To achieve four marks for aesthetics/ characteristics, you would therefore need to provide four different, fully explained and appropriate specification points.

Quality standards

When you explain how the product can meet quality standards you need to refer to size, dimensions and the use of tolerances. You should also refer to the relationship between quality, cost and scale of production. For example, a one-off product may use more

Task
Describe the retail market and the needs of the target market group for each of the following products:

- the Hot Bertaa kettle designed by Philippe Starck (Figure 1.21)
- a Swatch watch
- a knock down self-assembly computer desk.

expensive or unusual materials than a high volume product, although both levels of production would make use of a quality system of some kind.

All products need to be manufactured to the correct size and dimensions to ensure that component parts fit together well and the product is capable of performing its function. All the component parts therefore need to be designed and manufactured to a high standard with precision and accuracy. This is where standards such as British Standards (BS) come in. There is an enormous range of published BS which are used by manufacturers to help them produce a quality product. Although you are not expected to quote a BS number, it is always preferable to explain the relevance of a standard, such as the use of a BS to test the strength and stability of furniture.

Successful manufacturers incorporate the use of a quality management system (QMS) in product design and manufacture in order to achieve a quality product. You could therefore refer to the use of a QMS or total quality management (TQM). One aspect of TQM is the use of quality control (QC) checks which use agreed tolerances to check the accuracy of dimensions and sizes in order to manufacture identical products. You could also quote the use of ISO 9000 which is an internationally agreed set of standards for a QMS. ISO 9000 ensures that a manufacturing customer receives the product that has been agreed. For example, a domestic iron manufacturer that is ISO registered would only buy in component parts from a supplier that was also ISO registered, because they would know that the components would meet an agreed BS. Any manufacturer that has a QMS in place can apply for a KiteMark or offer a warranty or guarantee of product quality.

Safety

Safety is an essential feature of all manufactured products, many of which have to comply with safety legislation before they can be sold. Safety standards are set by British Standards (BS) to ensure the safety of the user.

Products such as toys, garden tools and children's outdoor play equipment are rigorously tested to ensure that they will not cause injury through normal use or misuse. This includes the safety of components like hinges, catches, paints and finishes which must be non-toxic.

Products like kettles and toasters are tested to ensure electrical safety and for the working life of the controls. A domestic iron needs to have tamperproof screws to prevent access to electrical connections.

A product that displays a KiteMark is independently tested at regular intervals to make sure it complies with a relevant safety standard. The KiteMark symbol shows potential customers that the product is safe and reliable. When a product is sold in the European Union (EU) it has to meet safety standards set by the EU. Manufacturers who claim to meet these standards can use the CE mark, but if the product is found not to comply with the safety standard, it can be seized and the manufacturer, importer or supplier prosecuted.

In this section you will need to make and explain points that are specific to the product in question, rather than making general statements. For example British Standards (BS) in relation to food processors might be related to the safety of the cutting blades or related to electrical safety when blending liquids. You will not be expected to quote a BS number, but you must make sure that what you explain is appropriate to the product. Other points about safety need explaining, e.g. rather than stating that the product needs to have a KiteMark, you could explain that the product needs to meet a relevant safety standard and pass regular tests in manufacture to be awarded a KiteMark.

Task

A one-off product such as a custom-made garden seat made from a rare hardwood is likely to be made to a high quality and be very expensive to buy. On the other hand, a mass produced garden seat from a local do-it-yourself store is likely to be made from lower cost hardwood and be a fraction of the cost of the one-off, although it would have been produced to meet BS through the use of the manufacturer's quality assurance system.

1 Describe how a designer-maker could ensure that the custom-made garden seat was a high quality product.
2 Describe how the manufacturer of a mass produced garden seat could achieve a quality product.

Task

Describe the safety features of a knock-down portable computer desk, with reference to the following criteria:

- compliance with safety standards
- ergonomics
- ease of assembly
- safety when opening the desk drawers
- electrical safety
- finish
- safety of use and disposal.

Think about this!

In the Product Analysis examination paper the product specification headings will be given so you do not have to commit them to memory.

Remember to address at least four of the headings so you have the opportunity to achieve the seven marks available. You can still address all seven headings to gain seven marks, but must explain each point.

The specification statements require well justified points about how the product should be designed. Remember that the product specification is not a description of the given product, but criteria which define what the product should be like. The given scale of production is important, because it influences many aspects of the product specification.

Figure 1.2 Public seating

Task

The public seating shown in Figure 1.2 is made from recycled plastic and aluminium. The extruded plastic seat lengths can be fabricated to bespoke lengths and curvatures, depending on the client's requirements. The cast aluminium frame is made in two styles, with and without a backrest, to allow for further customisation. Draw up a product design specification for the seating.

b) Justify the use of materials and components (6 marks)

In this section you will be asked to justify the use of materials and components used in the product given in the exam paper. There are two parts to the question with three marks allocated for each part.

You will be asked to justify the use of either two different materials or two different components or one material and one component. In your response you will need to give reasons why the working properties and characteristics of the given materials or components make them suitable for the product and its function. Simply listing the properties of the given material is not enough to gain the available marks. When you undertake product analysis as part of your course, keep a reference book handy so you can look up materials properties to help you decide why the material is suitable for the product.

Working characteristics of a range of materials and components

Physical/mechanical properties

In order to explain the suitability of a material for the product given in the Product Analysis exam, you will need to understand the material's physical and mechanical properties. For example medium density fibreboard (MDF) is durable and readily available in large sized sheets which makes it suitable for the mass production of a flat-pack self-assembly desk.

The physical and mechanical properties of resistant materials make them suitable for different types of manufacturing processes and different types of products.

- Physical properties describe the handling characteristics of a material, including its feel.
- Mechanical properties describe how the material reacts to forces acting upon it.

Wood, metal and plastics may have different mechanical properties but all of them can be deformed. Laminating wood, for example, increases its strength, a mechanical property. Other materials such as plastics and metals have the ability to change into a molten or plasticised state at certain temperatures. It is important to differentiate between physical and mechanical properties and to be able to apply them to woods, metals and plastics. Table 1.2 lists some common physical and mechanical properties.

Table 1.2 *Physical and mechanical properties*

Physical	Mechanical
Appearance, corrosion resistant, chemical resistant, density, electrical conductivity, insulation, fusibility, optical properties (how easily light passes through), thermal conductivity insulation	Brittleness, ductility, durability, elasticity, hardness, malleability, plasticity, strength, toughness

Aesthetics

Aesthetics refers to all the ways in which we use and interact with products, whether by sight or touch. These days the decision to buy a product is often based on the appearance of the product, rather than its technology, because many products have similar functional characteristics. The success of one product over another is therefore often dependent on its aesthetic characteristics and the user's subjective experience of it. For example, owning a certain type of vacuum cleaner or toaster can say something about you. When you refer to the aesthetic properties of materials you will need to explain how their working properties impact on the shape and form of the product, using terms such as those shown in Table 1.3.

Table 1.3

Words related to texture	Words related to colour	Shape and form of the product
Hard, soft, abrasive, smooth, textured	Mellow/dull, bright/vivid, neutral/ colourless, dark/sombre, pastel/light	Functional, engineered, stylish, sleek, modern, traditional

The properties of metals and alloys

Metals can be divided into three main categories: ferrous, non-ferrous and alloys.

- Ferrous metals contain iron. They are almost all magnetic and unless treated corrode very easily.
- Ferrous alloys such as mild steel and stainless steel are made from a mixture of iron and carbon. Iron is soft and ductile and carbon is hard and brittle. By varying the amount of carbon used, steels with different hardness can be produced.
- Non-ferrous metals such as copper, aluminium and zinc are pure metals that contain no iron.
- Non-ferrous alloys include brass which is made from a mixture of copper and zinc.

Metals are ideally suited to manufacturing processes such as casting, extrusion, milling and turning, grinding, spark erosion and forging. However, it is not possible to apply all of these manufacturing processes to all metals. For example, aluminium, brass, copper and zinc alloys cast well. Table 1.4 shows the physical and mechanical properties and end-uses of a range of metals.

Figure 1.3 This hand blender has a stainless steel detachable shaft. Stainless steel is a good choice because it resists wear, will not corrode (rust) and is easy to clean. Stainless steel is strong, durable, safe and hygienic to use in cooking.

Table 1.4 *The physical and mechanical properties and end-uses of a range of metals*

Material	Physical properties	Mechanical properties	End-use
Mild steel (ferrous alloy)	Poor resistance to corrosion (rusts)	Tough, ductile and malleable, good tensile strength, easily joined by welding or brazing, cannot be hardened and tempered	Furniture, filing cabinets, car bodies, lamps, nails, screws, nuts and bolts, brackets
Medium carbon steel (ferrous alloy)		Tough, harder than mild steel, but less ductile	Springs and axles
High carbon steel (ferrous alloy)		Very hard, difficult to cut, malleable, can be hardened and tempered	Drills, hammers, cutting tools, files, saws, chisels
Stainless steel (ferrous alloy)	Resists wear and corrosion	Hard, strong, durable and tough, lightweight, difficult to cut and file	Cutlery, kitchen sinks, kettles
Copper (non-ferrous pure metal)	Good conductor of heat and electricity	Malleable and ductile, easily joined, polishes well, expensive	Cables, car radiators PCBs
Aluminium (non-ferrous pure metal)	Corrosion resistant, good conductor of heat and electricity, good fusibility	High strength/weight ratio, lightweight, malleable and ductile, difficult to join, polishes well	Aircraft parts, castings, window frames, saucepans
Zinc (non-ferrous pure metal)	Good corrosion resistance	Ductile and easily worked	Die casting alloys, coating for steel
Brass (non-ferrous alloy of copper and zinc)	Corrosion resistant, good conductor of heat and electricity, good fusibility	Harder than copper, casts and machines well, polishes well, cheaper than copper	Bath taps, plumbing fittings, marine fittings, screws, electric plug connector pins, candlesticks, clocks

Task

Look at two household products that explain the use of different metals.

1 Investigate the properties of the different metals and explain why they are suitable for their end-use.
2 Draw up a product design specification for one of these products.

The properties of plastics

Plastics are also known as polymers because of their special structure of interlinked chains of molecules. Most early plastics were so called because they were 'plastic', meaning soft and pliable. The very plastic nature of plastics and the suitability of plastic materials for vacuum forming, injection moulding and blow moulding, enables the development of an enormous range of different product shapes. Plastics can be divided into two main categories; thermoplastics and thermosetting plastics.

- Thermoplastics are the most common type of plastic, made from long tangled chains of molecules which have very few cross links. When thermoplastics are heated they become soft, allowing them to be formed into different shapes and then return to their original shape on reheating. This is known as plastic memory. Thermoplastics generally soften at low temperatures (as low as 100 °C), making thermoplastic products unsuitable for use in high temperatures.
- Thermosetting plastics are made from long chains of molecules which are cross linked, resulting in a very rigid molecular structure. Thermosetting plastics can only be heated up and re-formed once, after which they are permanently set in a shape. They can be used in temperatures in excess of 400 °C.

Tables 1.5 and 1.6 show the properties and end-uses of common thermoplastics and thermosetting plastics.

Table 1.5 The properties and end-uses of thermoplastics

Thermoplastic	Properties	End-use
Acrylic	Rigid, hard, durable with uniform strength, glossy, clear, has good optical properties, available in many colours, easily scratched, weather resistant, non-toxic, good electrical insulator, easily machined and polishes well	Baths and bathroom furniture, car indicator covers/reflectors, signs, transparent boxes/lids
Rigid polystyrene (HDPS)	Light, hard, rigid, non-toxic, water resistant, brittle with low impact strength, often transparent, toughened HDPS can be in range of colours, is impact resistant, can be recycled	Model kits, disposable cups and plates, body of food blender/food processor, remote controls, telephones, childrens toys
Expanded polystyrene (LDPS)	Buoyant, lightweight, good sound and heat insulator	Sound and heat insulation, food packaging
PVC	Rigid or flexible, hard, tough, lightweight, good chemical and weather resistance, good electrical insulator	Water pipes, guttering, window frames, disks
PET	Very tough with high tensile strength, impact resistant, clear, has good optical properties, good chemical/temperature resistance, alcohol and oil resistant, can be recycled	Mineral water and soft drinks bottles, toasters, electric kettles
Low density polyethylene (polythene) (LDPE)	Tough, durable, robust, impact resistant, lightweight, can be soft and flexible, resistant to chemicals/weather, good electrical insulator, available in wide range of colours, can be recycled	Squeezy shampoo and washing-up-liquid bottles, kitchen bowls, food storage containers/lids, water reservoir of domestic iron, toys, carrier bags
High density polyethylene (polythene) (HDPE)	More rigid and harder than LDPE, surface has waxy feel, waterproof, resistant to chemicals, can be sterilised, can be recycled	Buckets, bowls, wheelie bins, milk crates, bleach and medicine bottles
ABS	Durable, high impact strength, lightweight, tough and scratch resistant, good chemical resistance, high quality of surface finish	Telephones, electric kettles, food processors, toys
Polypropylene	Clear, light, rigid, hard, good impact resistance, smooth, shiny, good chemical resistance, can be sterilised, good resistance to work-fatigue	Medical equipment, syringes, containers with integral hinges, door handles, electric kettles

Table 1.6 The properties and end-uses of thermosetting plastics

Thermosetting plastic	Properties	End-use
Epoxy resin	Clear, rigid, very strong, especially when reinforced with glass or carbon fibres, good resistance to wear and chemicals, good adhesive	Adhesive for unlike materials, e.g. metals to plastics. PCBs, surfboards, motorbike helmets
Urea formaldehyde	Stiff, hard and brittle, good electrical insulator	Electrical plugs and fittings, adhesive

Task

1 Using Table 1.5 to help you, list the physical and mechanical properties of acrylic, HDPS, LDPS, PVC, PET and polypropylene.
2 State the type of plastic suitable for use in the following products. Explain three reasons why each plastic is suitable for the product:
   • shop sign
   • drinks bottle
   • child's toy.

The properties of woods

As a natural resource, hardwoods and softwoods produce timber with a number of disadvantages, such as knots and irregularity of grain. Timber can also suffer from changes in moisture content, leading to warping and twisting if not properly seasoned. Wood is also prone to decay and fungal and pest attacks. Timber is relatively expensive to buy and does not come in large sizes, although it can be machined and joined in many ways.

Wood can be produced in standard stock sizes and sections, suitable for manufacturing into products. The use of standard sizes is cost-effective for product manufacture because it reduces the need for initial cutting to a workable size.

• Hardwood is a close-grained, strong, tough timber from deciduous trees that carry their seeds in fruit. It is slow growing (60–100 years to mature) and therefore expensive.
• Softwood is a more open-grained timber from cone bearing coniferous trees, that are evergreen with needles. Although it is fast growing (20–30 years to mature) and ideal for growing commercially, it produces weaker timber that can split easily. Softwood is less expensive to buy because it can produce long straight lengths with little waste on cutting.

The properties and characteristics of timber can be categorised by their grain, colour, texture, hardness and elasticity. Hardwoods generally have a greater mechanical strength than softwoods. Table 1.7 shows the properties and end-uses of hardwoods and softwoods.

Table 1.7 The properties and end-uses of hardwoods and softwoods

Wood	Type	Properties	End-use
Beech	Hardwood	Close-grained, hard, tough and strong, works and finishes well but prone to warping	Workshop benches, rolling pins, cutting boards, wooden bowls, mallets, toys, chairs, stools
Jelutong	Hardwood	Uniform grain with few knots, pale cream, soft, fine, shapes easily	Pattern making, carving, drawing boards
Iroko	Hardwood	Cross-grained, durable, heavy, oily	Substitute for teak, used in furniture, veneers, garden gates
Pine or Red Deal	Softwood	Straight-grained, long fibres, fairly strong, but knotty and prone to warping, easy to work, readily available and inexpensive	Roof joists, skirting boards, country-style furniture
Cedar	Softwood	Lightweight, knot free, soft, straight silky grain, durable against weather, insects and rotting, easy to work but expensive	Timber cladding, garden sheds and fences

Table 1.8 *The properties and end-uses of plywood, blockboard and MDF*

Manufactured board	Properties	End-use
Plywood	Made from odd number of veneers glued with grain in alternate directions, two outside layers in same direction, generally made from birch, strong and fairly inexpensive	Boat-building (exterior waterproof quality ply), drawer bottoms, shutters, door panels, bent plywood chairs
Blockboard	Made from strips of wood glued together and covered with heavy veneers, solid but lower uniform strength than plywood but cheaper to make	Tabletops, shelves, firedoors
MDF	Very stable and dense with smooth faces, easily cut and shaped, can be joined with wide range of knock down fittings, takes range of surface finishes, paints well	Flat-pack furniture, kitchen units, heat and sound insulation

The properties of manufactured board

Manufactured boards are available in large, wide sheets up to 3 metres x 2 metres. They are relatively inexpensive and because there is no grain running through them they are more stable. Manufactured board can be finished by painting and staining, but when used in furniture is often veneered or covered with plastic laminates which give the impression of a solid wood finish. Table 1.8 shows the properties and end-uses of plywood, blockboard and MDF.

The properties of composites

Composites are made up of two or more different materials combined by bonding with glues or resins. The resulting materials have improved mechanical properties and excellent weight/strength ratios, enabling the reduction of weight in products. Glass reinforced plastic (GRP) is commonly available as matting and carbon fibre is used to produce strong lightweight structures. Table 1.9 shows the properties and end-uses of GRP and carbon fibre.

Task

Compare one piece of furniture made from softwood, one made from hardwood and one made from manufactured board.

1 Investigate the properties of the softwood, hardwood and manufactured board and explain why they are suitable for their end-use.
2 Draw up a product design specification for one of these products.

Task

Modern tennis rackets are often made from carbon fibre. Give three reasons why this material is used in preference to wood.

Standard components

It is generally more economically viable for manufacturers to 'buy in' standard components from specialist suppliers. For

Table 1.9 *The properties and end-uses of GRP and carbon fibre*

Composite	Properties	End-use
Glass reinforced plastic (GRP)	High tensile strength, lightweight, durable, good corrosion resistance	Small boats, exterior casings
Carbon fibre	Stronger than GRP, lightweight	Sports equipment such as tennis rackets, golf clubs and skis, body armour and protective clothing for the military

Table 1.10 The characteristics of a range of standard components

Standard component	Characteristics
Nuts and bolts	Made from low or medium carbon steel, tightened with spanner, to give strong mechanical joints, general purpose temporary fixing
Rivets	Made from soft iron, ductile and easy to work, frequently with countersunk or snap heads, used to permanently join metal, acrylic and wood
Pop rivets	Hollow rivets, used to join sheet metal when impossible to reach both sides
Gears	Toothed wheels that transmit forces and motion, compound gear trains enable large speed changes, worm and bevel gears transmit rotary motion through 90°, bevel gears used in hand drills, rack and pinion gears convert rotary motion to linear
Bushes and bearings	Support rotating shafts
Cams	Convert rotary motion into reciprocating motion

example, a manufacturer of electrical kettles might buy in the water heating elements, the mains lead socket and the standard mains electrical lead. The kettle manufacturer's business is to design and manufacture kettles, and while their volume of production is likely to be high, the company is not in the business of producing the individual kettle components. These will be made in standard forms and sizes by specialist companies who will manufacture and supply components in very high volumes at a lower unit cost than would be possible by the kettle manufacturer. Table 1.10 shows the characteristics of a range of standard components.

Task

Analyse a kitchen tap or electric plug to see how many component parts are used. Explain why manufacturers use standard components.

Finishes, properties and quality

Surface finishes are used to improve a product's functional and aesthetic properties, to improve its useful life and to improve the overall quality of the product. For example, a steel or brass bathroom tap is often coated with chrome to give it a more durable and shiny surface.

- Functional finishes protect the product from oxidation, scratching or tarnishing. For example, finishes on metals reduce corrosion and wood finishes reduce attack by damp or infestation. Plastics generally do not require finishing but may suffer discolouration when exposed to sunlight.

- Aesthetic finishes using colour can create an image or style, make a product look heavy or light and give a sense of quality.

Table 1.11 shows the characteristics of a range of finishes. In the Product Analysis exam, it is important when justifying the use of a specific material, to think about the relationship between materials properties, any applied surface finish or coating and the required level of quality of the product. For example, the required product quality may be different for a one-off product and a high volume product.

Task

Look at Figure 1.4 below and justify the use of:
(i) polystyrene in the body of the hair dryer (3)
(ii) chrome plating for the nozzle.   (3)

Figure 1.4 The body of this hair dryer is manufactured from polystyrene (HDPS) and the nozzle is chrome plated.

Table 1.11 *The characteristics of a range of finishes*

Finish type	Characteristics	End-use
Preservatives	Oil based creosote improves resistance of wood to damp, fungus decay and attacks from pests	Garden sheds, fences. Furniture.
Paints (surface coating)	Oil based gloss paints in wide range of colours are durable and waterproof, polyurethane paints are tough and scratch resistant	Outdoor products. Childrens toys.
Varnishes (surface coating)	Gloss, satin or matt finish made from synthetic resins, gives tough, waterproof, heatproof finish	Country-style furniture. Childrens wood toys.
Electroplating (surface coating)	Gives metals such as brass and copper a coating of durable and decorative metal such as chromium or silver	Metal products.
Anodising	Gives aluminium and its alloys a consistently high quality finish, coloured dyes can be added before final lacquering	Kettles, bike frames.
Self finishing	High volume processes include die casting, blow moulding, injection moulding and extrusion, plastics require little or no finishing due to use of high quality moulds, textured moulds give different textures	Plastic products.
Surface decoration	Decoration by engraving, burning pattern into wood or by application of vinyl graphics	Wood and metal products.

c) Give four reasons why the product is one-off, batch or mass produced (4 marks)

In this section you will be asked to give reasons why the given product is manufactured either as a one-off or batch or mass produced. Four marks are available, so you will need to explain four appropriate reasons for the given scale of production. Your responses should be applied to the product in question, rather than being general statements about one-off, batch or mass production. For example, a product such as the table shown in Figure 1.5 combines high quality craft skills with the use of expensive seasoned oak. Users are therefore likely to value the table more highly than a mass produced item and be prepared to pay more for it. The table will also take longer to manufacture and fewer of them will be produced, both good reasons why it would need to be sold at a higher price than a mass produced product.

Scale of production

The scale of production is one of the most important decisions to be made when developing a product, because it has an impact on all design and manufacturing decisions, including:

- the number of products manufactured
- the choice of materials and components
- the manufacturing processes, speed of production and availability of machinery and operators
- production planning, the use of just in time (JIT) and stock control including the use of ICT

Figure 1.5 *This table, called 'The Plank', combines high quality craft skills with the use of seasoned oak. The table folds out completely into a hinged, solid piece of oak.*

- production costs, including the benefits of bulk buying, the use of standard components and the eventual retail price.

One-off production

One-off production includes single, often high cost products, manufactured to a client specification such as bespoke furniture or exclusive jewellery. One-off products are often very high cost because a premium has to be paid for the unique features, more expensive or exclusive materials, time consuming hand production and finishing processes involved.

Bespoke production is often achieved by one designer-maker and quality is checked as the work progresses. The tools and equipment may be less automated than in high volume production, but the end product is often more individual and high quality.

Large size one-off products like the London Eye (Figure 1.6) are designed and manufactured by a team of people across the world, each working on individual aspects of the product. In the manufacture of this type of product, accuracy and user-safety are of primary importance. Materials and production costs are likely to be very high, although use may be made of some standardised components. Production planning and the use of quality control (QC) would be critical for the London Eye to function as planned. The production team would also make use of ICT in design,

Figure 1.6 *The London Eye was manufactured as a one-off product, despite its size*

production planning, JIT and manufacture, to enable the product to be manufactured on time and to budget.

> ### Task
> 1 Explain the benefits to the client of having a piece of furniture manufactured as a bespoke product.
> 2 Give four reasons why a large scale one-off product such as the Millennium Bridge is manufactured as a one-off product.

Batch production

Batch production involves the manufacture of identical components or products in specified, predetermined 'batches', which can vary from tens to thousands. The tooling, machinery and workforce must be flexible to enable a fast turn around so production can be easily adapted to another product manufacture. Batch production makes use of flexible manufacturing systems (FMS) to enable companies to be competitive and efficient. Production cells, CNC manufacturing, automated parts handling and assembly enable production downtime to be kept to a minimum.

Batch production results in a lower unit cost than one-off production because economies of scale in materials buying enables cost savings and identical batches of consistently high quality products are manufactured at a competitive price.

High volume production

The high volume production (mass production) of most consumer products makes use of faster, more automated manufacturing processes and a largely unskilled workforce. High volume products are designed to follow mass market trends, so the product appeals to a wide target market. Production planning and quality control (QC) in production enables the manufacture of identical products. Production costs are kept as low as possible so the product will provide value for money. For example, the mass production of a domestic iron might make use of:

- bulk buying of polyethylene granules or screws to reduce production costs
- standard sizes of screw forms and a standard process such as injection moulding to ensure cost-effective and efficient manufacture
- high cost specialist tools, equipment and jigs to enable efficient manufacture

- fast production of the component parts, using a dedicated production line and automated processes
- quality control to enable manufacture of identical irons that meet specifications.

Figure 1.7 *This sandwich toaster is mass produced from rigid polystyrene (HDPS) and uses electric heating elements in the top and bottom parts.*

Task

Give four reasons why the toaster in Figure 1.7 is mass produced.

Factfile

In-line production and assembly makes use of low-cost unskilled labour. Most assembly lines operate on a 'just in time' (JIT) basis in which ICT is used to plan the ordering of materials and components, so they arrive just in time for production. JIT is often used in quick response manufacturing (QRM), where products are produced quickly in the exact quantities needed to fulfil demand. JIT and QRM reduce the need and the costs of keeping stock.

Production cells are small teams of people working together, who are responsible for producing high quality products. Fully automated production cells include CNC machines and robot parts handling. Cells are used in QRM because they increase productivity and efficiency, enabling the fast changeover for new products and improved quality.

Most modern manufacture relies on the use of ICT for information handling, stock control and production planning to enable increased productivity and competitive manufacture.

Task

Remember that in the Product Analysis exam you need to provide four different, fully explained points about the scale of production in order to achieve the available marks. Use the following questions about the scale of production to help you:

- Is the product designed to follow mass market trends?
- Does the product appeal to a wide target market or a single user?
- Is the product value for money?
- Is the product high cost or is it sold at a low retail price?
- Does the production make use of standardised materials, components and processes?
- Does it use specialist tools, equipment, jigs or patterns?
- Is the product fast or time consuming to manufacture? What impact does this have on costs?
- Do the production costs enable the bulk buying of materials and components?
- Does the product make use of production planning and quality control (QC) in production to make identical products? How is this achieved?
- Is the product made by quick response manufacture? How is this achieved?
- Are just in time (JIT) and stock control features of the product manufacture? How are they achieved?
- Is the product made in large quantities, with a dedicated production line, using automation or robotics?
- Is the product batch produced in specified quantities, using CAD/CAM to enable a fast turn around to adapt production to another product manufacture?
- Is the product made for a specific client, using specialist materials and processes?

d) Describe, using notes and sketches, the stages of manufacture for the product, including references to industrial manufacturing methods (16 marks)

This section is the most demanding on the Product Analysis paper, the one that carries the most marks and the one where you should spend the most time. In this section it is even more important that you plan your responses fully enough to ensure that sufficient relevant points are identified and explained. Note where the most marks are awarded and allow enough time to achieve the available marks. You are directed to use the following headings in your answer:

- preparation (of jigs, patterns, tools and equipment)
- processing
- assembly
- finish.

Using these headings will enable you to structure your responses. Remember that one word or generalised comments will gain few if any marks. Examiners are looking for knowledge and understanding of the stages of manufacture of the *given* product, so the use of technical terms about industrial manufacture is essential. You do not need to include detailed references to quality control and safety testing in this section.

Preparation (of jigs, patterns, tools and equipment)

Preparation deals with the preparation for the manufacture of the given product, *not* the lead up research, design and prototyping stages. You are expected to apply your knowledge and understanding to the product in question, i.e. either a one-off, batch or high volume product. Depending on the type of product, you will need to refer to the use of jigs or patterns, specialist tools or the use of CNC equipment.

Buying in materials

In all levels of production, preparation for manufacture incorporates the selection and buying in of the most suitable materials and components. The best material for the job is not necessarily the most expensive because in many cases there needs to be a compromise between quality and cost. In high volume manufacture in particular, there needs to be a continuous supply of cost-effective materials of known performance and of an acceptable quality (i.e. the chosen material must be fit for its purpose). Buying in materials for different levels of production depends on the following factors:

- the required aesthetic, physical and mechanical properties
- the scale of production and related cost/quality requirement. Is the product cheap and cheerful or a bespoke piece of jewellery?
- the availability of a supply of reliable, cost-effective materials for high volume production.
- the availability of specific high quality materials for one-off production
- the suitability of the material for the manufacturing process. For example, thermoplastics are suitable for injection moulding
- the required dimensional accuracy of the finished product. Can the material be precision cut?
- surface finishes appropriate to the required product quality. Does the material require electroplating?

Figure 1.8 *Preparation for injection moulding of electric drill parts involves the design and manufacture of moulds.*

27

Making aids

In high volume production, preparation is mainly concerned with the manufacture of making aids, such as jigs, patterns, special tools or moulds. These make the flow of products through the factory smooth and uninterrupted, enabling efficient manufacture. For example, chipboard has reliable properties and is produced in standard sizes, ensuring economical cutting prior to further processing.

The preparation of manufacturing aids is very costly and therefore mainly associated with mass production. For example, split moulds comprising two or more sections, suitable for injection moulding the plastic parts of an electric drill, must be of good quality as any imperfection in the mould surface will be replicated on the finished product. The drill mould must also be manufactured to a very high degree of dimensional accuracy, with correct draft angles to ensure that the formed drill parts release easily. Any mould used for a plastic product made by vacuum forming, blow moulding or casting (or metal products made by forging) must also be of good quality for the same reasons. Sample formed drill parts are generally made and tested before commencing full mass production, to ensure that the drill parts fit together accurately, so the drill will be of an acceptable quality and within the specified tolerance. The costs of preparing these moulds can run into hundreds of thousands of pounds which is why these processes are ideally suited to high volume production runs.

The moulds for an electric drill are produced using milling and spark erosion.

- Milling is a wasting process carried out in both the vertical and horizontal axes, using multi-toothed cutters to remove the waste metal material from the mould. CNC machines enable intricate and complicated 3D sections of waste material to be removed.
- Computer controlled spark erosion is used to complete the 3D profiling of the metal mould. A small spark up to 1200 °C is pulsed at up to 10,000 times per second between two conductors, one of which is the metal piece being machined. With each pulse a tiny piece of metal is removed (eroded), allowing very fine detail and complicated shapes to be machined.

Preparation processes

Preparation processes used for metal, wood or plastic products, may include drilling, turning, laser cutting, forging, cutting or abrading.

- Drilling is used to cut holes in most materials using the correct bit, the work being held by special jigs. In high volume manufacture drilling is an automated process.
- Turning is the process of removing wood, metal or plastic using a single point or form tool while the material stock is being rotated in a lathe. Preparation of timber is essential before turning to make sure it is free from splits, with the corners cut or planed off.
  - Manual centre lathes requiring skilled operators are used in one-off and batch production. Although tooling costs are low, labour costs are high.
  - CNC lathes enable flexibility, fast turn around and short downtimes, making them suitable for batch and short production runs.
  - Automatic lathes with automatic material feeds and multi-spindles are used in the high volume production of components such as screws. Tooling costs are high both for CNC and automatic lathes, although labour costs are low.
- Forging such as drop forging is often quicker and more economical than machining components from solid metal. Drop forging uses two halves of a mould in which the metal is placed. An enormous force applied by a hammer action shapes the metal components. Although the cost of producing moulds is high, labour costs in drop forging are low.
- Cutting machines used in high volume manufacture are often computer controlled. These CNC machines are controlled by digital data sent directly to the machine control unit.

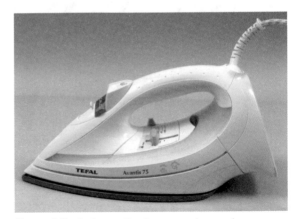

Figure 1.9 *A domestic steam and spray iron.*

- Laser cutting is computer controlled to enable the fast and accurate cutting of metals in complex shapes. The cost of all cutting machines is high although they enable the fast preparation of materials ready for processing.
- Abrading using disc, belt, orbital sanders or lathes is a wasting process, used to clean up and improve the finish of wood, metal and plastic components prior to processing.

> **Task**
> Describe the preparation stage of manufacture for the mass produced domestic iron shown in Figure 1.9. Include references to industrial manufacturing methods in your answer.

Processing

In the processing section examiners are looking for technical details about manufacturing processes, including the use of good quality annotated diagrams. Remember to match your responses to the marks available which may be different in each exam.

The available or chosen method of processing for a particular product has an enormous influence on the product design. New manufacturing processes have often led to major changes in the shape of products.

For example, at one time bearings were either bushed or used ball races which needed constant lubrication. With the introduction of sintering and later on, the use of polymers, the need for lubrication was removed. This reduced maintenance requirements and changed the shape of many commonly used kitchen appliances. The shape and style of toasters has changed over the years as a result of the use of plastics and processes such as injection moulding (Figure 1.10). You will therefore need to be familiar with a number of common manufacturing processes, such as die and sand casting, injection moulding, blow moulding and vacuum forming. The use of CNC machines is a feature of many of these automated processes.

Die casting

Complex shapes such as kitchen taps and shower heads are almost impossible to produce in any other way except by casting. This process involves molten metal being poured into a preheated high carbon steel or graphite mould called a die. When the metal has solidified the die is opened and the casting is removed.

In gravity die casting the molten metal is poured into the reusable mould and gravity causes it to fill all the cavities in the mould. This process is used for the high volume production of components made from non-ferrous metals such as copper and aluminium, while carbon steels are cast using graphite dies. The process is suitable for symmetrical

Figure 1.10 *The shape and styling of modern kitchen appliances depends on the materials and processes used in their manufacture.*

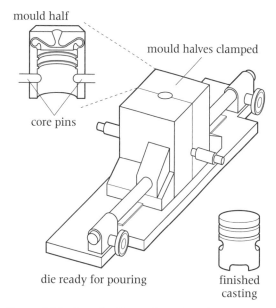

Figure 1.11 *Gravity die casting of a piston*

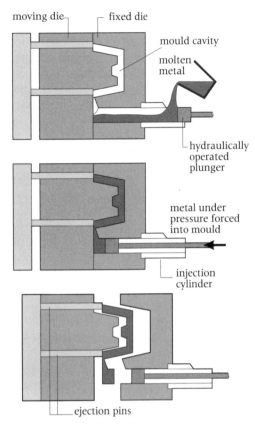

Figure 1.12 *Pressure die casting*

components because the die can be split into two halves and can be 'cored' to make hollow forms.

Pressure die casting is used for more intricate and complicated shapes. The molten metal is forced into the die under great pressure ensuring that the whole mould cavity is filled. Pressure die casting involves the following processes:

- the molten metal is fed into the machine and forced into the mould cavity using a hydraulic ram or Archimedean screw
- dwell time allows for the molten metal to solidify
- the two part mould is opened and the product is removed using ejector pins
- the mould is cleaned and closes again whereupon the whole process is repeated.

In gravity and pressure die casting 'flashing' sometimes occurs when the metal leaks out between the two sections of the mould. One of the major advantages of die casting is that it produces high quality castings with a smooth surface finish and fine detail clearly reproduced. For example, pencil sharpeners do not need surface finishing and

will not rust or tarnish because they are made from zinc based alloys. Another advantage of die casting is that the dies can be used many hundreds of thousands of times, making the initial high cost of the dies worthwhile.

Sand casting

Although commercial sand casting can be highly automated for manufacturing large batches, it is much slower and involves many more stages than die casting, so it is often used in low volume manufacture. A range of metals can be cast, although sand casting tends to be used mainly for steel, aluminium and its alloys. Sand casting involves the use of a wooden mould called a pattern, the same shape as the component to be cast. Sand casting involves the following processes:

- the pattern of the required component is made from wood
- the pattern is packed into damp sand in two steel boxes (the cope and drag) with sprue pins
- the cope and drag are split and the pattern removed, leaving a perfect impression in the sand
- the sprue pins are removed and the sprue holes opened up
- the cope and drag are put back together
- molten aluminium is poured in through the sprue holes into the empty cavity
- dwell time allows for the molten metal to solidify
- the cope and drag are broken out to reveal the cast product.

Sand casting has a low initial set up cost and is ideally suited to products that do not require

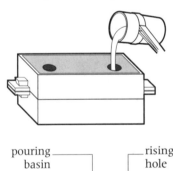

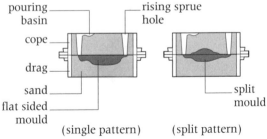

Figure 1.13 *Sand casting in aluminium*

high levels of accuracy, such as metalwork vices. Although the pattern and sprue pins can be reused, a new sand mould has to be made each time, so the whole process is slow. Cast products also need surface finishing.

Injection moulding

Injection moulding is the most common manufacturing process for containers such as washing up bowls or buckets and casings for television sets. It is best suited to thermoplastics, although some thermosetting plastics and composites can be used. Initial tooling costs to make the mould are high, making the process unsuitable for one-off or small batch production. Injection moulding is therefore commonly used for high volume production because it uses highly automated CNC machines, making the process low cost, quick and efficient. Injection moulding is suitable for complex shapes with holes and for multipart dies for small products like containers and lids. Integral hinges can be moulded into the product by thinning the plastic. The dies themselves are usually made from steel as one-off or small batch products. Injection moulding involves the following processes:

- the production of a good quality mould, which is critical to the product quality. The mould is usually designed with tapers to allow for removal. Multipart dies allow for screw threads to be moulded
- thermoplastic granules are fed into the hopper
- the granules are forced under pressure by the Archimedean screw thread through the heating element
- polymerised material collects in a shot chamber and is ejected into the mould cavity
- dwell time allows the plastic to cool and solidify, sometimes using water to help cooling
- the mould opens and ejector pins release the formed product

- the mould closes in preparation for the process to be repeated.

In injection moulding, production rates are very high. Labour and finishing costs are low because little finishing is required other than the removal of sprue pins and runners and the occasional excess plastic. All waste can be recycled into the process.

Task
1 Examine the shapes of a simple pencil sharpener and a hand drill.
2 Explain how and why the properties of the different materials used in these products influence their manufacturing processes.

Blow moulding

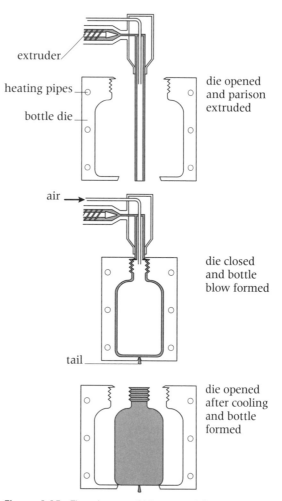

Figure 1.15 *The stages of blow moulding, used for milk, soft drinks, cooking oils and disinfectants bottles*

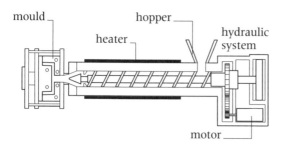

Figure 1.14 *Injection moulding is used in many plastics products, such as kitchen blenders, mixers and irons.*

Blow moulding is similar to glass blowing and is used for the high volume production of plastic bottles and containers. This highly automated process is extremely expensive to set up as the moulds need to have a very high quality finish. Blow moulded plastic bottles are very low cost to produce, because they have hollow rounded shapes with thin walls that reduce weight and materials costs. The blow moulding process can produce up to 2500 bottles per hour using automated CNC machines, so labour costs are low. Blow moulded containers need not be symmetrical and can integrate handles, screw threads and undercut features. Blow moulding involves the following processes:

- a hollow tube of thermoplastic, called a parison, is extruded downwards between a split mould
- the mould closes and grips both ends of the parison
- hot compressed air is blown into the parison forcing it to expand to take on the shape of the mould, including any relief details, such as threads and surface decoration
- dwell time allows for the plastic to cool and solidify
- the mould is opened and the container is ejected
- the whole process is repeated.

Other than surplus material being removed at the tail, no finishing is required apart from applying labels.

Vacuum forming

Vacuum forming is used to produce simple shapes from thermoplastic sheet using polymers such as high density polystyrene (HDPS), polyethylene, PVC, and acrylic. This automated process uses CNC machines for the high volume production of food packaging and products such as acrylic baths and car dashboards. Set up costs are very high because the moulds need to have a very high quality surface finish. All vertical surfaces must be slightly tapered and all sharp edges and corners must be rounded off. It is also necessary to incorporate vent and air holes to avoid pockets of air becoming trapped as the forming process takes place. Vacuum formed packaging is very low cost to produce, because it has thin walls that reduce weight and materials costs. Vacuum forming involves the following processes:

- a flat thermoplastic sheet is clamped and heated until it becomes very flexible
- the sheet is blown and stretched
- a platform pushes the mould up into the softened sheet

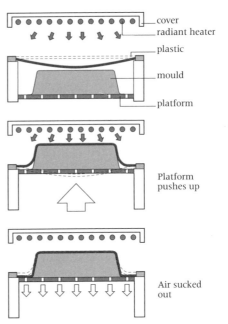

Figure 1.16 *Vacuum forming is used to produce food packaging such as yoghurt pots or chocolate box trays*

- air is sucked out from below the sheet, forcing the softened sheet down over the mould
- dwell time allows for the plastic to cool and solidify
- cold air is blown back up to help release the formed shape from the mould
- the formed shape is removed from the mould and the process repeated.

In vacuum forming, production rates are very high and unit costs low. Little finishing is required other than the removal of waste, which can be recycled.

Task

1 Examine the shapes of a yoghurt pot, a milk bottle and a sandwich toaster.
2 Explain how and why the properties of the different materials used in these products influence their manufacturing processes.

Assembly

In the Product Analysis exam you will be asked to produce an appropriate order of assembly for a *given* one-off, batch or high volume product and refer to the assembly joining processes. You could use a flow diagram to describe the order of assembly, but remember to use full sentences and to match your responses to the available marks.

Design and assembly

Considerations about the assembly of a product need to take place early on in the design process, as the product design needs to take into account the materials and manufacturing processes to be used. For example, the initial design will need to take into account how the component parts align and the order in which they need to be assembled. In some instances, a push fit is adequate for the parts to fit together, but in other cases permanent or non-permanent fixings, such as rivets, nuts and bolts may be used.

In high volume production, designing for manufacture is directly related to designing for cost. The main aim of this is to minimise component and assembly costs, to minimise product development cycles and to enable high quality products to be made. If a new sandwich toaster can be made using existing equipment, the costs and technical risks in using new machinery can be reduced. If the sandwich toaster needs new injection mouldings to be made, the design of these parts must be finalised early in the design cycle. If any new component (that might give the toaster a competitive edge) is going to be difficult to make, prototypes will need to be made.

Manual or high speed automatic assembly is the joining together of parts and sub-assemblies to make a finished product. Sometimes the parts are finished before assembly or require minimal finishing, such as plastics components. On the other hand the sheet metal parts and rivets used in an animal feeding trough, will need to be hot dip galvanised after assembly to seal the joints and prevent corrosion. You need to be aware of two joining processes used in assembly:

- mechanical assembly processes
- chemical joining processes.

Mechanical assembly processes

Mechanical assembly processes include semi-permanent and permanent fastenings.

- Semi-permanent or temporary fastenings, including nuts, bolts and screws are the most common methods of joining materials where the joint might have to be occasionally dismantled. Self-tapping screws are used when one side of the work is inaccessible or when joining dissimilar materials. They are used to secure sheet metal, plastics and composite materials. Washers and locking devices prevent the screws from working loose.
- Permanent fastenings are those in which one or more of the components have to be destroyed to separate the joints. This includes rivets, which are made of ductile materials and rely on deformation to fasten and hold components in place.

Chemical joining processes

Chemical joining processes include solvent welding and adhesive bonding.

- Solvent welding cements are used to join thermoplastics such as polystyrene and acrylic.
- Thermoplastic and thermosetting plastic adhesives are used extensively in industry. Thermoplastic adhesives, used to join wood, metal and plastics, soften when heated and have good resistance to moisture. Although thermosetting adhesives (epoxy adhesives) cannot be softened and provide high strength joints, they have low impact strength and tend to be brittle.

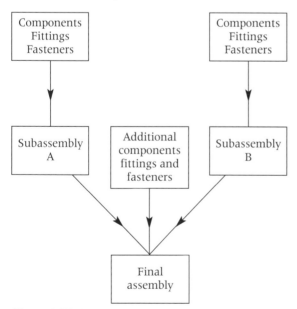

Figure 1.17 *Assembly of components and subassemblies*

Task

1 Explain the difference between permanent and semi-permanent mechanical joints and give an example of a product where each might be used.
2 Name and give reasons for your choice of adhesive to join a) a model kit and b) a wooden coffee table.
3 Draw a flowchart to show the assembly of a kitchen hand blender and a sandwich toaster.

Finish

The last part of section d) deals with the finish given to a product, whether it be surface coating, applied finishes, self-finishing or surface decoration. The analysis of a range of manufactured products made using woods, metals and plastics will help you understand different types of finishes and the reasons for applying them.

Finishing is the final process in the manufacture of a product and is a very important aspect of quality. In high volume and batch production, random quality checks are made on complete assembled products as part of the ongoing quality assurance system. Although finishes vary according to the product and materials used, the general reasons for their use include protection against corrosion or degradation, resistance to surface damage or to provide surface decoration to improve the appearance, add style or brand logos to the product. Some finishes may be added to provide information about the product, such as instructions on the product assembly or for fire or electrical safety. In general finishes should:

- be colourfast with a uniform colour and texture
- not run, peel or blister
- resist environmental and operating conditions (corrosion or mistreatment)
- resist physical damage (wear or scratching)
- resist staining or discolouration
- be easy to keep clean.

Task

1 Identify and compare six examples of products and analyse the surface finish of each. Use the following questions to help you:
   - What kind of material is the product made from?
   - Is the finish coated or anodised?
   - Does the surface finish result from any manufacturing process?
   - Was the finish applied before or after assembly?
   - How was the finish applied?
2 Select a range of products such as a kitchen water filter, a wooden garden bench, a workshop machine vice or a sandwich toaster. Describe, using notes and sketches, the stages of manufacturing for each under the following headings:
   - preparation
   - processing
   - assembly
   - finish.

e) Discuss the importance of quality in the manufacture of the product (8 marks)

In this section you will be asked to demonstrate your understanding of the importance of quality in design and manufacture. You will need to explain each point you make. For example, stating that the use of tolerance is important will gain few if any marks. You will need to explain why tolerance is important for the product in question and give an example of how it might be used. Remember to avoid discussing safety in this section.

Quality control in production

Quality assurance (QA)

There is no such thing as absolute quality, because the concept of quality changes over time. The attitude of companies towards quality must therefore be constantly reviewed if they are to satisfy consumer expectations, which are influenced by:

- the product design, its appearance and the image it gives the user
- its build quality, performance in use and value for money.

Customer satisfaction in which cost and quality are in harmony is an aspect of quality assurance (QA), which covers every area of product development from design to delivery to the customer. The use of QA ensures that identical products are manufactured on time, to specification and budget. Manufacturers of high volume products that demonstrate the use of a total quality management (TQM) system throughout the company, can apply for ISO 9000, the international standard of quality. ISO 9000 approved companies only buy in standard components from other approved suppliers. TQM gives them control over raw materials, a record at every production stage to aid product/process improvement, a reduction in waste/reworking and customer satisfaction. TQM means that quality is built-in and monitored at every stage of production, to enable the product to be made 'right first time'. The use of a TQM system means that the company's reputation is enhanced, so it will get repeat orders and increase its profitability.

Although a system like TQM is not likely to be used in the manufacture of a hand made chair, it would be used in the production of a large scale one-off product, such as the Millennium Bridge over the Thames. Different aspects of TQM include the use of making jigs and patterns and the use of quality control (QC) to ensure accurate and consistent production. For example, in injection moulding, the accuracy of dies is essential for ensuring that a domestic iron is made consistently and all the component parts fit together accurately when the product is assembled.

Quality control (QC)

Quality control is the practical means of achieving quality assurance. It is concerned with monitoring the accuracy of production for conformance to specification, at critical control points (CCPs) in the product's manufacture. QC ensures the manufacture of identical products with no faults and provides feedback to the quality assurance system, to make sure that it is working properly. QC makes use of inspection and testing against manufacturing specifications and against agreed quality standards.

- Specifications provide clear details about materials, dimensions and tolerances, processes and assembly.
- Tolerance is the numerical difference between the limits in size that the design will tolerate and still function as required. For example the dimension of a shaft might be specified as 50 mm with a tolerance of +/– 0.05 mm. This means the shaft can actually be 0.05 mm bigger or 0.05 mm smaller and yet still function correctly and to its quality specification.
- Inspection examines the product component or material to determine if the specified tolerance limits are being met. It takes place during preparation, processing, assembly and finish, where final inspection

monitors the quality of the materials, dimensional accuracy, appearance and surface finish. Random sampling involves the inspection of a small batch of the finished products. The overall product quality is then determined using statistics.

Task

Analyse an 'own brand' product such as a hand drill.

1 Write a report on the quality assurance system that could be used by the manufacturer, identifying and describing the key factors of the system, including:
   - critical control points
   - quality control techniques used
   - the role of inspection.
2 Justify the use of a quality assurance system in one-off production and high volume manufacture.

Quality standards

Quality assurance (QA) involves the use of quality standards (QS), which enable manufacturers to meet the requirements of the users. The aim of QA is customer satisfaction, which is concerned with the relationship between performance, price and aesthetic appeal. All manufacturers want to produce saleable products. A product such as a bicycle, that was considered state of the art 50 years ago would not be a saleable product today, which is one of the reasons why QS are continually developing, to keep up with technological change.

QS are agreed by the customer (such as a DIY retailer of 'own brand' products) or laid down by organisations such as the British Standards Institute (BSI), European Standards (EN) or the International Standards Organisation (ISO). Agreed QS and those laid down by organisations are incorporated into the product specification.

Testing against external quality standards

Testing is concerned with the performance, durability and life expectancy of the product. In quality control, quality indicators (QIs) are used at critical control points (CCPs) to check for conformity to specification. QIs are variables or attributes that are capable of being monitored.

- Tolerance is a variable factor because it is concerned with dimensions that can be measured, such as length, weight or performance. Test results are compared with the specification.

- Attributes cannot be measured, they are either right or wrong. Visual inspection of a watering can, for example, checks if it is the correct colour or if it leaks. If it leaks it is rejected, if it does not leak it will do its job and is said to conform to its specification.

Labelling requirements

Most labelling requirements relate to labels, signs, symbols and warnings about safety, found on packaging of products, such as toys, upholstered furniture or plastic products.

The Kitemark (see Figure 1.18) is awarded if a product meets a given standard *and* the manufacturer has a quality system in place to ensure that every product is made to the same standard. Independent testing houses, approved by the BSI, test products at regular intervals and confirm that they comply with the relevant standard. If you see a Kitemark symbol on a product, you will know that it has undergone a series of tests to make sure that it conforms to the QS in its specification, so you know that the product is safe and reliable.

Figure 1.18 *The BSI Kitemark and European CE marking*

> ### Task
> Discuss the importance of quality in the manufacture of a wooden dining chair, a galvanised watering can and a portable CD player, using the following headings:
>
> - quality control in production
> - quality standards.

f) Discuss the health and safety issues associated with the product and its production (8 marks)

In this section you are asked to demonstrate your understanding of the principles of health and safety legislation and good manufacturing practice. Make sure that you match your responses to the marks available, explaining each point you make.

Safe use of the product

Product safety and usability are of prime importance in today's market, where users regard safety as a basic requirement of a product's performance. For example, in the 1950s American cars were sold on looks alone, whereas today's cars include airbags and side impact bars as standard. Cars are also increasingly liable to environmental legislation, whether it be to minimise fuel consumption, reduce the use of non-renewable materials or design for recycling.

Guarantees

Manufacturers today are expected to guarantee a product's reliability, performance and safety. Typically, a product such as a food processor (Figure 1.19) would be supplied with a warranty to cover the product for 12 months from the date of purchase. It would also have displayed on the packaging a list of features that form part of the specification of performance. Consumers these days expect that the products they buy perform as specified, so the provision of warranties is essential for any manufacturer that wants to stay in business.

Figure 1.19 *Electrical products are supplied with warranties.*

A food processor is potentially very dangerous as it has a stainless steel blade which rotates at very high speeds. It therefore has a series of safety factors designed into it:

- the blades will only rotate if the lid is locked in place
- the motor stops immediately if the lid or the mixing bowl are removed during operation
- the food container is high sided to stop fingers getting down to where the food is placed
- a pusher is used to push foodstuffs down for grating or cutting
- there are non-slip feet on the underside and no dangerous parts protrude
- there is a waterproof casing with carefully sealed bearing and motor housings, to make it safe when processing liquids
- instructions for use identify ways of avoiding injury when handling and cleaning blades.

Labelling
The CE marking shown on products sold within the EU means that the product has met the required legal, technical and safety standards. If the product is tested and found to fail the standard, it can be withdrawn from sale and the manufacturer prosecuted. The Kitemark is another guarantee that a product is safe and reliable. Special labelling requirements apply to toys for children under the age of 36 months. For example, BS EN 71 describes how toys must be accompanied by appropriate clear and legible warnings (such as suitability for the age of the child or about a choking hazard) in order to reduce risks in their use.

Task
Identify how the design of a product such as an electric hedge trimmer has safety factors designed into it. Make reference to the following:

- electrical and operating safety
- protruding parts
- handling/cleaning the tool.

Safety procedures in production

Principles of health and safety legislation
The Health and Safety at Work Act (1974) provides a body of law dealing with the health and safety of people at work and the general public who may be affected by the work activity. The legislation exists to ensure the provision of safe working conditions which reduce the risks of accidents. This legislation also includes:

- The Factories Act (1961)
- COSHH (Control of Substances Hazardous to Health)
- The Management of Health and Safety at Work Regulations (1992).

Principles of health and safety at work
The 1974 Act states that risk assessment is a legal requirement, which means that all manufacturers must have a health and safety system in place. Not only are employers and employees responsible for ensuring safety at work, but so are manufacturers of equipment and all suppliers of materials and components. Employers are responsible for the health and safety of their employees and employees must follow the safe working practices set out by the employer, with guidance from the Health and Safety Executive (HSE).

Making risk assessments
Risk assessment means identifying hazards that may cause potential harm to employees and users. The risk that a hazard may occur must be evaluated and the chance of injury and potential damage that could occur must be eliminated or controlled. Risk assessment used in manufacture could include the use of:

- health and safety regulations and risk assessment procedures
- health and safety notices placed around the workplace
- staff training in the safe use of machines, tools and materials
- guards and emergency stop buttons on machines
- machine servicing and up-to-date log books
- the correct use of personal protective equipment (PPE), such as clothing or goggles
- appropriate ventilation, heating, light and noise levels
- COSHH data, first aid instructions and fire safety signs.

Task
Draw up the key stages of production for a hand drill and identify the risk assessment procedures necessary to manufacture it as safely as possible.

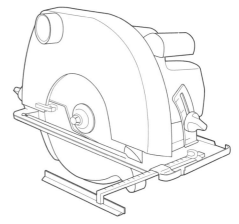

Figure 1.20 A circular saw

g) Discuss the appeal of the product (8 marks)

This section asks you to discuss the appeal of the given product, using headings such as 'form', 'function', 'trends/styles' and 'cultural'. The headings may vary in each exam, depending on the product in question, so you will need to match your responses to the available marks. Remember to use the headings to structure your answer. You should approach this section from the point of view of the buyer, so ask yourself 'Why would the user buy this product?' Remember that this section is *not* a repeat of section a) so do *not* write out another product design specification, which will gain few if any marks.

Product appeal

Trends and styles are very important criteria in product development these days. There is also a need to use new technology, to understand the market and to continually re-innovate to prevent products from becoming out-of-date. Even for technical products like mobile phones or hand-held PDAs, aesthetics, market appeal and function are vital to the product's form and use. The economic success of most manufacturers depends on their ability to identify target market group (TMG) needs and to create products that meet these needs. These days the TMG may be global and cultural differences are becoming increasingly important. Environmental issues are also set to become a market driver as legislation clicks

in. In the exam you will need to discuss the following:

• form and function, which relate to the product's design features and technical performance. How do they meet user requirements? Who are the TMG? Are they adults or children, male or female? Why is the product suitable for them? What are

Figure 1.21 The 'Hot Bertaa' aluminium kettle was designed by Philippe Starck. Although it is widely recognised as a 'design classic', it is very difficult to fill and pour from the conical shaped spout. The handle, which is an integral part of the pouring spout becomes very hot to hold.

the specific characteristics that make it more appealing than any other product?

- trends/styles which relate to the aesthetic appeal of the product. In what way does the style of the product appeal to the TMG? How does if fit in with their lifestyle? What kind of image does it give to the user? Does the product's style and colour follow current market trends? Is this a selling point?

- cultural, which can include other values issues that influence the design of the product. Is it recyclable? Does it have a Kitemark or a warranty? Is it designed to meet British, European or International legislation? What kind of retail outlet would sell it? Is it cheap and cheerful or high quality? Is it expensive or value for money?

Task

1 Identify a current best-selling product and evaluate its appeal.
   - State the TMG for the product and the image it gives the users.
   - Explain the characteristics that make it more appealing than any other similar product on the market.
2 Compare the key design features of a kettle or toaster manufactured by two different manufacturers.
   - List and compare the aesthetic and performance characteristics of each product.
   - Draw up a list of TMG needs and explain how each product meets them.
   - Explain which product is the best buy and why.

Quality of written communication (3 marks)

Remember that three marks are available for the 'Quality of your written communication'. If you always use the headings given in the exam paper to structure your answer, you will be more likely to organise and present your responses clearly and logically. When you work through this unit keep a technical notebook where you write definitions of technical terms so you use them appropriately in the exam. Three marks can make a difference between grades.

Exam preparation

Practice exam question

Figure 1.22 shows a desk with three drawers.

Figure 1.22 *A desk with three drawers*

The computer desk is:
- sold as a flat pack for self assembly
- made using beech laminated board
- made using black lacquered steel for the legs and drawer handles
a) Outline the product design specification for the desk. Address at least **four** of the following headings:
  - function/purpose
  - performance
  - market
  - aesthetics/characteristics
  - quality
  - safety   (7)
b) Justify the use of:
  - beech laminated board   (3)
  - black lacquered steel for the legs and drawer handles.   (3)
c) Give **four** reasons why the desk is mass produced.   (4)
d) Describe, using notes and sketches, the stages of manufacture for the desk under the following headings:
  - preparation (of tools and equipment)   (3)
  - processing   (7)
  - assembly   (4)
  - finish   (2)

  Include references to industrial manufacturing methods in your answer.

  Do **not** include detailed references to quality control and safety testing in this section.
e) Discuss the importance of quality in the manufacture of the desk, using the following headings:
  - quality control in production   (4)
  - quality standards   (4)
f) Discuss the health and safety issues associated with the desk and its production under the following headings:
  - safe use of the product   (4)
  - safety procedures in production   (4)
g) Discuss the appeal of the desk under the following headings:
  - form   (3)
  - function   (2)
  - trends/styles/cultural   (3)
h) Quality of written communication   (3)

Total: 60 marks

UNIT 2

Product development I (R2)

Summary of expectations

1. What to expect

You are required to submit one coursework project at AS. This project enables you to build on the knowledge, understanding and skills you gained during your GCSE course. At AS level you are expected to take more responsibility for planning your work. Your AS project should comprise a product and a coursework project folder. It is important to undertake a project that is appropriate and of a manageable size, so that you are able to finish it in the time available.

2. What is a resistant materials project?

An AS Resistant Materials Technology project should:

- reflect study of the 'technologies' involved in the AS Resistant Materials Technology Specification
- be manufactured using materials listed in Unit 3A (Classification of materials)
- ensure that at least two thirds of the work focuses on resistant materials, both in the practical outcome and the coursework folder
- include a functioning product that matches its specification.

For example, an AS Resistant Materials Technology project could include the use of systems and control. In this case the design and practical work should focus on the use of resistant materials and their manipulation. Any systems and control aspect would require a lower level of research and understanding than the dominant resistant materials aspect. An element of 'black box technology' would be acceptable in this kind of project, but there would need to be enough understanding of the systems and control aspect to enable design decisions to be made.

3. How will it be assessed?

The AS project covers the skills related to designing and making. It is assessed using the criteria given in Table 2.1.

You must attempt to cover all the assessment criteria A–G. The G criterion has been included to reflect that your project meets all the requirements of the

Table 2.1 AS coursework project assessment criteria

Assessment criteria	Marks
A Exploring problems and clarifying tasks	10
B Generating ideas	15
C Developing and communicating design proposals	15
D Planning manufacture	10
E Product manufacture	40
F Testing and evaluating	10
G Appropriate project	10
Total marks	110

Specification (see 'What is a resistant materials project?'). It is very important to check the appropriateness of your project with your teacher or tutor *at the start of the project*. If you take account of how the marks are awarded when planning your work, you will be able to spend an appropriate amount of time on each part of the project. This will give you more chance of finishing in the time available and increase your chance of gaining the best possible marks. Your AS project will be marked by your teacher and the coursework folder will be sent to Edexcel for the Moderator to assess the level at which you are working. It may be that after moderation your marks will go up or down.

4. Choosing a suitable project

As a student designer your choice of AS coursework project is very important, because you need to balance designing and making a successful product with meeting the needs of the project assessment.

Remember that the level at which you should be working is one year on from GCSE. Do not be too ambitious in your choice of project, as testing and evaluation cannot properly take place on incomplete work.

At AS level you are expected to take a more commercial approach to designing and making products that meet needs that are wider than your own. This could mean designing and making:

- a one-off product for a specified user
- *or* a prototype product that could be batch or mass produced for users in a target market group.

The key to success is to choose a project that is both enjoyable and challenging, so that you will feel inspired to finish it in the time available.

If you identify a realistic user need and a problem to be solved, you can start to focus on the kind of product that you could design and make to solve the problem. The needs of others is therefore a good starting point for design. It will enable you to ask questions about the purpose and potential for a product and how it will benefit the user(s).

Whatever kind of product you design will need to be planned and you will need to include details of how this single product will be manufactured in your school or college workshop. Even if you are designing for batch or mass production, you will still only be making *one* of them. You are *not* required to manufacture the product in quantity, although you may need to produce identical components for use in the product. You will, however, need to detail in your production plan the changes necessary in the manufacture of your one single product, if it was to be made in quantity.

5. The coursework project folder

The coursework project folder should be concise and include only the information that is relevant to your project. It is essential to plan and analyse your research and be very selective about what to include in your folder. This will help you make decisions about what you intend to design and make.

Do not be tempted to waste your valuable time finding out information that has no relevance to your project, because you will not gain any more marks for it.

Your coursework folder should include a contents page and a numbering system to help its organisation. The folder should comprise around 20–26 pages of A3/A2 paper. The title page, contents page and bibliography should be included as extra pages.

Table 2.2 gives an approximate guideline for the page breakdown of your coursework project folder.

Table 2.2 *Coursework project folder contents*

Suggested contents	Suggested page breakdown
Title page with Specification name and number, candidate name and number, centre name and number, title of project and date	extra page
Contents page	extra page
Exploring problems and clarifying tasks	4–5
Generating ideas	3–4
Developing and communicating design proposals	5–6
Planning manufacture	3–4
Product manufacture	2–3
Testing and evaluating	3–4
Bibliography	extra page
Total	20–26

In the section on 'Product manufacture' it is essential to include clear photographs of the actual manufacture of your product. This will provide photographic evidence of modelling and prototyping, any specialist processes you have used including the use of CAD/CAM, and show the stages of manufacture.

Please note, however that the guideline for the page breakdown of your coursework folder is only a suggestion. You may find that your folder contents vary slightly from the guideline because of the type of project that you have chosen.

6. How much is it worth?

The coursework project is worth 40 per cent of your AS qualification. If you go on to complete the whole course, then this unit accounts for 20 per cent of the full Advanced GCE.

Unit 2	Weighting
AS level	40%
A2 level (full GCE)	20%

A Exploring problems and clarifying tasks (10 marks)

Look at Figure 2.1 and consider the questions:

1. Identify, explore and analyse a wide range of problems and user needs

Your choice of AS coursework project is very important because you are expected to take a more commercial approach by designing and making a product that meets needs that are wider than your own. This could mean designing and making a one-off product for a single specified user, or designing and making a product that could be batch or mass produced for users in a **target market group**. Whichever type of product you design and make, you will need to explore and identify a realistic need or problem through investigating and analysing the needs of people in different contexts. You should also be prepared to consult with others, including your teacher or tutor, to ensure that they help you choose a suitable project.

Exploring and identifying the needs of users

The needs of users change according to **demographics**, expectations and **lifestyle**. In other words, the kind of products that people want to use change according to their age, and their expectations change according to the kind of lifestyle they aspire to. Many manufacturers and retailers target potential customers and attempt to match their lifestyle needs with products. They often do this by using market research to identify the buying behaviour, taste and lifestyle of potential customers. This can establish the amount of money they have to spend, their age group and the types of products they like to buy. New products can then be developed to match customer needs.

Therefore, the identification of a need is tied up with finding out what people want. The context in which you do this can vary – you may, for example, decide to investigate new trends in sport, different people's lifestyles or demographics such as investigating the needs of people involved in sport, designing to meet the taste and personality of a specific target market group or designing for the very young (or old!).

Task
Evidencing industrial practice: finding out about the needs of users
The needs of your users or target market group can provide a good starting point for design. Manufacturers often build up 'customer profiles' to help establish the characteristics of products that customers want. You can use a similar practice. Write a customer profile to describe target market groups for the following products. In doing this you could think about customers' lifestyles, values and tastes.

a) racing bike   c) camping kettle
b) portable CD player   d) table lamp

Identifying and analysing a realistic need or problem

The characteristics of products must also change if they are to fulfil the developing needs of users and sell into a market at a profit. Once the requirements of users are known they can be analysed and problems which give rise to the need for new products identified. Often a new product may be developed from an existing one by modifying its **aesthetic** or **functional** characteristics to meet changing user needs. This kind of product development often involves redesigning to add value to a product – to improve its performance, function or appeal. Many 'new' products are developed in this way and may use existing technology in a new context or take a different approach to a problem. Cars, electric toasters, vacuum cleaners and furniture are often designed as a result of this.

Figure 2.1
What problem does this product solve? What is the target market for this product? What are its key design features? How does this product meet the needs of its users?

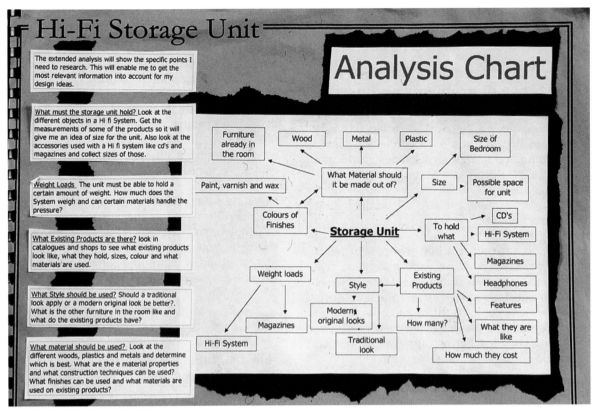

Hi-Fi Storage Unit

Analysis Chart

The extended analysis will show the specific points I need to research. This will enable me to get the most relevant information into account for my design ideas.

What must the storage unit hold? Look at the different objects in a Hi fi System. Get the measurements of some of the products so it will give me an idea of size for the unit. Also look at the accessories used with a Hi fi system like cd's and magazines and collect sizes of those.

Weight Loads The unit must be able to hold a certain amount of weight. How much does the System weigh and can certain materials handle the pressure?

What Existing Products are there? look in catalogues and shops to see what existing products look like, what they hold, sizes, colour and what materials are used.

What Style should be used? Should a traditional look apply or a modern original look be better?. What is the other furniture in the room like and what do the existing products have?

What material should be used? Look at the different woods, plastics and metals and determine which is best. What are the e material properties and what construction techniques can be used? What finishes can be used and what materials are used on existing products?

Furniture already in the room — Wood — Metal — Plastic — Size of Bedroom

What Material should it be made out of? — Size — Possible space for unit

Paint, varnish and wax

Colours of Finishes

Storage Unit

To hold what — CD's — Hi-Fi System — Magazines — Headphones — Features — What they are like

Weight loads — Style — Existing Products

Modern original looks — How many? — How much they cost

Magazines — Traditional look

Hi-Fi System

Figure 2.2 *Analysis of a need or problem*

Sometimes a new product is developed to fulfil a need in a completely new situation – in this case a product may be described as innovative or inventive. This kind of product development may arise through the desire for adventure, through new types of leisure activities, through the needs of people in dangerous situations or through developments in technology. Some of these new situations can create opportunities for product development to meet new challenges, such as trekking to the Poles, taking part in performance sports, ballooning round the world or space exploration! Figure 2.2 shows how one student identified a need.

Clarifying the task

Once you have identified user needs and a problem to be solved, you can start to focus the problem by asking questions about the kind of product that you could design and make to solve the problem. You can think about the purpose and potential for the product – how will it benefit users? Are there any products currently on the market that fulfil a similar need? What is the price range of these products? What kind of materials do they use? What kind of materials and processes could you use? What are current product design

trends? Asking questions like this will help you clarify what you are trying to achieve and enable you to write a design brief.

To be successful you will:

- Clearly identify a realistic need or problem.
- Focus the problem through analysis that covers relevant factors in depth.

---

2. Develop a design brief

Developing a design brief will focus your mind on what you want to do. The design brief should develop from your exploration and analysis of user needs and problems, and from your identification of a potential product that is feasible for you to make. The design brief needs to be simple, concise and explain what needs to be done, but it should not include the solution to the problem. In other words, it should give you direction but not be so precise and specific that you are not left with any room for development.

Task
Evidencing industrial practice: developing a design brief

The design brief should be simple, concise and explain what needs to be done, without going into too much detail, e.g. 'Design and make a product to transport garden rubbish'.

a) For the design brief above identify the type of product that is to be designed, what it should do and the range of potential users.

b) Choose three different products and write a design brief for each, that identifies the product type, its purpose and the target market group.

Try not to be too ambitious when you write your design brief, because even the simplest product idea has a habit of becoming more complex as it develops! Use your design brief to help plan your research, so that you can target what you need to find out.

To be successful you will:
• Write a clear design brief.

3. Carry out imaginative research and demonstrate a high degree of selectivity of information

Research
Your research needs to be targeted and it needs planning in order to find out useful information that will help you make decisions about what you intend to design and make (see Table 2.3). Read your design brief and your analysis of the problem – this will help your planning. For example, the design brief 'Design and make a product to transport garden rubbish' would lead to research into the needs of gardeners of different ages and to the investigation of existing rubbish transporters, including research into their design, the materials, components and manufacturing processes used and the quality, cost and safety needs of users.

Task
Evidencing industrial practice: market research

Produce a market research report that identifies the buying behaviour, taste and lifestyle of potential customers. Find out the size of the target market group, preferred brands and the competition from existing products.

You should undertake both **primary** and **secondary research** using a range of sources, such as the ones listed in Table 2.3. Use the research ideas above and your research planning to target the research you need to undertake. This will depend on the type of product you intend to design and make – you are not expected to research everything listed in Table 2.3.

Writing a bibliography
Reference all your secondary sources of information in a bibliography and include:

• sources of any information found in textbooks, newspapers, magazines
• sources of information from CD-ROMs, the Internet, etc.
• sources of scanned, photocopied or digitised images.

Table 2.3 *Research ideas and where to find information*

Research ideas	Information sources
Market trends, design and style trends, **niche markets**, new product ideas, user requirements, buying behaviour, lifestyle, demographics	Market research, window shopping, shop surveys, visits, the work of other designers, art galleries/museums, user surveys, questionnaires, product test reports, consumer reports, people, the Internet
Materials, components, systems, processes, construction technology, scale of production, product performance requirements, product quality, product price ranges, value for money	Analysis of existing products, materials testing, books, newspapers, electronic media, CD-ROMs, databases, the Internet, exhibitions, reports, magazines, catalogues, libraries, local colleges, industry, people
Quality control and safety procedures	Books, safety reports, 'Design and Technology Standards for Schools', information via the Internet, industry
Values issues, e.g. cultural, social and environmental	Keep up with the latest news, events, films, exhibitions, cultural and social issues. Use the Internet to find out about company values and about environmental issues

Product analysis

In industry product analysis is often used to obtain information about the design and manufacture of competitors' products. Analysis can include data research using catalogues or trade literature and analysis of the products themselves, either by eye or using physical analysis of the product's component parts. You can analyse commercial products that are similar to the product type that you intend to design and make. This can provide data about materials, components, processes and construction. It will also develop your understanding of quality of design and manufacture and of the concept of value for money.

At this stage of your project you may find that some activities need to be carried out simultaneously. For example, research and the analysis of the problem are often bound together – some analysis may be necessary in order to focus some of the research, while analysis of the research is necessary if the gathered information is to be useful when making decisions about what to design.

Analysing research

You will need to analyse your research and select *useful* information that is *relevant* to the design of your intended product. Do not be tempted to include pages of irrelevant information to 'pad out' your project folder, as this will gain you no extra marks. The Moderator needs to see evidence of your ability to be selective and demonstrate how your research has linked into the problem drawn out from your analysis. Your research analysis should, therefore, provide you with a good understanding of the problem and the desired aesthetic, mechanical and performance requirements of the product you intend to design and make. This will enable you to move on to the next stage in the development of your product – writing a design specification.

To be successful you will:

- Carry out a wide range of imaginative research, selecting information that will help you make decisions about what to design and make.

4. Develop a design specification, taking into account designing for manufacture

In the same way that analysis and research are often bound together, the design brief, the research process and the development of a product design specification are all linked and

Factfile

A design specification is detailed information that guides a designer's thinking about what is to be designed. It is used to help generate, test and evaluate design ideas and to help develop a **manufacturing specification.**

may be developed simultaneously. Your design specification should include measurable characteristics that will help you design with manufacture in mind. It needs to include enough detail to develop feasible design ideas, but leave room for creative thinking. Use the following checklist to help develop your design specification:

- the product purpose, function and aesthetics
- market and user requirements
- the expected performance requirements of the product, materials and components
- the kind of manufacturing processes, technology and scale of production you may use
- any values issues that may influence your design ideas, such as cultural, social or environmental
- any quality control and safety procedures that will constrain your design
- time, resource and cost constraints you will have to meet.

You are expected to identify an *appropriate* scale of production, such as a one-off product for a specified user, or a product that could be batch or

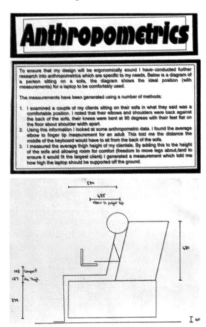

Figure 2.3 *Student research into a problem*

mass produced for a target market group. The scale of production will impact upon all your design and manufacturing decisions. For example, a one-off product for someone with limited mobility would need to meet the requirements of one person and may be a more complex product or one that is more complicated to manufacture. A batch or mass-produced educational toy would need to meet the requirements of a range of children *and* their parents but may require processes to be simplified for ease of manufacture. Figure 2.4 shows part of a specification for a workstand.

Your design specification should guide all your design thinking and provide you with a basis for generating design ideas. The specification can change and develop as research is carried out, often starting as an outline specification until the final design specification is reached. This is used as a check when testing and evaluating design ideas and provides information about the product that can help to monitor its quality of design. The design specification is therefore an essential document that sets up the criteria for the design and development of your product. Specification criteria can also be used later on to guide your thinking when developing a manufacturing specification.

> **To be successful you will:**
> • Write a clear design specification.

Specification

Primary specification points:

❑ The unit must make a laptop and a work stand easy to use on a sofa.

Justification: This requirement was stated in the design brief.

❑ The unit must be rigid and stable.

Justification: This point was determined through the client questionnaire.

❑ The product must be found to be aesthetically pleasing/attractive to my clients.

Justification: This point was determined through the client questionnaire.

❑ The unit must fit in aesthetically with its surrounding environment.

Justification: This point was determined through the client questionnaire.

❑ The product must be safe to use with no sharp edges.

Justification: This point was determined through the client questionnaire.

❑ The unit must be designed and manufactured to an excellent standard with extra attention given to the finish.

Justification: This point was determined through the client questionnaire.

❑ The unit must be completed by spring 2001.

Justification: The unit is required for external inspection during the spring.

Secondary specification points:

❑ A mug must be held securely in a convenient position for use.

Justification: This point was determined through the client questionnaire.

Figure 2.4 *Part of a student specification for a laptop workstand*

B Generating ideas (15 marks)

1. Use a range of design strategies to generate a wide range of imaginative ideas that show evidence of ingenuity and flair

Using your design specification

You are expected to generate a range of feasible design ideas, based on the criteria that you have set up in your product design specification. Sketches need to be lively and include annotation to explain your thinking. Remember to practice sketching and annotating ideas as this will help you in your coursework and in the Unit 6 Design examination. Your design specification should be a great help when designing, as it is much easier to develop ideas from a starting point than starting from nothing!

Imagine starting with a blank sheet of paper and being able to design anything you like. Where do you start? How do you know what is required? No designers work like this because, firstly, there is not enough time to work in this way and, secondly, products are designed for people who have definite likes and dislikes and lifestyles that demand products with specific aesthetic, functional and performance characteristics.

Many designers say that designing becomes easier when there are limitations under which to work because these limitations provide a framework within which to design.

Inspiration for design ideas

All sorts of sources can be used for inspiration – your design specification and research, of course, but you may also decide to base some aspects of your ideas on a theme. Try using some of the following to inspire your work:

- natural forms
- an artist or the work of other designers, e.g. Starck
- an art or design movement, e.g. Art Nouveau

- a theme, e.g. 'miniature' or 'techno'
- influences from exhibitions, music or films
- new technology, e.g. using new materials or processes.

You can use product analysis to inspire your design work. It is a good way of collecting information about a product type – about materials, components, manufacturing processes, style, colour, quality and price. If you work out the design specification for an existing product, this can often help you develop a specification for your own product. However, you must ensure that any product you develop in this way is truly original and not simply a copy of an existing product.

Generating ideas

It is often a good idea to keep handy a notebook for quick sketches – these can be pasted or scanned and pasted into your coursework project folder, rather than be redrawn (your project folder should show evidence of creative thinking rather than stilted copied-out work). This may mean a certain untidiness, but you will find it more inspiring if you approach your initial design work in a similar way to using a sketch book – use hand-drawn sketches, colour ideas and written notes to show your ideas, which can be developed and modified later. At this stage the examiner is looking for evidence of your design thinking and later on to see how you develop these ideas. It is not always necessary to develop a wide range of totally different ideas, although you should always try to produce variations related to what the product looks like, with alternative ideas of how it will function, especially if there are moving parts.

2. Use knowledge and understanding gained through research to develop and refine alternative designs and/or design detail

Evidencing the influence of research on your design ideas should not be a problem, as this influence should come through naturally from the design specification, which in itself is based on research and analysis. Also, you should be using your research and specification as inspiration for ideas – so be sure to make this explicit when you are developing your initial ideas by adding brief notes to explain your thoughts. Figure 2.5 shows how one student researched her project and provided the evidence for this.

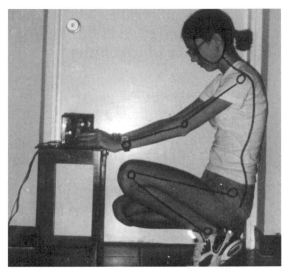

Figure 2.5 *This student investigated the strain on the spine when bending to tune a radio at different heights*

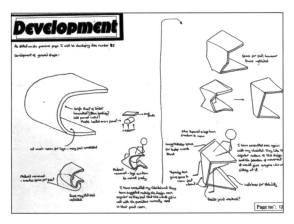

Figure 2.6 *The influence of research on design*

As you experiment with first ideas and gradually refine your thinking, you may find that you start to think about the possible materials or processes you could use, to work out if your ideas are feasible.

You may also start to play around with combinations of ideas or work on the fine detail of some of your ideas. Making use of the information you acquired during your research phase should enable you to develop and refine alternative ideas to the stage where you can select one (or possibly two) that are the most promising.

Factfile

Designing different types of products
The type of product being designed will influence the research you need to do and the kind of ideas that you produce. For example, ideas for the design of a child's desk may be concerned with the shape and form of the desk in relation to its function and age/size and interests of the child.
Ideas for a clock may be concerned with the mechanical/electrical control systems as well as its form and function.

To be successful you will:
• Demonstrate effective use of appropriate research.

---

3. Evaluate and test the feasibility of ideas against specification criteria

As you sketch your first ideas you should refer back to your design specification to see if you

are going in the right direction, to see if there is any aspect that you have missed or to look for more inspiration. Make sure that you use your design specification as a tool for measuring the appropriateness of your design ideas. Always make evaluative comments on decisions made. Make sure you demonstrate your technical knowledge and use technical terminology, rather than making general references such as 'made from plastic' or 'I don't like the look of it'. At AS level you are required to justify the rejection or selection of ideas. It is always helpful to talk to others at this stage, as talking over your ideas often provides the step forward you need. There are a number of options here – discussing your ideas with a teacher or tutor, presenting your ideas to a small group of fellow students or talking to potential users of your product. In industry this would be a normal part of product design and development, in order to determine the feasibility of ideas, ease of manufacture and market potential. You should evaluate your ideas against the design specification so that you are able to justify, using written notes, why your chosen design is worth developing.

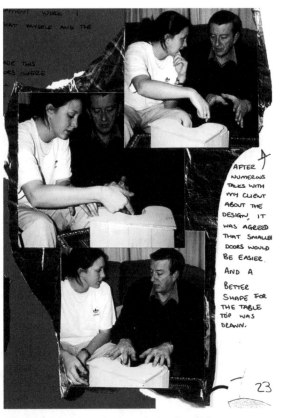

Figure 2.7 *Why a chosen design is worth developing*

During the course of your design development you may find that there are some aspects that you need to find out more information about. You may need to modify your design specification in some way if, for example, you find after evaluating ideas against the design specification, there are some aspects that are not feasible.

C Developing and communicating design proposals (15 marks)

1. Develop, model and refine design proposals, using feedback to help make decisions

Your aim should be to develop your ideas until you produce the best possible solution to your problem. This can be done by modelling, **prototyping** and testing. Modelling your design proposal in 2D and 3D will provide you with information about its feasibility. You can also get feedback by finding out what potential users think about your ideas. Ask them a range of questions, based on the requirements of the design brief and specification. The feedback you receive should help you make decisions about the aesthetic and functional characteristics of your design proposal. You can then refine your ideas if necessary, until you find the best possible solution.

2. Demonstrate a wide variety of communication skills, including ICT for designing, modelling and communicating

You should use a variety of 2D and 3D communication skills to develop, model and refine your design proposal (see Figure 2.8). Communication skills can include writing, drawing or using **ICT** for word processing or CAD. Modelling will enable you to see how your design proposal will perform or what it will look like before making any final decisions. The

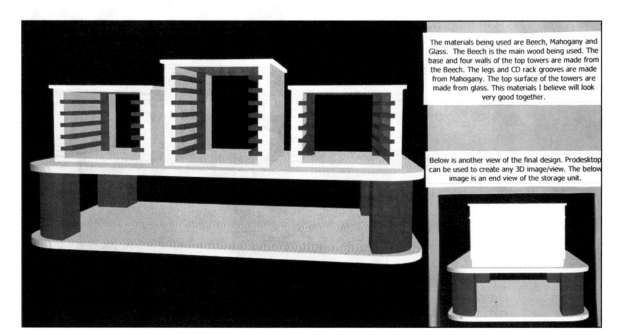

The materials being used are Beech, Mahogany and Glass. The Beech is the main wood being used. The base and four walls of the top towers are made from the Beech. The legs and CD rack grooves are made from Mahogany. The top surface of the towers are made from glass. This materials I believe will look very good together.

Below is another view of the final design. Prodesktop can be used to create any 3D image/view. The below image is an end view of the storage unit.

Figure 2.8 Modelling ideas can help to make decisions about the feasibility of your design proposals

modelling method you use will depend on the type of product you are designing and the aspect of its design which is to be modelled. You should use materials which are quick and easy to cut, shape and join, and could use construction kits or computer modelling. The use of computers for **2D and 3D modelling** is an essential part of industrial product design.

2D modelling
2D modelling techniques can include, for example, drawing **pictorial** or **exploded views**, using cut and paste, or using computer-aided design (CAD) software. Using CAD, you can scan in your image and try out different variations, or use parametric software to trial 'what if?' scenarios. However, you should only use CAD if it is appropriate and you will not be penalised for its non-use. Sometimes it is more appropriate to use hand-drawn techniques, e.g. when thinking through the development of an idea. You should try to develop both hand and computer skills. Working models in 2D can be made from strip and rod materials to test the function or accuracy of mechanisms. Sometimes you need to produce a number of models before a mechanism functions well.

3D modelling
You should use 3D modelling and prototyping techniques to test your design proposal before manufacture. Modelling by hand to make 3D working mock-ups can involve using different materials such as:

- card, lightweight materials, sheet materials, soft timbers, foam board, high density foam, clay
- components and/or construction kits.

If you are including any systems and control elements in your product, remember that your focus should be on two thirds resistant materials. Any modelling you do could incorporate the use of 'black box technology', although you would need to have enough understanding of the systems and control element to enable you to make design decisions. If in doubt, consult with your teacher or tutor.

Sometimes it is only necessary to model one part of a product. For example, a product with moving parts may only need to have the mechanism modelled in 3D to test its physical or mechanical characteristics (see Figure 2.9); the aesthetic characteristics could be modelled in 2D, using drawings or CAD.

Your modelling and prototyping should help you plan:

- the most appropriate manufacturing processes
- how long each different process might take

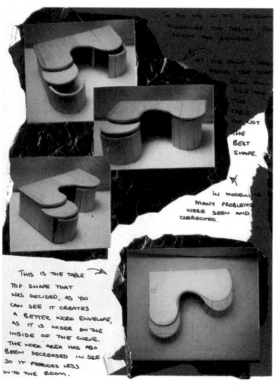

Figure 2.9 *3D modelling prior to manufacture*

- the materials, components, equipment and tools you need
- the order in which to assemble the component parts
- how easy the product will be to manufacture in the time available – do you need to simplify anything?
- any forward ordering of materials, so they are ready when you need them
- estimated costs of materials and manufacture
- where and how you will check the quality of your product.

As your design proposal develops, it will become more refined until you reach the best possible solution – your final design proposal.

> **To be successful you will:**
> - Use high-level communication skills, with appropriate use of ICT.

3. Demonstrate understanding of a range of materials/components/systems, equipment, processes and commercial manufacturing requirements

You are expected to demonstrate an understanding of the materials, components and/or systems that are appropriate to the manufacture of your product. Modelling and prototyping should enable you to do this because it enables you to test and trial materials and components. Selecting the most suitable materials is vital to the success of your project. Your materials and components should be appropriate to your chosen scale of production. For example, you may need to choose special materials for a one-off product or more cost-effective materials for a product that could be batch or mass produced.

Selecting materials

Technologists have difficult decisions to make when selecting the right material for the job, especially when new materials are appearing all the time! Deciding which materials to use in a product design is not easy. Making good choices requires understanding of a wide range of materials. When choosing materials you need to take into account the following:

1. Materials availability
- How rare or common is the material?

- How simple, easy or safe is its manufacturing process?
- Does the material come in standard forms and preferred standard sizes?

2. Moral and social issues
- Is the material harmful to work with or use, even though it has some very useful properties?
- Should you take the risk and use the material or not?
- Does the production of the material exploit a labour market in any country?

3. Cost
- What are the processing and delivery costs of the material?
- How much will it cost to store the material? Is it possible to use just-in-time ordering of materials to reduce storage costs?
- What are the costs of waste materials? Can these be recycled?

4. Method of production
- Are the material's properties appropriate to the chosen method of production?
- How many products need to be made?
- Will the combination of materials and the production method produce a high-quality product?

When choosing materials you should also consider influences on the product styling:

- What is the product's purpose? What is it for? What should be its durability and life span?
- What is the product's function? How is it required to work? What does it need to do?

Other considerations include the aesthetic requirements of the product. You should consider:

- form, such as the 3D shape and size
- visual properties, such as colour, reflection, transparency and surface pattern
- textural properties, such as how rough or smooth, including surface detail and the finish used.

The final choice of materials is often a compromise, which means that it partly satisfies all the product requirements, but does not completely satisfy them all! In some cases some requirements are more important than others, such as cost being more important than function. It is only when all the information is collected that a decision can be made. There is rarely one correct answer or absolute best material. Usually, there are several materials that will do the job.

Figure 2.10 *Final proposal drawing*

Illustrating the final design proposal

You should clearly illustrate your final design proposal, to show what your product will look like, how it will work and how it will be made. You should use an appropriate graphic style. This could be hand- or computer-generated. You will not lose marks if you choose to use hand techniques as opposed to using ICT. However, you could enhance your design and technology capability by using a range of computer techniques, such as using word-processing or CAD software. You are not required to know how to use a specific language, computer or software package, but should use what is appropriate and available.

You should annotate your final design proposal, using appropriate technical terminology. Identify the materials, components and processes required to manufacture your product. This may require you to produce front or back views of your product, or to produce exploded views to explain any design detail. Your annotation should demonstrate an understanding of the working characteristics of your chosen materials, components and processes. This information should be related to your chosen scale of production. For example, if you design a one-off

product for an individual user, it may require the use of special materials, processes, tools or equipment. If you design a product intended for mass production, it may require the use of easily available materials, or processes that reduce waste or that need to be simplified for ease of manufacture. Remember that if you are designing for an individual or for mass production you will still only be making one product in your workshop.

> **To be successful you will:**
> • Demonstrate a clear understanding of a wide range of resources, equipment, processes and commercial manufacturing requirements.

Factfile
Illustrating the final design proposal

Professional product designers aim to illustrate the final design proposal in the most convincing way possible. To do this they use a variety of techniques such as:

• 2D and 3D presentation drawings
• engineering drawings and schematics
• detail drawings of parts of the design
• photographs of small-scale and full-scale models
• written reports

The technique chosen to illustrate the final proposal needs to be suitable for the client's budget, for the type of information to be communicated and for the character of the product. It is often a good idea to use a style of presentation that supports the image of the product. For example a child's toy could be presented in a simple, colourful style, whereas a more technical style might be more suitable for a high-tech product.

4. Evaluate design proposals against specification criteria, testing for accuracy, quality, ease of manufacture and market potential

You should test your final design proposal against the design specification to evaluate how it will meet its quality requirements, how easy it will be to manufacture and how it will meet user requirements. The use of

Figure 2.11 *Evaluation of design proposals*

feedback from an individual user or users in a target market group will give you some idea of your product's market potential. Remember to include evaluative comments about your product in your design folder. This evaluation should enable you to justify why this is the best solution to the problem, by explaining:

- how your design proposal meets the specification
- how it will meet the aesthetic, functional, cost and quality requirements of users

- how easy it will be to manufacture in the time available
- the availability of any specialist equipment and your skill level in using it.

> **To be successful you will:**
> - Objectively evaluate and test design a proposal against the specification criteria.

D Planning manufacture (10 marks)

1. Produce a clear production plan that details the manufacturing specification, quality and safety guidelines and realistic deadlines

You are expected to produce and use a production plan that explains how to manufacture your product, within realistic deadlines. This involves providing details of how to make the product, taking into account quality and safety requirements. Realistic deadlines are those that are achievable. They should match the making of the product to the time available.

The work that you have already done on modelling, prototyping and testing should help you to plan your product manufacture. Prototyping enabled you to decide on the manufacturing processes you will use, if you need to prepare any jigs or patterns to aid manufacture, the quantities of materials and components you require and how all the different component parts will be assembled.

Other planning decisions may involve:

- how easy the product will be to manufacture in the time available
- if it is necessary to simplify anything
- how the product could be manufactured if you were to make it in high volume
- if any special materials or tools are required and the safety procedures you need to observe.

Producing a production plan

Your production plan should be made before you manufacture your product. It is worth remembering that you will not be awarded marks for a production plan made after manufacturing the product. Your production plan should include a manufacturing specification and a production schedule, which give clear and detailed instructions for making your product.

a) A manufacturing specification includes:
  - a product description

- accurate exploded, orthographic, isometric or working drawings with clear assembly details, dimensions and tolerances
- quantities and estimated costs of materials and components
- finishing details.

b) A **production schedule** can be produced in table form and should identify:

- the individual tasks within the manufacturing process
- the sequence of tasks in logical order
- the tools and equipment required for each task
- the estimated time each stage of manufacture/process will take
- **critical control points** in the product's manufacture where quality is to be checked
- **quality indicators** such as defined **tolerances** to show how quality will be measured
- safety requirements.

Part of a production schedule is shown in Figure 2.12.

The production plan is a key part of your quality assurance system, because it

Figure 2.12 Part of the production schedule

WHAT I WILL DO / WEEK NUMBER	INTENDED
ONE	Cut rails for frame. Cut rails for legs.
TWO	Cut joints for each corner of table - rails & legs
THREE	Cut rest of joints. Glue together back of frame
FOUR	Glue together, RHS of frame & LHS lower level & LHS
FIVE	Cut door 1 shape from pine block.
SIX	Sand & shape door frame shape - Cut in half so there is 2.
SEVEN	Cut sides for frame, glue door 1 together.
EIGHT	Rout ply wood, for all around base, to look like panelling. Fit ply to door frame 1.
NINE	
TEN	Cut frame for second door - in the same way.
ELEVEN	Fit panelled ply to back & sides of frame - Glue & pin
TWELVE	Fit ply to door frame 2.
THIRTEEN	Cut table tops & sand edges.
FOURTEEN	Cut & fit shelf into RHS lower level. Fit table top on. Fit doors
FIFTEEN	Fit table tops on. Sand down & Wax.
SIXTEEN	Test & Evaluate.

documents all the information required to manufacture your product. It identifies the key stages of production where you will check for quality to make sure that your product conforms to specification. Using quality control will make sure that if your product was made in high volume, each product would be made to the same standard. Remember to record the critical control points where you will check for accuracy and the quality indicators you will use, such as the tolerances and dimensions you identified in your manufacturing specification. You should also record how you use testing, inspection and safety procedures during manufacture.

Task

Evidencing industrial practice: planning manufacture

Use the following to help you plan manufacture:

- Ensure your materials are easy to work and handle.
- Check that the performance characteristics of your chosen materials meet the design specification.
- Forward order materials and components if necessary.
- Produce a manufacturing specification and a work schedule.
- Specify any safety requirements and procedures.
- Specify where and how you will check for quality.
- Make sure that you follow your production plan and record any changes you make.

---

documents all the information required to manufacture your product. It identifies the key stages of production where you will check for quality to make sure that your product conforms to specification. Using quality control will make sure that if your product was made in high volume, each product would be made to the same standard. Remember to record the critical control points where you will check for accuracy and the quality indicators you will use, such as the tolerances and dimensions you identified in your manufacturing specification. You should also record how you use testing, inspection and safety procedures during manufacture.

c) An estimate of product costs

Estimating product costs means producing an accurate price for the product, which would make it saleable *and* create a profit. In industry cost levels depend on the method of production, which must be easy and fast so that labour costs are as low as possible. You can cost your product in set stages:

i) Work out **direct costs**, like materials and labour costs (how long your product takes to manufacture at a set rate per hour).

ii) Work out **overhead costs**, like rent, heat and electricity (these are often worked out as a set percentage of labour costs).

iii) Add together the direct and overhead costs, to give the total manufacturing cost.

iv) Work out your manufacturing profit (a set percentage of the total manufacturing cost).

v) Add together the total manufacturing cost and the manufacturing profit to give the selling price.

d) Setting realistic deadlines

Realistic deadlines are those that are achievable. Following a production plan will help you meet your production deadlines, but be prepared to modify your planning if you make any changes to your product or manufacturing processes during manufacture. Any modifications should be noted in your production plan, so make sure that you leave enough space to do this.

To be successful you will:
- Produce a clear and detailed production plan with achievable deadlines.

---

2. Take account of time and resource management and scale of production when planning manufacture

Planning is an important part of any project and many of the activities that you undertake will overlap because designing and manufacturing are complex and interrelated activities. Also, the number of weeks that you have available will depend on your timetable, e.g. you may have a set number of weeks where you concentrate totally on your coursework project or you may

Tasks

1 Planning

Use the following questions to help you plan your production:

a) Will my materials, components, tools and equipment be available when I need them?
b) How will my scale of production affect my manufacturing processes?
c) Can I use standard components, parts or materials to simplify my task?
d) Will the quality and quantity of my materials and components match my manufacturing specification?

2 Production planning

Using a Gantt chart is a good way of planning a project because it gives you a picture of the whole project at a glance . It can be used to plan:

- a whole project over the total number of weeks available
- the detailed manufacture of your product.

Produce a Gantt chart for your project:

a) Draw up a table with the dates across the top.
b) In the left-hand column, put in order a list of tasks to be done.
c) Note any tasks that can be done at the same time.
d) Plot the tasks against the time you have available.

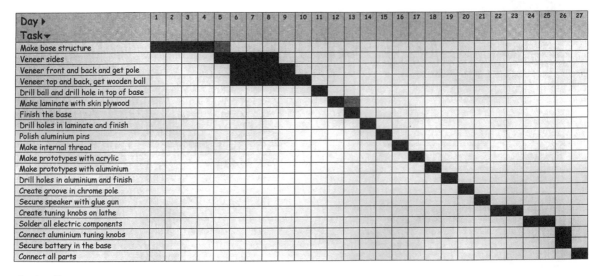

Day ▶ Task ▼	1	2	3	4	5	6	7	8	9	10	11	12	13	14	15	16	17	18	19	20	21	22	23	24	25	26	27
Make base structure																											
Veneer sides																											
Veneer front and back and get pole																											
Veneer top and back, get wooden ball																											
Drill ball and drill hole in top of base																											
Make laminate with skin plywood																											
Finish the base																											
Drill holes in laminate and finish																											
Polish aluminium pins																											
Make internal thread																											
Make prototypes with acrylic																											
Make prototypes with aluminium																											
Drill holes in aluminium and finish																											
Create groove in chrome pole																											
Secure speaker with glue gun																											
Create tuning knobs on lathe																											
Solder all electric components																											
Connect aluminium tuning knobs																											
Secure battery in the base																											
Connect all parts																											

Drying times
Four hours
Twenty-four hours

Figure 2.13 *A student produced this Gantt chart to help her plan her project*

have less time during the week but more weeks overall. In other words, your coursework project time may be short and fat or long and thin!

Remember to use your production plan as a working document in which you record any subsequent changes you have to make, if for example, delays occur. Any realistic amendments to the production plan will provide you with useful data to refer to in your end of project evaluation.

Planning materials

One of the most important reasons for planning is to make sure that materials, components, tools and equipment are available when required and in the appropriate quantity and quality. Check out your requirements well in advance. As far as quality of materials is concerned, you should ensure that they meet your specification requirements. For example, if you are planning the manufacture of a one-off product for a client you may require the use of special materials or more time consuming complex processes, so take this into account. On the other hand, if you are planning a manufacturing prototype you may need to consider using standard sizes or standard components to reduce costs – or to simplify manufacturing processes to ensure fast, cost-effective manufacture.

Help! What if my production plan goes wrong?

The purpose of your production plan is to guide you through your product manufacture, so you use your time well.

- Sometimes you may come across delays, such as having to wait for a component to arrive or for the use of a piece of equipment.
- The first thing you must do is not panic, but record any problems you have in your production plan. You can then adapt your manufacture to meet the changed circumstances.
- If you use a Gantt chart for planning you will easily see your progress, so you can monitor things as you go along.
- If you are held up for any reason, make a note of it in your production plan and get on with something else!

To be successful you will:
- Demonstrate effective management of time and resources, appropriate to the scale of production.

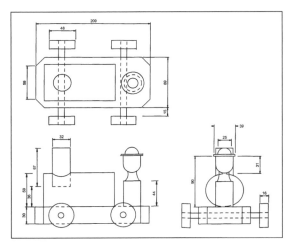

Figure 2.14 *Working drawing using CAD*

3. Use ICT appropriately for planning and data handling

The aim of using Information and Communications Technology for planning and data handling is to enhance your design and technology capability. You will not be penalised for non-use of ICT, although you should use it where appropriate and available.

When planning and data handling, good use of ICT could include using word-processing, databases, spreadsheets or CAD software for a range of activities that may include:

- organising and managing data
- production planning using colour-coded Gantt charts, diagrams or flowcharts
- producing manufacturing specifications
- producing accurate **working drawings**
- working out quantities and costs of materials and components.

An example of working drawings produced using CAD software is illustrated in Figure 2.14.

To be successful you will:
- Demonstrate good use of ICT.

E Product manufacture (40 marks)

1. Demonstrate understanding of a range of materials, components and processes appropriate to the specification and scale of production

Demonstrating understanding of materials

You are expected to demonstrate an understanding of the working characteristics of the materials and components appropriate to the manufacture of your product.

To a certain extent you have already demonstrated understanding of the materials, components and processes needed to manufacture your product. You modelled, prototyped and tested materials, components and processes. You annotated your design proposals and explained the working characteristics of suitable materials, components and processes. In your planning you specified the materials, components and processes required to make your product. You are ready to demonstrate further your knowledge and understanding of materials and components through the actual manufacture of your product.

Scale of production

Your product will be either a one-off for an individual user or a product that could be batch or mass produced. Even if you are designing for batch or mass production, you will still only be making *one* product. You are *not* required to manufacture your product in quantity, although there may be times when two or more identical components will have to be made. Remember to detail in your production plan the changes necessary in the manufacture of your

one single product, if it was to be batch or mass produced.

A batch or mass produced product requires a different approach throughout its development to a one-off product designed for a single user. A product designed to be batch or mass produced will have a wider target market group and may require the use of standardised materials, fewer component parts and more simplified processes. It will, however, still need to be made and finished to the highest quality. By contrast, a one-off product for an individual user may need to be made to specific dimensional requirements, using specialised or more expensive materials and more complex processes; hence this type of product is often made to order by a 'designer-maker' at a higher cost.

Whichever type of product you make, there will be other complications such as constraints related to the materials, tools and equipment available to you. If problems occur with the availability of resources, for example, you may have to change your original choice of materials

Figure 2.15 *Work in progress, showing a skill*

or adapt the processes you use. If this happens, do not forget to record any changes in your production plan and justify any new choices of materials, components or processes.

Task

Approaches to manufacturing

A different approach is required when planning the manufacture of a product at a different scale of production. For one of the following products draw up a table to show the key stages of manufacturing the product as a one-off for an individual user and as a product suitable for batch or mass production:

- a child's wall clock
- a table light for a home office.

For each scale of production, think about materials preparation, processing, assembly and finishing.

To be successful you will:
- Demonstrate clear understanding of a wide range of materials, components and processes.

---

2. Demonstrate imagination and flair in the use of materials, components and processes

---

Task

Practise the techniques and processes you aim to use during manufacture, so you can improve your skills. You may:

- experiment with working, shaping and joining materials
- use mock-ups to trial joints and structures
- experiment with processes to improve aesthetic qualities such as materials finish.

Be prepared to modify your manufacturing processes if necessary or to adapt details of the product design, e.g. changing the type of joint or method of joining. Keep all your experimental work in a small box, so you can refer to it if necessary. You can evidence your experimental work by including a photograph in your folder.

One clear way that you can demonstrate imagination and flair is in the way you handle materials and processes. An understanding of how materials behave and processes work, will enable you to show your skills and ability. This will result in the production of a quality product – one that:

- is attractive to the market
- is well made from suitable materials
- functions well
- is enjoyable or fun to use
- would sell at an attractive price
- is manufactured for safe use and disposal, without harm to the environment.

This is quite a list of considerations, but if you check you should find that you have taken most of them into account in your design and manufacturing specifications. At this stage, prior to manufacture you have the opportunity to hone your skills – to experiment with and trial materials, components, techniques and processes – so you can demonstrate your ability through the manufacture of your product.

To be successful you will:
- Demonstrate imagination and flair.

---

3. Demonstrate high-level making skills, precision and attention to detail in the manufacture of high-quality products

Demonstrating high-level making skills

Demonstrating high-level skills involves making the best use of available materials and components, appropriate to your design proposals. It also involves using tools and equipment with accuracy, confidence and skill. If you practise your existing skills before manufacturing your product, you should gain an understanding of your ability in relation to your expectations for your product. If your ability falls below your expectations, you have two options, either improve your skills or adapt the process. Improving your skills will result in improving the quality of your work, so you produce a high-quality product.

The making of high-quality products also depends on planning quality into your design and manufacturing process. Refer to your design and manufacturing specifications and to your production plan, where you should find references to quality. Your production plan should identify the key stages of manufacture,

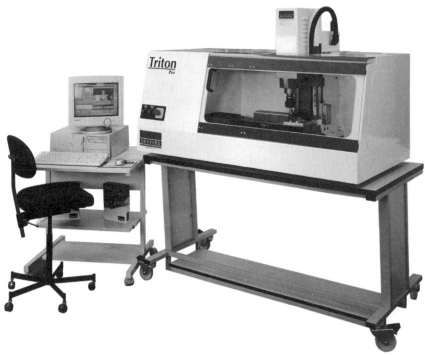

Figure 2.16 *A CNC milling machine attached to a PC*

where you can monitor the accuracy of your work as it progresses, checking against the dimensions and tolerances you detailed in your working drawings.

> **To be successful you will:**
> • Demonstrate demanding and high-level making skills that show precision and attention to detail.

4. Use ICT appropriately for communicating, modelling, control and manufacture

> ### Factfile
> **Using ICT in manufacture**
> The increasing use of ICT has had an enormous impact on manufacture, through the use of CAD/CAM systems. CAD/CAM enables the efficient design and manufacture of products and the control of manufacturing equipment. Computer-aided manufacture (CAM) automates production, repeats processes easily and precisely and enables the production of cost-effective products.

You can use ICT to help your product manufacture, where it is appropriate and available, but you will not be penalised for its non-use. You are not expected to know how to use specific equipment or programs, but you should understand the benefits of using ICT for manufacture.

Different uses of ICT include:

• using software to model **'virtual' products** on screen before manufacture, saving time and costs, because it reduces the need to make expensive manufacturing prototypes
• communicating information between CAD software and **Computer Numerically Controlled** (CNC) equipment
• using CNC machines for fast, accurate production processes
• communicating manufacturing information between the design office in one location and the manufacturing site in another.

Figure 2.16 shows a CNC milling machine attached to a PC.

If you do not have easy access to CAM equipment you could use a printer or a plotter to print out working drawings, or to cut out a component parts drawing and use it as a template for making identical components.

If you do have access to specialised CAM equipment you can use CAD to produce design ideas and then export the digital data to CNC equipment for producing accurate component parts for your product.

> **To be successful you will:**
> • Demonstrate good use of ICT.

5. Demonstrate high level of safety awareness in the working environment and beyond

Safety in manufacturing means the safe design, manufacture, use and disposal of products. Manufacturers must follow safety procedures and check standards, regulations and legislation related to product design. This ensures that products are safe for the manufacturer, the consumer and the environment. Legal requirements, such as the Health and Safety at Work Act 1974, and Reporting of Accidents 1986, ensure that safe production processes are followed to prevent industrial accidents. Safe production means identifying all possible risk and documenting safety procedures to manage and monitor the risk.

A question of safety

Ask the following questions at key stages of design and manufacture:

- What could go wrong?
- What could cause things to go wrong?
- What effect would this have?
- How can I prevent things from going wrong?

You need to demonstrate a similar awareness of safety at all stages of design and manufacture, by making safety a priority in your work.

1. At the research and design stage you should take account of designing with safety in mind, both for you, the maker, for your intended user(s) and for the environment. This may involve researching safety regulations related to your product. Safety features should be identified in your design specification.
2. Your production plan should identify specific safety features related to manufacture, including safety guidelines for your chosen materials and the tools, equipment and processes you may use. Modelling and prototyping before production will enable you to test for safety against the criteria that you have identified.
3. During the manufacturing process you should follow safety guidelines related to safety with people, materials, tools and equipment.

> **To be successful you will:**
> - Demonstrate high-level safety awareness.

F Testing and evaluating (10 marks)

1. Monitor the effectiveness of the work plan in achieving a quality outcome

Your production plan is a key tool in monitoring the quality of your product. You should record any changes you make to the product itself or to any processes you use during manufacture. You may not need to make any changes, but if you do, however minor, they should still be recorded because they could have an impact on the quality of your product. Recording any changes would also enable you to make an identical product to the same standard.

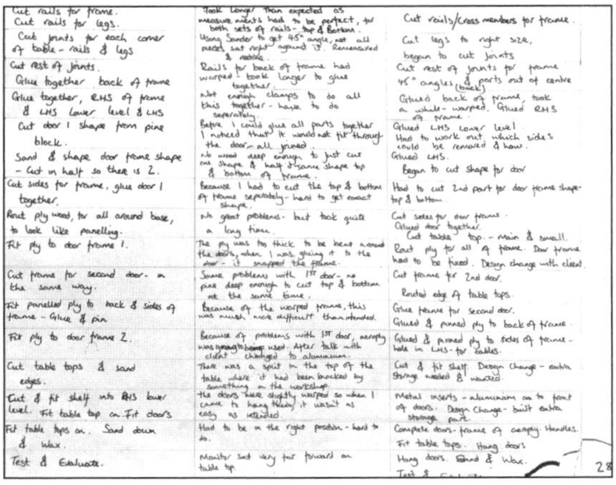

Sometimes completely unforeseen problems can arise through, for example, using a process that is new to you. Other reasons for making changes could be through not having the right materials, components, tools or equipment available when you want them, or because you are running out of time. If you do have to make any changes, make sure that you explain what you have done and why – write it down straight away before you forget or do a quick sketch to explain in your production plan any change in design or product manufacture. Recording any changes to your product will make it easier to evaluate its quality of design and manufacture.

Figure 2.17 *Your production plan is a key tool in monitoring the quality of your product*

> **To be successful you will:**
> - Make effective use of your work plan to achieve a high-quality outcome.

2. Devise quality assurance procedures to monitor development and production

Task

Evidencing industrial practice: the meaning of quality

In industry quality means:

- conforming to the specification
- ensuring fitness for purpose
- making products with zero defects
- making products right first time, every time
- ensuring customer satisfaction
- exceeding customer expectations.

Use the following questions to help your quality planning:

- Do you aim for fault-free work?
- Do you know what standards are expected?
- Do you check the quality of your work against the specifications?
- Does your work meet the specifications?
- Are you pleased with your work?
- Can you do it any better?

Figure 2.18 *Testing the product is essential to meet the requirements of the specification and the user(s)*

Quality planning is a key process during product development and manufacture and you should devise your own **quality control** procedures to monitor quality. Check that you can meet the quality requirements outlined in your design specification and check your product for quality at critical points in its manufacture, using quality indicators. These are categorised as 'variables' or 'attributes'.

- Variables are measurable characteristics which can vary within set limits, such as keeping within a tolerance of +/-0.5 mm. Checking tolerances may involve the use of an accurate measuring device, such as a Vernier gauge or a micrometer. Variables can include length, width, height, diameter, position, angles and mass.
- Attributes are either acceptable or unacceptable characteristics. They make use of inspection using sensory tests of vision and touch to check characteristics such as colour or texture. For example, if the colour is meant to be blue, green won't do!

Remember to record how you use quality control checks and inspection during manufacture.

To be successful you will:
- Devise clear quality assurance procedures.

3. Use testing to ensure fitness-for-purpose

Testing to ensure fitness-for-purpose means testing that the product's performance meets the requirements of the specification and the user(s). Inspection and testing are essential and the techniques that you use will depend upon the product type. Materials testing can include mechanical tests for strength, testing for physical properties or inspecting for visual appearance. Process testing can include inspecting for faulty processing or testing mechanical parts. The final inspection can include the product's function under normal working conditions, testing for conformance against specifications and visual appearance.

You should record the results of any testing and inspection done during and after manufacture:

- Test the performance of the product against the design and manufacturing specifications
- Test that the quality of the product is suitable for user(s); check against user requirements in the specifications.

To be successful you will:
- Make effective use of testing to ensure fitness-for-purpose.

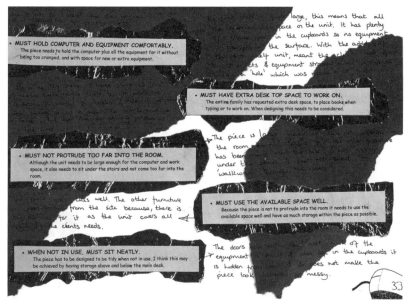

Figure 2.19 *Evaluation against specifications and feedback from users is an effective way of judging the success of a product*

4. Objectively evaluate the outcome against specifications and suggest appropriate improvements

You should be as objective as possible when justifying the success of your product against the design brief and specifications. Being objective means taking an unbiased view of your product. This can sometimes be difficult, as you will have been closely involved in its design, development and manufacture. It is easier to be objective if you use standards against which to judge your product – these standards are the design brief, the design and manufacturing specifications and the quality criteria identified in the production plan. Make sure that you evaluate the success of your product against user needs, using feedback to evaluate how well the product works, how it looks and how well it meets requirements.

Objective evaluation should provide you with feedback on the success of your product, which will help you decide how and if it can be improved. Your suggestions for improvement should be based around the product's aesthetic and functional success, its quality of design and manufacture and its fitness for purpose.

> **To be successful you will:**
> • Objectively evaluate the outcome and suggest appropriate improvements.

G Appropriate project (10 marks)

The G criterion has been included to reflect that your project meets all the coursework requirements. It is very important to check the appropriateness of your project with your teacher or tutor at the start of your project to make sure that it will enable you to address all of the assessment criteria by which your project will be marked. After your teacher or tutor confirms that your project is appropriate, you will still need to keep an eye on the assessment criteria in order to achieve all the available marks. You will also need to take account of feedback from your teacher or tutor in order to improve your work as it progresses. Remember to include photographic evidence of your modelling and prototyping and the product manufacture, especially to highlight difficult techniques or hidden details. This could include, for example, photographs of moulds or jigs that may have been crucial to the manufacturing process.

Student checklist

1. Project management

- Take responsibility for planning, organising, managing and evaluating your project.
- Include photographic evidence to show hidden details or to demonstrate the processes you used at each stage of manufacture.
- Include only the work related to the assessment requirements.

2. A successful AS coursework project will:

- identify a realistic need and solve a problem for your specified user(s)
- include relevant information that summarises your research
- show the influence of research on your design decisions
- demonstrate a variety of communication skills, including appropriate use of ICT
- be a manageable size so you can finish it on time
- focus on at least two thirds resistant materials (listed in Unit 3A)
- evidence understanding of industrial practices
- include clear photographs of modelling, prototyping, testing and manufacture
- detail the manufacture of one product and show how it could be manufactured in quantity
- manufacture a functioning product that matches its specifications
- allow time to evaluate your work as it progresses and modify it if necessary
- be well-planned so you can meet your deadlines.

3. Evidencing industrial practices in coursework

- Use industrial terminology and technical terms.
- Use designing activities similar to those used in industry, i.e. develop a design brief, use market research, modelling and prototyping, etc.
- Use manufacturing activities similar to those used in industry, i.e. use a production plan, quality control, test against specifications, etc.

4. Using ICT in coursework

- Develop the use of ICT for research, designing, modelling, communicating and testing.
- Develop the use of ICT for planning, data handling, control and manufacture.

5. Producing a bibliography

- Reference all secondary sources of information in a bibliography, e.g. textbooks, newspapers, magazines, electronic media, CD-ROMs, the Internet, etc.
- Reference scanned, photocopied or digitised images. Do not expect to use clip art at this level.
- Do not expect marks for any work copied directly from textbooks, the Internet, or from other students.

6. Submitting your coursework project folder

- Have your coursework ready for submission by mid-May in the year of your examination.
- Include a title page with the Specification name and number, module number, candidate name and number, centre name and number, title of project and date.
- Include a contents page and numbering system to help organise your coursework folder.
- Ensure that your work is clear and easy to understand, with titles for each section.

7. Using the Coursework Assessment Booklet (CAB)

- Complete the student summary in the CAB *and remember to sign it!* This should include your design brief and a short description of your coursework project.
- Ensure that the CAB contains a minimum of three clear photographs of the whole product, with alternative views and details.
- Your candidate name and number, centre name and number and 6298/01 should be written in the CAB, by the product photographs and *on the back of each photograph.*

Help! What if my project goes wrong?

- If your Unit 2 coursework project doesn't meet your expectations, don't worry! You can retake the unit and the better result will count towards your final grade.
- If you find yourself in this situation your teacher or tutor will be able to advise you on the best way forward.

Materials, components and systems (R301)

Summary of expectations

1. What to expect

Unit 3 is divided into two sections:

- Section A Materials, components and systems
- Section B consists of three options, of which you will study only one.

Section A is compulsory and builds on the knowledge and understanding of materials, components and systems that you gained during your GCSE course.

2. How will it be assessed?

The work that you do in this unit will be externally assessed through Section A of the Unit 3 examination paper.

You are advised to spend 45 minutes on this section of the paper.

3. What will be assessed?

The following list summarises the topics covered in Section A and what will be examined:

- Classification of materials and components:
  - ferrous metals, non-ferrous metals and alloys
  - thermoplastic and setting polymers
  - hardwoods, softwoods and manufactured boards
  - composites, synthetics and manufactured materials
  - ceramics, glass and concrete
  - microstructure of materials
  - classification of components.
- Working properties of materials and components:
  - hand and commercial processes
  - finishing techniques
  - product manufacture.

- Testing materials:
  - principles and techniques of testing before manufacture
  - comparative testing
  - British, European and International Standards.

You should apply your knowledge and understanding of materials, components and systems to your Unit 2 coursework.

4. How to be successful in this unit

To be successful in this unit you will need to:

- have a clear understanding of the topics covered in Unit 3A
- apply your knowledge and understanding to a given situation or context
- organise your answers clearly and coherently, using specialist technical terms where appropriate
- use clear sketches where appropriate to illustrate your answers
- write clear and logical answers to the examination questions, using correct spelling, punctuation and grammar.

5. How much is it worth?

This unit, with the option, is worth a total of 30 per cent of your AS qualification. If you go on to complete the whole course, then this unit accounts for 15 per cent of the full Advanced GCE.

Unit 3 + option	Weighting
AS level	30%
A2 level (full GCE)	15%

1. Classification of materials and components

Metals and alloys; ferrous and non-ferrous metals

The major proportion of all naturally occurring elements are metals and they form about one quarter of the earth's crust by weight. Aluminium is the most common (8 per cent), followed closely by iron (5 per cent). With the exception of gold, all metals are found in the form of oxides and sulphates. The ores have no pattern of distribution around the world but some countries have larger deposits than others.

Metals are divided into three basic categories:

1. Ferrous – the group which contains mainly ferrite or iron. It also includes those with small additions of other substances – mild steel, cast iron. Almost all are magnetic.
2. Non-ferrous – the group which contains no iron – copper, aluminium and lead.
3. Alloys – metals that are formed by mixing two or more metals and, on occasions, other elements to improve properties. They are grouped into ferrous and non-ferrous alloys.

In order to obtain the metals in any useful form, they have to be extracted from the ore before processing can take place. Mining or quarrying removes the ore from the ground, whereupon it is crushed which removes much of the unwanted earth, clay or rocks. The metal, now in a concentrated form, is roasted which causes the ore to change chemically into an oxide of the metal. The remaining stages of reduction break the chemical bond between the metal and the oxygen in the ore to leave a pure metal ready for further processing.

The production of ferrous metals

During the reduction process of iron, the ore coke, in the form of carbon and limestone, is fed into the blast furnace and heated to 1600°C. The limestone is used to extract the impurities from the ore to form a molten slag which floats on the iron and is tapped off separately.

The iron at this stage is called pig iron and it is still too impure for general use and needs further refining. In its molten state the pig iron, which contains about 3–4 per cent of carbon, is transferred into a further converter furnace which is more able to control the carbon content and any further impurities.

To make steel, the carbon content needs to be reduced significantly and this is normally done in the basic oxygen furnace where large volumes can be handled. Essentially, oxygen is blown into the liquid to combine with the carbon and

other impurities. Lime is added again which acts as a flux and removes the impurities to float on the surface as slag.

After careful checking and analysis of the composition of the melt, it is either poured into ingots, poured directly into castings or directly into a continuous casting machine. This latter process aims to increase efficiency since the metal is already in its molten state. From larger ingots or billets, the steel is removed to the mill and reheated before being rolled to form rods, flats, square tubes or channel sections.

The result of hot rolling gives a black oxide film and this type of steel is called black mild steel (see Figure 3.1.1). Bright drawn mild steel (BDMS) is oiled and re-rolled cold before being drawn through dies to create the accurate sizes.

Alloy steels are formed to create metals with enhanced properties. Mild steel is generally alloyed with such metals as chromium, tungsten and nickel. Whereas basic carbon steels lose their hardness at higher temperatures, high speed steels retain their hardness and cutting edge even at red heat. Resistance to corrosion can also be increased, as in stainless steel, which contains 12 per cent chromium and some nickel.

Micro-structure

Metals usually have one or two loose electrons in their outer electron shell and therefore they are quite likely to become easily detached. The **metal crystals** have a regular arrangement held together by electrostatic attraction. It is this movement of electrons which accounts for metals' high electrical and thermal **conductivity**. This mobility also leads to a degree of **plasticity** in metals in the form of ductility and **malleability**. Once a bond is broken another is formed.

Figure 3.1.1 Mild steel being hot-rolled

The production of non-ferrous metals

Aluminium is only available commercially in the form of bauxite, a hydrated form. It is very difficult to break down and therefore a process of electrolysis is needed. This is very expensive in terms of electrical energy. Firstly, the bauxite is crushed, mixed with caustic soda and then heated under pressure, whereupon it melts. Once filtered and washed it is roasted to produce alumina before it passes through the electrolysis stage. The proportion of aluminium is alloyed to improve its strength and hardness. Copper ores contain about only 4 per cent copper and they undergo similar processing to that of the production of aluminium to extract the pure metal. Crushing, floating and the addition of lime all help in the removal of impurities before the final stages of electrolytic refining.

Micro-structure

With the exception of mercury, all metals are solid at room temperature. In their molten form they are held together only by weak forces of attraction which mean they lack cohesion and will flow. As the metal solidifies, the energy is reduced within each atom, giving out heat, and the atoms arrange themselves according to a regular pattern or **lattice structure**. Their overall properties are affected by this lattice structure. Most metals crystallise into one of three basic types of lattice, as shown in Figure 3.1.2:

- close-packed hexagonal (CPH)
- face-centred cubic (FCC)
- body-centred cubic (BCC).

Iron is a very important metal since it changes from BCC to FCC at 910°C. Above 1400°C it changes back to BCC again. In the FCC form it absorbs carbon which is essential in the process of steel making. When cooling the changes occur in reverse.

A pure metal solidifies at a fixed known temperature with the formation of crystals, in either a cube or hexagonal structure. On further cooling, the crystals continue to grow as **dendrites** until each one touches its neighbour. At this point grains are formed and boundaries become visible when viewed under a microscope.

> ## Task
> Define the materials that are used in the manufacture of the blade for a carving knife, and a cold chisel. Explain how the properties and composition of each material contribute to the function of the product.

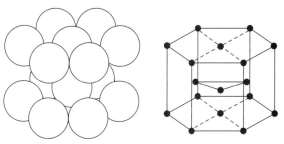

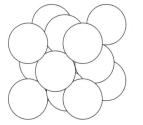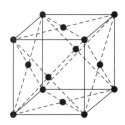

a) close-packed hexagonal (CPH)
zinc, magnesium
(weak, poor strength to weight ratio)

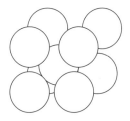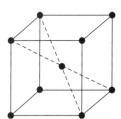

b) face-centred cubic (FCC)
aluminium, copper, gold, silver, lead
(very ductile, good electrical conductors)

c) body-centred cube (BCC)
chromium, tungsten
(hard, tough)

Figure 3.1.2 *Different metallic structures*

Table 3.1.1 on page 68 summarises the working properties and uses of common metals.

Thermoplastic and setting polymers

Thermoplastic and thermosetting plastics cover a wide and diverse range of substances that exist in both a natural and synthetic form. Natural resources such as cellulose from plants, latex from trees and shellac, a type of polish extracted from insects, play only a small part in the plastics industry. Synthetic resources, especially crude oil, supply the majority of the raw material for the production of plastics. This single resource of hydrogen and carbon account for the majority of plastics.

Table 3.1.1 *The working properties and uses of common metals and alloys*

Material	Melting point °C	Composition	Properties	Uses
Cast iron	1000–1200	Pig iron, scrap steel, various additions dependent upon use	White cast iron – very hard and brittle Grey cast iron – easily casts and good corrosion resistance	Heavy crushing machinery Bench vices
Steels	1400	Alloys of carbon and iron	Dependent upon carbon content and other elements	
Low carbon steel		Less than 0.15% carbon	Soft, ductile, malleable	Wire, rivets cold pressings
Mild steel		0.15–0.3% carbon	Ductile and tough Cannot be hardened and tempered	General construction steel, car bodies, nuts and bolts
Medium carbon steel		0.3–0.7% carbon	Harder than mild steel, less ductile	Springs, axles and shafts
High carbon steel		0.7–1.4% carbon	Hardness can be improved by heat treatment	Hammers, cutting tools and files
Alloy steels Stainless steel		Medium carbon steel + 12% chromium + 8% nickel	Corrosion resistant	Kitchen sinks, cutlery
High speed steel		Medium carbon steel + tungsten, chromium and vanadium	Retains hardness at high temperatures Brittle but can be hardened and tempered	Lathe tools, drills and milling cutters
Aluminium	660	Pure metal	Malleable and ductile Very conductive of heat and electricity	Aircraft, boats, window frames and castings
Duralumin		Aluminium + 4% copper + 1% magnesium	Work hardens, ductile and machines well	Aircraft parts
LM4 casting alloy		Aluminium + 3% copper + 5% silicon	Increased fluidity and improved hardness Good corrosion resistance	General purpose casting alloy
Copper	1083	Pure metal	Malleable and ductile Excellent conductor of heat and electricity	Wire, central heating pipes, car radiators and PCBs
Brass	927	65% copper + 35% zinc	Corrosion resistant Casts well Good conductor of heat/electricity	Casting, ornaments and marine fittings
Bronze	900–1000	90–95% copper + 5–10% tin Sometimes includes phosphor	Harder and tougher than brass Hard wearing Corrosion resistant	Castings, statues bearings
Lead	327	Pure metal	Soft and malleable Corrosion resistant Easy to work Immune to attack from chemicals	Protection against radiation from X-rays Roof coverings and flashing
Tin	232	Pure metal	Soft Corrosion resistant	Tinplate and soft solders
Zinc	420	Pure metal	Ductile and easily worked A layer of oxide prevents it from further corrosion	Coating for steel (galvanising), rust-proof paints, die casting

The refining of crude oil in a fractioning tower is the process that gives rise to the product hydrocarbon naphtha which is subsequently cracked into fragments using heat and pressure to form ethylene and propylene. In naturally occurring compounds, the molecules, consisting of only a few atoms, are short and compact. In plastics, the molecules do not stay as single units but link up with other molecules to form large chains of giant molecules. This process is called **polymerisation**.

Plastics are subdivided into two main groups with the formation of the chains the key feature that separates them:

1. Thermoplastics. These plastics are made up from long chains of molecules with very few cross-linkages. The smaller cross-links are known as **monomers** and the polymer chains are held together by a mutual attraction known as Van der Waals forces (see Figure 3.1.3a). This physical attraction is weakened by the introduction of heat. As the molecules move, they become untangled and the material becomes pliable and easier to mould and form. When the heat is removed the chains reposition and the material becomes stiff once again. Thermoplastics have a plastic memory, which means they have the ability to return to their former state after heating provided that no damage or chemical decomposition has happened during the heating process. Polythene, polystyrene and polypropylene are all examples of thermoplastics. Polythene is extensively used in the production of toys and carrier bags; polypropylene is used for containers with built-in hinges and chair shells where its good resistance to work fatigue is exploited.

2. Thermosetting plastics. Thermosets set with heat and thereafter they have little plasticity. During the polymerisation process the molecules link both side to side and end to end. This cross-linking process, known as covalent bonding, makes for a very rigid material, and once the structure has formed it cannot be reheated and changed (see Figure 3.1.3b). Polyester resin is used in with fibre glass and for paper weights. Urea formaldehyde is a stiff, hard, strong plastic and it is used for electrical fittings and some home-appliance parts such as knobs.

3. Elastomers. There is a third group of plastics and these are elastomers and they fall between the two basic groups. A limited number of cross-links allows some movement between chains. Rubber is a type of elastomer

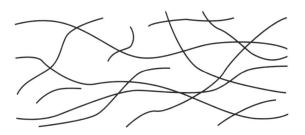

Figure 3.1.3a *Van der Waals bonding – low density polythene*

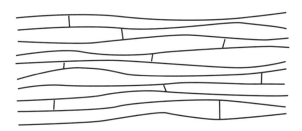

Figure 3.1.3b *Covalent bonding – polyester resin*

and it is used to make tyres for cars, flexible joint couplings and can also be used to dampen vibrations.

Glass reinforced plastic (GRP)

Glass reinforced plastic, often referred to as fibreglass, consists of strands of glass that are set in a rigid polyester resin. The strands are woven into matting which is available commercially in different weights. The polyester resin, albeit a thermosetting plastic, exists in a liquid form that has a catalyst or hardener added to it along with a coloured pigment for decoration purposes. The glass fibre strands provide the basic strength while the resin with its additives bonds the fibres together and provides a very smooth surface finish.

In order to achieve a high standard of finish from any GRP work, a high-quality mould must first be produced. The external or 'finished' side of the work must be finished to a very high standard since any defect or imperfection in the mould will be replicated in the finished piece.

The mould can be made from virtually any material but quite often medium density fibreboard (MDF) and hardboard are used with the additional use of wire and plaster of Paris for complicated shapes. If a porous surface has been used it is essential to seal the surface prior to use and a proprietary mould sealer should be used. It is quite common to make a full-size model of the finished piece which is then used to produce the GRP mould. In order to be able to remove the work from the mould it should be made with tapered sides and it should have no undercuts. A release agent is also essential and the mould should be coated several times before lay up proceeds. Good mould design should see no sharp corners and large flat areas should be avoided.

The stages in laminating follow a structured process and can be broken down into basic stages:

- Polish mould with the releasing agent.
- Prepare matting into appropriate sizes.
- Mix gel coat with pigment, hardener and catalyst.
- Apply gel coat to an even thickness of 1 mm.
- Wait about 30 minutes before stippling matting over mould making sure it is wet through.
- Build up successive layers to the appropriate thickness.
- Full curing takes approximately 24 hours before separation can take place.

GRP is used in a vast range of products where its great strength to weight ratio can be fully utilised. This means that much stronger shapes and products can be built that weigh much less than when being produced by other means. It is also very resistant to corrosion. GRP is used to make sailing boats and canoes. Some high-speed train front nose cones are also made from GRP.

Injection moulding

Injection moulding is probably the most widespread and versatile process used commercially for producing moulded plastic products, from bowls and buckets to television casings and dustbins. Although the cost of a typical mould is high, the unit cost per component produced becomes very small for high volumes making it an ideal process for mass-produced components. The process is best suited to thermoplastics but a few thermosetting plastics are used depending upon the conditions and environment the product is to be used in.

The process is quite simple since the material is heated to a plastic state and injected into an enclosed mould under pressure. The mould is opened and the product is removed with the use of ejector pins. Injection moulding is a highly automated process that produces high-quality products that require no further finishing other than to remove any sprue pins, gates and runners which are chopped off and reused. The

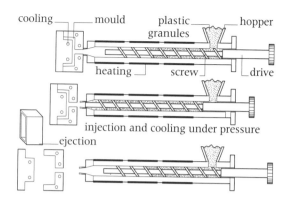

Figure 3.1.4 Injection moulding

machine itself consists of a hopper into which is fed the plastic granules, a heater and a rotating screw mechanism. The screw mechanism acts as a ram that injects the plasticised material into the mould before it is allowed to cool (see Figure 3.1.4).

Blow moulding

Blow moulding is the process used to form hollow products and components. A hollow length of plastic called a parison is formed by extrusion and is lowered down between an open split mould. The mould is then closed to seal up the free end of the parison and compressed air is blown into the mould forcing the plastic to the sides of the mould cavity where it is chilled causing the plastic to set (see Figure 3.1.5). Blow moulding is another highly automated process that produces little waste and requires only the flashing to be trimmed. It is estimated that some 1.5 billion PET (polyethelene teraphthalate) plastic bottles are made and thrown away each year in the UK. Like injection moulding, the initial mould cost is high, as is the machinery, but with components being produced in the volume of the PET bottles it is easy to see how the unit cost is very low.

Task

Think about the environmental issues and impact that the production of PET bottles cause, from the actual production of the plastic to the disposal of the bottle once its contents have been consumed.

Vacuum forming

Vacuum forming is used to produce simple shapes from thermoplastic sheet. It is possible to vacuum form acrylic. However, the ideal degree of plasticity in acrylic is not reached until a temperature of 180°C. Unfortunately, at 195°C

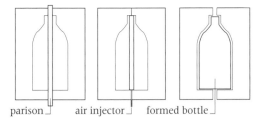

Figure 3.1.5 *Blow moulding*

acrylic starts to degenerate, therefore making it quite difficult to achieve a uniform heat across the whole sheet. However, 'Perspex TX' is an extruded form of acrylic and this becomes plastic at 150°C making it much more suitable for use in industry when products as large as baths can be formed. More commonly used materials include high-density polystyrene, ABS (acrylonitrile-butadiene-styrene) and a flexible grade of PVC (Polyvinyl chloride).

Vacuum forming requires a mould of the finished component to be produced first and this must be to a high standard with the sides tapered slightly to between five and ten degrees to ease the removal of the formed component once completed. The process works by removing the air trapped between the mould and the sheet, thus reducing pressure below the trapped material. Atmospheric pressure pushes the heated plasticised sheet on to the mould. The plastic sheet to be vacuum formed should be clamped around its edges in an airtight plate with a rubber

seal. Heat is applied by elements normally housed in a hood that is held above the material.

When a material has reached its plasticised state the heaters are removed and the pump is used to expel the air below. There is, however, one basic problem with vacuum forming and that is that on deforming the material it can become quite thin. One technique used in industry to overcome this problem is that when the material reaches its plasticised state, it is blown to uniformly stretch the whole surface before the mould is raised on the table and the air expelled.

The whole process can be summarised into four basic stages:

1. The plastic is heated using radiant heaters.
2. The plasticised material is then blown to stretch it.
3. The table or platen is raised into the dome area.
4. The air is expelled causing atmospheric pressure to force the plastic material down on to the mould (see Figure 3.1.6).

Vacuum-formed products range from acrylic baths to the plastic packaging found around Easter eggs.

Fusion

Plastics can be fused together to form strong joints. Sheet plastics can be fusion welded using ultrasound, where tiny vibrations cause a rise in temperature at a localised point, and with the application of pressure the two separate pieces become fused. It is also possible to fusion weld rigid sections together by heating them at the joint with a hot-air torch and adding a filler rod of the same material. The process can be used where adhesives cannot because of the risk of chemical attack which would render the joint useless. Recently, many novelty products such as inflatable postcards and clocks have been manufactured using this fusion welding process.

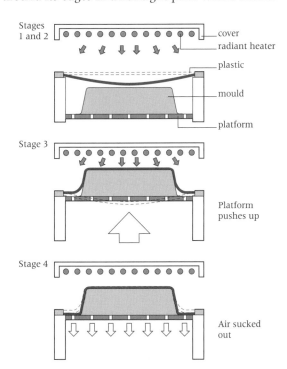

Figure 3.1.6 *Vacuum forming*

Task

Assess critically the methods used in a variety of plastics-forming processes, using the questions below to guide you. If possible, watch a video that shows industrial and commercial processes. Also try handling some products made by these forming processes.

- How was the force applied?
- How was the heat applied?
- How easily is the process controlled?
- How complex is the mould?
- Is any finishing necessary?

Hardwoods and softwoods and manufactured boards

Characteristics and faults of wood

The many different species of tree provide an enormous wealth of materials, which are put to many uses. However, any naturally occurring material inevitably produces variable quality, and wood is no exception to this. As a material it can be cut and shaped in numerous ways and this is one of its major advantages. Regrettably, the irregularity of grain, knots, warping and twisting are all disadvantages. Wood is also prone to biological attack from insects and fungi.

To a certain extent some of these irregularities have been minimised by rapid growth in the area of manufactured boards, which have reduced the demand for prime quality timber, but they should not be regarded as a cheap substitute. They present in many ways their own problems and cost and strength comparisons are sometimes misleading. Table 3.1.2 considers the advantages and disadvantages of manufactured boards.

Table 3.1.2 Advantages and disadvantages of manufactured boards

Advantages	Disadvantages
Large standard-sized sheets	Difficult to join
Uniform thickness	Exposed edges often need to be treated
Stable in most atmospheric conditions	Thin sheets become easily distorted unless held by a frame
Grained boards have good strength to weight ratio	Adhesives can blunt cutting tools quickly
Thin sheets can be bent easily	

Faults and defects affect the overall strength and durability as well as mar the visual appearance. Defects can be caused by a variety of factors:

- Shrinkage. After **conversion** and **seasoning**, shrinkage affects the shape of the cut board. Movement cannot be entirely eliminated since any change in temperature or humidity will result in some change, although converting the wood using the quarter-sawn method can lessen the impact. Movement exists in three main forms:
  - warping: a **cupping** across the width of the board
  - bowing: along the length of the timber
  - twisting: a twist from side to side along the length of the timber.
- Splits. Logs will develop a radial split if they are allowed to dry out before seasoning. Splits in seasoned timber occur because it has been dried out too quickly through the end grain. Quite often, in a timber mill the end grain of trees and sawn timber are painted to stop this rapid drying-out process.
- Knots. These are natural irregularities formed between the junctions of branches. They inevitably weaken the structure but they are considered as either 'live' or 'dead' knots.
- Irregular grain. Knots also contribute to variations in the grain direction which can lead to serious weaknesses especially where short grain occurs. It also makes for difficult working of that section.
- Shakes. Separations in adjoining layers of wood are known as shakes. They include:
  - heart and star: caused by shrinkage
  - cut and ring: strains of the wind, or felling or seasoning
  - thunder: thinner hair-line cracks formed perpendicular to the grain, commonly found in African timbers.
- Fungal attack. This type of attack causes the wood to decay which results in total loss of strength and weight.
- Dry rot. This thrives in damp conditions where there is no air circulation. The wood is attacked by fine strands, which reduce the wood to a dry powder, and leaves a musty smell.
- Wet rot. External timbers subjected to both wet and dry conditions decompose and become alternately spongy when wet and brittle when dry.

Characteristics and working properties of timber

The characteristics and working properties of timbers can be broken down into categories. Knowledge in each of these areas will help you to identify timbers in your work. They are:

- weight
- texture
- durability
- colour
- odour
- ease of working.

Micro-structure

A tree essentially consists of two major parts, the inner or 'heartwood' which gives rise to strength and rigidity, and the outer layers or 'sapwood' which is the region of growth where food is stored and transmitted. Growth is a seasonal process where layers are seen as concentric growth rings, known more commonly as annual rings. As the tree grows the wood tissue grows in the form of long tube-like cells which vary in shape and size. These are known as fibres and are arranged roughly parallel along the length of the trunk and give rise to the general grain direction. This variation in cell size, shape and function leads to the botanical distinction of hardwoods and softwoods (see Figure 3.1.7):

- Softwood structure, e.g. Scots pine, red cedar, spruce:
  - Tracheids: these are elongated tubes which become spliced together in the direction of growth and make up the grain. Sap and food pass through smaller openings known as pits that age harden as the tree grows older.
  - Parenchymas: smaller than tracheids, these make up the remaining cells.
  - Resin canels: evident in the majority of conifers. They carry away waste products in the form of resin and gum.
- Hardwood structure, e.g. oak, mahogany, beech:
  - Fibres: these constitute the bulk of hardwoods. They are not in any regular pattern or formation and they are much smaller and more needle-like than tracheids in softwoods.
  - Vessels/pores: they form long tubes within a tree which carry food. They are used to

distinguish one type of hardwood from another.
  - Parenchymas: these are more prominent in hardwoods and in oak they become quite thick, up to 30 cells thick, and are seen as the familiar 'silver' flashes within the grain.

Sources of different types of wood

The prime source of the world's supply of commercially grown softwood is the northern hemisphere, but particularly the colder regions that stretch from North America, Scandinavia and Siberia and parts of Europe. Conifers are relatively fast growing and produce straight trunks which make for economic cultivation with little wastage. With careful management of forests it is possible to control the supply and demand of softwoods. Being relatively cheaper than hardwoods they are used extensively for building construction and joinery. What waste that is produced is used in the manufacture of fibre boards and paper.

Britain imports almost 90 per cent of its timber needs since it is one of the least wooded countries in Europe. The imported boards are usually supplied debarked or square edged ready for further processing at the saw mills.

There are thousands of species of hardwoods grown across the world and many are harvested for commercial use. Most broad-leafed trees grown in temperate climates such as Europe, Japan and New Zealand are deciduous and lose their leaves in winter with the exception of a few like holly and laurel. Those grown in tropical and sub-tropical regions like Central and South America, Africa and Asia are mainly evergreen which means they grow all year round and reach maturity quicker. Hardwoods generally are more durable than softwoods and offer much more variety in terms of colour, texture and **figure**. Since they take a relatively longer time to grow they tend to be more expensive than softwoods with the really exotic timbers being converted into veneers which allows for much greater use of a limited supply.

Conversion

Once a tree has reached full maturity it is felled (cut down). This process is normally carried out during the winter months when growth is dormant and less sap and moisture are in the tree. All branches are removed which makes transportation and storage easier. With timber grown in the UK the bark is normally left on until the logs reach the saw mill and this stops rapid drying out occurring and prevents some of the defects as a result. Conversely, imported

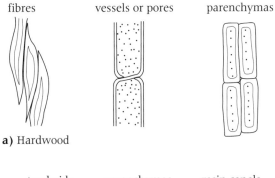

fibres   vessels or pores   parenchymas

a) Hardwood

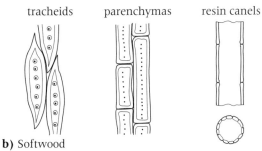

tracheids   parenchymas   resin canels

b) Softwood

Figure 3.1.7 *Hardwood and softwood cells*

timber is often stripped of bark to avoid any risk of insect contamination. Conversion is the term given to the process of sawing logs into commercially viable timber.

Ultimately, the figure and stability of the sawn timber is determined by the plane of the saw in relation to the annual rings. However, this is reflected in the price paid for the timber since some methods of conversion are more wasteful than others. There are basically two methods of cutting used in the conversion process (see Figure 3.1.8):

- slab, plain or through and through
- quarter (radial) sawn.

Slab, plain or through and through conversion is the simplest, quickest and cheapest of the two methods. The process makes a series of parallel cuts through the length of the log resulting in parallel slices or slabs. The thickness of the slabs can be varied as the log is cut and this type of cutting is frequently used on softwoods where the logs tend not to be that large in diameter.

Quarter (radial) sawn is a much more time-consuming process and involves much more manual handling. It is also a much more wasteful process. However, the timber produced tends to be better in quality and is much more stable in that it is less likely to move, warp, bow or twist.

Essentially, quarter sawing tries to make the annual rings as short as possible and at 90 degrees to the cut surface. This type of cutting results in the grain's figure being exposed and this is quite noticeable in an oak where the silver grain is exposed.

Seasoning

Drying or seasoning wood is the process of removing the excess water and much of the bound moisture from the cell walls. As the wood dries water is lost from the cavities until only the cell walls contain moisture. This is known as the fibre saturation point and it occurs at about 30 per cent moisture content. On further drying moisture is lost from the cell walls and shrinkage starts. At some point the loss of water

stops and the wood is in balance with the relative humidity of its surroundings and this point is called the equilibrium moisture content (EMC). It is important, however, to reduce the moisture content to less than 20 per cent since this has a number of implications:

- It makes the timber immune to rot and decay.
- It makes the timber less corrosive to metals.
- It increases overall strength and dimensional stability.

Not all moisture should be removed from the timber. Depending upon the use to which the timber is to be put there are recommended levels of moisture content as shown in Table 3.1.3.

Table 3.1.3 Recommended levels of moisture content

Moisture content	Uses
Below 18%	General outdoor use such as fences and sheds
Below 10%	Indoor use in centrally heated homes: stairs, door frames and skirting boards

Seasoning can be carried out in two different ways: natural-air seasoning and kiln seasoning. Natural-air seasoning, as its name suggests, is where slabs of timber are stacked and natural air is allowed to flow around them. It takes an average of one year to season 25 mm of thickness in this way. Kiln seasoning uses steam to heat and remove the excess moisture in a controlled environment. Very precise levels of moisture content can be achieved using this method.

Composites, synthetics and manufactured materials

When two or more materials are combined by bonding, a composite material is formed. The resulting material has improved mechanical and other properties and, as with most composites, it will have excellent strength/weight ratios. Composites consist of a reinforcing material that provides the strength and a bonding agent, termed the 'matrix', in the form of glues or resins.

Wood is a natural composite in that its fibres, which provide the strength, are held in a matrix of lignin, the glue.

Initially, glass fibre was the most widespread form of reinforcing material and was available in a variety of forms: a string of fibre woven together, loose strands, or, most commonly, in a non-woven matting of short strands. Glass fibre

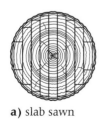
a) slab sawn

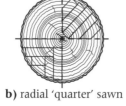
b) radial 'quarter' sawn

Figure 3.1.8 Slab and radial sawn logs

is held in matrix of polyester resin and it is best suited to large structural items such as boat hulls, septic tanks and pond liners. There are a number of inherent dangers with GRP work and they all necessitate careful consideration.

Think about this!

Consider the following environmental issues:

- Polyester resins contain styrene and can cause skin irritation.
- Catalysts (hardeners) are usually peroxides and these too can cause skin irritation and they will cause damage if they come into contact with the eyes.
- Toxic gases in the form of 'styrene' are given off and can cause respiratory problems in the throat and nose.
- Fibres themselves can cause irritation to the skin.
- When cutting or finishing any GRP work the dust generated can cause respiratory problems in the nose and throat.
- Styrene vapours present fire hazards.

'Formica' is a layered composite that uses melamine formaldehyde resin to bond layers of paper together, the outside one being a decorative pattern or colour. A clear hard heat protective resin is finally added over the top layer and then the whole sandwich is heated under pressure where the resin cures and strong cross-links are formed.

'Tufnol' is another type of the layered composite that consists of woven linen impregnated with a phenolic resin. It is extensively used for gears, bearings and slides in machines.

More recently, carbon fibre has been developed in a similar form to that of glass fibre. Carbon fibres are, however, much stronger and are used in structural components for aircraft, propellers, protective clothing, body armour and sports equipment such as golf clubs, skis and tennis and squash rackets. The extensive use of fibre glass in the aircraft industry has led to major weight reductions of between 15 per cent and 30 per cent which has resulted in better fuel economy. The manufacturing processes involved with the use of carbon fibre are almost identical to that of GRP work. Carbon fibres are also available in various forms but most frequently they are laid up using resin to produce strong lightweight structures.

One of the most widespread and commonly used composite materials is medium density fibreboard (MDF). The fibres are made from wood waste that has been reduced to its basic fibrous element and reformed to produce a homogeneous material. Fibres are bonded together with a synthetic resin adhesive to produce the uniform structure and fine textured surface. There are various types of MDF board, which have a less dense central core but still retain the fine surface.

This type of fibreboard can be worked like wood and with a veneered surface it makes an excellent substitute. It finishes well with a variety of surface treatments and it is available from 3 mm to 32 mm thick and in sheets 2440 mm by 1220 mm wide.

As is the case with all composites there are some dangers involved in the use of them. As a result of the very fine fibres, particles and synthetic resin adhesives great care must be taken when undertaking any form of cutting, drilling or sanding. Respiratory equipment should be used since the dust can cause irritation of skin and to the throat and nasal passage and in school/college a dust extractor must also be used.

Tasks

1 Find out what COSHH stands for.
2 Assess the risks involved in the use of MDF and GRP.
3 How are those risks controlled?
4 List the safety precautions that should be taken when using MDF and GRP.

Ceramics, glass and concrete

Ceramics

Most ceramics are brittle and hard since they are chemically bonded by either covalent or ionic bonding. They are far less ductile than most metals and easily fractured at the slightest attempt to deform them. As a general group of materials, the following are all considered to be ceramics:

- glass products
- bricks
- roof tiles
- sanitary ware (toilets and basins).

Ceramics are also able to withstand high temperatures, pressures and have good resistance to chemical corrosion. Modern ceramics are capable of operating at much higher temperatures and are now being used as replacements for alloy steels as components in combustion engines. They are also used on the nose cone of the US space shuttle to insulate and protect the crew and their instruments on re-entry to the Earth's atmosphere where surface temperatures on the nose cone can reach 1500°C.

Ceramics are manufactured from three main materials: clay, sand and feldspar (aluminium potassium silicate). To this combination fluxing agents are added to lower the temperature needed in their manufacture and refractory compounds are added to increase resistance to temperature. Once all the components have been finely ground to a powder they are mixed into shape and fired to a temperature between 700°C and 2000°C.

Glass

Glass is made from silica sand, lime and sodium carbonate. Other materials can be added in order to produce various types of glass:

- Coloured glass – oxides of transition metals such as iron, copper and nickel are added.
- Lead glass – lead oxide is added to produce higher values of refractive index, used for cut glass and neon signs.
- Borosilicate glass – contains a high proportion of boron oxide and this type of glass is sold under the trade name of 'Pyrex'.

The raw materials for glass are fed into the furnace where they are heated to 1500°C. Once molten, they are tapped out in a continuous flow and floated on to a bath of molten tin that has a perfectly smooth surface. As the glass comes from the production line it is cut to size and this type of glass is known as plate glass. Glass has many uses because of its transparency and resistance to chemical attack. It is brittle and is much stronger in compression than in tension. In the construction industry, buildings can be made with glass walls that allow light in but reflect light so that people cannot see through. The other type of glass used in the construction industry is safety glass and there are two types:

- Laminated glass consists of two thin sheets of plate glass with a sheet of non-brittle plastic material trapped between them. They are bonded with an adhesive and the plastic centre holds fragments together if the glass is broken.
- Tempered glass has been annealed to give a low stress uniform structure. It is heated to

400°C and it becomes very tough and much stronger in compression and it is used in doors and vehicle windows.

Concrete

Concrete is an artificial stone which is made from a combination of cement, water and aggregates. The proportion of cement to aggregate is governed by the strength required for a particular situation. It can vary from 1:10 for a very 'lean' mixture and 1:3 for a very 'rich' mixture. Concrete is relatively cheap and has good compressive strength that makes it an ideal material for use in the building industry and civil engineering. Various additives are available which allow rapid hardening, low temperature hardening and slow hardening. Cement additives are used where resistance to sea water or acid attack is required.

For structural members such as beams and column supports plain concrete would not be adequate. With the addition of steel reinforcements in the form of rods or mesh, the compressive strength is further increased and the cross-section of the member can be reduced. As a material in the construction industry it has many uses, including:

- foundations
- structural load-bearing columns
- lintels for use above doors and windows.

Tasks

1 Consider how the strength of concrete is affected by the addition of larger and smaller aggregate.
2 Why might ceramics be a good choice of material to use in car engine blocks?

Classification of components

Screw thread forms

There are several different types of screw thread, each used for very specific purposes but essentially they have three main uses:

- converting rotary to linear motion
- obtaining a mechanical advantage
- fastenings.

Screw threads have two basic forms: the V-thread and the square thread. The most common type of screw thread is the 'V' type and it exists in the form of an isosceles triangle with a crest and a root either rounded or flattened (see Figure 3.1.9a).

Table 3.1.4 *ISO metric screw thread sizes*

Nominal Dia	Pitch
3	0.5
4	0.7
5	0.8
6	1.0
8	1.25
10	1.5

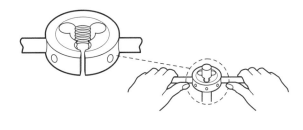

The square thread takes its name from the profile shape of the thread (see Figure 3.1.9b). It is not as strong as the V-thread but it allows a large force to be applied and it is therefore used in vices and cramps. Buttress threads are used where a force has only to be applied in one direction (see Figure 3.1.9c). They are commonly used in woodwork vices that are fitted with a quick release mechanism and a half nut for rapid opening and closing. Acme threads are used extensively for the transmission of motion with an engaging nut as on the centre lathe (see Figure 3.1.9d). Here the tool post moves automatically along the bed until the tool reaches the end of the cut and the nut is disengaged.

Nuts and bolts
Made from low or medium carbon steel, bolts are forged or machined and the threads cut or rolled. Sometimes they are also made from high tensile steel, alloy steel or stainless steel, and in some cases they are protected from corrosion by galvanising.

Coach bolts and studs are two other forms of bolts. Coach bolts are mainly used for fastening metal parts to wood and have a domed head with a square underneath it that acts as a locking device. A stud is a headless bolt with a thread at each end and a plain middle.

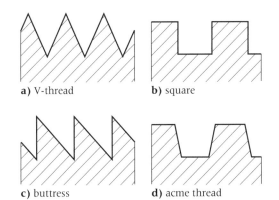

a) V-thread   **b)** square

c) buttress   **d)** acme thread

Figure 3.1.9 *V-, acme, square and buttress thread*

'drunken' thread
the die is not square to
the axis of the rod

Figure 3.1.10 *Thread cutting*

A nut is a collar and must fit the bolt with the same thread form and it should be of the same thread diameter. Nuts can be hexagonal or square in shape and are normally forged with a chamfer cut on one or both faces. In a special type of nut a ring of fibre or nylon is inserted in a groove inside the nut and provides extra frictional forces when the nut is fitted.

Theory of thread cutting
The process of cutting an external screw thread is termed threading and requires two basic hand tools, a split die and a die stock. The die is held in the die stock by a number of screws. The rod to be threaded should be a nominal size (e.g.10 mm diameter for an M10 thread). It is essential to check the die is square to the axis to ensure that the thread does not become 'drunken'. Once cutting, each turn clockwise should be followed with a turn anti-clockwise to break off the swarf. To aid the cutting a lubricant should be used and a general proprietary type is suitable for steel. For aluminium and copper, paraffin should be used. Brass and plastics require no lubricant.

Rivets
Riveting is a simple way to make a permanent joint between two or more pieces of metal, either in the form of a hinge pin or in a rigid form as in a ship's plating. For general engineering purposes, rivets are normally made from soft iron and are therefore ductile and easy to work by hammering or pressing. Rivets exist

in many different forms but the three most common types are countersunk headed, flat headed and snap or round headed (see Figure 3.1.22 on page 88). The choice of rivet to be used depends solely on the materials being joined and the location of the joint. In general, access is required on both sides when riveting but this is not always possible. In these circumstances a different process has to be used called pop riveting. This process was developed for the aircraft industry where extensive use of thin sheet material is joined with access generally only available from the one side. However, since the joint is hollow it is relatively weaker than conventional rivets but much lighter in weight as they are normally made from aluminium alloys.

Gears

A gear is a toothed wheel with a special shaped profile. This allows it to mesh with other gears, thereby transmitting forces and motion, when fixed on driving and driven rotating shafts within machines. Two gears connected together form a gear train, where each gear turns in the opposite direction when fixed to a parallel shaft. If the gears are different sizes, then they will turn at different speeds and this is termed the velocity ratio (VR). An idler gear inserted

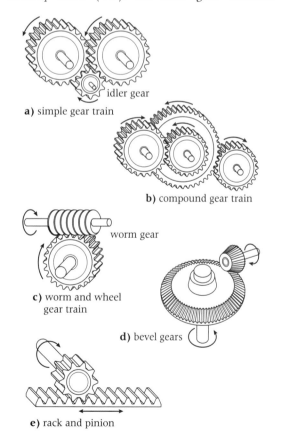

a) simple gear train

b) compound gear train

worm gear

c) worm and wheel gear train

d) bevel gears

e) rack and pinion

Figure 3.1.11 Gear systems

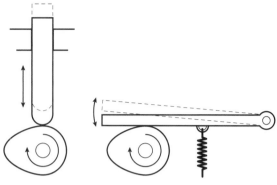

Figure 3.1.12 Cams and followers

between the driver and the driven gear will result in the two external gears turning in the same direction without affecting the overall velocity ratio. As several gears are introduced on to identical shafts and mesh with other gears a compound gear train is formed and large speed changes can be achieved. Worm gears and bevel gears are special gears that transmit rotary motion through 90 degrees. Large speed reductions can be achieved with the worm gear since the driver, the worm gear itself, is regarded as only having one tooth. Therefore, the velocity ratio is purely dependent upon the size of the driven gear. Bevel gears need different sized gears to achieve any speed change, as is the case with the hand drill.

A rack and pinion allows rotary motion to be converted into linear motion as can be seen on the pillar drill. When the hand wheel is rotated the chuck moves down in a linear fashion.

Cams

A cam is a mechanism that is normally used to convert rotary motion into a reciprocating motion (although the cam itself may have an oscillating motion). The cam is fixed to, or is part of, a rotating shaft and a follower is held against it either under its own weight or by a spring. As the cam rotates the follower moves depending upon the shape of the cam. Followers vary in shape and their use depends upon the type of cam they are being used with. The four main types are: knife-edge, flat, roller and roller and rocker.

Bushes and bearings

All rotating shafts need to be supported and bearings and bushes provide the engineering solution to this problem. Two different load types present two different problems to be contained: radial load and axial load. A radial load is simply caused by the rotating shaft whereas an axial load is a combination of a radial load with an extra load being pushed along the shaft into the bearing itself.

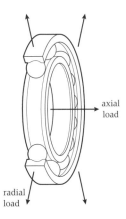

Figure 3.1.13 *The ball bearing*

Bearings come in many forms, each having a specific use and application, but the most common types are plain bearings, roller and ball bearings. Friction is a problem in bearings and it is overcome with lubrication. In situations where contamination could be a problem from lubricants, like the food industry, nylon or other plastic materials are used.

A bush is the simplest form of bearing and it is basically a cylindrical sleeve that fits into a hole and acts as the bearing surface. Quite often a different material is used to that from the shaft material and brasses, bronze, white metal and plastics fall into this group.

Stock sizes/standard sizes
All materials and fixings are supplied in a range of sizes. Metals are available in a huge range of

sections and the availability of sizes should be considered as part of your design work. You need to take into consideration exactly what sizes are available. Timbers in sheet format are produced in standard sizes:

- 2240 mm × 1220 mm
- 1220 mm × 610 mm.

Sections of softwood timber are available in a variety of machined sizes and a catalogue should be consulted to see what sizes are available prior to manufacture. Hardwoods tend to be sold by volume once the dimensions that are required have been specified. Plastics are commercially available in sheet form with the most common size being 1000 mm by 600 mm for acrylic. Small extruded sections like those made for model making can also be purchased.

All fixings are sold with a description of their size and material. There are almost endless sizes of screws available made from different materials and with different heads.

Task
Look around the workshop and try to identify different forms of screw thread. Identify what type they are and work out why they have been used in that situation.

Carry out the same exercise, only this time look for different types of gears. Identify what type of gear it is and why it has been used in that situation.

2. Working properties of materials and components related to preparing, processing, manipulating and combining

Alloying metals
In their pure form, most of our useful metals are soft and ductile. Pure copper and aluminium are excellent materials as electrical conductors and both can be drawn into thin wires. Unfortunately, while ductile, these pure materials, together with zinc, are comparatively weak. While it is possible to increase strength by cold working, it is usually necessary to increase strength and hardness by alloying.

An alloy is a metal compound produced by combining a metal with one or more other elements. The object of this being to improve the properties of one of these metals, or in some cases, to produce new properties that none of the original metals possessed in their pure state.

Alloying alters the properties of the base metal and can:

- change the melting point
- increase strength, hardness and ductility
- change electrical and thermal properties
- enhance resistance to oxidation and corrosion
- change colour (as is the case with brass and copper)
- give rise to better castings.

In its pure state, iron is soft and ductile and carbon is brittle. Yet with the addition of less than 0.5 per cent carbon, a new material is formed with different mechanical properties, namely steel. The amount of carbon introduced into pure iron gives rise to essentially three different grades of steel:

- low carbon steel – less than 0.3 per cent carbon
- medium carbon steel – 0.3–0.6 per cent carbon
- high carbon steel – 0.6–1.7 per cent carbon.

Task

Try filing and cutting a piece of each of the three grades of steel and record your findings.

When the carbon content is below 0.2 per cent the steel remains ductile, which allows it to be deep drawn and therefore suitable for a whole range of applications from car-body panels to washing-machine drums. As the carbon content increases, the mechanical properties change significantly. The hardness increases with the addition of carbon but there is a compromise as the ductility decreases. The inclusion of the other elements such as tungsten, chromium and nickel give rise to a change in other properties.

Compared with carbon steels that lose their hardness at high temperatures, these new alloys, or high-speed steels, retain their hardness and therefore are used as cutting tools such as drills and milling cutters.

Resistance to corrosion is increased in steel with the addition of 12 per cent chromium and some nickel to form stainless steel. Table 3.1.5 lists the composition, properties and uses of some alloys.

Table 3.1.5 *Common alloys, composition, properties and uses*

Alloy	Composition	Properties and uses
Mild steel	Fe, 0.15–0.35% C	Tough, ductile and malleable. Cannot be hardened and tempered Nails, nuts and bolts
High carbon steel	Fe, 0.8–1.5% C	Very hard, less ductile Can be heat-treated Hammers, chisels and screwdivers
Stainless steel	Medium carbon steel +12% Cr +8% Ni	Hard and tough Corrosion resistant Cutlery and sinks
Brass	65% Cu, 35% Zn	Casts well. Good corrosion resistance Boat fittings

Mechanical properties

A mechanical property is associated with how a material reacts when a force is applied to it. The material will deform in one of two ways: elastically or plastically. **Elastic deformation** describes the behaviour of the material that returns to its original shape and form once the deforming force has been removed. **Plastic deformation** occurs when the deforming force permanently deforms the material even after the deforming force has been removed. This property allows materials to be pressed into new shapes that they retain once the force has been removed. The extent to which material can undergo permanent deformation in all directions under compression without cracking or rupture is known as malleability. Lead is a very malleable material and it is still used to make joints watertight on roofs.

Extensive deformation can in some instances lead to fracture. However, some materials can undergo extensive deformation without fracture and these materials are said to be ductile. Copper, aluminium and silver are all very ductile and can be drawn through a die into thin wires. Permanent reduction in cross-section is achieved without causing any rupture or dislocations within the material. Conversely, those materials that exhibit little or no deformation before fracture are termed brittle.

Toughness, however, is the ability to withstand sudden impact and shock loading. A tough material will also resist cracking when subjected to bending and sheer loads. Hardness is the ability to withstand wear, scratching or indentation. It is an essential property in all cutting tools. Diamond is the hardest of all materials but tungsten carbide is a much cheaper manufactured alternative for use in cutting tools. The strength of a material is defined as the ability of the material to withstand forces without permanently bending or breaking it. Strength can be broken down into five main areas:

- tensile strength – the ability to resist stretching or pulling forces
- compressive strength – the ability to withstand pushing forces trying to crush it
- bending strength – the ability to withstand the forces attempting to bend it
- shear strength – the ability to resist sliding forces acting opposite to each other
- torsional strength – the ability to withstand twisting forces under torsion or torque.

Heat treatment and work hardening

Heat treatment is the process of heating and cooling materials in a controlled fashion in order to change their properties and characteristics. Naturally, the temperature to which the metal is heated and the rate of cooling are fundamental to all heat treatment processes. Basically, all heat treatments fall into five main areas although there are many different ways in which these processes can be carried out.

The hardening of steels is achieved only when the carbon content is above 0.4 per cent and full hardness will be achieved when the carbon content is above 0.8 per cent. The process is carried out by heating the steel to just above its upper critical temperature (720°C for a steel with a carbon content of 0.83 per cent), before it is quenched in water.

Once the metal has been hardened, it is capable of cutting other materials and resisting wear. It is, however, very brittle and will break if a load is applied. By slightly reducing the hardness at this stage a more elastic and tougher material will be produced that retains its cutting edge. This process is known as **tempering**. The fully hardened steel is polished so that when reheated a coloured oxide can be seen on the surface, and as the appropriate temperature and colour is reached the work piece should be quenched in cold water. The temperature to which the piece is heated is entirely dependent upon the use to which it is to be put and Table 3.1.6 gives some examples.

Normalising is a process that is used to obtain a uniform grain structure throughout the whole work piece such as a forged component. The process of normalising is relatively simple and involves heating the work piece to just above its upper critical temperature, allowing it to soak for a period of time to attain a uniform temperature throughout, before being allowed to cool to room temperature in still air. The grain will have been refined and the work piece will now be more ductile and possess greater toughness.

When a work piece has been deformed by cold working (hammering, bending, rolling) **work hardening** takes place and deforms the structure. This process of work hardening has some advantages with regard to the manufacture of certain components. For example, when copper has been drawn to make tubes it has been work hardened. It has to be annealed at certain stages during this process, but if a final draw is not made after it has been annealed it remains too soft, and it will break. A final draw slightly work hardens the structure allowing it to be successfully bent without breaking.

Annealing is a process that restores the crystal structure allowing the relief of internal stresses to take place at relatively low temperatures. As the temperature increases, a point is reached when new crystals begin to grow, the size and growth of which essentially depend on the temperature the work piece is heated to and the length of time it is held at that temperature. Once soaked, the piece should be allowed to cool very slowly in either an oven or a sand box where it can retain the heat.

Age hardening is almost exclusive to aluminium alloys. This range of age-hardenable alloys are known as Duralumins and they contain in varying degrees elements such as copper, manganese, magnesium, silicon, iron and zinc. Despite what this term might imply, the alloys harden by the application of heat rather than by the passing of time. They must be heated uniformly to the correct temperature in order to achieve a hard, strong structure. If they are over heated then the initial gain in hardness and strength is lost.

Table 3.1.6 *Tempering colour chart*

Colour	Temperature (°C)	Uses
Light straw	230	Lathe tools, scalpels, scribers
Dark straw	240	Drills, taps and dies
Brown	260	Hammer heads
Purple	275	Chisels, saws
Blue	290	Springs, screwdrivers

3. Hand and commercial processes

Fabrication/manufacture

Fabrication is the term that is used to describe the process of joining both similar and dissimilar materials together. The joining of wood to wood can be broken down into three main areas and these are framed, box and edge-to-edge joints.

Frame joints tend to form the main structural components of most furniture and will need to be fixed at the corners and at other places if strength is to be increased or twisting opposed. The theory behind any jointing process is to achieve the greatest possible gluing surface area and this is achieved by cutting and removing the wood in various configurations. Sometimes the exposed joints are also cut in certain ways for decoration purposes.

Box joints are used where the width of the timber to be joined can be as big as 225 mm to 300 mm. In natural timbers joints can be cut but with commercially made boards a range of knockdown fittings are available.

Again, with this jointing technique the main objective is to increase the gluing area which gives rise to greater strength and less chance of the wood moving. Various types of box joint can be used in the fabrication process with the most common types being butt and lap, dovetail, comb or finger joints and housing joints (see Figure 3.1.14).

Edge joints are used either to make wider board sections from natural wood or to cover exposed unattractive edges on manufactured boards. For joining solid wood, simple butt joints, biscuit joints, tongue and groove or dowel joints can be used. Edging manufactured boards can be done with iron-on edge strip or by simply butt jointing in a solid wood section to the exposed edge.

Lamination

This fabrication process involves thin strips of wood being deformed or bent around a former and stuck together on the contacting surfaces. Once dried they cannot move since this would involve the strips straightening and slipping over one another. Straight timbers can also be laminated where they become very strong mechanically and they are often used as major structural members within buildings where the

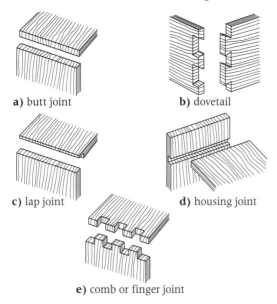

a) butt joint   **b)** dovetail

c) lap joint   **d)** housing joint

e) comb or finger joint

Figure 3.1.14 *Butt, lap, dovetail, comb and housing joints*

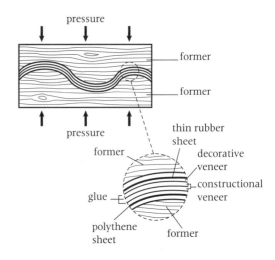

Figure 3.1.15 *Lamination process*

aesthetic characteristics of the timber can be exploited. Once a former has been made it can be used over and over again to produce batches or mass-produced items.

Glass reinforced plastic

Glass reinforced plastic (GRP) is another fabrication process which can be described as laminating. Layers of glass strands matting are fixed together over a former using polyester resin as the glue.

Sheet metalwork

Sheet metal is a versatile material and can be formed into boxes, trays, pipe work and ducting. The material is bent or folded into the desired shape using a rawhide mallet and folding bars. It can be fixed at the seams which overlap by riveting, or any of the processes that involve heat such as soldering or spot welding. As this is such a labour intensive process it means that it is normally confined to very specialist jobs. Where larger production runs are required presswork is normally used, as in the production of car body panels.

Processes

Casting

Pouring molten metal into a mould that contains a cavity of the required shape produces a casting. Initially, the mould or pattern needs to be made of the component to be cast and it should be slightly oversized to allow for shrinkage of the casting on cooling. Most patterns are split along the centre line and are located with dowels to form a solid pattern. Patterns should avoid sharp corners and undercuts, and all vertical surfaces should be tapered to allow for easy extraction from the sand. The process of casting varies depending upon the type of pattern being used but essentially they will follow the same method (see Figure 3.1.16):

1. The sand needs to be damp enough to hold its own shape when clenched in the hand. If it is too wet it can be dangerous when casting and dry sand should be added and mixed. It should be sieved thoroughly and all lumps removed.
2. The drag (the bottom half of the casting flask) should be placed upside down on a moulding board and one half of the pattern should be placed flat side down on it. French chalk should be sprinkled lightly over the pattern to help release it later.
3. The sand should be sieved over the pattern to a depth of at least 30 mm and it should then be rammed down firmly. Once compact the drag should be filled and rammed once again before finally being levelled off.
4. The drag should be turned over and the cope fixed in place and the pattern should be assembled and lightly dusted once again. Sprue pins should now be inserted and these will ultimately create a cavity for the metal to run into. The sieving process is repeated and once again the sand should be compacted. Finally, a small well should be created around the top of one of the sprue pins.
5. The sprue pins should be removed and the cope and drag separated. Gates and basins should be cut into the sand in both the cope and the drag before the pattern is removed.
6. The mould box should now be reassembled and placed on the floor ready for pouring.
7. With the metal in a molten state, it should be fluxed and degassed to remove any impurities. These will form on the surface and should be removed before pouring commences.
8. The melt should be poured slowly and with an even flow into the small well. Once the metal has solidified, the sand can be broken but great care should be taken because the components and sand may still be hot.
9. Finally the casting will need to be fettled which involves cutting off the runners and risers and any flashes.

On a large-scale production site producing such items as engine blocks and metalwork vices casting is carried out on a continual basis. Casting can also be used to produce a single item in the school/college workshop but this makes it quite labour intensive since the mould will be used only once.

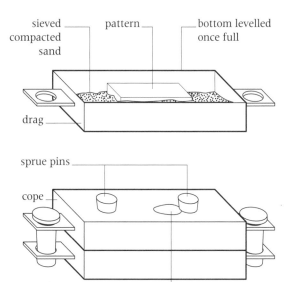

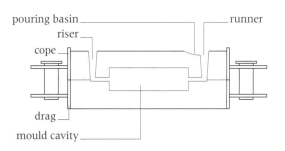

Figure 3.1.16 *The process of casting*

Task

Carry out a risk assessment for the casting process and list all the major hazards that you are likely to encounter when casting. Make a list of the steps that can be taken to ensure that the risks to the individual using this process are minimal.

Sintering

While most metals are cast as ingots or castings, sintering is the process used to form components from metals and other elements with very high melting points. This process also allows alloys to be made from metals that are not miscible in the liquid state. As a manufacturing process it can be used to mass produce components and the process can be divided into four stages:

1. producing the suitable powder mix with the correct amounts and any additives
2. compacting the powder in a shaped die under extreme pressure

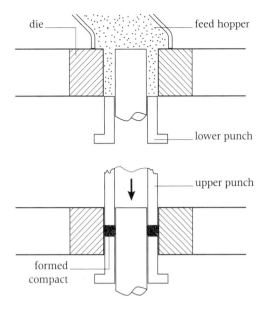

die — feed hopper

lower punch

upper punch

formed compact

Figure 3.1.17 *Stages in the compacting of metal powdered bearings*

3. sintering the compact at high temperatures to fuse the particles together
4. sizing and finishing (see Figure 3.1.17).

Sintered components are often used for bearings where, because of their porous nature, they are able to retain lubricating oil and become self-oiling, sometimes lasting the lifetime of the product in which they are fitted such as electric hand-power tools like drills and jigsaws.

Shearing

Shearing tools are very simple and are used to cut strip or sheet metal to length. Two hardened steel blades are used with a ground cutting edge on each. As pressure is brought to bear upon the material, a certain amount of plastic deformation occurs within the material being cut before the blade penetrates the metal and the cut is made. For an efficient shearing action clearance between the two cutting blades is essential. When incorrectly set burrs form or the metal tears. Scissors, tin snips and guillotines all use the shearing action to cut materials.

Stamping

Stamping is a process in which plastic deformation takes place by compression. Due to excessive forces involved the process is mainly confined to coins, keys, medals and shallow relief work. A small blank or preform is placed within a closed die as the punch or stamp is forced down. The material undergoes work hardening as it is forced into the die and the piece retains its shape once removed.

Spark erosion

Very hard materials and very complicated shapes and profiles can be cut by spark erosion. A small spark is used which jumps between two conductors, one is the work piece and the second is the tool. The sparks generated can be as hot as 1200°C and are generated up to 10,000 times a second. With each spark a tiny piece of metal is eroded. However, the major drawback with spark erosion as a process is that the tools, which are normally made from brass, wear out extremely quickly due to the erosion process itself. Injection moulding and extrusion dies are often made using the spark erosion process because of the very fine detail and complicated shapes that are required. In some instances the process is used to machine a single one-off component or profile cut three-dimensional pressings such as car body panels.

Laser cutting

The use of lasers to cut metals and other materials such as textiles provides a very accurate means of doing so since the cut widths can be as little as half a millimetre. When lasers are used to cut metals the temperatures reached actually melt the metal and therefore a jet of pure oxygen is used to blow away the molten metal. It also blows away the oxide film from the cut itself. The whole process is normally computer controlled where the profile to be cut has been programmed into the machine allowing it to be operated remotely and for greater accuracy. Large numbers of textiles items can be cut at once making it an ideal process for use in the mass production of clothing. It can also be used to cut a single very complex shape that could be cut in no other way.

Forging

Forging by either hand or machine drop forging produces strong tough components due to the grain being refined in the hammering process. It is sometimes quicker to forge components than to machine them from solid metal and it is also more economical as far as material consumption is concerned. The crucial factor in any forging is the control of the heat and mild steel should be worked at around 1200°C. There are some basic processes in forging. These are:

- drawing down – reducing the cross-section by increasing the length
- bending – forming a sharp or gradual bend
- punching and drifting – punching and tidying up punched holes
- twisting and scrolling – decorative features using traditional wrought ironwork.

Figure 3.1.18 *Drop forging*

Figure 3.1.19 *Milling*

Drop forging uses two halves of a mould called a die. Metal is placed into the die and shaped by an enormous force generated by the hammer action of the machine. In some instances the components can be forged in one 'hit' but more often the blank will pass through several dies. Hot forging of the type normally undertaken by a blacksmith is labour intensive and therefore would be limited to batch production. Drop forging is used to make products such as hip replacement joints by passing the preform through a series of dies.

Removal – milling

Milling is a wasting process that uses a multi-toothed cutter to cut metals and plastics. Each individual tooth on the cutter removes a chip of material as it passes over the work. It is common practice to 'upcut' mill which means that the work should be moved in the opposite direction to that of the rotating cutter. Milling can be carried out either horizontally or vertically and in each case the work is clamped firmly to the table below using 'tee' blocks and bolts. The table can be moved in three different

axes; X, along the length of the table, Y, across the width and Z, up and down vertically. The milling process can be used to produce large horizontal flat surfaces and vertical surfaces. Slots can also be machined and narrow slots as small as one millimetre wide can be achieved with a slitting saw on a horizontal mill.

With CNC milling, the labour costs are confined to setting up the program and maintaining the machine. CNC milling can be used repeatedly to cut components on long production runs or for cutting short or even one-off components which would otherwise be impossible to machine.

Drilling

Drilling is a process that is used to cut holes with a rotary cutting tool. A pillar drilling machine can be found in almost every school /college workshop and can be used to drill holes in any material if the correct bit is used. The most frequently used type of drill is a twist drill and they are normally made from high-speed steel (HSS) and these fall into two categories:

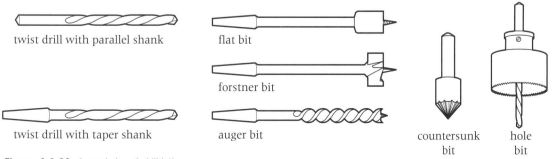

twist drill with parallel shank

flat bit

forstner bit

twist drill with taper shank

auger bit

countersunk
bit

hole
bit

Figure 3.1.20 *A variety of drill bits*

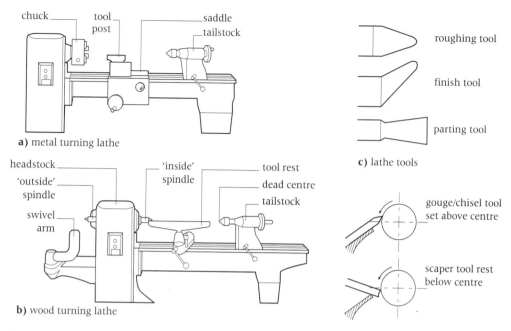

Figure 3.1.21 *Metal turning and wood turning lathes*

- parallel shanks – up to about 20 mm in diameter
- taper shank – having a morse taper that fits directly into the machine.

Other types of drill bits used in the workshop are:

- flat bits – used to drill deep holes in wood
- forstner bits – produce flat clean holes in wood
- auger bits – used in a carpenter's brace, best suited to deep holes
- countersink bit – provides a 90-degree conical recess for screw heads to sit in
- hole saws – a circular toothed cutting ring ranging from 20 mm to 150 mm in diameter.

The drilling of components can be carried out manually using jigs to hold the work accurately or in a school/college workshop used to drill one-off items that have been measured and marked out.

Turning

Turning on either a wood or metal lathe uses a single point cutting tool held against the rotating work to turn cylindrical objects. The tool can be moved parallel to the work, at right angles or in any combination of these movements to produce tapers or curves. Turning manually either wood or metal one can produce bespoke items, or with the aid of templates, small batches of identical products. CNC lathes produce identical items that are produced with very low labour costs although the initial investment costs are high.

Task

Analyse a G-clamp and a sash clamp, with respect to the processes that have been used to make them.

Wood turning

A wood lathe (see Figure 3.1.21b) offers two very different turning opportunities. On the outside a faceplate can be used for turning bowls, while on the inside between centres, slimmer, longer objects can be turned such as candlesticks and stair rails. The theory of cutting is not dissimilar to that of the metal lathe, the main difference is that the tools are hand-held. The three basic turning tools are:

- gouges – these cut large quantities away quickly and are used for rough shaping
- chisels – used for final shaping and fine finishing
- scrapers – good for beginners, slower than gouges but they do not leave a good surface.

Preparation of timber is essential before turning commences regardless of the type of turning you are undertaking. Timber should be free from splits and corners should be cut or planed off. When bowl turning a wooden spacer should be used between the blank and the faceplate. Once ready to turn, the tool rest should be set at the correct height for the tool being used and the correct spindle speed selected.

Metal turning

There are a number of ways of holding work on a centre lathe when machining:

- 3-jaw self centring – the most common type used in school/college workshops; can be fitted with reverse jaws to hold large cylindrical components
- 4-jaw chuck – each jaw is moved independently and holds square or irregular shapes
- face plate – castings and irregular shapes can be bolted to it
- between centres – used for long components.

Lathe tools are available in a variety of forms each having their own specific application as shown in Table 3.1.7. A metal turning lathe can be seen in Figure 3.1.21a.

Grinding/abrading

Abrasives can be used on all types of woods, metals and plastics. Disc sanders, belt sanders and orbital sanders are all commonly found in workshops and they work by moving abrasive papers over the work. Certain plastics can also be used on these machines.

Polishing with emery cloth, wire wool and various pastes on a buffing wheel, can abrade metals.

Grinding of metals is carried out by either a disc grinder, offhand grinder or a surface grinder. Each of these methods uses discs that have been made from abrasive powder that have been cemented together. The first two methods are essentially used for cleaning up and finishing, while surface grinding is a precision machining process that grinds very hard metals to a smooth and accurate finish.

Table 3.1.7 *Types of lathe tool and their applications*

Tool	Application
Right-hand knife	Used to face the left-hand edge or to cut a shoulder to the left
Left-hand knife	Used to face the right-hand edge or to cut a shoulder to the right
Round nose	Used to cut in any direction or to produce a radiused corner
Parting	Moved at right angles to the work in order to cut it off
Form	Specially ground profiles to cut any shape
Knurling	Pressed into the surface to produce a textured pattern
Boring	Single point tool used to turn inside an existing hole

Addition and joining

Joining processes can be categorised as follows:

- Permanent – once made they cannot be reversed without causing damage to the work piece.
- Temporary – although not always designed to be taken apart, they can be disassembled if needed without causing damage.
- Adhesives – these fall into two groups, natural and synthetic. The synthetic types tend to be toxic substances and therefore need to be handled with care. It is thought that most adhesive bonding can be classified as a chemical reaction.

Adhesives

- Polyvinyl acetate (PVA) – a popular white woodworking glue. It is easy to use and strong providing the joint is a good fit. It is not waterproof.
- Synthetic resin (cascamite) – much stronger than PVA and is supplied as a powder to be mixed with water. It is a good joint filler and it is waterproof making it ideal for external use.
- Epoxy resin (araldite) – a two-part resin and hardener that needs to be mixed in equal parts. It takes a while to harden fully, and is expensive.
- Acrylic cement (tensol cement) – available in various forms with Tensol 12 being the most common. It is ready for immediate use.

Contact adhesives

Used for large areas such as sheet material. Two surfaces are coated and left for 15 minutes. On contact with the other surface adhesion is instant.

Rivets

Rivets are used extensively in sheet metal work although they can be used to join acrylic and wood (see Figure 3.1.22). Conventional rivets are available in various forms in addition to pop rivets which are hollow and used widely in the aircraft industry.

Wood screws provide a temporary method of fixing unless, of course, the materials have been glued together. They can be used for joining wood to wood and metal or plastic to wood. Screws are classified by their length, gauge size, head type and material. They are normally made from steel or brass with the steel type undergoing a number of surface treatments such as chrome plating or galvanising to increase its resistance to corrosion.

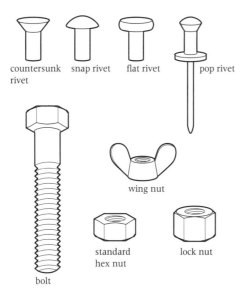

Figure 3.1.22 *Nuts, bolts and rivets*

Nuts and bolts

Nuts and bolts are another method of fixing materials temporarily (see Figure 3.1.22). Bolts are commonly available with hexagonal heads, and together with nuts of matching thread size and form, lock together to form strong mechanical joints.

Task

Using a series of annotated sketches show the main stages of the following processes:

- pop riveting
- making a fruit bowl on a wood lathe
- sticking two pieces of acrylic together.

Heat processes

All heat processes used for joining materials are permanent and the processes differ according to the heat source, temperature and materials being joined.

- Soldering. This is generally restricted to light fabrication work and can be broken down into different types of soldering depending upon the material involved:
  - Soft soldering – about 200°C – is used for making joints in brass, copper and tin plate.
  - Hard soldering – about 625°C – produces much stronger joints but a gas-welding torch is needed because of the temperatures involved.
  - Silver soldering – between 625°C and 800°C – allows soldering to be undertaken in

different stages since subsequent joints can be carried out at lower temperatures.

- Brazing. This is a hard solder with a melting point of 875°C. The filler rod is an alloy of copper and zinc and this is an ideal process for use with mild steel. When soldering or brazing there are a few essential tips which should always be adhered to:

  1. Make sure the joint area is very well cleaned.
  2. Let the solder flow once heated.
  3. The solder/braze should melt on the metal and not in the flame.
  4. Use a soft flame at the start in order not to blow away the flux.

- Welding. Whereas soldering processes simply make use of the filler material to 'stick' the materials together, welding is carried out at such a high temperature that it melts the parent material and the filler rod melts into the joint making it extremely strong. There are many ways in which this fusion process can be carried out.
- Oxy-acetylene. Oxygen and acetylene are mixed together from separate cylinders through a blowpipe. The filler rod is held manually and inserted into the molten pool to form the joint.
- Arc welding. A big current is used as the source here via an electrode that is used as the filler rod. The work piece needs to be earthed to the transformer. When the gap is small enough between the work and the filler rod, an arc is produced which generates the heat source required to melt the work and filler rod.
- MIG Welding. Metal inert gas (MIG) uses a continuous filler rod that acts as the electrode, and an earthing clamp to complete the circuit. Again, the arc is struck between the work and the electrode to provide the heat source. The inert gas acts as a shield around the arc to prevent oxides forming on the surface around the weld.
- Spot-welding. This process is used extensively in the fabrication of car bodies since it is a quick and clean process requiring no timely preparation (see Figure 3.1.23). Two large copper electrodes are used to conduct large currents through the thin metal sheets where a small nugget weld is formed.
- Ultrasonic welding. Metals as well as thermoplastics can be fabricated using this process. A probe is placed on the surface of the material and vibrations through it create a temperature rise through friction and as pressure is applied a bond is formed.

Figure 3.1.23 *Robots spot-welding cars on a production line*

Figure 3.1.24 *Anodising*

Tasks

1 Describe the difference between permanent and temporary fixings and give two examples of each.
2 Heat can be used in many ways to join metals. Produce an information sheet aimed at GCSE students on two different methods of joining metals using heat.

Finishing techniques for function and decoration

The relationship between finishes, properties and quality is one that the designer should consider very early on as one of the major design considerations.

Finishes in their various forms are used to improve the product's functional properties, aesthetic qualities and generally serve to improve quality overall. For example, bathroom fittings and taps are coated with chrome to give them a cleaner, more durable and attractive surface. Motorway barriers are plated with zinc to give them a galvanised finish which will resist corrosion. Tin cans are made from cheaper sheet steel but they are plated with tin to stop them rusting and contaminating the food.

Surface coating

Anodising

Anodising is a surface treatment associated with aluminium and its alloys. The whole product is immersed in a solution of sulphuric acid, sodium sulphate and water. The product itself is used as the anode and lead plates are used as a cathode. When a direct current (DC) is passed through the solution a thin oxide film forms on the component. When finally washed in boiling water, coloured dyes can be added before the surface is finally lacquered. As a process it can be used to finish components to a consistently high-quality finish.

Painting

Before any metal surface can be painted, the surface needs to be degreased and cleaned with paraffin. A primer should then be applied and this can be sprayed on or brushed on depending upon the circumstances. For a professional finish an undercoat should be applied before the final topcoat. 'Hammerite' is a type of paint that requires no surface preparation other than to remove any old flaking paint prior to application. It is a one-coat application for ferrous metals and is available in a wide range of colours in either a smooth or 'crackle' finish.

Painting wood also involves the application of a number of coats. Prior to any painting, all knots should be sealed to prevent any resin from escaping. In between coats the surfaces should be rubbed down with fine glass paper. Topcoats are available in various forms:

- Oil based – commonly known as gloss paints, these are available in a wide range of colours. They are durable and waterproof and are excellent for use on products that are outside such as window frames and doors. Certain paints used on boats never need rubbing down for repainting.
- Emulsion – available in vinyl or acrylic resin, these paints are water based but not waterproof.
- Polyurethane – tough and scratch resistant, these paints harden on exposure to air. They are used widely on children's toys.

Painting, other than spray painting, is very time consuming in its application. Great care also needs to be taken to ensure an even application over the entire surface. It does, however, allow you the flexibility to create original pieces by way of choice or mix of colours therefore creating a range of one-off finishes.

Varnishing

Varnishes are a plastic type of finish made from synthetic resins. They provide a tough waterproof and heatproof finish. Polyurethane varnish is available in a range of colours with different finishes; gloss, matt or satin. They are best applied in thin coats with a light rub down with wire wool in between. New varnishes based on acrylic dry more quickly, have less odour and brushes can be cleaned in water. As they do not use solvents, they are environmentally friendly.

Preservation methods

Wooden products that are used outside such as fences and garden sheds need to be protected from the wet, insects and possibly fungal decay. Creosote is an oil-based preservative that is widely used on timbers for external use. This type of product is purchased already treated where it will have been dipped in a bath or pressure treated to absorb the solution. For furniture use, hardwoods and tanalised softwoods are used. Tanalised timber has been treated with preservatives that have been driven into the wood under pressure.

Self-finishing

Plastics generally require a little finishing on the edges and no surface finishing. This is mainly due to the exceptionally high quality of moulds used in the various manufacturing processes. Textures can be introduced to the mould surface and will subsequently be manifest in the final moulded products (see Figure 3.1.25).

Surface decoration

Engraving

Most materials can be engraved with special tools or by a chemical reaction. Hand-held tools such as chisels are used on the more resistant materials, while etching with acids permanently engraves the surface of metals. Some techniques are now computer controlled allowing a multitude of fonts and styles to be quickly converted and output. A variety of materials such as woods, metals and even composite materials

Figure 3.1.26 Engraved glass goblet

such as reconstituted stone can all be cut with the appropriate tooling.

Pyrographic methods

Woods can be decorated by burning patterns into the surface. A tool similar to a soldering iron is fitted with various shaped bits. These are then heated and pushed into the surface allowing total flexibility and creativity over the finished design (see Figure 3.1.27).

Transfer techniques on plastic

Vinyl is used widely by sign writers to create large and decorative designs and images for signs and vehicle graphics (see Figure 3.1.28). Data prepared on CAD packages is quite easily output to plotters and cutters before being transferred to a backing material. This process, however, is not a direct transfer process like screen-printing. This versatile process can be applied to many surfaces and circular items too. It is essential first to generate an artwork that is then transferred on to stencil film with the use of ultraviolet light. The

Figure 3.1.25 Plastic toy made in a mould

Figure 3.1.27 Pyrographic design on a breadboard

Figure 3.1.28 *Vehicle graphics using vinyl*

stencil is then fixed below a mesh and the work piece held below the whole arrangement. Inks are then applied and squeezed through the mesh and artwork on to the work piece. The process can normally be repeated at great speed industrially where such items as T-shirts and ceramics can be painted and over printed using different colours.

Spray paints

Spray painting offers a quick solution to covering large surface areas evenly. Used extensively in the car industry and now controlled by computers and robots, this process produces a high-quality surface finish. Layers of paint are built up to provide a hard surface and one that protects the material below from corrosion and oxidation.

Etching

With the use of acids, designs and patterns can be made on the surface of metals by etching. An acid resistant such as paraffin wax or a mask is applied to the areas not to be exposed. The acid then chemically attacks the metal surface to leave a contrasting surface texture or finish.

Product manufacture

Within any design work a major consideration is the eventual scale of production. In a drive to reduce the cost of manufacture products are often made in large quantities. This plays a significant part in the design of a product as it must allow it to be mass produced. Most production processes are based on one-off production, batch production, and/or high-volume or mass production.

One-off production

One-off production is used for very different reasons and it depends entirely on the nature of the product. Much of the work that you undertake at school/college will be of this one-off type. A space rocket or a motorway bridge will also fall into this category since there would only be the one produced. In these situations criteria such as safety and reliability are much more important than cost. Other 'one-offs' exist in the form of jewellery, bespoke furniture and in interior design where the emphasis is not on function but more on aesthetics (see Figure 3.1.29). Cost in these circumstances has a greater significance but there is still a premium to be paid because of the originality factor: the product is unique and its production is labour intensive.

Batch production

Batch production can be described as the production of identical products of specified quantities in 'batches'. Batches can vary from a few products to several thousand and changes in market demand can be met easily with little time delay because everything involved in the production process – tooling, machinery and people – is kept as flexible as possible. Once batches of products are complete tooling and machines are again available for use on the production of the next batch. Ranges of furniture can fall into this category where the legs may be identical, but the tops and any draws could be different sizes. Once a particular batch has been produced, the tooling can be changed to make the next size.

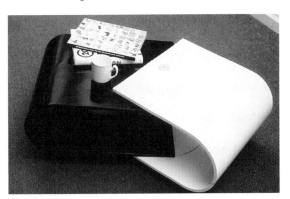

Figure 3.1.29 *Much of the work you undertake will be one-off production*

Task

From a selection of items such as those listed below look at and record the type of surface finish each product has and work out why each finish was used for that particular set of circumstances.

- Kitchen taps
- Dog-food bowl
- Bread board
- Empty tin can
- Child's wooden toy

Table 3.1.8 *Comparison of manufacturing processes*

	Labour costs	Equipment costs	Economic size
Sand casting: manual	High	Medium	+1
automated	Medium	Medium	Any volume
Injection moulding	Low once the mould has been produced	High cost of machinery and mould	High volume in runs of thousands
CNC milling: one-off	High	High	+1
mass production	High cost initially to set up the program and machine	High	Any volume of production but the more produced the cheaper the unit cost becomes

Mass production

Mass production is the term for high-volume production with long runs following expensive 'tooling up' costs. Continuous production operates 24 hours a day and requires high investment in equipment, although it has low labour costs in terms of skilled operators. Examples of continuous production could include steel making, oil refining and chemical production.

The most appropriate choice of manufacturing process is determined by several factors:

- the time allowed to make the product
- the number to be manufactured
- the availability of machinery and skilled workers where appropriate.

A comparison between three different manufacturing processes is shown in Table 3.1.8 to demonstrate the economics of materials processing.

Task
In your work for Unit 2 think about how slight changes in the design of the product could allow your product to be batch or mass produced. You need to demonstrate an understanding of commercial manufacturing processes and how they could be applied to your work in the development stages of your portfolio.

4. Testing materials

British and International Standards

The testing of products and components is strictly governed by British Standards and other International Standards organisations around the world. The British Standards Institute (BSI) is one of the largest independent testing organisations in the world. It is responsible for testing products from children's toys and equipment to medicine bottles and bicycle helmets. It is also responsible for drawing up new testing procedures.

Products that have been tested to British Standards and pass carry a safety mark to recognise this fact.

Carry out tests on your own work!
Your coursework project in Unit 2 should involve testing of some description. You should, however, as with any design work, consider the standards to which you have to design to. The relevant standards should be consulted in the design stages.

Safety testing under controlled conditions

Any testing carried out by the BSI, or on your own work, should be carried out under controlled conditions. It is essential that the tests are identical, so that when testing a range of products, they will all be subjected to, for example, being dropped from the same height or being hit with the same force.

Fire testing
Fire testing obviously needs to be carried out under controlled conditions. Fire regulations are an important aspect that have to be considered when using many modern plastics and textiles since some very toxic gases can be given off when burning. Many of these materials have now been banned and special grades of upholstery foam have to be used for furniture and bedding, and special finishes are used to improve resistance to fire.

The use of information and communications technology in testing

As information and communications technology (ICT) has developed, testing is increasingly being carried out using computer modelling. Traditionally, car safety was tested using a crash dummy. Now, complicated computer programs are being used to simulate how the car will react when hit in a number of ways and this means that the cars no longer have to be destroyed during testing.

Virtual reality modelling

Virtual reality modelling is providing a very useful tool in the visualisation of architectural design. Buildings can be modelled on screen to show the internal and external organisation and layout. This technique can also show how a building may look in different materials and at different times of the day and year as the weather and position of the sun changes.

Test programmes before manufacturing

ICT has also allowed manufacturers to run test programmes to assess the viability of making and manufacturing in the long term. They are able to assess tooling costs and times and how they might need to hold the work during machining.

Testing of products sometimes involves testing them to destruction and although this is appropriate for smaller products, it is not possible on aircraft or ships. In this case, computer models are used with results that were obtained from testing smaller scaled versions. Testing would be carried out in wind tunnels or water tanks and the results gathered would be used to build the computer models for the full-sized product.

Ultrasound testing

Ultrasound testing is used to inspect items such as alloy wheels or welded underground pipes that cannot be tested to destruction. A frequency between 500kHz and 20MHz is passed through the component, and where a flaw exists a reflection is caused on the ultrasound vibration.

Standard destructive tests and comparative testing in the workshop

Standard destructive tests and comparative testing can be carried out in your school/college workshop. A tensometer can be used to carry out tensile testing of materials. In order that a fair test is undertaken, the specimen pieces have to conform to British Standard sizes. The force applied and extension of the material is recorded and can then be plotted on a force-extension graph (see Figure 3.1.30). The tensometer can also be used to test the strength of joints, the bending of materials and their compressive strength. With special tooling they can also be used to test the hardness and shear strength of materials.

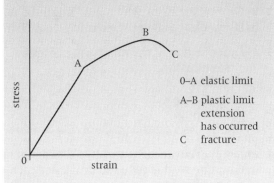

Figure 3.1.30 Force/extension graph

0–A elastic limit

A–B plastic limit extension has occurred

C fracture

Table 3.1.9 Standard destructive tests and comparative testing in the workshop

Test	Method	Reason
Tensile	Tensometer	If a material is not strong enough for its purpose it would fail in use. The tensometer measures tensile strength of materials to determine what limits they can be put to.
Hardness	Brinell Vickers Rockwell	Materials must be capable of withstanding wear and indentation. If the incorrect material is chosen the product may fail. These three tests measure a material's ability to withstand scratching or resistance to indentation.
Toughness	120D impact test	The measurement of resistance to shock loading. The material may break and fracture if not tough enough, again leading to component/product failure.
Ductility	Bend tests	If a material is too ductile it may stretch or deform, resulting in mechanical failure of the component or product.

Exam preparation

You will need to revise all the topics in this unit, so that you can apply your knowledge and understanding to the exam questions. In preparation for your exam it is a good idea to make brief notes about different topics, such as 'Ferrous metals, non-ferrous metals and alloys.' Use sub-headings or bullet point lists and diagrams where appropriate. A single side of A4 should be used for each heading from the Specification.

It is very important to learn exam skills. You should have weekly practice in learning technical terms and in answering exam-type questions. When you answer any question you should:

- read the question carefully and pick out the key points that need answering
- match your answer to the marks available, e.g. for two marks, you should give two good points that address the question
- always give examples and justify statements with reasons, saying how or why the statement is true.

Practice exam questions

1 a) State the meaning of two of the following forms of surface finishing or coating:
  - anodising
  - painting
  - varnishing
  - engraving
  - etching. (2)
  b) Using a product example, briefly describe the term 'self finishing'. (3)

2 a) Give two reasons why a gear might be used in a machine or engine. (2)
  b) Using clear diagrams, explain two different types of gear systems. (4)

3 a) Describe two of the following processes:
  - sand casting
  - milling
  - spark erosion
  - abrading. (4)
  b) Briefly describe the purpose of a bearing. (2)

4 a) List two advantages and two disadvantages of converting timber. (4)
  b) Give one working characteristic for each of the following:
  - hardwoods
  - softwoods. (2)

5 When turning on a wood lathe, preparation of timber is essential. List five essential things that should be checked for before turning commences. (5)

6 Describe in detail one of the following processes:
  - annealing
  - work hardening. (5)

7 a) Explain the difference between thermoplastic and thermosetting polymers, giving one example of how each is used. (4)
  b) With the aid of clear diagrams, describe two of the following processes:
  - injection moulding
  - blow moulding
  - vacuum forming. (6)

8 a) Explain why testing before manufacture is an important process. (3)
  b) Describe the purpose of British Standards. (2)

9 Explain why computer modelling is increasingly used as a testing aid. (5)

Design and technology in society (R302)

Summary of expectations

1. What to expect

Design and technology in society is one of the three options offered in Section B of Unit 3 of which you will study only one. This option builds on the knowledge and understanding of how design and technology affects society, that you gained during your GCSE course.

2. How will it be assessed?

The work that you do in this option will be externally assessed through Section B of the Unit 3 examination paper. The questions will be common across all three materials areas in product Design. You can therefore answer questions with reference to **either**:

- a Resistant Materials Technology product such as a Bauhaus table lamp;
- a Graphics with Materials Technology product such as an Art Nouveau perfume bottle;
- **or** a Textiles Technology product such as a cushion using a William Morris fabric.

You are advised to spend **45 minutes** on this section of the paper.

3. What will be assessed?

The following list summarises the topics covered in this option and what will be examined.

- The physical and social consequences of design and technology on society.
  - The effects of design and technological changes on society.
  - Influences on the development of products.
- Professional designers at work.
  - The relationship between designers and clients, manufacturers, users and society.

- Professional practice relating to the design management, technology, marketing, business, ICT.
- The work of professional designers and professional bodies.
- Anthropometrics and ergonomics
  - The basic principles and applications of anthropometrics and ergonomics.
  - British and International Standards

4. How to be successful in this unit

To be successful in this unit you will need to:

- have a clear understanding of the subject knowledge covered in this option
- apply your knowledge and understanding to a given situation or context
- organise your answers clearly and coherently, using specialist technical terms where appropriate
- use clear sketches where appropriate to illustrate your answers
- write a clear and logical answer to the examination questions, using correct spelling, punctuation and grammar.

There may be an opportunity to demonstrate your knowledge and understanding of design and technology in society in your Unit 2 coursework.

5. How much is it worth?

This option, with Section A, is worth 30 per cent of your AS qualification. If you go on to complete the whole course, then this unit accounts for 15 per cent of the full Advanced GCE.

Unit 3 + option	Weighting
AS level	30%
A2 level (full GCE)	15%

1. The physical and social consequences of design and technology on society

The effects of design and technological changes on society

Design and technology has improved the lives of millions of people world-wide, but the changes brought about by developments in technology have resulted in far reaching physical and social consequences.

The benefits of technology are countless – imagine your life without electricity, television or computers! Many of the products that we take for granted today are available as a direct result of developments in mass production and technology (see Figure 3.2.1). Mass production may have improved our lives, but it has also brought unforeseen consequences – one simple example being a concern about the adverse influence of computer games on children. On a larger scale, there is growing awareness of the need for sustainable technology. More people are now aware of the problems arising from the over-use of the world's natural resources, the consequences of pollution and the impact that global manufacturing has on the lives of many people world-wide.

Mass production and the consumer society

The history of design as we know it began with the industrial revolution and the invention of the steam engine in the mid 1700s. As a result of this invention, coal mining, iron and steel and machine production took on a new importance and set the scene for the development of industrial mass-production. The steam engine led to the development of

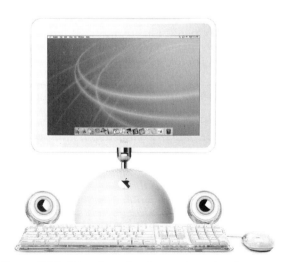

Figure 3.2.1 *IMac from Apple creates a lovely shape for the workplace*

machinery, transport and trade. This fostered the need for the design of new products, but design was no longer to be in the hands of individual craftspeople. Expensive and time-consuming hand work could now be replaced by machine work. Products, once exclusively made for the rich, could now be made at an affordable price for ordinary working people.

The steam engine led to the development of machinery, transport and trade. This fostered the need for the design of new products, but design was no longer to be in the hands of individual craftspeople. Expensive and time-consuming hand work could now be replaced by machine work. Products, once exclusively for the rich, could now be made at an affordable price for ordinary working people.

Mass production

The main characteristic of mass production was that the production process was simplified into a limited number of tasks. The craftsperson became 'redundant', replaced by low-skilled factory workers who performed simple repetitive tasks.

What started out as a wonderful opportunity for ordinary people to find work and gain access to inexpensive consumer products, ended in misery for many. The reduced requirement for skills meant lower wages and the employment of women and children in 'sweatshop' factories. The resulting poverty led to worker uprisings and the development of trade unions, aimed at combating poor living conditions, poverty and the increasing pollution brought about by industrialisation.

Assembly lines

The story of mass production would not be complete without reference to the introduction of the moving assembly line. In the United States of America, industrial production developed at a much faster pace than anywhere else and the first automatic assembly lines were in use by the mid nineteenth century. The first assembly lines were used in slaughter-houses, then in the sewing machine industry and later in automobile manufacturing. Assembly lines made mass production easier and faster, enabling products such as cars to be made more cheaply and be available to a much wider market.

Design tradition

Although the technical advances of the nineteenth century brought about new production methods and new products, there was no tradition of design

Figure 3.2.2 *Heavy, overdecorated Victorian furniture*

Figure 3.2.3 *The Remington 1, the first mechanical typewriter, 1876*

for mass-produced products. Instead, poor quality utensils and furniture were decorated to imitate the traditional styles of hand-made products. You may have seen examples of the heavy, over decorated furniture that was typical of the Victorian era (see Figure 3.2.2).

Design for mass production

During the second half of the nineteenth century trade unions demanded changes to the poor living conditions of factory workers and the design of simple, inexpensive consumer goods that were appropriate for their lives. The poor quality, over-decorated, over-sized furniture that was currently being mass produced was totally inappropriate for the cramped housing conditions of the majority of workers. As a result, furniture for factory workers became a new area of design. These changes in the concept of design for mass-production were long overdue. They mark the beginning of modern design history. The connections between form, function and products began to be recognised. They are the same ones that we use today in design and technology.

Design in the USA

In contrast to Europe, the concept of design in late nineteenth century USA was more technical and functional. The increasing mechanisation included not only production methods, but the products themselves. Products such as the sewing machine, the microphone, the telephone and the mechanical typewriter were mass produced (see Figure 3.2.3). Many of these products were totally functional and lacked any kind of decoration. The concept of 'styling' didn't exist at that time, mainly because there was no competition from similar products and therefore no competing market to sell into.

The development of the consumer society

In both the USA and Europe, the early years of the twentieth century were decades of uncertainty. War, revolution and economic crises resulted in massive unemployment, poverty and housing shortages. For the well-off, however the lifestyle was much the same and culture, entertainment, sport and social life continued. In the USA, jazz, swing and the Charleston dominated the dance halls. Popular culture and the age of Hollywood would become an enormous influence on lifestyle, fashion, design and even morality.

As international commerce and transportation systems developed, new opportunities for product design came about, such as luxury ships, aeroplanes, hotels, theatres and department stores. The gradual spread of electrification brought about the design of innovative new products using new technology and new materials. In the 1930s, most middle class American homes owned consumer goods such as radios, refrigerators, toasters and washing machines. As the standard of living improved, the demand for new products increased. Advertising became an important new industry, using market research, packaging and product styling to sell the new products. Design became an important marketing tool. This was used to great effect after the Wall Street crash of

1929, when product 'styling' was used to motivate people to buy. Designing aesthetically appealing products was one strategy used to promote consumerism. Another was called 'streamlining', which developed from research into aerodynamics for cars and planes. After the 1930s, the availability of new materials such as plywood, plastics and sheet metal enabled rounded 'streamlined' shapes to be applied to many products and it came to represent 'modernity', 'speed' and 'improved efficiency'.

Another more controversial strategy was that of 'planned obsolescence', in which advertising played a major role. New updated product models were continually brought onto the market to increase demand for the 'latest', technically up-to-date model. Some products were even designed to wear out after a time!

Task

These days legislation and standards ensure that good quality products are manufactured. This was not the case in the past when planned obsolescence was designed into some products. Consumers were encouraged to throw away the old and buy the new, better product. Explain your views on consumerism and the 'throw away' society.

The 'new' industrial age of high-technology production

In the twentieth century, developments in materials technology, together with changes in lifestyle have revolutionised product design. New materials such as aluminium, stainless steel, heat-resistant glass, polyester, polypropylene and silicon have enabled new ways of designing and manufacturing. In particular, the development of digital computers in the 1940s and the silicon chip in the 1960s, have enabled cheap portable computer technology, which has transformed modern industrial society.

Miniaturisation

The most important technological development in recent years has been in the field of microelectronics. Not only have products have become smaller through advances in microchip technology, but previously unimaginable multi-functional products have been developed.

These include the first transistor radios and televisions in the 1950s and colour video

Figure 3.2.4 *The Psion Series 3 palm-top computer provides an address book, diary and data transfer using infra-red technology to another computer or printer*

recorders in the 1960s. By far the most influential product in the 1980s was the 'Walkman', which had an unprecedented impact on people's lifestyles. Current developments include portable CD players, multi-functional fax, e-mail and Internet browser telephones and Palm-top computers.

In the past it was easy to recognise the function of a product, such as a typewriter or a watch. Nowadays, the impact of miniaturisation may mean that products effectively 'disappear', in that the product no longer visually represents its function, or the function is not clear. The designer then has to convey this function by other means. If a calculator is built into a wristwatch, is the product designed as a calculator or a watch? How is the purpose of such a product made clear?

Case study: Swatch of many functions

Swatch watches were first marketed in the early 1980s when the Swiss watch industry was fighting for survival against Japanese market expansion. Swatch decided to target the lower

Figure 3.2.5 *Interactive watches, similar in style to this one, will allow the wearer to access the Internet and talk to a PC*

end of the market in order to produce affordable watches that were designed around the concept of style and fashion. The technological aspect took a back seat.

Now things have changed and the marketing climate is different. Technology is now a major driving force for design, having become seriously 'trendy'. The most recent developments by Swatch are interactive watches with so-called 'access technology'. This type of watch can act as a ski pass and metro ticket. It has already been in use in European ski resorts.

The next development for Swatch is the 'Internet Swatch', which has the potential for you to e-mail, access data from a PC, book tickets and browse the web from your watch! Swatch is also working on 'Swatch Talk', a watch that also acts as a mobile phone. The aim is to make people who wear the Swatch brand feel 'up-to-the-minute', with the opportunity to be permanently connected to the net, allowing mobility and interactivity.

Figure 3.2.6 *Globalisation includes having to design products for someone in another country. These 'adaptive spectacles' were designed for the developing world. The lenses are easily adjusted by the wearer to correct their vision – no sight test is required*

Task
Investigate other high-tech products that are interactive. How many functions does the product have? Why is it necessary for one product to have more than one function? Explain how the styling of the product enables the customer to understand the purpose of the product.

The global market place
The need to be competitive means that many companies sell their products all over the world. It can sometimes be a problem to design for unfamiliar markets or design products that will sell across different countries. Many companies have design teams situated throughout the world so they can design for a particular local market. Other companies use focused market research to discover the needs of specific niche markets.

Products that sell across the global market sometimes have to be remodelled to include different design features depending on where they are to be sold. Remodelling may involve many factors including:

* increasing the amount of recyclable materials used in the product
* whether a plug is fitted or not
* the fitting of different visual displays
* using devices to suppress noise levels.

Increasingly products are sold under the same name in different countries. For example, a kitchen cleaner recently changed it's name to Cif to harmonise with the rest of Europe.

Global manufacturing
Global manufacturing is closely linked to the growth of multinational companies, which operate in more than one country. In the past, multinationals were mainly associated with mineral exploitation or with plantations, such as for cotton or food. Since the 1950s, many multinationals have been involved in global manufacturing, especially of cars and electrical goods. Today, global manufacturing is growing at an increasing rate, mainly due to international competition and developments in Information and Communications Technology (ICT). Global manufacturing covers a wide range of activities, such as:

* petroleum (BP, Exon)
* motor vehicles (Ford, General Motors)
* electrical goods/electronics (Philips, Sony, Hitachi)
* financial services (Barclays)
* food and hotels (Coca Cola, McDonalds, Trust House Forte)
* textile and garment manufacturing (DuPont, Marks and Spencer).

High-speed revolution
The high-speed information revolution that has come about through developments in ICT will continue to increase international competition.

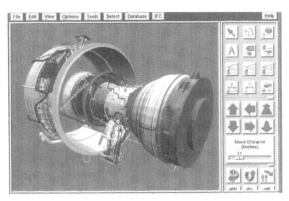

Figure 3.2.7 *The skills of designers, engineers, suppliers and many others were used in the development of engines for the Airbus A330 plane. This would be impossible without the use of electronic communications which enables collaboration with partner companies across the world*

For many companies, competition means reducing labour and material costs. Global manufacturing is a means of doing just this, since moving manufacturing to another country can make use of lower labour costs, thus reducing one of the highest costs of manufacturing. The trend towards global manufacturing often includes designing products like electrical goods or cars in one country and manufacturing in another. This is increasingly cost effective because of improved electronic communications. Large-scale products such as aircraft engines may be designed and engineered by teams working together across the world and assembled using component parts that are sourced from supply chains in different countries.

Issues related to global/local production

Issues related to local/global production are concerned with the effects of the global economy and of multinationals on quality of life, employment and the environment. While the head offices of many multinationals are often located in developed countries (such as Western Europe), some multinationals are based in newly industrialised countries (NICs) such as Singapore or Taiwan. Developing countries, such as those in Africa or Asia, have generally welcomed multinationals and the benefits that locating manufacturing there brings. However, there are disadvantages for both developed and developing countries in global manufacturing.

Advantages of global manufacturing for NICs and developing countries:

- It provides employment and higher living standards.

- It may improve the level of expertise of the local workforce.
- Foreign currency is brought into the country to improve their balance of payments.
- It widens the country's economic base.
- It enables the transfer of technology.

Disadvantages of global manufacturing for NICs and developing countries:

- It can cause environmental damage.
- The jobs provided may only require low-level skills.
- Managerial roles may be filled by employees from developed countries.
- Most or all of the company profits may be exported back to developed countries.
- Multinationals may cut corners on health and safety or pollution (which they could not do in their home country).
- Multinationals can exert political pressure.
- Raw materials are often exported or not processed locally.
- Manufactured goods are for export and not for the local market (where many could not afford them anyway).
- Decisions are made in a foreign country and on a global basis, so the multinational may pull out at any time.
- With increased mechanisation, there is a reduced need for the local workforce.

Influences on the development of products

The design and manufacture of products is a complex affair. Why some products are successful, why they are made as they are and how they are used and disposed of are issues that affect every one of us. How do we choose which products to buy? Do we really need all of them? How do we recognise a well-designed product? Why is design important?

The Design Council recently conducted a survey of 800 UK manufacturers about the contribution of design to the UK economy. The results were very clear. Ninety two per cent of businesses agreed that design helps to produce a competitive advantage and 87 per cent believed it increases profits and aids diversification into new markets.

Design is clearly important. It is interesting to note that in sixteenth century England the word 'design' meant a 'plan from which something is to be made'. Today, we normally use the term 'design' to mean the drafting and planning of industrial products. One outcome of industrialisation has been the requirement for the profession of the 'designer'.

Task

Global manufacturing highlights the many moral and ethical questions, the so-called values issues, that are inherent in product design and manufacture. Investigate further one of the following issues related to global economy manufacturing, to find out who are the winners and losers in terms of jobs, quality of life, and the environment:

1 What are the effects of the global economy on lifestyles in developing countries? Is it ethical to advertise products that many people cannot afford? Should developed countries impose their values on traditional cultures?
2 Do multinationals have a responsibility to society and the environment? What are the effects of building new factories and transporting raw materials and products? What are the effects on energy demands in NICs and developing countries? Should multinationals follow sustainable manufacturing practices?
3 The effects of deforestation and over-use of the world's natural resources are plain to see. How can we avoid the effects of global warming or the loss of bio-diversity in many countries?
4 Moving manufacturing away from developed countries causes unemployment there. As competition increases, many NICs are also affected by further relocation of manufacturing, such as the move from Hong Kong to China. How can the threat of unemployment be overcome in a global economy?
5 Developing countries have to pay off debts to world financial institutions rather than spend money on food and development in their own countries. This may mean a country exporting food to pay debt during a famine. Is this ethical?

Influences on design

For a company to make a profit, product design must be market led and market driven. It must take into account the needs of the target market group and the various influences of market trends, including colour and style. For many consumers these days, design has become an important means of self-expression. Consumers choose products not just for what they do, but for what they tell the world about them. Products are no longer simple, functional artefacts. We buy a diver's watch not because we want to spend hours under the sea, but because a high performance product has a sense of glamour. We buy a chair not just as a comfortable product to sit on, but also because it can express a sense of tradition or modernity.

Now that products are mass-produced and sold in millions, the primary purpose of the designer is to inject a sense of personality in a mass-produced object. For example, the first telephone or early typewriters were the result of mechanical solutions and nobody had any preconceived idea of what they should look like. These days, when products are mass produced and sold in millions, it is the primary purpose of many designers to give the product a sense of personality.

Task

Compare the design styles of a product such as the radio. What did the first radio look like in comparison with models today? Explain the differences in terms of the materials used, shape, form, styling and colour. Is it easy to see how to use the product? How big are the controls?

Product reliability and aesthetics

Product reliability is no longer an issue. Most products carry guarantees and there is consumer legislation to support product quality and safety. Most brands within a given product category perform equally well. The main reason for buying a product is how it looks – its aesthetic qualities. The product's function, relating to its performance is often taken for granted. The job of the designer then, is increasingly to give a product and therefore the consumer an image. Should the product look traditional, retro, or high-tech? At the same time, the consumer should understand how the product works, so that it is obvious how to operate it.

Form and function

The connection between form and function has been one of the most controversial issues in the history of design. When products were first mass-produced in Victorian times they were highly decorated to look like hand-made products, whether the decoration was appropriate or not. The development of 'reform' groups such as the Arts and Crafts Movement gradually brought about a change in the concept of design. The form of products was to be simplified and the products well made from suitable materials. At the turn of the nineteenth century, developments in materials and technology enabled the production of innovative new products such as the telephone. Many of these products were so innovative that no one knew what they should look like! The development of mass production required that products be standardised, simple and easy to produce. The supporters of functionalism therefore suggested that the form of a product must suit its function and not include any excessive decoration.

From the functionalism of the early twentieth century, as far back as even the 1970s, the functional requirements of mass production were used as a benchmark for the form of an industrial product. In other words, for a product to be mass produced at a profit, it needed to be simple and easy to produce.

The argument about form and function still continues. As a student designer, you are asked to simplify your designs for ease of manufacture. One of the many reasons for doing this is to give you time to manufacture your product. The concept of form and function is complex. Think about the design of modern products and of the development of styling to market them. Think about developments in the technical design of products. Think about marketing and image. These days a product is thought to have three basic functions:

- its practical and technical function, if it works efficiently
- its aesthetic function, how it looks, its styling
- its symbolic function, or the image it gives the user.

It is recognised today that design fulfils not only technical and aesthetic functions, but it is also a means of communication. Design tells the onlooker something about the user.

Figure 3.2.8 *Harley Davidson bikes can be customised*

Task
The Harley-Davidson has become a cult bike for many people. The bike is sold in a standard form, with the opportunity of customising it by buying interchangeable parts. Describe the image that such a product is perceived to bring to the user.

- Aesthetic properties relate to how a product looks, matching its styling with its end-use. As a student designer you need to develop an 'eye' for aesthetic characteristics, such as balance, line, shape and form, texture and surface pattern. Scale too is an important factor; some designers develop products by using change of scale as a starting point.
- Colour is a most essential characteristic of many products, as it is often the first thing we notice about the product. Colour is a powerful marketing tool, which can encourage consumers to buy. Colour in home ware products changes less frequently than fashion products.
- Mechanical properties relate to product performance, e.g. using ductile and tough mild steel for car body parts.

Task
Explain why image and style are increasingly important to the design of products. Choose two products that illustrate your answer. Explain why both are attractive to the consumer.

Design and culture
Throughout history, designers have been influenced by what they see and the products they use. All designers need starting points for design, whether they specialise in industrial, graphic, textile, or fashion design. The work of other artists and designers, both today and through history, have often provided such starting points.

The design movements that are included in the next section are some of the key ones in relation to the development of design. In a book of this type, it is impossible to include every possible influence on design – added to which all designers are influenced by different things. You will therefore need to read around the content of this section. You may also already have favourite designers or design influences that you will be able to draw upon when you answer the exam questions for this unit.

The Arts and Crafts movement

William Morris (1834–96) believed that it was essential to understand the production process in order to be a designer. This belief became one of the founding principles of the Arts and Crafts Movement with which Morris was closely associated. In 1875 he set up Morris & Co which produced furniture, stained glass, wallpaper, fabrics, carpets and pottery. Morris was opposed to mass-production because he believed that manufacturers were more concerned with quantity than quality. Morris saw the effects of industrialisation as polluting the environment, giving poor working conditions and producing low quality mass-produced products. He and others in the Arts and Crafts Movement believed in a return to workshop production using traditional techniques and the importance of the craftsperson creating the product. Morris believed in artistic design, based on simple natural forms.

The Arts and Crafts Movement introduced a new direction in design, reviving an interest in simple, practical design. Comfortable wooden chairs, like the ladderback or Windsor, which had been used to furnish simple country cottages, now found their way into the homes of the wealthy. This type of simple undecorated furniture created a demand for simplicity of design and fitness for purpose, representing the values of 'truth to materials and form'. The Arts and Crafts Movement had an important influence on Art Nouveau and the Bauhaus Movements. In this sense, it can be said to form the basis of modern design and through its influence on Scandinavian design, to have influenced much of the design in Europe (see Figure 3.2.9).

Art Nouveau

Art Nouveau was an important design movement in France around 1900 and soon developed into an international movement. The main characteristic of Art Nouveau styling was its use of flowing lines, stylised climbing plants and water lilies. In Scotland, Charles Rennie Mackintosh was also inspired by geometric forms based on Japanese art.

Art Nouveau was an influential decorative style used in architecture, wrought ironwork, glass, furniture, fabrics and wallpaper. The

Figure 3.2.9 *The Arts and Crafts Movement still influences design today, as can be seen in this rush seated chair*

Figure 3.2.10 *This Porte Dauphine Metro entrance, made from cast iron and glass was designed by Hector Guimard*

entrances to some metro stations in Paris are typical of the Art Nouveau style (see Figure 3.2.10) Although Art Nouveau designers were much more interested in using modern materials and mass production, some considered themselves to be artists and rejected industrial production methods. Their designs were only available to the wealthy, such as Rene Lalique jewellery made from semi-precious stones, glass and gold. Art Nouveau could be described as fitting in somewhere between art and industry. Although it encouraged a return to craft work and used some mass production techniques, some say that it delayed the development of modern industrial design. Around 1910 the Art Nouveau style virtually disappeared.

Task
Investigate two different products, one from the Arts and Crafts Movement and the other from the Art Nouveau Movement. Compare and contrast the form, decoration and styling used in their design.

The Bauhaus (1919–1933)

In Germany, the Bauhaus school became the centre of modernism and functionalism. It laid down design principles that still influence the teaching of design and industrial design. Many of its products still look modern today. The principal aims were to use modern materials and to combine the concepts of form and function.

The Bauhaus was founded and run by Walter Gropius between 1919 and 1928. The basis of Bauhaus education was a preliminary apprenticeship centred on free experimentation with colour, form and material. The goal was to offer an equal education in artistic and handicraft skills that were linked to industry. After the preliminary course, students chose one of the commercial workshops for carpentry, pottery, metalwork, textiles, stage design, photography or commercial art. Bauhaus training was given by important artists such as Johannes Itten, Lyonel Feininger, Paul Klee, Georg Muche and Oscar Schlemmer. This was the first time that so many artists were involved to this extent in the teaching of design.

In 1922, Laslo Maholy-Nagy was appointed director of the Bauhaus metal workshop and instructor of typography. He designed all the Bauhaus books and opened a graphics studio in Berlin in 1928. He experimented with light, film and plexiglass, developing the dimmer switch in 1930.

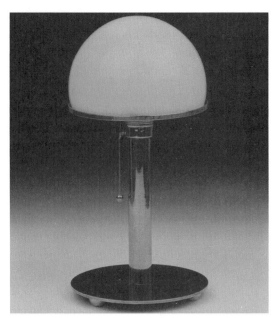

Figure 3.2.11 *This Bauhaus table lamp, first made in 1923–1924, was one of the most successful to come from the Bauhaus metal workshop. It was made from industrially produced metal and glass. Although originally hand made, it is mass produced today*

As the Bauhaus developed its influence, the first industrially useful designs were produced in the metal workshop. Students were encouraged to use new materials such as steel tubing, plywood and industrial glass. The aim was to produce economical mass-produced products, such as table lamps, metal teapots and chairs.

The Bauhaus was closed in 1933 by the Nazis in an effort to stop modernism in design. Gropius and Maholy-Nagy moved to the USA in 1937 and the New Bauhaus was founded. There the Bauhaus style became known as the 'International Style', which was mainly concerned with architecture. However, architects such as Le Corbusier and Alvar Alto also designed furniture which followed the principles of the Bauhaus.

Task
The work of other designers and artists has always been used as a starting point for design work. It is a part of design development to build on what has gone before. Choose an artist whose work you find attractive or inspirational. Try to decide what it is that you like about it. Make sketches of the aspects of the work that you like and try to integrate these aspects into design work for your next project.

Figure 3.2.12 In 1920s Paris, many artists were inspired by developments in art and technology. Fernand Leger was also influenced by the teachings of the Bauhaus and by Cubism as can be seen in his 1924 painting 'Elements Mecaniques'

Figure 3.2.13 Early radios were designed to look like furniture, but with the introduction of plastics they began to have a style of their own. This 1932 Art Deco style radio was made from Bakelite in a bold, circular shape

Art Deco

Art Deco originated in France and its design style was thought to be highly modern and elegant. It was influenced by the Cubist painting of Picasso and Braque, African and Egyptian art. Art Deco focused on exclusive designer made products, using geometric shapes, zig-zag patterns, chevrons and sunbursts and expensive ivory, bronze, crystal, and ebony. The movement was at its height in the 1920s and 30s and although it was initially opposed to mass production, its extravagant style gradually made use of more modern materials. It influenced the design of many mass-produced products made from new materials such as aluminium, chrome, coloured glass and Bakelite. Art Deco was a popular style for interior design and architecture.

New Art Deco materials

Aluminium, plywood and Bakelite were used extensively in mass produced Art Deco products, such as jewellery, cigarette cases, perfume bottles and radios. Bakelite, invented in 1907, was first used as a substitute for wood and was carved out of solid blocks. It was, however, perfect for moulding into the smooth, streamlined shapes of 1920s and 30s electrical products because it was malleable, durable and inexpensive (Figure 3.2.13).

Modern design and styling

In the 1940s and 50s 'Italian style' products became all the rage. The Vespa scooter, the Fiat 500, the Lancia, Alpha Romeo and Ferrari

Figure 3.2.14 The Vespa scooter was famous all over the world

Figure 3.2.15 *The 1969 Valentine portable typewriter designed by Ettore Sottsass for Olivetti. It is made from pillar-box red moulded plastic with yellow caps on the ribbon spools*

cars, furniture, espresso machines and fashion products were set to become sought after design classics. In the 1950s and 60s new synthetic materials were used to create colourful furniture which was durable, easy to clean and relatively inexpensive. In the 1960s, design was seen as being an essential part of Italian culture and designers differentiated products by giving them names. For example, the Sottsass 1969 typewriter was called 'Valentine', giving the product a sense of personality.

Youth culture

In the 1960s youth culture had an enormous impact on fashion and design. For the first time young people were seen as an emerging group of consumers, different from their parents. Powerful television advertising and the use of new materials, shapes and bright colours led to the development of mass consumerism. Pop music and the 'hippie' movement influenced commercial art, graphic design, fashion and interior design. Images from daily life, such as soup cans or comics became a part of art (Andy Warhol) and design. New products appeared, such as the mini-skirt, the mini car and the first type of beanbag chair.

By the early 1970s other influences had an impact on design. The combination of space exploration and science fiction films suggested infinite technical opportunities for product design. For example, the film *2001: A Space Odyssey* and television programmes like *Star Trek* inspired designers to create futuristic products. As production technology developed, small production runs became possible. This moved the emphasis away from mass production towards meeting individual needs.

Memphis

Memphis was an Italian design group led by Ettore Sottsass. Originally an architect, Sottsass became a consulting designer for the typewriter manufacturer Olivetti. Memphis was the most important design group of the 1980s and designed a variety of furniture, glass and ceramic products specifically for mass production (Figure 3.2.16). Memphis designers loved the fast changes brought about by fashion and their witty, stylistic design was influenced by comic strips, films and punk music. They combined materials such as colourful plastic laminates (such as melamine and formica), glass, steel, industrial sheet metal and aluminium. Many products were inspired by children's toys. In the 1980s the Memphis group introduced a new importance to design, so that the status of design itself grew and took over a key role in the development of individual lifestyles.

Design after Memphis

A number of designers, such as Ron Arad, Jasper Morrison and Tom Dixon, moved away from functionalism and focused on one-off design, using concrete, sheet metal, plywood and rubber. Other designers, concerned about

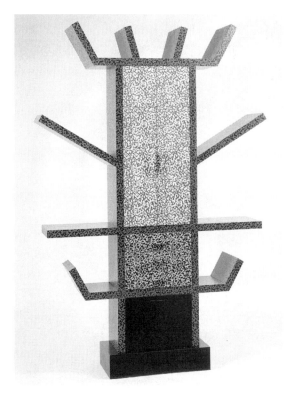

Figure 3.2.16 *The Casablanca sideboard, designed in the Memphis style by Ettore Sottsass*

built-in obsolescence, started to use recycled materials and to design more energy-efficient products. For example, the French 'super designer' Philippe Starck designed some furniture that can be recycled through the use of screw fixings rather than gluing the component parts together. Some of his other products use ecologically sound materials, like his television set made from MDF, which gives the product a more human face than using hard edge black plastic.

New materials, processes and technology

In the twentieth century, developments in materials technology and changes in lifestyle revolutionised product design. New materials such as aluminium, stainless steel, heat-resistant glass, polyester, polypropylene and the silicon chip enabled new ways of designing and manufacturing. This led to the development of multi-functional products that look 'technical'. These high tech products are more durable, easier to clean, and more exciting to use. Designers like Michael Graves and Philippe Starck have created many multi-functional products that have 'street cred'; products that provide function with image.

The development of digital computers in the 1940s and the silicon chip in the 1960s, has enabled cheap portable computer technology, which has transformed modern industrial society. The most important technological development is in the field of microelectronics, enabling products to become smaller through advances in microchip technology.

Smart materials

Smart materials can be plastics, metals, textiles, ceramics or liquids. Their physical properties can be altered in response to an input or changes in their surroundings. Examples of smart materials include the following:

- Piezo-electric actuators, used in greetings cards, to produce a sound from an electrical signal when the card is opened.
- Shape memory alloys, made to change their shape at specified temperatures, for

Figure 3.2.17 *This multi-functional chest of drawers contilevers out to form a table*

example to open greenhouse windows when it gets too hot.
- Smart wire, which contracts when an electrical current is passed through it, giving a useful pulling force. Used in locks or small robots.
- Smart links, a new silicon material, consisting of a thick walled tube of ultra-low hardness, placed over a 3 mm rod to make flexible joints. It can transmit rotary movement, serving as a universal joint, a flexible hinge or a coupling.
- Smart grease, a sticky lubricant using motion control gel to transform the behaviour of a mechanism. For example smart grease placed between the wheel and bearing in a simple motor will make it turn very slowly at a uniform speed, providing stored energy.
- Smart ceramic material, that absorbs light energy and re-emits it. Used for glow in the dark products, such as watches, emergency signs or torches.
- Thermochromatic materials, containing billions of microscopic liquid crystal capsules that change colour at specified temperatures. Used in kettles, feeding spoons, thermometers and battery test strips.

Modern production techniques

Modern materials require the development of new manufacturing processes and components, such as the following:

- The combination of powder metallurgy and injection moulding, to produce very small, accurate components with superior mechanical properties.
- The new process of friction stir welding, to improve the welding of aluminium extrusions and plates. This is used globally by the automotive and aerospace industries.
- A new aluminium self-clinch fastener for BMW cars, used to attach aluminium bumpers. It is stronger than using steel nuts and makes the bumper recyclable.

Developments in plastics

In the 1950s the use of plastics such as acrylic, PVC or polypropylene revolutionised the furniture-making industry. Plastic could be made in any colour and was malleable, light, inexpensive and modern. Plastic products were durable and could be produced in any shape or size using a moulding machine.

The popularity of plastic had a downturn after the 1973 oil crisis. It was no longer called modern or high tech, but cheap, tacky, tasteless and un-ecological. Plastic's popularity may improve in the future with the development of new eco-friendly biopolymers, processed from the maize plant.

- Enpol, a fully biodegradable plastic with comparable strength and cost to polythene, uses 2.5 times less materials to achieve the same performance as conventional plastics.
- Eco Foam, made from chips of foamed starch polymer is water soluble, reusable and free from static. It can replace polystyrene packaging materials

Computers and design

The development of powerful user-friendly home computers and Information Communications Technology (ICT) has enabled changes to the function of many consumer products. For example a multi-functional wrist computer, designed in 1988 included a compass, watch, telephone and city map. Digital technology features in many modern products like refrigerators, cameras and video players, but its biggest impact is in the use of computers for design and manufacture. CAD/CAM has enabled the development of new types of production and processes, especially for high tech products. Modern software programs enable product simulation on screen and the modification of technical data, without the need to produce physical prototypes. For example, the design of car components, including ergonomic studies are done using computer simulation.

Miniaturisation

The invention of the silicon chip has transformed modern industrial society. Without microchips a computer would be the size of a living room and a pocket calculator the size of small car! By the 1970s, thousands of electronic components could be printed on top of a single silicon chip measuring only 5 mm square. This requires a tiny amount of sand and very little energy in use.

Micro and Nano technology are being used in exciting developments, such as the world's smallest silicon gyroscope. This is tough and rugged because it is solid state with no mechanical moving parts. In medicine Nano machines can travel round the body and clear blood clots. The interface between humans and machines is set to become one of the most challenging aspects of the future.

Eco design and environmentally friendly processes

Consumers have grown accustomed to the benefits of mass production and the supply of inexpensive, well designed, easily available products. Unfortunately mass production is not sustainable. Environmental legislation, such as the banning of lead from electronics by 2008 is encouraging the use of low-tech sustainable technology, recycling and the reuse of materials.

For a product to be eco-friendly, it must be durable and recyclable *and* have an aesthetic appeal. For example:

- with a few minutes winding, the Freeplay flashlight produces a steady, reliable light source without the need to consume toxic batteries (see Figure 3.2.18)

Figure 3.2.18 *The Freeplay wind-up flashlight*

- the recycled pencil is made from recycled polystyrene cups
- electric and solar cars have been developed to reduce emissions, and reduce the weight of the car through an increased use of plastics and alloys. The well designed car uses little fuel, produces few emissions, lasts a long time, is easily repaired and at the end of its life can easily be broken down and recycled.

> **Task**
>
> Try to imagine what life will be like in 2050. What kind of lifestyle will we have? What kind of products could be made to function without the use of electricity, for example? Describe some new products that can be developed now to improve our lives in the future.

2. Professional designers at work

The relationship between designers and clients, manufacturers, users and society

The role of the designer

These days product designers need to be creative *and* have an understanding of technology, so they can develop products that match the quality, price and availability requirements of the consumer. Product design incorporates the identification of needs and opportunities, generating design ideas, using an understanding of materials and process technology and satisfying consumer demand.

In large companies designers usually work in a design and production team. A small company may employ only one designer, but very few work totally alone. It is the responsibility of everyone in a company to get the product to market on time and to budget.

Good designers take account of their company design policy, resources, target market profile and marketing objectives. For many industry sectors effective marketing is about branding, image and developing a competitive edge.

The role of design and production teams

Design and production teams include creative and open-minded thinkers, problem solvers, technicians and financial planners. A designer fulfils some of these roles but it is the responsibility of the whole team for ensuring that the product can be produced efficiently to time and budget. The team also has to make sure that consumers are assured of safe, high quality products.

In order to develop a product that matches the quality and price requirement of the target market, designers and production teams need to undertake some or all of the following activities:

1 Identify needs and opportunities:
- use market research to identify target market needs
- research existing and new materials, processes and technology
- develop a design brief and specification, including aesthetics, performance requirements, production constraints and quality standards relevant to the product.

2 Design, including the use of CAD:
- generate and develop ideas
- test the feasibility of ideas, models and prototypes against specifications and market needs.

3 Production planning:
- produce working drawings and specification sheets
- plan the timing of key production stages
- produce a production schedule
- plan resource requirements and production costs
- plan quality checks during production.

> **Task**
>
> Describe the role of the designer within a production team involved in the manufacture of the chest of drawers shown in Figure 3.2.17.

The aesthetic role

Many consumers are concerned with how a product looks and the image it gives them. With this in mind, the role of the designer is increasingly to give a product a 'personality'. The aesthetic role is therefore one of creating and developing innovative, attractive products that meet market needs. Designers also need to be aware of future market needs, moral, cultural, social and environmental issues and the competition from other products.

Function and technical role

All products must be designed with function and performance in mind. Some products, such as seat belts, are produced specifically for their functional performance rather than for aesthetic qualities. The functional role of the designer therefore is to keep up-to-date with technical information about materials, processes and finish and to understand the competition from other functional products.

Economic and marketing role

Consumers want to buy innovative, attractive products at a price they can afford. The economic and marketing role of a designer is therefore to design marketable products to a price point. In other words designers must work to target production costs, which are established at the start of a project. Target production costs are based on a study of the design, development and manufacturing costs of the product. They are also checked against the cost of existing similar products. In this role the designer needs to be aware of the market into which the product is to be sold and should have a clear understanding of production processes and costs.

Organisational and management role

In the past, the design development process was consecutive, with each department contributing to the overall process before handing over the product to the next department on its way to production. In this scenario, the organisational and management role of the designer is limited. Many companies these days use the concept of concurrent manufacturing. This brings together all the different departments (marketing, design, production, quality assurance, etc.) to work concurrently on product development. Designers are increasingly involved in the whole organisation and management of the product and generally work as part of a design and production team. This team shares all the information about the product, using software such as Product Data Management (PDM). This enables fast and easy communication between design, production, suppliers and clients and results in a faster time to market of products that meet customer needs.

Case study

The cordless Quattro VP 2000, from Black & Decker was launched into a highly competitive market in 1998. It has a Power Handle with a motor, gearbox, switch and battery source. Different heads can be plugged into the Power Handle to convert it into a drill, screwdriver, sander or saw. The heads contain all the gearing and mechanisms necessary to produce the required output.

Identifying the need and opportunity

The DIY tools market requires the development of multi-functional products that can be sold at a competitive price. The original idea for the Quattro VP2000 came from Black & Decker's innovation and marketing departments. Using the latest advances in technology, the company took the opportunity to develop a multifunctional power tool that would be attractive to the DIY market.

Market research

The marketing department carried out a considerable amount of market research for the Quattro VP2000. This identified the market demand for this type of multipurpose tool and helped them develop initial specifications for the product.

Design development

Black & Decker had already developed a very successful multifunctional sander, which was used as a benchmark for developing the new

Figure 3.2.19 *This cordless Black & Decker drill developed from the original idea for the Quatro VP2000*

Quattro VP2000. The project followed the company standard implementation process, which included modelling the prototype using laser-solidified liquid resin. This was used to test the engineering concepts and to get customer feedback on the design of the system. The design and production teams worked closely together to ensure that the project was completed within the allocated 15 month timescale. Some features of the Quattro VP2000 were patented during the product development stage to protect it from copies.

The success of the product

Black & Decker thought people would find the tool packaging attractive and hoped they would feel as if they were buying a 'magic box of tricks' with all the different interchangeable heads. They were right! Sales have been very successful since the product's launch into the DIY market. Features such as rechargeable batteries and the safety lock to prevent accidental operation are also proving highly successful.

Future developments

Since the success of the Quattro VP2000 a more powerful model with an upgraded battery has since been developed (see Fig 3.2.19). New models based on the original idea are currently being developed.

Professional practice relating to design management, technology, marketing, business, ICT

Design and marketing

Although market research is often done by the marketing department, all designers need to be aware of market trends. Sometimes individual designers establish a product need, such as James Dyson who developed the Dual Cyclone vacuum cleaner.

One of the key features of successful marketing is the development of a marketing plan aimed at the needs of the target market group. It involves developing a competitive edge through providing:

- well-designed, reliable, high quality products at a price consumers can afford
- products with a desirable image that will appeal to the market.

Target market groups

Successful product development needs a clear target market group. This is often decided by market segmentation, which divides the target market into different groups. There are many ways of dividing up consumers into market segments, including:

- age; using demographic information to target a specific age group
- level of disposable income; targeting the available spending power of consumers
- lifestyle; targeting the lifestyle and brand loyalty of specific consumers
- product end-use; targeting market-specific products such as multi-purpose tools or furniture.

Marketing plan

A marketing plan can be used to promote products and brands using retailers, newspapers, TV, radio and the Internet. A successful marketing plan uses market research to find out:

- consumer needs and demand
- the age, income, size and location of the target market group
- the type of product customers want and how much they will pay for it
- economic trends affecting the market, such as spending power in relation to home mortgage interest rates
- the competition from existing products
- the time required to develop and market the product, such as launching a product just before Christmas.

Efficient manufacture and profit

On average, 80 per cent of a product's cost results from its design. Design management is therefore an essential element of efficient manufacture. It provides the profit that is essential for funding the research and development of new or improved products. Efficient manufacture involves the efficient use of resources, using the most suitable materials and manufacturing processes.

Capacity and efficiency

Organisations generally look at the forecast demand for a product and use this to find the production capacity needed. If capacity is less than demand, orders are not met and potential customers are lost. If capacity is greater than demand, there is spare capacity and under-used resources. The basic measure of manufacturing performance is therefore capacity. This is defined as the maximum numbers of products that can be made in a specified time. All processes have limits on their capacity, such as factory output per week or machine output per hour.

If, for example a manufacturing process has a capacity of 200 units per week, this is the maximum number of units that can be made. If the manufacturing process is idle for half the time and actually makes 100 units, the utilisation of its capacity is 50 per cent. If it uses 25 hours of machine time to make these 100 units, the productivity is four units per machine.

When measuring the efficiency of a manufacturing process a comparison needs to be made between the actual output of products with the possible output. If for example an office worker can process five documents per hour, but actually processes four documents, their efficiency is 4/5 = 0.8 or 80 per cent.

Modifying design and manufacture to achieve efficiency

Many companies analyse the manufacture of existing products to find out if the product design can be modified to improve manufacturing efficiency. The aim is to reduce production costs by creating designs that use less material or energy during manufacture and to reduce the production of waste.

Changing the product design and manu- facture to increase efficiency may involve using:

- a simpler design with fewer components to reduce assembly time
- different materials to reduce their weight or the quantity used
- materials that result in less waste
- materials that use less energy during manufacture
- different shaped components to make them easier to machine or mould
- different machining of components to reduce the production of waste

Figure 3.2.20 *The efficient L48 solar lantern uses a pyhotovoltaic panel to charge a battery that provides up to four hours light*

- a simplified or different speed production process so it is more efficient.

Factfile
'De-materialisation' is the process of reducing a product's material content and achieving the product function in another way.
'Lightweighting' is making a product lighter while maintaining its function.

The furniture company Avad concentrates on the efficient manufacture of well designed products. Throughout the manufacturing process Avad tries to eliminate unnecessary components and minimise waste. Their first product was a shelving unit, which required an inefficient and expensive production process using glue and metal fixings. They had to find a new way of fixing the shelves to their supports. The solution was a design that used a totally glue and fixing-free joint system that formed an important part of the product. The redesign of the product resulted in a simplified, cost and time efficient production process and the manufacture of good looking shelving that is real value for money.

Using disassembly to achieve efficiency

Taking a product to pieces can make it easier to analyse its materials use. Disassembly can provide information about how the product is manufactured and how it could be made more efficient.

- Are the materials easily identifiable? Has too much material been used? How can it be reduced?
- How is the product held together; with glue, screws or snap-fits? Can the number of fixings be reduced?
- Have the materials been used to increase the product weight to give an impression of added value? How can the weight of the product be reduced?

Kettle disassembly

A kettle may have a specialist screw in its base, but this can generally be removed with care by pliers. Kettles generally function efficiently but how they are used often means that too much water is boiled and then reboiled, resulting in an over consumption of electricity. Redesigning a kettle to reduce the amount of electricity used could include the following:

- improve the water level indicator so that the user needs to boil less water
- design a variable temperature kettle, for when the water does not need to be boiling
- install a temperature gauge so there is less need to reboil the kettle
- insulate the kettle, so that heat is not lost as quickly.

Task

Choose a product that can be disassembled easily:

- A telephone can usually be levered gently apart after removal of all the screws.
- A torch is usually simple to take apart.

Carefully disassemble the product and keep a record of how it fits together, so that you can put the product back together again! Analyse the materials, components and processes used to manufacture the product. Redesign the product to make it more efficient to manufacture or use.

Aesthetics, quality and value for money

Aesthetics

Industrial products, such as tyres or oil filters are made solely to meet performance requirements, however, the impact of aesthetics on the design of industrial and technical products is increasing. In the car industry for example, colour and style forecasting is used to predict the future aesthetic needs and wants of consumers.

Quality and value for money

In a competitive market no product will sell if it is of poor quality. Consumers expect to be able to buy reliable, high quality products at a price they can afford. Good quality for the consumer is often described as 'fitness-for-purpose'. This can be evaluated through a product's performance, price and aesthetic appeal. All of these criteria must be met if a product is seen to be 'value for money'.

Quality for a manufacturer means meeting the product specification and finding a balance between profitable manufacture and the needs and expectations of the consumer. This often involves juggling the competing needs of function, appearance, materials and cost. Quality is therefore an important issue because there often has to be a compromise between quality and cost. There will always be a need for products at different cost levels, to meet the different spending needs of consumers.

Values issues related to design

Values issues are inherent in designing and making and in many ways are a 'driving force behind design'. One example is the increasing interest in the environment and the fact that one of the many roles of the designer is to design with recycling in mind.

As with other aspects of designing, there is often a conflict between values held by the designer, the client and the user.

- Cultural and social values are related to the way in which aspects such as fashion and lifestyle affect design. Trends in colours used for clothes, for example, influence colours in cars, furniture and interior design. Social influences from the media such as film, television and music also influence design. Exhibitions also stimulate a revival of interest in design influences such as a recent exhibition of Art Nouveau.
- Economic issues mean that there is a need to reduce costs and maximise profit if companies are to survive. This, and developments in ICT, have led to a shift in manufacturing away from traditional areas to new developing countries where labour costs are cheaper.
- Values issues are often very sensitive and companies need to approach these issues with great care. The clockwork radio, designed by Trevor Davis, was designed to help those living in poorer countries of the world by providing a communications link at low cost. When production started, it was based in South Africa and was largely done by people with physical disabilities. In December 1999, the company involved announced that production was being moved to China to save on production costs. This one decision covered a wide range of values issues.
- When operating in the global market place companies have to be careful to use product names which do not cause offence to religious or cultural views. Consideration also needs to be given to the ethics of imposing values from the traditional industrialised nations on those countries which do not have the same tradition. For example, computers that are advertised on television world-wide are no use to people who do not have electricity, but who require the basic essentials of life. Is it moral to advertise such products and to create a demand for them?.

Figure 3.2.21 *The 'Rover' chair designed by Ron Arad in 1981*

The work of professional designers and professional bodies

Professional designers

It is impossible in a book of this type to include information about every influential product designer. The following designers are therefore intended as a starting point. It is not necessary for you to study every designer listed, you could study the work of two or three designers whose work you admire. Keep a sketch book with a collection of images and notes about their work, including the kind of materials they use, the types of product they design and the market they design for.

Ron Arad (1951–)

Arad originally studied architecture in Israel and later studied in London. His view of designing is that it is essentially a form of expression for himself and for the client. Arad's early work was intended to represent the decay of the post-industrial scene and this accounted for his choice of materials - industrial materials and recycled parts, making extensive use of concrete and steel sheet metal. Arad came into the public eye with the design of his 'Rover' chair in 1981 – a chair which used recycled leather seats from Rover cars (see Figure 3.2.21). In 1981, Arad founded One-Off Ltd, producing individual pieces of furniture and he is now one of the most creative designer-makers (see Figure 3.2.22).

Mario Bellini (1935–)

Bellini is one of the most influential Italian designers who trained as an architect in Milan.

Figure 3.2.22 *The 'bookworm' bookcase, designed by Ron Arad in 1992. As with many other successful ideas, this is a very simple idea of a continuous strip of sheet metal formed in a one-piece curve*

In the early 1960s he moved into product design, working at a time when Industrial Design was becoming increasingly important in Italy. Since 1963, Bellini has worked as a consultant designer for Olivetti, the Italian typewriter company. He has also worked for the furniture company Cassina, the car makers Fiat and Lancia and the design group Artemide. His approach to design is based more on instinct than philosophical ideas

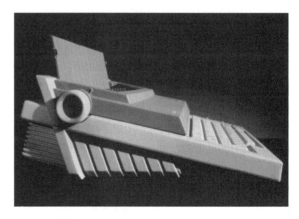

Figure 3.2.23 *Bellini typewriter*

(Figure 3.2.23). Bellini was able to incorporate more sophisticated technology and miniaturisation into his product design. For example, his 1970 design for the Totem Stereo had speakers that rotated out on a pivot to reveal the record deck hidden below. Bellini's work frequently makes use of interesting forms, luxurious materials and a high level of finish.

Joe Colombo (1930–71)

Colombo originally trained as a painter in Milan and in 1962 established his own design studio, concentrating on furniture and interior design. He was one of the outstanding designers of the 1960s and was a master of plastic design. His futuristic shapes were inspired by space travel and science fiction and he produced innovative compact 'living systems' – minimal-space living areas inspired by ideas related to space travel.

His most famous piece of work is the 'Universale' chair designed in 1965 for Kartell. The design was one of the first attempts to make an injection-moulded chair in one piece (see Figure 3.2.24).

Colombo saw the role of the designer very much as a shaper of the environment in which people live. Many of his ideas were innovative

Figure 3.2.25 Tom Dixon's 'S' chair

and radical, making clever use of new materials and processes.

Tom Dixon (1959–)

Tom Dixon was one of a group of designers in the 1980s, including Ron Arad and Jasper Morrison, who were inspired by Punk and worked with recycled materials and welded metal. These designs combined aspects of art, craft and sculpture and were known as 'creative salvage'. Dixon was self-taught and developed more commercial designs in the late 1980s. The organic curve of the 'S' chair is based on a sketch of a chicken and he worked on over fifty prototypes (see Figure 3.2.25). These were made using rush, wicker, old tyre rubber, paper and copper.

Throughout his career, Dixon was not approached by any British manufacturer, but in 1987 the Italian company Capellini bought the 'S' chair design and mass produced it. In 1994, Dixon opened his SPACE shop and in 1996 launched a new product range called Eurolounge. In 1998, Dixon was appointed head of design at Habitat. He is re-instating a Habitat workshop for the design team to work on new ideas and prototypes. At Habitat, Dixon aims to reproduce some design classics and to put into production designers' prototype products.

James Dyson (1947–)

One of Dyson's early products was the Rotork Sea Truck, a marine vehicle that could carry a three-ton load at 50 mph. Other products include the Wateroller, a lawn roller which used water to give it weight and the Ballbarrow, a redesign of the traditional wheelbarrow.

Figure 3.2.24 'Universale' chair designed by Joe Colombo in 1965. The hole in the back is purely practical since it assists in removing the chair from the mould

Dyson spent five years and made more than 5000 prototypes to develop the highly successful Dual Cyclone vacuum cleaner, produced for the mass market in 1993. The cyclonic system uses the principal of centrifugal force to suck up air and revolves it at eight hundred miles an hour through two cyclone chambers, until the dust drops to the bottom of a transparent cylinder.

Charles Eames (1907–78)

Eames was an American who trained as an architect and later moved into furniture design. He was one of the best-known furniture designers of the twentieth century. Eames collaborated with the manufacturer Herman Miller, for whom he designed innovative furniture made from bent plywood, chrome steel tubing and finishes made of synthetic materials. His prototype chair 'La Chaise', made from hard rubber with a synthetic covering, was designed in collaboration with his brother Ray (see Figure 3.2.26). Eames thought of himself as an architect, saying that 'I can't help

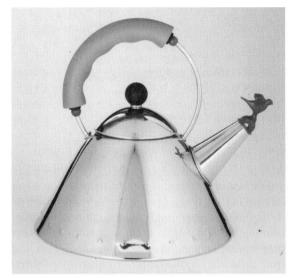

Figure 3.2.27 *The Graves kettle, produced in 1985 for Alessi is made from steel with a polyamide handle. The plastic bird mounted on the spout sings when the kettle boils*

but look at the problems around us as problems of structure – and structure is architecture'.

Michael Graves (1934–)

Graves is another architect who has also worked on the design of products – mainly furniture and ceramics. His early work was inspired by ideas from art history particularly classicism and cubism. Graves is one of the leading exponents of post-modernism and has designed in the Memphis style for Alessi.

Jasper Morrison (1959–)

Morrison trained as designer at the Kingston School of Art and Design in London. During the early 1980s, he produced a range of designs

Figure 3.2.26 *This 1948 prototype chair 'La Chaise' shows an unmistakable similarity to the sculptures of Henry Moore*

Figure 3.2.28 *Wine rack by Jasper Morrison*

including his 'Handlebar' table, constructed of wood, two bicycle handlebars and a circular glass top. Morrison designs for companies such as Vitra, Cappellini and Artemide. Some of his most important pieces were his storage units, known as the 'Universal' range, designed for the Italian company Cappellini.

Morrison is a designer who is committed to practical, simple ideas, which he has successfully developed, paying close attention to detail and high-quality making (see Figure 3.2.28). He is known for his minimalist plywood furniture with untreated surfaces.

Philippe Starck (1949–)

The French designer Philippe Starck was described as the 'super-designer' of the twentieth century. He happily borrows design styles from the past, such as 'streamlining' or Art Nouveau. Starck uses unusual combinations of materials such as plastic with aluminium, glass with stone or fabric with chrome. In the early 1980s he designed the interior of the Café Costes in Paris, including a three-legged chair, which has come to signify modern restaurant design. He designs saleable, relatively inexpensive products for mass production. These include many well-known products such as his Juicy Salif Lemon Press (Figure 2.1), lighting (the Miss Sissi Table Lamp) and every day products such as furniture, televisions, water taps, clocks and toothbrushes. Starck also designs some furniture that can be recycled and often uses ecologically sound materials such as in the MDF television set shown in Figure 3.2.29.

Figure 3.2.29 *This MDF and plastic television designed by Philippe Starck gives the product a more human face than using hard edge black plastic*

Ettore Sottsass (1917–)

Sottsass is one of Italy's best-known designers, whose work spans over 40 years. In each decade, he has produced innovative work that seems to express the period. In 1981, Sottsass launched the design group Memphis, producing exciting and witty new designs that sometimes look like funny children's toys. They mixed plastic laminates with expensive wood veneers in bright primary colours. Sottsass's influences came from 1960s pop and his fascination with the ancient structures of Indian and Aztec art. Sottsass has worked on a wide range of products such as typewriters, furniture, computers, glass products, lighting and many more, for international companies including Knoll, Cleto Munari and Artemide. Many younger designers have worked with Sottsass, who has been described as one of the most influential designers of the late twentieth century.

Professional bodies associated with designing

The Crafts Council

The Crafts Council is a national organisation for the promotion of crafts. It provides exhibitions, a shop selling crafts and books, a Reference Library, the National Register of Makers with contact information for over 4000 UK craftspeople and Photostore, a visual database containing over 40,000 images of selected high quality craft work. Major craft exhibitions often go on tour around the country.

The Crafts Council can help designer/ makers by providing practical help and advice on business matters and as a source of information and reference materials. Potential clients can obtain information about craftspeople and see illustrations of their work. Students can also use the same information to research contemporary design and craft work as a source of products for evaluation and inspiration.

The Design Council

The Design Council aims 'to inspire the best use of design by the UK, in the world context, to improve prosperity and well being'. The Council does this through the use of events, publications, research, educational resources and case studies which highlight examples of design and innovation in action. Annual events include Design in Business Week and Designers into Schools Week, which brings the real world of design into the classroom, by enabling Design & Technology students to work with professional designers. This initiative gives students a unique opportunity to build their creativity and problem solving skills and helps them see Design & Technology as a creative force shaping everyday experiences.

The Engineering Council
The Engineering Council (EC) was created in 2002 as the main professional body for engineers, technologists and technicians. The Council supports designing and making in schools and colleges through the Neighbourhood Engineer Scheme and the Women into Science and Technology programme (WISE).

3. Anthropometrics and ergonomics

The basic principles and applications of anthropometrics and ergonomics

Ergonomics
Ergonomics is the science of designing products for human use, and matching the product to the user. It has a role in designing everything from furniture to cars and its application makes products usable. Ergonomics is therefore an essential part of the design process. Sometimes products are matched to a single user, where the product is customised to suit one person. The main objective for ergonomists is to improve people's lives by increasing their comfort and satisfaction when using products. When ergonomics is applied to the workplace it can help improve productivity and reduce errors and accidents.

Anthropometrics
Anthropometrics is a branch of ergonomics that deals with measurements of human beings, in particular their shapes and sizes. For many products, complex data is required about any number of critical dimensions relating to the human form, such as height, width or length of reach when standing or sitting. In some products a single critical dimension is all that is needed. In general, products are matched to a target population of users who come in a variety of shapes and sizes.

Using anthropometric data
When applying anthropometric data to a design problem, the designer's aim is to provide an acceptable match for the greatest possible number of users. This is achieved by the use of anthropometric data. Many companies use anthropometric data charts from the British Standards Institute (BSI), which are available in simplified form from the *Compendium of Essential Design and Technology Standards for Schools and Colleges* (see your department copy or visit www.bsi.org.uk/education). Simple data charts relating to measurements for men, women and children can also be found in the clothing sections of mail order catalogues. In your own designing you may need to collect your own data if you are designing for a specific individual or for a small target market group.

Statistical data available from the BSI is associated with average heights, in which only one person in twenty is shorter than average (the fifth percentile) and only 5 per cent of people are taller than average (the ninety-fifth percentile). The BSI anthropometric data therefore covers the 90 per cent of the population who fall between the fifth and the ninety-fifth percentile. For example, if you design a chair which has to be comfortable for 100 people with a range of heights from 1.5 metres to 1.9 metres, designing to fit the whole range of sizes would be difficult. According to the principles applied by the BSI, you would need to ignore the smallest five people and the tallest five people and design the chair to fit the remaining 90 people in the group. This principle is applied to the design of most products.

Ergonomic considerations
Ergonomic methods are used to improve product design by understanding and/or predicting how humans interact with products. The methods used focus on different aspects of human performance, taking either a quantitative or qualitative approach.

- The quantitative approach predicts the physical fit of a product to the body, encompassing workload, speed of performance and errors.
- The qualitative approach predicts user comfort and their satisfaction with the

product, so it has the optimum interaction with the user.

When designing a product it is very important to decide on the kind of people you are designing for. For example, what is the target market and market segment? Are you designing for men, women or children, are the users able-bodied or disabled, are they young or old, are they normally sighted or do they have impaired vision, are they expert users or first time buyers?

The profile of the end-user population can often help when designing a product. For example, The Royal National Institute for the Blind (RNIB) developed a battery-operated or mains driven Talking Scientific Calculator, designed to meet the needs of visually impaired students. The idea for the calculator came from the RNIB's work with visually impaired people and from requests from mathematicians, who needed a device that would help visually impaired students when taking exams. The easy-to-use Talking Scientific Calculator helps students to study and take exams without any help. The calculator is designed with no visible display, but includes 50 functions on a custom-made, 40-key tactile keypad. The PIC based technology allows the calculator to be programmed to 'speak' different languages. The custom-designed membrane keypad uses many visual and tactile keys for ease of use. The calculator can be connected to a computer or printer to provide a record of an exam.

The interaction between users, products, equipment and environments

All types of products that are designed so their dimensions match those of their users will suit their end-user better. Equipment needs to be designed so it can be operated easily and safely by 90 per cent of the population. Safety considerations require easy operation but must also ensure that equipment is not operated by mistake.

Figure 3.2.30 shows some of the measurements that need to be taken into account when designing products. It is very important when designing office furniture, for example, to make sure that the correct ratio is used between the height of a chair and table and the position of a computer monitor and keyboard, to enable users to work comfortably. Many people who are outside the fifth to the ninety-fifth percentile have to learn to be adaptable when using products. Conditions such as back pain or

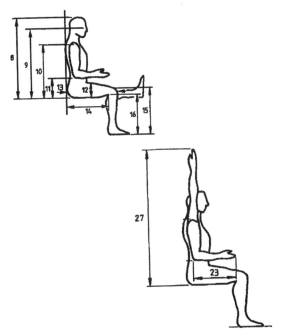

Figure 3.2.30 *The numbered dimensions on these human figures can be found in BSI anthropometric charts in the Compendium of Essential Design and Technology Standards for Schools and Colleges*

Repetitive Strain Injury (RSI) are commonly caused by using equipment that is not the correct size for the user.

In a well-designed table the headroom, knee room and elbow room must accommodate the dimensions of the largest person. The height of the table from the floor should therefore be not less than the knee height of the ninety-fifth percentile user. Similarly, in a well-designed chair, the height of the seat from the floor should not be greater than the knee height of the fifth percentile user. This will enable a short person to reach the floor with their feet to enable good blood circulation.

- The height of a table from the floor that is suitable for a ninety-fifth percentile user will also suit 95 per cent of the population.
- The height of a seat from the floor that is suitable for a fifth percentile user will also suit 95 per cent of the population.
- However, even with these dimensions in place, problems will still occur for the very tall and the very short people.

Human dimensions are also important in the design of environments from bedrooms to kitchens to primary school to sports venues. When designing vehicles, designers need to take account of the different height and reach of male and female drivers. The height and position of seats, the steering wheel and mirrors must be adjustable to allow the driver to be comfortable for long periods of time and to easily see the road in front and behind. All the controls, switches and foot pedals must be suitable for a range of sizes of hands and feet (see Figure 3.2.31).

British and International Standards

The British Standards Institution (BSI) is the world's leading independent standards and quality services organisation. It works globally with manufacturers to develop British, European and International standards. The BSI belongs to the International Organisation for Standardisation (ISO). CEN is the European Committee for Standardisation, which harmonises technical standards in Europe, in conjunction with the BSI.

Setting standards

Most standards are set at the request of industry or to implement legislation. The setting of standards, testing procedures and quality assurance techniques enable companies to meet the needs of their customers. Tests are carried out against set standards for a wide range of products manufactured in the UK and overseas. Some British Standards are also agreed European and/or International Standards. Any product that meets a British Standard is awarded a Kitemark, as long as the manufacturer has a quality system in place to ensure that every product is made to the same standard.

The relationship between standard measurements and the design of products

Whatever project you are working on, standard measurements probably exist in relation to the product you are making. Sometimes a single critical dimension is all that you need, whereas other designs may need the lengthy and complex calculation of data. When designing a one-off or custom made product, it may be necessary to use specific dimensions. For example, fitted furniture for an awkward alcove would need to be made to critical dimensions for it to fit in the space available. When designing mass produced products, however, it is usually necessary to match the product to a range of users who come in various shapes and sizes. Information about standard measurements may be found in the 'Compendium of Essential Design and Technology Standards for Schools and Colleges' and through the BSI website on www.bsi.org.uk/education.

Ergonomic considerations for designs and models

There are a number of considerations to be taken into account when designing.

- It is a fallacy to think that just because your product is the correct size for you, it will be right for everyone.
- Designing for the 'average' user doesn't mean that a product will be suitable for everyone. Since average dimensions only take account of 50 per cent of the population, the other half may find the product unsuitable or difficult to use.
- Although people are adaptable, it should not be used as an excuse for bad design. Problems like back pain, for example, are often the result of using furniture that requires unsatisfactory working positions.
- Many products are sold for their aesthetic properties and may be designed without reference to anthropometric data, because it is expensive to buy.

Figure 3.2.31 *One of the main features of the Ford Ka, apart from innovative design is its exceptional ergonomics which make the car extremely practical*

Exam preparation

You will need to revise all the topics in this unit, so that you can apply your knowledge and understanding to the exam questions. Some questions may ask you to give answers related to a product example. If you cut out and save newspaper and magazine articles about products, it will help keep you up-to-date with the latest information.

In preparation for your exam it is a good idea to make brief notes about different topics, such as 'Mass production and the consumer society'. Use sub-headings or bullet point lists and diagrams where appropriate. A single side of A4 should be used for each heading from the Specification.

It is very important to learn exam skills. You should have weekly practice in learning technical terms and in answering exam-type questions. When you answer any question you should:

- read the question carefully and pick out the key points that need answering
- match your answer to the marks available, e.g. for four marks, you should give four good points that address the question
- always give examples and justify statements with reasons, saying how or why the statement is true.

Practice exam questions

1 a) Briefly describe the characteristics of mass production. (4)
  b) State what is meant by the following terms:
    (i)   assembly line (3)
    (ii) consumer society. (3)
  c) Describe how high technology production has enabled the development of one modern product. (5)

2 a) These days products are manufactured on a global scale.
    (i)   Give **three** reasons why products are often manufactured overseas. (3)
    (ii) Outline the importance of ICT to global manufacturing. (4)
  b) Describe the impact of global manufacturing on:
    (i)   the environment (4)
    (ii) employment. (4)

3 a) State the meaning of **two** of the following terms:
    (i)   form
    (ii) function
    (iii) style. (4)
  b) For many consumers today, design has become an important means of self expression. Give your views on this issue. (6)
  c) The work of other designers has often provided a starting point for product design. Using **one** product example describe how **one** designer has used materials in an innovative way. (5)

4 a) Explain why a product designer needs to have a good technical understanding in order to design for manufacture. (5)
  b) Give **one** example of how a product could be modified to improve **one** of the following:
    (i)   its aesthetic appeal
    (ii) its environmental impact. (6)
  c) Describe what is meant by **two** of the following terms:
    (i)   capacity
    (ii) efficiency
    (iii) profit. (4)

5 a) Describe the ergonomic considerations that must be taken into account when designing. (5)
  b) (i) Explain the term 'anthropometrics'. (4)
    (ii) Using **one** product example, explain the importance of anthropometric data to product design. (6)

6 a) Describe how a product can achieve a Kitemark. (3)
  b) Outline the benefits to a manufacturer of working to set standards. (7)
  c) Outline the importance to the consumer of a manufacturer working to set standards. (5)

UNIT 3B2 CAD/CAM (R303)

Summary of expectations

1. What to expect

CAD/CAM is one of the three options offered in Section B of Unit 3, of which you will study only one. This option builds on the knowledge and understanding of the use of ICT and CAD/CAM you gained during your GCSE course, depending on which focus area you studied. If, however, these materials are completely new to you, don't worry. This unit will take you through from first principles.

2. How will it be assessed?

The work that you do in this option will be externally assessed through Section B of the Unit 3 examination paper. The questions will be common across all three materials areas in product Design. You can therefore answer questions with reference to **either**:

- a Resistant Materials Technology product such as a kettle component produced by rapid prototyping;
- a Graphics with Materials Technology product such as digitally printed signage;
- **or** a Textiles Technology product such as circular weft knitted fabric.

You are advised to **spend 45 minutes** on this section of the paper.

3. What will be assessed?

The following list summarises the topics covered in this option and what will be examined.

- The impact of CAD/CAM on industry:
  - changes in production methods
  - global manufacturing
  - employment issues
  - trends in manufacturing using ICT.
- Computer-aided design:
  - CAD techniques

  - common input devices
  - common output devices.
- Computer-aided manufacture:
  - CNC machines
  - the use of CAM when producing products
  - advantages/disadvantages of CAM.

4. How to be successful in this unit

To be successful in this unit you will need to:

- have a clear understanding of the topics covered in this option
- apply your knowledge and understanding to a given situation or context
- organise your answers clearly and coherently, using specialist technical terms where appropriate
- use clear sketches where appropriate to illustrate your answers
- write clear and logical answers to the examination questions, using correct spelling, punctuation and grammar.

There may be an opportunity to demonstrate your knowledge and understanding of CAD/CAM in your Unit 2 coursework. However, simply because you are studying this option, you do not have to integrate this type of technology into your coursework project.

5. How much is it worth?

This option, with Section A, is worth 30 per cent of your AS qualification. If you go on to complete the whole course, then this unit accounts for 15 per cent of the full Advanced GCE.

Unit 3 + option	Weighting
AS level	30%
A2 level (full GCE)	15%

1. The impact of CAD/CAM on industry

The need for manufacturing companies to develop competitive products is vital for their own economic survival and the prosperity of their workforce and the other businesses in their community. Eventually, most products can be designed better or updated because of advances in technology or produced more economically by improvements in production methods. Designers and others use the computer-based tools within a computer-aided design (CAD) system to create, develop, communicate and record product design information. Computer-aided manufacture (CAM) is a rapidly evolving set of technologies that translate design information into manufacturing information. CAM helps to plan manufacturing processes. The system of process planning combines a range of sub-systems including computerised sensing and control systems, robotics and computer-driven machinery; CAD/CAM is where the two systems are integrated. The type and degree of integration will depend on the scale of production and other operational or commercial considerations.

Creating or responding to change?

Computer integrated manufacture (CIM) is an increasingly effective way of integrating CAD/CAM technologies. The development of computer-based design and manufacturing technologies is providing a driving force for change. They also provide an effective mechanism for responding to changes in external factors, such as a fluctuating market demand (see Figure 3.3.1).

The pressures for change

Modern manufacturers of mass-produced items market and sell their product families, such as washing machines and cars, across the world. This creates pressure on the design processes, the manufacturing processes and the organisation of the production facilities. A product may have to be remodelled to include different design features depending on where it is to be sold. There may be specific market or local need. In some countries local legislation imposes material or health and safety restrictions on manufacturers. Multinational manufacturers often face a challenge from local manufacturers of similar products. These product differences are classed as design variants. They could range from the amount of recyclable materials used in the product, to whether a plug is fitted or not, to the fitting of different visual displays or devices to suppress noise levels. Another pressure for change is that product lifetimes are becoming shorter, especially in areas such as telecommunications and information systems. Manufacturers now have to develop and produce products within a much shorter time scale. New technologies and materials are also increasing the technical complexity of products and how they can be manufactured. Figure 3.3.2 shows the effect of pressures to improve the production process.

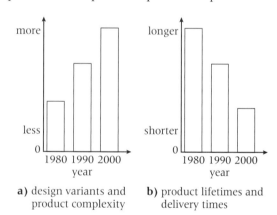

a) design variants and product complexity

b) product lifetimes and delivery times

Figure 3.3.2 *Pressures to improve the production process*

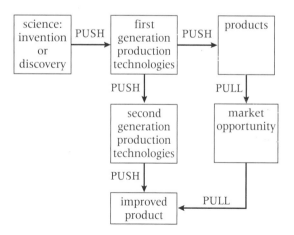

Figure 3.3.1 *Changes in production methods are either pushed by the development of new technologies or pulled by the demands of the market*

Task

Select a common household product. Write down what requirements can be placed on the design by the buyer and what constraints are imposed on the design by other factors. These might include specific legal requirements or technological considerations such as the use of microprocessors.

Changes in design and production methods

A fully featured CAD system provides the means to develop design concepts and ideas from the simplest to the most complicated product. Different parts of a product can be rapidly designed and put together in an assembly drawing. They will also be drawn to standard conventions. Fully featured systems support work in 2D and 3D including the development of photorealistic images and 'virtual products'.

Photorealistic images

The growth of the Internet and the development of web sites to advertise and sell products have increased the pressure on software designers to improve the 'real life' quality of product images. These images are described as photorealistic. Modern CAD systems allow greater control over the quality of these images, typically through the use of an object or image browser. One of the key features will be the ability of the software to represent different material qualities such as metallic and non-metallic surfaces. A CAD system such as Pro/DESKTOP™ will also allow the designer to 'virtually' control the level of lighting as well as the type of camera lens in order to create a photorealistic image. Designers can choose varying intensities of room lighting; daylight conditions; spot or flood lighting. Camera lenses available include fisheye, wide-angle and telephoto. These determine how much of an image can be seen and from what distance.

Virtual products

The comparatively recent introduction of 3D CAD systems allows the creation of virtual reality environments and products. A virtual product can be viewed from any angle at any distance. Products with moving parts can be seen in operation 'on screen'. These are generally kinematic motions that do not take account of the mass of the object or the other physical forces acting on it. They do not represent a complete model of how the product will behave in 'reality'.

We will return to the subject of photorealistic images and virtual products later in this unit.

Managing design changes

In the more sophisticated CAD applications that require larger amounts of computer memory the software keeps track of what are called design dependencies. This means that when one value on a part or assembly is changed, all the other values that depend on it are also automatically and accurately redrawn. This is known as parametric designing.

The benefits of CAD/CAM product modelling

Combining 3D CAD systems with computer-aided modelling techniques such as Rapid Prototyping (RPT) allows the creation of physical models as soon as the 3D digital model is designed (see Figure 3.3.3). This reduces potential communications problems in the product development team. A further benefit is that potential errors or technical and tooling problems are found out more quickly. Changes to a product design in the later stages of its development are potentially very costly in terms of time and reworking costs.

Task
Construct a simple organisational chart indicating the main stages in the design process, as you understand it. Identify how the computer can be used at each stage in the process indicating what features make them useful or how they might have a limited application.

Computer Numerically Controlled (CNC) machines

CNC is in widespread use in modern industry and especially in automated production systems. Computer Numerically Controlled (CNC) machines are controlled using number values written into a computer program. Each number or code is assigned to a particular operation or process. CNC machines are now easier to use because of improvements in the machine-operator interface. Computer programs, some-times called 'wizards', eliminate the need to

Figure 3.3.3 *3D digital model*

learn elaborate CNC machining codes. Most CAD/CAM software is now capable of generating the NC machining codes known as 'G' and 'M' codes from the digital data created from a drawing. Examples of 'G' and 'M' codes are shown in Table 3.3.1.

Table 3.3.1 Examples of 'G' and 'M' codes

Code no.	Type	Description
G00	Rapid traverse	The tool moves from point 1 to point 2, along the shortest path available The feed rate (speed of movement of the tool) is usually set to run as fast as possible
G01	Point-to-point positioning	The tool moves from point 1 to point 2, in a straight line, with a controlled feed rate
M00	Stop program at this point	
M02	End of program	
M03	Spindle on clockwise	Code is followed by a number prefixed by the letter S, denoting the spindle speed
M05	Stop spindle	
M06	Change tool	Code is followed by a number prefixed by the letter T, denoting the number of the tool you wish to change to
M30	Program end and rewind to start of program	

These codes can be shown on a screen as the product is either 'virtually manufactured' as a simulation or in reality on the CNC machine. The numbers or codes are easily changed from within the CAD software when required. Most CNC machines also have the capability to be programmed manually from an adjacent keypad (see Figure 3.3.4).

The benefits of CNC machines
- Products are made accurately and at speed.
- They provide increased operational flexibility as they can be employed in batch and mass-production systems.
- They can be used reliably in situations requiring continuous operation or conditions that are hazardous to human operators.
- They are economical to operate but at a high initial cost.

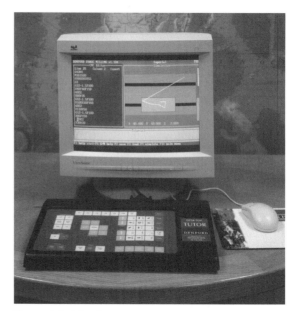

Figure 3.3.4 CNC machine with numerical keypad

Additional advantages and the disadvantages of CAM are discussed on pages 148–9.

Computer integrated manufacturing (CIM)
Traditional approaches to manufacturing involve a linear or sequential approach in which the product passes through a series of predefined stages. In this system, often referred to as 'over the wall', process planning and the handling of production data are relatively straightforward activities but design errors or manufacturing problems can occur at many points along the line. This extends the time taken to design and manufacture a product and bring it to market. As we have seen earlier, product life cycles are reducing significantly and with the globalisation of manufacturing there are severe competition pressures. These are forcing companies to look at more efficient ways of operating such as concurrent engineering.

Concurrent engineering
In this manufacturing system a product team is organised so that all the manufacturing activities within a company are represented. These multi-disciplinary teams share their expertise right from the start of a product's life. They work together at the development stage to reduce errors. A manufacturing engineer will immediately be able to tell a design engineer whether the part that he or she has designed can be manufactured or not rather than waiting until the 'completed' drawing is received.

The role of computers in flexible manufacturing systems (FMS)

Software applications in a flexible manufacturing system (FMS) allow a central computer to process production data in order to sequence and control a network of machines and materials handling systems in order to better meet changes in demand The data can also be used in many other ways. They can be used to judge progress against 'world-class manufacturing' quality criteria such as 'right first time every time'.

The move to Total Quality Management (TQM) means that product quality is no longer the responsibility of one department. This new organisational culture of continuous improvement (CI) through concurrent engineering cannot exist without effective computer-based communications.

CAD and CAM systems generate vast amounts of digital data that can be used at different stages in an integrated manufacturing system. Relational databases and other data storage methods enable data to be tracked, stored and retrieved as required. Data can be used to plan CNC and other manufacturing operations – computer-aided process control (CAPP). These 'new' data combined with other data generated from the CAD model can be used to manage the production processes, a technique known as computer-aided production management (CAPM).

Figure 3.3.5 shows a systems model of the use of software applications within CIM.

Global manufacturing

We are living through a high-speed information revolution that is not only making the world a smaller place but also increasing international competition and creating pressures on manufacturing companies to respond or die. The trend towards cooperative and integrated working is increasingly more cost effective because of improved communications and data exchange systems that are not limited by geographical boundaries.

There are now many examples of products that are designed and engineered by teams working across the globe and assembled using

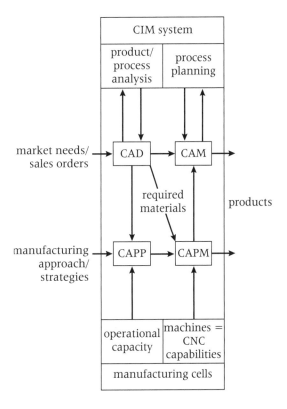

Figure 3.3.5 *A systems model of the use of software applications within CIM*

component parts that, because of increased specialisation, are sourced from supply chains in different countries. The London Eye is a feat of modern engineering and is an example of this method of manufacturing (see Figure 3.3.6). The project management team drew on specialist expertise and suppliers based in many different countries.

Figure 3.3.6 *The London Eye – an engineering project that drew on manufacturing expertise from around the world*

Task

Analyse the major components that make up the London Eye. Find out where they were designed. Where were the parts manufactured? How was the manufacturing organised?

Employment issues

CAD/CAM technologies are directly affecting patterns of employment in manufacturing right across the globe. The numbers of people involved in manufacturing are declining as automated systems take over. For those that are left, their jobs have changed significantly (see Figure 3.3.7). For instance, as we have seen, CNC machines can be controlled directly from a central computer system which means that some shop-floor jobs consist of nothing more than 'machine minding'; correcting faults that arise or replacing materials that have run out. With developments in automation, robotics and artificial intelligence it is likely that there will be even less human involvement in the production processes of the future.

Employment trends on the design side

CAD systems reduce the need for large and labour-intensive drawing offices where historically drawings were hand-drawn by skilled technicians. However, the effective use of CAD requires workers who have high levels of computer and visual literacy alongside creativity and problem-solving skills. The increased use of

Figure 3.3.7 *Manufacturing cell at a Ford plant*

CAD and CAM systems has raised significant issues around initial and on-going training issues. The effective introduction of these new ways of working relies on the willingness of employees to adopt more flexible approaches to work and the recognition that they will need to retrain or update their skills as systems continue to develop.

Employment trends on the processing side

CAM operators now have to be trained to operate different machines and carry out many processing operations within their manufacturing 'cell' or work centre. They have to be good 'team players' offering help to others as required. Gone are the days of rigid demarcation and narrow specialisation when for instance lathe operatives were not allowed to set up and use another machine in the factory. This method of redeploying workers to the area of greatest need is a feature of modern production systems. These systems reduce queues for machines, remove potential bottlenecks on the production line and so reduce processing times. They are not viable without a skilled, trained and flexible workforce.

In the UK there are severe shortages of these multi-skilled, multi-function operators in many areas of manufacturing. When this is combined with the flexibility offered by computer-based systems, often companies can relocate their manufacturing operation to another part of the world. Design and development can remain in one country while manufacturing operations move abroad. This has a devastating impact on local and regional employment prospects. Until recently, large Japanese manufacturing companies offered 'jobs for life' but Japanese workers are now also feeling the pressure on their jobs from emerging manufacturing centres in Taiwan and other Pacific Rim countries. Figure 3.3.8 shows the worldwide distribution of manufacturing.

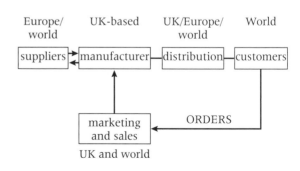

Figure 3.3.8 *The worldwide distribution of manufacturing*

The impact of CAD and CAM technologies on industrial innovation

The globalisation of manufacturing industry means that considerable research and development time is being spent on developing innovative manufacturing systems that fully integrate the use of CAD/CAM with artificial intelligence or 'expert' systems, information systems and databases. Innovation is a process involving three types of technologies:

- Critical technologies are the 'building blocks' from which products develop. CAD/CAM approaches will be involved in the continued development of computerised sensing and control systems, materials handling, storage and retrieval systems and the development of industrial robots.
- Enabling technologies such as CNC machines are needed to make use of critical technologies.
- Strategic technologies are concerned with the decision-making process. In manufacturing this can range from decisions about capital investment in new products, the most effective factory layouts and facilities, to the future use and potential benefits of systems based on artificial intelligence.

The drive for profitability

There is much research and development activity into data manipulation systems because a company's continued existence in 'volume' manufacturing relies on the establishment of efficient, cost-effective and 'quick response' systems. Effective CIM systems that include CAD and CAM reduce the 'lead time' from product development to market; time to market is a key factor in profitability.

Task
Explain what you think is meant by this sign on the wall of a manufacturing cell at a car production plant: 'Work smart – being busy doesn't mean being productive'.

---

2. Computer-aided design

A computer-aided design system is a combination of hardware and software that enables designers from all manufacturing disciplines to design everything from pens to space stations. In the case of the International Space Station it not only allows thousands of drawings to be drawn and cross-referenced to each other but also provides a means of keeping track of the millions of components required to assemble it.

The need for computing power

In general terms, CAD requires a powerful central processing unit (CPU) and a large amount of memory. Until the mid-1980s, all CAD systems operated on specially constructed 'dedicated' computers. The processing power of personal computers has improved so dramatically that professional quality CAD systems such as ProDeskTop™ can be operated effectively on local area networks (LANs) and wide area networks (WANs), general-purpose office workstations and on personal desktop and laptop computers.

The components of a CAD system

The following are the main components of a CAD system; you will consider them in more detail later in this option.

Hardware

This term describes all the physical components of a CAD system including the input and output devices. There are three main categories of computer that can be used in a manufacturing situation:

- Mainframe computers have high processing speeds and the memory required for handling and storing the large amounts of data that large manufacturing organisations generate. A mainframe computer is accessed via a network of computer terminals connected to it. The networks can be local area networks, intranets or wide area networks.
- Minicomputers are smaller versions of the mainframe system used by large organisations mostly in networks.
- Microcomputers, desktop or laptop personal computers (PCs) are used for individual computing needs or as machine control units (MCUs) for controlling a range of CNC machines.

Data storage devices include: the hard and floppy disks, CD-ROM and DVD and other external storage devices such as zip drives.

Input devices include: keyboard, mouse and tracker-ball, graphics tablet and stylus, digitiser, puck and mouse, digital camera and video, 2D and 3D scanners.

Output devices include: monitor, printers, plotters and cutters, CNC machines, Rapid Prototyping systems (RPT).

Software

The Operating System (OS) provides the platform to run all the application programs. It is also used to manage the files in the computer. There are a number of operating systems available such as Unix, Windows, DOS and MAC-OS (Apple computers).

There are many CAD software applications based on these operating systems. All CAD software, whatever the operating system, provides the data for the graphic display and the other output devices such as printers and plotters.

A modern CAD program contains hundreds of functions that enable you to accomplish specific drawing tasks. A task may involve drawing an object, editing an existing drawing, displaying a specific view of the drawing, printing or saving it, or controlling any other operation of the computer. The software will contain a number of menus, commands and functions that enable you to specify exactly what you want to do and how you want to do it. The edit functions also act as convenient drawing aids enabling faults to be corrected easily electronically. The software may also have a number of specialised functions such as providing animated 3D views or the printing of different layers which is useful in electronic drawings where the circuit can be on one layer, the components on another. Drawings can be plotted with specific colours, pen thickness, and line types. In some CAM programs such as Denford's MillCam™ different colours are used to indicate the different depths of cut.

Graphical user interface (GUI)

This is a two-way link between the user and the computer. It provides an on-screen display giving visual clues to help the user communicate with the computer. The GUI allows the user to enter data through commands or functions that are selected from menus; by keyboard stokes (e.g. Ctrl+P); from toolbars buttons and on-screen icons and text or dialogue boxes. GUIs also allow a range of users with different operational requirements to set up their own preferred working environment such as specifying dimensions and text that match industry standards such as ANSI, ISO and BSI. An example of a typical CAD window is shown in Figure 3.3.9.

Standards for CAD systems

A format, programming language, or operating protocol only becomes an officially recognised standard when it has been approved by one of the recognised standards organisations mentioned above. However, you will find that many of the CAD/CAM standards are in fact accepted standards because they are widely used and recognised by the industry itself as being the standard. Some examples of such standards that you will come across include:

- Hayes command set for controlling modems
- Hewlett-Packard Printer Control Language (PCL) for laser printers
- PostScript (PS) page description language for laser printers
- Data Exchange Format (DXF), a graphic file format created by AutoDesk and used on many CAD systems.

Common formats for storing CAD data

- Windows Metafile Format (WMF)
- PICT – the standard format for storing and exchanging graphics on Apple computers
- Tagged Image File Format (TIFF)
- Hewlett Packard Graphics Language(HPGL)
- Virtual Reality Modelling Language (VRML)

Managing CAD data

All CAD applications have a range of data management options. Drawings can be stored either on a hard disk or on a central network server. Drawing files are often quite large taking up a lot of memory. Some applications allow files to be compressed (zipped) to take up less of the system memory. Files are managed in directories and subdirectories. The software should also be able to translate drawings created by other CAD programs. Data Exchange Format

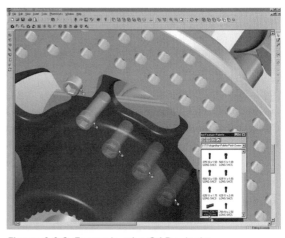

Figure 3.3.9 Example of a CAD window

(DXF) is one of the common data translation formats used by CAD programs. There are a number of other data formats available. Initial Graphics Exchange Specification (IGES) is an international standard, which defines a neutral file format for the representation of graphics data across different PC-based CAD systems.

Tasks

1 Find out and record what the initials ISO, ANSI and BSI stand for.
2 Give three examples of standards that might apply to CAD/CAM resources, equipment or software.

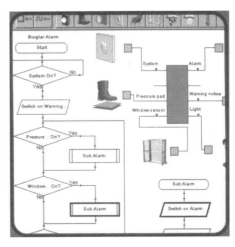

Figure 3.3.10 *Flowchart using Crocodile technology*

Computer-aided design models

All 2D and 3D CAD systems are based on the fundamental need for a designer to work with a 'model' of a product design. These systems are classed as interactive graphics systems because the user has control of the image on screen; data can be added, edited, modified and deleted. The generation of digital models or virtual products removes the pressure to produce a physical model too early in the product development process. The virtual product becomes the designers' main means of communicating and talking about their ideas with others in their team. Creating a digital product model requires a system that is capable of processing mathematical functions and making complex calculations in order to produce models and manipulate graphic images in 2D and 3D. These images and models are either generated by vector or raster graphics.

Using vector and raster graphics in CAD systems

In systems using vector and object-oriented graphics geometrical formulae are used to represent images as a series of lines. Raster graphics represent images as 'bit maps' and the image is composed of a pattern of dots or picture elements (pixels). Draw programs create and manipulate vector graphics. Programs that manipulate bit-mapped or raster images are called paint programs. Vectored images are more flexible because they can be resized and stretched. In addition, images stored as vectors look better on screen or paper, whereas bit-mapped images always appear the same regardless of a printer or a monitor's resolution or picture quality. Another advantage of vector graphics is that representations of images often require less memory than bit-mapped images

do. CAD programs employ a combination of these two graphics. Vector graphics are used to draw lines and produce 3D shapes; raster graphics are used for the rendering of surfaces and textures.

The different uses of CAD-generated models

Engineering designers use CAD systems in a variety of ways depending on the properties to be modelled. They are concerned with how the product will function, how the parts go together (structure), its form (shape) as well as the materials, surface finishes, dimensions and operational tolerances that are needed. In the case of electronic systems, flow diagrams and a modelling of the system will perhaps come first. This is followed by the generation of detailed drawings that show the relative positions of components on the circuit board (see Figure 3.3.10). The 'systems' engineers then supply the necessary manufacturing data to the 'manufacturing' engineers. They use it to determine how to set up the CNC machines that automatically insert and fix components on to the circuit boards.

The basic operating characteristics of CAD programs

- The user is able to interact with and manipulate images on screen.
- Displays can be divided into two or more windows, sometimes referred to as tiles or panes.
- Each window can contain a different view of the assembly or the different sub-assemblies.
- Models can be repositioned or edited independently in each window, the effects of one action affecting all relevant views.

- When working with multiple windows only one of the windows remains current or active; other windows are activated by clicking on them.
- The coordinates that make up the multiple views to create a 3D model are calculated automatically.
- Models can be displayed or viewed from any direction or viewpoint.
- Standard projections are supported including orthographic (1st and 3rd angle), oblique, isometric and perspective.
- Pull-down or pop-up menus contain the various commands that allow text, dimensions and labels to be added. Features such as line styles and use of colour can be adjusted. Most CAD packages have keyboard shortcuts for drawing and other features such as Ctrl+G for grouping a collection of individual elements in addition to the standard word-processing shortcuts, e.g. Ctr+P for printing.
- Primitives are predefined graphic elements. Most CAD packages have a library of 2D and 3D vectored objects that can be drawn, stretched and resized. Typical primitives are:
  - 2D: lines, polylines, arcs, polyarcs, circles, ellipses, splines, Bezier curves, and polygons
  - 3D: cones, cylinders, prisms, pyramids, and spheres.

Comparing the benefits of 2D and 3D drawings

Historically, 2D CAD drawings have been used to develop, share and exchange product designs by electronic means such as e-mail or local and global networks. The development of affordable 3D CAD systems that do not rely on powerful mainframe computers is providing a means to communicate and exchange much more design information. 3D facilities allow complex screen images or virtual products to be rotated, sectioned, measured and annotated to create a range of digital data. This data can be used via CAM to support an increasing range of CNC and automatic processing operations.

Using design data

In modern CIM systems design data can also be shared with the suppliers of materials, components and sub-assemblies, as well as the workers and machines on the production lines. Product data can be used directly or converted into other file formats for a variety of other uses, such as product and sales presentations, company reports, marketing materials and brochures that are made available at a company web site on the World Wide Web. The web sites often provide e-mail addresses to offer the possibility of a two-way communication with retailers and customers. Virtual Reality Modelling (VRM) and the use of 'knowledge-based' expert systems via the Internet are growing in importance for all the purposes described above and more. Multimedia approaches will be covered in more detail later in this unit and in Unit 4 Section B Option 2.

The importance of CAD modelling

CAD modelling is now a key part of the industrial design process for the following reasons:

- Designs can be developed and electronically shared with others which enables a fast turn-around of ideas. A team of specialists often designs product assemblies. The first stage in the process might involve drawing the overall layout in 2D. The design constraints can then be applied along with the way the different components need to move (kinematics) if this is necessary. The basic solid model properties are added and the top-level layout is complete. The specialist teams work on their particular components or features. If there are any design changes, these take place on the top-level layout so all the design teams are updated automatically.
- Ideas can be tested, evaluated and modified at all stages at any point in the process.
- The need to produce a range of costly prototypes or samples is reduced. Photo-realistic images can be created and modified without the need for physical models and expensive photography.
- Products and processes can be simulated or animated and then evaluated on screen. This means that development time, design costs and the use of resources is significantly reduced.

2D and 3D geometric models

Geometric modelling is concerned with describing an object mathematically (algorithm) in a form that a CAD or graphics program can display visually. Geometric models are sub-divided based on the amount and kind of information they store. The three divisions are wireframe, surface and solid models (see Figure 3.3.11).

Wireframe models

Wireframe models in 2D or 3D are most effective for sheet metal products and simple frame constructions without a great thickness of material. In a wireframe model an object is

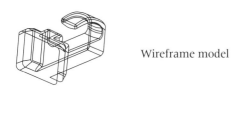

Wireframe model

Solid model

Surface model

Figure 3.3.11 Applications of 3D modelling techniques

represented as a collection of points, lines and arcs. Wireframe models can be ambiguous and difficult to 'read' or interpret. A realistic form is only achieved by the generation of a lot of data, which increases image-processing times. Dimensions, annotations, and other 'attributes' of the object may be stored but there are no visible surfaces. This means that surface or solid properties cannot be computed and rendered images cannot be generated. Additionally, 3D-wireframe object's lack of information about points inside the object and the geometric data that are produced is incompatible with the requirements of CNC programs.

Surface models
Surface models in 3D can provide more machining data than wireframes and generate a more realistic 'picture' of the model. This technique is an alternative to solid modelling but provides less data. Surface models, either flat or curved, are created by 'patches'. Polygons define contours and surfaces. As with the wireframe, the surface model contains no data about the interior of the part.

Solid models
Solid models in 3D can produce full digital mock-ups and a comprehensive data set including product assemblies. Solid models are

clear; there are no visual confusions as with the other models described. They provide complete representations of the properties of the solid.

Rendering
Rendering is the process of adding realism to a computer model by adding visual qualities (see Figure 3.3.12a). These include colour; patterns and textures; surface shading with and without light sources; hidden line removal and hidden surface removal. Hidden line removal is an important drawing function as it removes lines from the drawing that would normally not be visible from the chosen viewpoint making the model less ambiguous. The semi-hidden function displays 'hidden' lines in the 'dashed' line style (hidden detail) which you will be familiar with in engineering drawings. Hidden surface removal is a technique for filling shapes on the model with colour to improve visual understanding.

Other uses of rendered images
Rendered images are also used in advertising, sales literature, assembly illustrations, operational instructions and other information sources. The degree of realism that can be achieved is dependent on the quality of the available software and hardware, the designer's creative and visual abilities and the time available.

Shading
CAD software has a range of available shading options. The three most common are as follows:
- Flat shading is quick and simple. The surface of the object is divided into small polygons that are all shaded uniformly. This type of shading gives the object a faceted appearance. The curved surfaces are represented as a series of flat surfaces rather than a smooth curve.
- More realistic effects are achieved by graduated shading which removes the sharp edges created by flat shading and replaces it with a gradually changing shading pattern.

a)   b)

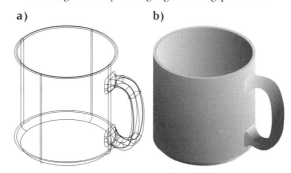

Figure 3.3.12 Rendering and sweep techniques

• Phong shading is the most accurate as it incorporates 'highlights'. Each pixel on the shaded portion can be assigned a brightness value. As a result, the rendering quality and visual realism are very good but phong shading is time consuming and slows down the processing of images.

Sweep techniques

Sweeping refers to a class of techniques used for creating curved or twisted solids (see Figure 3.3.12b). Sweep techniques involve drawing a profile along a specified path. The profile is usually a closed geometric form such as a 'D' shape. The path indicates how or to where the profile will be 'swept'. Moving the profile along the path that can be linear, circular, radial, spiral or some other configuration then creates the solid. Handles on a cup or a threaded part are examples of profiles that can be generated by sweeping.

Textures

Textures can have the 2D qualities of colour and brightness and they can have the 3D properties of transparency or reflectivity. Textures can be mapped electronically around any 3D model, a technique known as 'texture mapping'. Textures are an important part of creating ever more realistic images but they use lots of memory and image processing can be slowed down.

Constructing accurate drawings within a CAD system

To describe an object accurately all the appropriate 2D orthographic views and 3D visualisations must be drawn. Production drawings communicate all the information necessary for the production of products and assemblies. All production drawings, whether CAD or manually generated, can be classified into two major categories:

• Detail drawings are drawings of single parts and include the additional information such as dimensions and notes relating to materials, finish, weight, or standard tolerances that are required to manufacture the part or parts.
• Assembly drawings document all the necessary parts needed to assemble a product and how they fit together. The dimensions in an assembly drawing usually refer to the spatial relationships of different parts to each other rather than the size of the individual parts. An assembly drawing may be a multi-view drawing or a single profile view. Ballooned letters or numbers are attached to leader lines to 'reference' or identify the parts in the assembly. The letters or numbers also identify the part in a list which is usually placed to the bottom right of the drawing. The 'parts list' provides information regarding the name of the part, what material it is made from and 'no-off', the minimum number of each part that is required. Standard 'off-the-shelf' parts and components like nuts and bolts are also included in the parts list.

Dimensioning and annotating a drawing

Accurate information about the size of the product and its components and sub-assemblies is provided by dimensioning and annotating a drawing. Different types of features require the use of different dimension formats. CAD systems can provide linear, angular, cylindrical and radial dimensioning. Notes are added to drawings to provide additional information about the project. They are used to indicate specific surface finishes or materials; or other special manufacturing requirements such as the size or depth of holes.

The importance of dimensioning standards

In any manufacturing system it is important that all the people reading a 'drawing' interpret it in exactly the same way, but dimensioning practices may vary by company or by country. A set of international standards (ISO) has been developed to specify acceptable dimensioning practices. CAD systems offer standard dimensioning formats allowing the fundamental principles of dimensioning to be followed. Some are listed below:

• Each feature of an object is only dimensioned once in the view in which that feature is most clearly seen.
• Each dimension should include an appropriate tolerance.
• Dimensions should be located outside the boundaries of the object wherever possible and there should be a visible gap between the object and the start of a dimension line.
• Crossing of dimension lines should be avoided wherever possible.
• Dimensions should refer to solid rather than hidden lines.
• Dimensions should be placed as close as possible to the feature they are describing.
• When dimensions are 'nested', the smaller dimension should be placed closer to the object.

Task

Produce a series of drawings for your project folder to demonstrate your capability in using the techniques described above using a CAD program that you have access to.

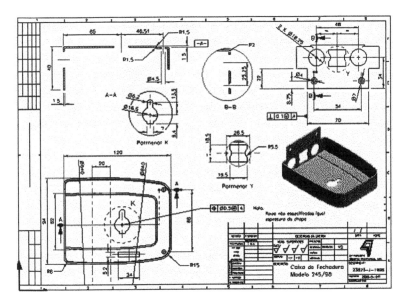

Figure 3.3.13 *Standard dimensioning formats*

Figure 3.3.13 shows some standard dimensioning formats.

Sections

Sections are an essential aid to understanding the complexity of a product. They should make a drawing easier to understand. Standard views show clearly all the exterior features of objects, but if the interior features are shown just as series of dashed lines (hidden lines) it can cause confusion to less expert readers of the drawing. In a CAD drawing, as in manually produced drawings, sectioning cuts the object with an imaginary plane (cutting plane), making interior features, which were hidden, visible. The generation of sectioned views is quick and relatively easy when using a CAD program. The solid parts of the object in contact with the cutting plane are cross-hatched. CAD systems will allow many types of section view to be drawn. The choice of method depends on the internal complexity of the object.

Virtual reality (VR) techniques

Virtual reality is an emerging technology that combines computer modelling with simulations in order to enable a person to interact with or be immersed in an artificial 3D visual or other sensory environment. Three-dimensional 'virtual products' can be created and viewed from different angles and perspectives.

Virtual Reality Modelling Language (VRML) is a specification for displaying and interacting with 3D objects on the World Wide Web using an Internet browser with a VRML plug-in or one that supports it. The development will have a significant impact on all industrial sectors but especially manufacturing. For instance, potential customers will be able to download virtual products and examine all aspects of them offline anywhere in the world. There are many other exciting developments that are beyond the scope of this book, but here are two examples for you to find out more about:

- Virtual manufacturing is a rapidly developing technology being pioneered by research teams all over the world. One of those teams, based at the University of Bath, produced this definition in 1995: 'Virtual Manufacturing is the use of a desk-top virtual reality system for the computer-aided design of components and processes for manufacture'. In their system, a user wearing a helmet with a stereoscopic

Tasks

1 Using a CAD program, generate some simple block shapes with holes, recesses and cavities.

2 Using either the views you generate above, or views supplied by your teacher, investigate how to produce:

a) a full-section view, i.e. show an entire orthographic view as a section view, with half the object removed

b) a half-section view, i.e. show one-half of the orthographic view as a section view

c) an offset-section view, i.e. a type of full section using two or more cutting planes that meet at 90-degree angles

d) a removed section view – this is similar to a revolved section but it is not drawn within the view containing the cutting plane line but is shown displaced from its normal projection position.

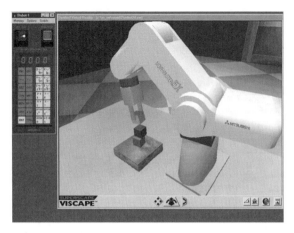

Figure 3.3.14 *3D website*

screen for each eye views animated images of a simulated manufacturing environment. The illusion of being there (telepresence) is caused by motion sensors that pick up your head movements and adjust the view on the screens accordingly, usually in real time. Real time is

---

Task

1 Connect to the Internet and visit or get details about the virtual manufacturing worlds at:

a) the University of Bath at
   www.bath.ac.uk/~ensab/Gmod/Vman
b) Denford Ltd at www.denford.com

2 Using the Internet, collect and record other examples of virtual products or virtual manufacturing.

---

the actual time during which something takes place. Simulations of manufacturing processes are usually accelerated to save time.
- Denford Ltd has created an innovative 3D website that uses virtual reality worlds to create a tour of its Professional Training and Development Centre where visitors can control a robot and try out trial versions of the company's CAD/CAM products (see Figure 3.3.14).

Creating total design concepts

Future developments in the use of multimedia including the technologies already discussed will have a profound impact on the creation of a 'total' design concept. In the future designers will have highly sophisticated multimedia 'toolkits' at their disposal. They will have access to an integrated 'on-screen' design-modelling environment that will include 'expert' systems that are directly linked to a range of production databases to analyse and plan for manufacture. Multimedia technologies such as CD-ROMs, Hypertext, the Internet and the WWW will allow the groups that are directly or indirectly involved in generating design ideas to work together and to share information effectively and efficiently. Multimedia applications will be enabling technologies and will include:

- communication systems such as voice and video conferencing, intelligent whiteboards and intranets that allow design sketches and images to be shared across different sites.
- information systems that use 'broadband' digital technology to allow designers in different locations to work on a design model at the same time. These technologies will lead to an increase in the use of applications such as VRML to present a total design concept or virtual product to all interested parties including the customer.
- organisational systems that support group design activity such as a workflow application which is an advanced form of e-mail that selectively routes electronic documents to people at a specified time according to their role in the design process.

Common input devices

As we have seen, CAD systems have to be both interactive and graphical in use. In addition to the keyboard such systems need input devices and a user interface, operating as an input/output device, that allows interaction with the computer-generated model. There are two types of interface in common use:

- Command-driven interfaces require specific commands or codes to be used in order to make something happen. These interfaces process data quickly and are flexible in use but they rely on operators trained in a particular code or command set. Incorrectly entered codes make it difficult to edit or revise the drawing. These types of interface are being gradually replaced by graphic user interfaces.
- Graphic user interfaces (GUIs), first developed in the 1970s, take advantage of the computer's graphics capabilities making the CAD program easier to use. Most GUIs use a WIMP format – windows, icons, mice and pull-down/pop-up menus operating environment. The user does not need to learn complex command codes. GUIs are effective in allowing the user to:

  – control the system by using set commands; by selecting functions via a series of windows; by a menu system; by screen icons or by direct actions such as 'clicking and dragging'

- receive information and feedback relating to what the system is doing, e.g. displaying an hourglass icon or progress meter
- enter data that will be used by the system in constructing the model
- select relevant data or parts of the model for the system to manipulate.

Operating characteristics of input devices

Input devices position or locate, point or pick or combine these functions. To signify that an action has to take place the user presses a button or switch that is provided on the input device. Many input devices produce analogue signals (A) that need to be converted into digital signals (D) in order to be processed by computers. This (A to D) process is completed using a device called a digital signal processor (DSP) which can also be used to produce an analogue signal for use by an output device (D to A).

Input devices used in CAD systems

The mouse

Invented in 1963, at the Stanford Research Centre, the mouse is the most common input device. It operates either mechanically or optically to control the movement of a cursor or a pointer on the graphic display. It allows the user to 'point' to a function and 'click' to 'execute' it. All mice contain at least one button and sometimes as many as three, which have different functions depending on what software is used. Some also include a scroll wheel for 'scrolling' through large documents. The big disadvantage of using a mouse is that a positional error will occur if the mouse is lifted from the surface that it is running on. It is also virtually impossible to trace a drawing from a paper sketch or drawing (see digitiser).

The trackball or tracker-ball

The trackball or tracker-ball is basically a mouse lying on its back. The cursor on the screen moves as a thumb or fingers, or even the palm of the hand rotates the ball. As with the mouse there are one to three buttons which are used like mouse buttons. Unlike a mouse the trackball remains stationary so it has the advantage of not requiring much space and it will operate on any type of surface. For both these reasons, trackballs are popular pointing devices for personal and laptop computers.

Table 3.3.2 shows the three basic types of mice and identifies the different ways in which mice and tracker-balls are connected to computers.

Digitisers

Digitising tables have a large working area, typically over A0 paper size, enabling users to enter large-scale drawings and sketches into a computer. They operate to a great degree of accuracy and avoid the positional problems described previously when using a mouse.

Table 3.3.2 Types of mice and computer connections

	There are three basic types of mice:	Mice and tracker-balls connect to computers in different ways:
	Mechanical – has a rubber metal ball on its underside that can roll in all directions. Mechanical sensors within the mouse detect the direction the ball is rolling and move the screen pointer accordingly	Serial mice connect directly to the RS-232C serial port or a PS/2 communication port. This is the simplest type of connection
	Optomechanical – similar to a mechanical mouse, but uses optical sensors to detect motion of the ball	PS/2 mice only connect to a PS/2 communication port
	Optical – uses a laser to detect the mouse's movement along a special mat with a grid that provides a frame of reference. Optical mice have no mechanical moving parts. They respond more quickly and precisely than mechanical and optomechanical mice, but they are also more expensive	Cordless mice are more expensive and do not physically connect to the computer. They rely on infra-red or radio waves to communicate with the computer On Apple Macintosh computers the mouse connects through the ADB (Apple Desktop Bus) port

Figure 3.3.15 *A graphics tablet*

A digitising table consists of a reactive electronic surface and a cursor (also called a puck) that has a window with cross hairs for pinpoint accurate placement and it can have up to 16 buttons to execute various functions. Each point on the table represents a fixed point on the computer screen. To determine the exact position of the puck the surface may have a grid of embedded wires, each carrying a coded signal. The puck has an electronic device that can pick up these signals which translate to give an exact position on the screen.

Graphics tablet

A graphics tablet is a tabletop digitiser consisting of a board (tablet) and pen (stylus) electronically connected to a computer (see Figure 3.3.15). The board contains electronics that detect movement of the pen. The advantage of this device is that the operator uses hand-drawing techniques in order to 'draw' ideas electronically. The drawing can then be manipulated in the normal way by the CAD software.

Digital camera

Digital cameras store images digitally rather than recording them on film. Once a picture or image has been 'captured', it can be downloaded as data into a computer system for manipulation within a CAD program or stored on a photo CD or printed on a dedicated digital printer (see Figure 3.3.16). The quality of a digital image is limited by the amount of memory in the camera, the optical resolution of the digitising mechanism, and by the resolution of the final output device. Established printer technologies have limitations but there are three printer technologies, 'thermo autochrome', 'dye sublimation' and digital printers that produce better images. We shall look briefly at all three in the section on output devices.

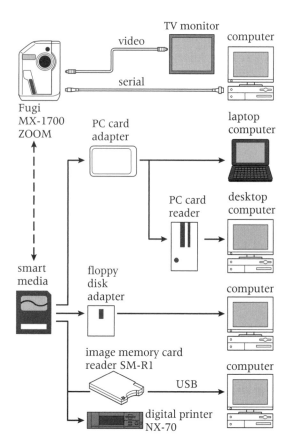

Figure 3.3.16 *Connecting a typical digital camera to a computer system*

The big advantages of digital cameras for designers and others are the operating costs; the speed of data conversion, because there is no film processing at the start of the process; and the image manipulation and editing that is possible. A digital camera allows an image to be in a CAD system for processing and image manipulation within minutes of shooting. Digitally enhanced images now appear in a whole range of media ranging from product presentations to Internet and print-based product catalogues. If the requirement is to get images in electronic form in the fastest possible time, then a digital camera is the best choice.

Task

Investigate the use of a digital camera and how the images are transferred from the camera to a computer. Once your image is on screen in what ways does your software allow the image to be edited? Produce a range of digital images for use in your project portfolio.

Digital video (DV)

A new generation of video cameras that are entirely digital are now on the market. In a digital video (DV) camera the output from the camera is already in a compressed digital format, so no analogue to digital conversion is required as with analogue video cameras. Images can be taken straight to a PC-based video editing system. Digital video systems allow the communication, control and interchange of digital, audio and video data. The benefits of applying these DV systems within CAD other than for video conferencing are an area of considerable research.

Scanner

A scanner is a device that converts light, analogue data, into the digital data that a computer can read. Scanners allow graphic images and text to be captured electronically for importing into design software where it can be manipulated in the same way as other visual data. It can be edited, stored and used to develop design ideas and specifications. Scanners are able to scan both 2D surfaces and 3D objects (see below). Developments in both the control technologies and the processing software mean that scanners are now much easier to operate. Many companies are developing scanners with 'one touch' operation for ease of use.

Types of scanner in common use in CAD

- Large drum scanner – capable of scanning both opaque documents and transparencies at high resolutions of over 400 dots per inch (dpi); expensive.
- Dedicated photo/transparency scanner for high resolution photographic images.
- Handheld scanner – low-cost small capacity devices with restricted scanning widths.
- Flatbed scanner – the most versatile and popular device.

Figure 3.3.17 *An arm scanner*

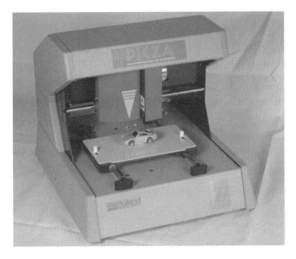

Figure 3.3.18 *A Roland scanning machine*

3D scanner

3D scanning or digitising involves creating a series of profile curves that define the surface characteristics and the physical geometry of a three-dimensional object. The digital data collected and recorded allows a 3D representation or model to be created within a computer. CAD and graphics software can then be used to blend and render surfaces to add colour, reflections, texture and other visual techniques to add visual realism. There are two different methods of scanning a 3D object, contact or non-contact.

Contact scanning systems

Mechanical tracking systems make a physical contact with the object with a probe that can be passed around and over the surface of the object. The tracking is done by a probe that is machine driven or manually operated. A typical manual system uses a mechanical arm that has digital sensors in each joint (see Figure 3.3.17). An operator moves the probe over the surface clicking and recording positional data as it moves over the object. These points generate the required profile curves. A machine-driven device common in UK schools and colleges is the Roland model, which can operate as a low-cost 3D scanner or as a small capacity CNC milling machine (see Figure 3.3.18). The scanned data can be exported in 3D DXF or VRML format for use in other software.

Non-contact scanning systems

Non-contact methods of 3D scanning mostly use a geometric technique known as triangulation to create the three-dimensional shapes. Laser scanners are non-contact and high-speed devices but they are expensive. These devices scan by either directing beams at various points to create a profile curve or by generating a 'laser

Figure 3.3.19 *Laser scanners in operation*

stripe profile' of the object (see Figures 3.3.19 and 3.3.20). The beams or stripes are reflected back to a series of sensors or into a video camera. In both cases an accurate surface representation is built up by scanning from different planes and angles and mathematically processing the digital data.

Ultrasonic scanners are also non-contact devices that 'bounce' sound waves off the surface of the object and triangulate the points in 3D. The devices are not portable or easy to set up. They are noisy in operation and do not provide a high level of accuracy.

Magnetic tracking scanners work on a similar principle to ultrasonic devices using magnetic fields to create the triangulated points. The major drawback of such systems is that they cannot scan any object with a metal part.

Common output devices

An output device is what makes a computer capable of displaying and manipulating pictures (graphics) or machining a variety of materials (CNC). Laser printers and plotters are 'graphic'

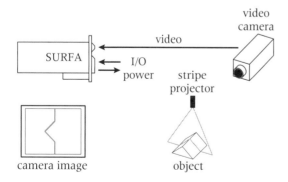

The SURFA board uses Digital Signal Processing of video data to capture surface shapes in real time at over 14,000 points per second.

Figure 3.3.20 *Laser stripe triangulation*

output devices because they permit the computer to output pictures. They produce 'hard copy' on paper or film. A monitor is an output device that can display pictures.

Linking CAD and CAM
CNC machines provide an interface between CAD and CAM. Numerically controlled (NC) machining processes were first developed in the USA in the 1940s. The motors and machining tables on the NC machines were originally driven from instructions provided on a punched card system and then from magnetic tapes. Programs generated and transferred from computers now control the operation of many NC machines, hence computer numerically controlled or CNC machines. There are a host of CNC machines including milling machines, lathes, drilling machines, presses and engravers. New classes of 'tool-less' CNC machines are in use in industry, e.g. CNC laser devices are increasingly being used in cutting and machining applications (see Rapid Prototyping in Unit 4, Section B Option 2).

Transferring data to output devices
Both CNC and graphic output devices are generally connected to the computer by either 'series' or 'parallel' cables, but some devices such as printers can be operated by infra-red and are therefore 'wireless'. The cables are connected into the computer via communication ports, the size, shape and number of connecting pins varying according to the specific make of computer. Almost all graphics systems, including CAD systems and animation software, use a combination of vector and raster graphics. Most output devices are raster devices.

Displaying graphics
The graphic capabilities of a monitor or display screen make it an important output device in any CAD system. There are many ways to classify monitors. The most basic is in terms of colour capabilities, which separates monitors into three classes:

- Monochrome monitors actually display two colours, one for the background and one for the foreground. The colours can be black and white, green and black, or amber and black. They are often used on the displays of a CNC machine where a colour image is not so important.
- A grey-scale monitor is a special type of monochrome monitor capable of displaying different shades of grey.
- Colour monitors can display any number from 16 to over 1 million different colours.

The importance of screen size for CAD work

The choice of screen size, or viewable area, is particularly important in a CAD system. Monitors that measure 400 or more millimetres from corner to corner are often called full-page monitors and are considered more suitable for graphics work. Large monitors can display two full pages, side by side.

The resolution of a monitor indicates how many pixels are on the screen. In general, the more pixels (often expressed in dots per inch – dpi), the sharper the image and the better the resolution.

Printers

A printer is an output device that prints text or graphics on to paper, card and film. Not all printers can produce high-quality images. The following printers are considered below:

- ink jet
- laser
- dye sublimation
- thermo autochrome
- digital.

Ink-jet printers

These non-contact printers produce low-cost, high-quality text and graphics in colour by combining cyan, magenta, yellow and black (CMYK). This is a distinct advantage over more expensive laser colour printing methods. They all use some sort of thermal technology to produce heated bubbles of ink that burst spraying ink at a sheet of paper to form an image. As the ink nozzle cools a vacuum is created and this draws in a fresh supply of ink for heating and spraying. The print head prints in strips across the page, moving down the page to build up the complete image with a resolution that can range from 300 to 1200 dpi. They are sometimes referred to as 'bubble jet' printers, which is actually the trade name of Canon's own ink-jet technology.

One disadvantage of the ink-jet printer is that the ink cartridges need to be changed more frequently and expensive specially coated paper is necessary to produce really high-quality images, which significantly raises the cost per page. Choosing the right paper for ink-jet printing is important. Some images, especially those with large areas of colour, can 'bleed' if the paper is too absorbent or too much ink has been applied. Bleeding causes images to blur as the colours merge and run together.

Another disadvantage of this system of printing is that images are easily smudged as some types of ink take a little time to dry. A further drawback might be that the diameters of the nozzles used in ink-jet printers are very small and can easily become clogged.

Laser printers

These printers use the same technology as photocopier machines. The printer receives data from the computer, which is processed and used to control the operation of a laser beam directing light at a large roller or drum. Altering the electrical charge wherever laser light hits the drum creates the required image. The drum then rotates through a powder called toner. The electrically charged areas attract the powder and the print is made when it is transferred on to the paper by a combination of heat and pressure. Laser printers produce very high-quality text and graphics.

Dye sublimation printers

These low-speed devices produce relatively expensive but high-quality graphic and photographic images. The four coloured inks or dyes (CMYK) are stored on rolls of film. A heating element turns the ink on the film into a gas. The amount of ink that is put on paper correlates to the temperature of the heating element. The temperature varies in relation to the image density of the original drawing or artwork. The reason that it produces images of such high quality is that the ink is applied as a continuous tone rather than as a series of dots and special paper is used that allows the dyes to diffuse into the paper to mix and create precise colour shades.

Thermo autochrome (TA) printing

This method is used to print high-quality images generated by a digital camera. The process is more complex than either ink-jet or laser printing. TA paper contains three layers of coloured pigment, cyan, magenta and yellow, each of which is sensitive to a particular temperature. Three passes are needed to get the three colours to show. The printer is equipped with both thermal and ultraviolet heads; the heat from the thermal head 'activates' the colour in the paper, which is then 'fixed' by the ultraviolet light.

Digital printers

These are used to produce photographic quality images from a digital camera without having to transfer data to a computer. The printers can be connected to a monitor for viewing and editing images and layouts. The widespread introduction of digital printers is limited at the time of writing because there are no agreed standards for them. Manufacturers of digital cameras will supply digital printers that match their range of cameras.

Printer classification

Printers are classified by the following:

- The quality of type they produce – either letter quality (as good as a typewriter), near letter quality, or draft quality. Ink-jet and laser printers produce letter-quality type.
- The speed at which they print. Printing speeds are measured in characters per second (cps) or pages per minute (ppm). The speed of printers within a particular class can also vary widely. Laser printers print at speeds ranging from four to 20 text pages per minute.
- The effectiveness of the methods used to create colour and more realistic images by employing techniques such as dithering, colour matching between the screen and what appears on paper, half toning and continuous tones.

Plotters

A plotter is a high-quality impact-printing device that draws images on paper or any other suitable medium directed by commands from a computer. There are two classes of plotter: vector and raster. Vector plotters produce an image as a set of straight lines, fill patterns are clearly visible and they operate comparatively slowly. All Raster plotters generate an image as a series of points. The way that the points are printed varies and the methods are beyond the scope of this book. These plotters produce very large full- colour drawings with a high degree of quality.

XY plotter

The term XY refers to the axes along which the plotting pen can travel. Plotters differ from printers in that they draw lines using a pen.

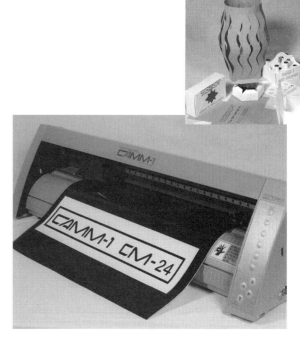

Figure 3.3.22 *A plotter-cutter and a range of cut products*

As a result, they can produce continuous lines, whereas printers can only simulate lines by printing a closely spaced series of dots. Multicolour plotters use different-coloured pens to draw different colours. Pens can be picked from a bank of penholders or changed individually as the different colours are called for. In general, plotters are considerably more expensive than printers. They are used in engineering applications where precision is essential. An XY plotter is shown in Figure 3.3.21.

Plotter-cutters

Plotter-cutters can plot drawings in the same way as the XY plotter described above but they can also produce cut shapes in card, vinyl and other sheet materials using thin blades that can be adjusted for depth and pressure of cut. This allows the plotter cutter to undertake finely controlled cutting techniques such as 'scoring' in which a card that is to be folded is only cut to a certain depth to make the subsequent folding easier. Plotter cutters are used in the production of advertising and promotional products as well as in sign making and similar processes. Figure 3.3.22 shows a plotter-cutter.

Engraving machines

Engravers also have a variety of uses ranging from sign making to the production of

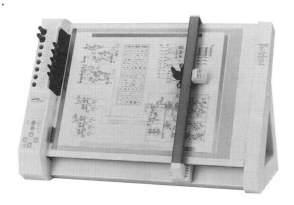

Figure 3.3.21 *An XY plotter*

jewellery, medals and 3D reliefs (see Figure 3.3.23). They can be relatively small devices that sit on a desktop or larger floor-standing machines. The machines can operate in the X, Y and Z axes. This allows the engraving of 3D surfaces and curves as well as lettering. Cheaper versions of CNC engravers for school and college have less control over the Z-axis of the cutting tool. This reduces the overall flexibility of the machine because it has to engrave at a fixed depth. One of the characteristics of an engraver is the high spindle speed that is needed because of the very small diameter of the V-point engraving tools. We shall return to CNC cutting speeds and feeds later in this unit.

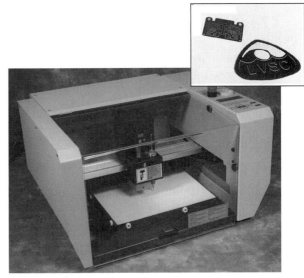

Figure 3.3.23 *A CNC engraver and a range of engraved products*

3. Computer-aided manufacture

The application of CNC machines

CNC machines are widely used in a range of industries. Because they can operate in more than one axis they can generate shapes ranging from straight lines to very complex curves. The technology and functionality of CNC machines has continued to evolve since they were first used in the 1970s. CNC machining centres allow a single machine to carry out more than one cutting operation, e.g. a CNC lathe can be provided with a milling attachment to allow both turning and milling operations. Processing flexibility is the key to the future development and profitability of CIM systems. Where they can be used machining centres offer reductions in processing times. Tool set-up times and tool changes are reduced when multiple machining spindles and tool-handling systems are used. A tool-handling system, sometimes called a tool magazine, allows all the cutting tools that are needed to be stored and loaded as the NC program directs.

CNC prototyping

The development of new 'tool-less' cutting technologies such as the use of lasers is further extending the range and complexity of products that can be manufactured. Rapid Prototyping (RPT) is an emerging CNC application that creates 3D objects using laser technology to solidify liquid polymers in a process called stereolithography.

Boxford Ltd in the UK has produced a relatively low-cost RPT system for schools and colleges based on a prototyping system called layered object modelling (LOM) (see Figure 3.3.24). Models are imported from a CAD program as in the industrial systems but the models are assembled from thin sticky backed paper. A CNC vinyl cutter cuts the slices (in the industrial process a laser is used). The layers of sliced paper are built up on a pegged jig to make the 3D prototype.

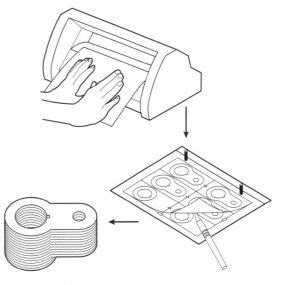

Figure 3.3.24 *Rapid Prototyping using CNC machines*

Operating characteristics of CNC machines

A computer-generated program is fed into a machine control unit (MCU) which includes a manual control keypad and in some cases a display screen. The MCU reads and converts the digital data it receives in order to control the analogue machining movements that the machine has to make. Movement is controlled by a series of servo systems or, in low-cost devices, stepper motors, called actuators. As the machine is operating the MCU is constantly receiving feedback information from sensing devices (transducers) or encoders on the machine. This information is used to correct any errors of spindle speed, feed rate or cutter position. This sensing and response mechanism is called closed-loop control (see Unit 4, Section B Option 2). Figure 3.3.25 shows a typical arrangement of a three-axis CNC machine and Figure 3.3.26 a typical CNC system.

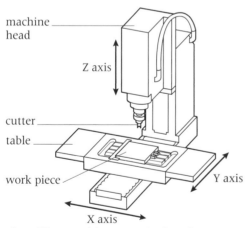

The milling machine moves in three basic directions, so that any part of the work piece can be reached by the rotating cutter. These three directions are called 'axes', or sometimes 'slides':

1 The table can move backwards and forwards – this is called the Y axis.
2 The table can move left and right – this is called the X axis.
3 The machine head and cutter (cutting tool) can move up and down – this is called the Z axis.

Figure 3.3.25 *Typical arrangement of a three-axis CNC machine*

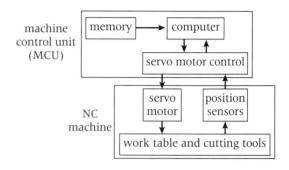

Figure 3.3.26 *A typical CNC system*

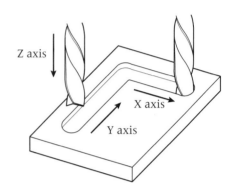

Figure 3.3.27 *Point-to-point cutting in three axes*

Toolpaths and cutting motions on CNC machines

- A cutting tool moves from 'point to point' as it moves between two specified positions. However, the toolpath between the points does not have to be a straight line, it can be an arc or a series of curves. CNC mills and routers use point-to-point control.
- Moving a cutting tool parallel to one machine axis is known as 'straight cutting'.
- Contouring allows both point-to-point and straight cutting in more than one axis, allowing complex curves and shapes such as spirals to be generated (see Figure 3.3.27).

The depth that the tool cuts in any one pass depends on the amount of material to be removed and the surface finish required on the finished article. The inside of a mould for a precision plastic product to be made by injection moulding has to have a finer surface finish than is needed on the outside. Roughing cuts remove large amounts of material and set out the basic profile and cut close to the different depths that are required. Finishing cuts provide the required final shape and surface finish. Finishing cuts are made in a number of ways. Depending on the functions available the cutter can:

- move in one direction, constantly lifting back from the end of the cut to the start
- constantly cut as it moves backwards and forwards
- follow the contours on the surface
- follow parallel paths over the surface of the object (see Figure 3.3.28).

> ### Task
> Determine what types of cut the CNC machines that you have access to are able to make. How should you compensate for the diameter of the cutting tool? Compile a table showing the results of your investigations.

Types of CNC machine
a) Lathes for operations such as parallel and taper turning, facing, drilling and thread cutting in metal and plastics.
b) Milling machines for operations such as profiling, pocketing and surface milling.
c) Routers and engravers for profiles and grooves.

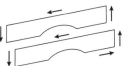

a) The cutter moves in one direction constantly lifting back from the end of the cut to the start

b) The cutter cuts constantly as it moves backwards and forwards

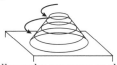

c) The cutter follows the contours on the surface

d) The cutter follows parallel paths over the surface of the object

Figure 3.3.28 *Tool paths for machining surfaces*

a) Lathe

b) Milling machine

c) Router

Figure 3.3.29 *Types of CNC machine*

d) Drilling and cutting machine

e) Pressing and punching machine

d) Drilling machines employing point-to-point motion to drill through and 'blind' holes.

e) Cutting machines, including flame, lasers and electric discharge devices such as spark erosion machines.

f) Pressing and punching machines for processing sheet materials.

These machines are illustrated in Figure 3.3.29.

Machining characteristics of CNC machines

On CNC machines either the tool or the work piece is able to move in up to five axes to generate the required point-to-point, straight or contoured tool paths, as shown in Figure 3.3.30.

Task

Refer to the manufacturers' instruction manuals or other reference sources for the cutting tools and CNC machines that you have available in the workshop. Look up the spindle speeds, feed rates and depths of cut for the x,y and z axes. Compile a table showing what the differences would be if you were CNC milling, engraving or turning mild steel, aluminium, MDF, polymer materials, engraving laminates and modelling wax.

Feeds, speeds and rapid traversing

The speed at which the cutting tools or the work piece move in relation to one another is either automatically or manually programmed using information extracted from a machining database.

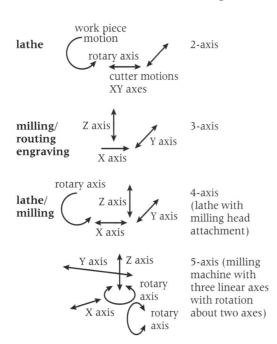

Figure 3.3.30 Tool paths

- The progress along the toolpath is called the cutter moving or feed rate and is measured in millimetres per second (mm/s). The feed rate is precisely controlled from the MCU using data provided from the remote computer and the feedback sensors on the machine. As a general rule, metals are machined with slow feed rates and small depths of cut, but slower feeds do not always result in a better finish

- Rapid traversing describes the way the cutter moves when it is not cutting any material. To work with maximum efficiency the tool is programmed to move quickly from the end of one cutting operation to the start of the next.

- The spindle holds the cutting tools and the speed at which it rotates the cutting tools is critical.

Spindle speeds

The cutter revolution or spindle speed is measured in revolutions per minute (rpm) and will vary according to the material being machined and the diameter of the cutter. As a general rule, the bigger the cutter diameter, the slower the spindle speed and the softer the material, the faster the spindle speed. On an engraving machine spindle speeds usually range between 5000 and 15,000 rpm. To give an example, acrylic is engraved at a spindle speed of 10,000 rpm with a depth of 0.2 mm at an XY feed of 15 mm/sec and a Z feed of 5 mm/sec.

CNC machines operating within CIM or FMS

If the computer sends instructions directly to the MCU that computer has always to be available and it is dedicated to that machine alone. Modern CIM systems download machining 'part programs' into the memory of the MCUs, as required, from a central computer that directs the operation of a series of manufacturing cells. This method, known as distributed numerical control (DNC), is essential to the effective operation of other parts of the CIM system such as the robotic systems that service the manufacturing cell. The stages in part programming will include the following:

1 The CAD program identifies the required machining motions.

2 Appropriately shaped tools are either suggested or selected from a tool library.

3 The tool paths calculations are generated mathematically.

4 The machining operations are simulated and displayed on the computer's screen.

5 Potential conflicts or collisions are identified and displayed for editing or correction.

6 A cutter file is produced.

7 The cutter file is downloaded or transmitted to the machine tool for cutting to begin.

The types of cutting tools on CNC machines

CNC machines use cutting tools that are similar to those used on their manual equivalents. The tools are held in collets. The choice of a cutter depends on the geometry or shape required and the cutting loads it has to withstand. Cutters are typically made from high-speed steel (HSS), tungsten carbide or ceramic materials (see Figure 3.3.31).

These materials can operate at high cutting speeds without losing their hardness. They can resist the heat generated as a result of friction during the cutting process. Tungsten carbide and ceramic materials are relatively expensive so these materials are only used on the cutting edges of a 'tipped' tool. Some cutters have removable blades for ease of maintenance and for sharpening purposes.

> ## Task
>
> Slot cutters, end mills, bull nose cutters and face mills are some of the cutters you might find on a CNC milling or routing machine.
>
> a) What features do they have in common?
> b) What are their respective advantages and disadvantages?
> c) What are the benefits of a collet rather than a chuck for holding the cutting tools?

Tool profiles

The geometry of the cutting tool determines what shape the tool generates and how the waste materials are moved away from the

Figure 3.3.31 *CNC cutter*

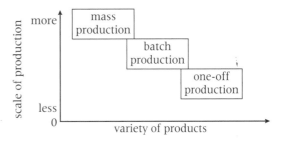

Figure 3.3.32 *Scale of production*

cutting edges. On a twist drill or a milling cutter 'flutes' force the materials up and away from the cutting operation. On a lathe tool the angled surfaces combine to move the cut material away. Routing cutters are small in diameter and can be half round or three-quarter round in shape. Engraving cutters are V-shaped.

Scale of production and the use of CAM

The choice to use CAM will depend on the intended scale of production, the number of identical components to be produced and the cost benefits that it can bring. There are essentially three categories of production:

- one-off production (sometimes called 'jobbing')
- batch production
- mass-production systems that include high-volume 'runs' or continuous operation (see Figure 3.3.32).

One-off production

This means that just one product is 'made to order' from specialist or niche manufacturers. Products made by this process are invariably more expensive to buy because they are individually designed, made and checked with few standardised components that can be bought in. The company has to have a highly flexible manufacturing facility and in some cases a highly skilled team of workers. To complicate matters slightly some one-off products such as a railway bridge that are 'engineered to order' will have thousands of components that are identical. These components can be 'sourced' from or subcontracted out to a volume manufacturer to be batch produced, but there is still only one final 'product'. Another type of one-off is when a company develops a prototype in order to try out a design idea or test the reaction to the product before committing to batch or mass production.

Batch production

This is a flexible system that is used to make a relatively small number of components or products. Components and parts are made in 'batches' and assembled. Once a batch run has been completed the machines can be reprogrammed and tooled up to make another batch of products. CNC machines are ideally suited to batch production because it is easy to reinstall the original cutting data and reset the cutting tools so that turn around time between batches is reduced.

Mass production

Set-up and break even costs can be higher than in the other two systems. Tooling up for high volumes or continuous operations reduces manufacturing costs. Mass-produced products vary in complexity ranging from a simple everyday item with only one component to cars that have thousands of components. A characteristic of mass production is that all the products are highly standardised.

Recent developments in production systems

Mass production companies are looking to develop more flexible systems based on the batch production principle. Earlier in this unit, we looked at the pressures for change including the demand for a greater variety of products and the move towards products that are 'customised' to meet the demands of a particular market sector. We have seen car manufacturers under pressure to reduce the costs of cars but at the same time offer a greater range of options as 'standard' rather than as 'optional extras'. Car manufacturers need flexible production systems to allow the car to be 'made to order'. Cars that are sitting in a stock compound waiting to be purchased are a costly overhead and a drain on the company's profits. Flexible manufacturing systems (FMS) are also employed when the scale of production cannot justify a fully automated production line or where there is a need to have a 'quick response' system (see Unit 4, Section B Option 2).

Advantages of CAM

CAM allows production processes including materials handling, retrieval and storage to be automated. Materials and components can be moved so that they are at the right stage of production at the right time. Automated handling and carrying systems allow people to be taken off tasks that are potentially hazardous to health. CAM systems are also able to operate in hostile environments and areas that are dangerous for human beings to be in such as nuclear power stations and chemical factories.

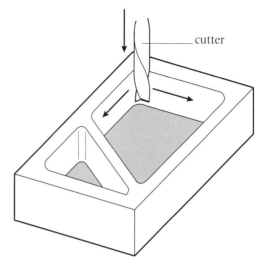

Figure 3.3.33 *Pocket machining*

Scale of production

CAM systems allow the scale of manufacturing to range from batch and mass to continuous production. The introduction of computer-controlled systems of manufacture such as 'just in time' (JIT) means that:

- CNC machines can be operated more flexibly allowing manufacturers to develop quick response systems
- production levels can be linked directly to the size of the customer order book
- the company is less likely to be damaged by sudden changes of demand in its particular market
- raw materials can be ordered as and when required, just in time, so avoiding large and costly stockpiles of materials and components that are not adding value to the process
- levels of finished products ready for distribution to retailers can be kept to a minimum.

Increased range of machining processes

On a processing level, prior to the introduction of CAM, numerically controlled machines could not be used to create really complex shapes. The development of CNC machines has increased the scope and range of machining possibilities. For example, in the aircraft industry profiling and pocketing techniques have developed to allow the machining of components from solid blocks to replace more costly and time consuming fabrication and assembly techniques (see Figure 3.3.33). Moulds for plastics can be surface milled from solid blocks.

Reduced manufacturing times

CAM can reduce manufacturing time from days to just a few hours. Cutter paths for complex shapes, such as double curves, are also easily developed, edited and tested through on-screen simulations at the design stage.

Operational reliability

CAM improves levels of operational reliability and the finished quality of products. Modern machining software can now generate and simulate tool paths that take account of collisions between the tool and the work piece which affect surface finishes and also other problems such as fouling against the work piece clamps and other fixtures.

Consistency in repetitive situations

CNC machines only need to be 'trained' once and they can do repetitive tasks rapidly with fewer errors than human operators can. Machines can operate 24 hours a day, do not need rest breaks or holidays and are not affected by other human constraints.

Improved productivity

Production 'throughput' is improved with lower processing costs and less waste of materials and resources. Manufacturing costs can be estimated with a greater degree of certainty, as production rates are more consistent than is possible with human-operated machines.

Disadvantages of CAM

Costs

The cost of buying and installing machines is high when compared to manually operated machines. For really high-volume mass production a purpose-built automatic machine may be a more cost-effective solution than the use of CNC machines.

Worker involvement

With developments in automation, robotics and artificial intelligence it is likely that there will be even less human involvement in the manufacturing and production processes of the future. This is a pattern that is repeated across the world.

Worker commitment

For some people CAM can create emotional and other problems at work. When CNC machines are controlled directly from a central system, some jobs consist of nothing more than 'machine minding' leading to poor job satisfaction and reduced productivity. Many companies are having to work hard to devise systems and develop employee schemes to maintain the interest, enthusiasm and cooperation of their workers.

Task

You might want to refer back to the first section of this unit to consider the employment issues surrounding the introduction of CAM in more detail. Explain what you consider the key issues to be.

Exam preparation

You will need to revise all the topics in this unit, so that you can apply your knowledge and understanding to the exam questions.

In preparation for your exam it is a good idea to make brief notes about different topics, such as 'Global manufacturing'. Use sub-headings or bullet point lists and diagrams where appropriate. A single side of A4 should be used for each heading from the Specification.

It is very important to learn exam skills. You should have weekly practice in learning technical terms and in answering exam-type questions. When you answer any question you should:

- read the question carefully and pick out the key points that need answering
- match your answer to the marks available, e.g. for two marks, you should give two good points that address the question
- always give examples and justify statements with reasons, saying how or why the statement is true.

Practice exam questions

1 a) Outline three reasons why the use of computers has enabled changes in design and production methods. (6)

 b) The use of CAD has changed the way designers work. Explain two of the following terms related to CAD:
 - 2D modelling
 - 3D prototyping
 - accurate drawings. (4)

 c) Describe the benefits to the manufacturer of using CAD in the design process. (5)

2 a) Describe what is meant by a CNC machine. (2)

 b) Outline two reasons why CNC machines improve the manufacture of products. (2)

 c) Describe the following terms:
 - computer integrated manufacturing (CIM)
 - concurrent engineering
 - flexible manufacturing system (FMS). (6)

 d) Explain the role of computers in a flexible manufacturing system. (5)

3 a) Describe how the following are used:
 - hardware
 - software
 - graphical user interface (GIU). (9)

 b) Explain how virtual reality techniques are helping designers to develop products. (6)

4 a) Explain and give an example of three input devices used in CAD systems (9)

 b) Outline the meaning of an output device. (2)

 c) Describe the benefits of using two of the following output devices:
 - laser printer
 - digital printer
 - XY plotter. (4)

5 a) Describe the benefits of using a CNC machine for prototyping a product. (4)

 b) Describe the following terms:
 - computer-aided manufacture (CAM)
 - just in time (JIT). (6)

 c) Explain the benefits of the use of CAM in mass production. (5)

Mechanisms, energy and electronics (R304)

Summary of expectations

1. What to expect?

Mechanisms, energy and electronics is one of the three options offered in Section B of Unit 3 of which you will study only one. You may have covered some of the option content in your GCSE course, depending on which focus area you studied. If, however, the content is new to you, do not worry. This unit will take you through from first principles.

2. How will it be assessed?

The work that you do in this option will be externally assessed through Section B of the Unit 3 examination paper. You are advised to spend **45 minutes** on this section of the paper.

3. What will be assessed?

The following list summarises the topics covered in this option and what will be examined:

- mechanical systems
- energy sources
- levers and linkages
- gear systems
- resistors
- potential divider
- diodes
- capacitors
- transistors
- relays
- circuit testing.

4. How to be successful in this unit

To be successful in this unit you will need to:

- have a clear understanding of the topics covered in this option
- apply your knowledge and understanding to a given situation or context
- organise your answers clearly and coherently, using specialist technical terms where appropriate
- use clear diagrams where appropriate ↓ illustrate your answers
- write clear and logical answers to the examination questions, using correct spelling, punctuation and grammar.

There may be an opportunity to demonstrate your knowledge and understanding of mechanisms, energy and electronics in your Unit 2 coursework. However, simply because you are studying this option, you do not have to integrate this type of technology into your coursework project.

5. How much is it worth?

This option, with Section A, is worth 30 per cent of your AS qualification. If you go on to complete the whole course, then this unit accounts for 15 per cent of the full Advanced GCE.

Unit 3 + option	Weighting
AS level	30%
A2 level (full GCE)	15%

1. Mechanical systems

We use **mechanical systems** each and every day, from using a handle to open a door, to the very complicated systems in operation in a motor car. Each one has been designed to perform a specific purpose. We take them all for granted and most of them go unnoticed. Mechanical systems form an essential role in industry; although processes may be mainly electronically controlled, it is basically mechanical systems providing the output. From lifting engines in the car industry on the production line to providing the forces to push plastic through dies for extrusion, mechanisms provide the transmission of forces and energy for useful work.

Common properties of mechanisms

Although each system is designed to perform a specific function there are some common principles behind all mechanisms. They all involve some kind of movement force and they require some form of input in order to achieve the desired output. For example, the basin tap in Figure 3.4.1 keeps the water from flowing through it and into the sink. The force applied when you turn the handle provides the input movement. The output movement raises a spindle and water flows through the seating and out of the spout. A screw thread is one of the most basic mechanisms and one of the most powerful. It can be used to lift enormous loads, yet it can also be used to provide very small, accurate movements as in the case of the tap.

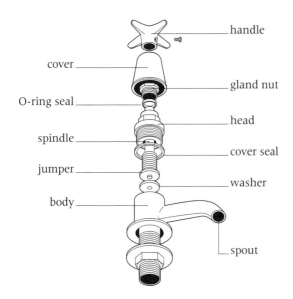

Figure 3.4.1 *Exploded view of washbasin tap*

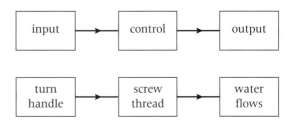

Figure 3.4.2 *Basic building blocks of a control system*

A screw thread changes the rotary motion into a linear output. This very basic system is best represented in the form of a block diagram as show in Figure 3.4.2.

Most systems are made up from smaller subsystems with each one carrying out specific functions. When connected they all contribute to the overall operation of the system. The most basic of systems is made up from three blocks: input, control and output.

Input

In a mechanical system the input is in the form of a movement. It may be by moving a lever or pushing a button. In electrical systems the inputs tend to be those that sense some change in the environment such as fluctuations in light levels, temperature or humidity.

Control

The control element is a signal processor. It normally changes the size of the input either mechanically, via gearboxes or levers, or electronically by transistors and amplifiers. It is also possible to change one type of input into a different type of output; electrical into mechanical, for example, as would be the case when the soil becomes too dry in a garden, a water pump is switched on.

Output

Outputs are the end result of the control systems and can be in the form of movements and audible visual warnings and indicators.

Task

Carry out a thorough analysis of the different types of control systems that exist within a bicycle. An example is illustrated below:

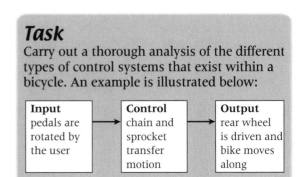

Input	Control	Output
pedals are rotated by the user	chain and sprocket transfer motion	rear wheel is driven and bike moves along

Open-loop systems

The systems that have been discussed so far are known as **open-loop systems**. They are connected up and processed one block after another in a linear fashion. There is no checking taking place to see whether actions have been carried out or not or whether a satisfactory condition or state has been arrived at.

When you heat water in a pan, it will simply boil and eventually evaporate in the form of steam. There is no checking to see what the temperature is or how hot it needs to be.

Closed-loop systems

A **closed-loop system** operates in a similar fashion to an open-loop system in that it moves sequentially through each block one at a time. The major difference, however, with a closed-loop system is that there is feedback built into the system and this is a method of checking to see that the action has been carried out correctly.

An example of this type of system is one which most of us take for granted, central heating. The input, or sensor, is in the form of a thermostat which measures the temperature of the air in the house and sends a signal to a control unit. A heating system also has a timer or programmer unit which turns the heating on and off at predetermined times during the day. When both of these inputs are sending signals to the control unit, the boiler and pump are switched on to heat and pump the water around the system. As the radiators get hotter, the air temperature rises and because of the feedback loop, the temperature of the environment is constantly checked and monitored. At the pre-set room temperature the thermostat will send a signal which will turn the boiler off and stop it heating the water (see Figure 3.4.3).

As already detailed, when the room temperature falls below a certain level the boiler is turned on to heat up the water and

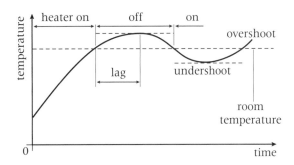

Figure 3.4.4 How room temperature changes as a result of lag

subsequently raise the ambient temperature in the house. As with any control system though, there is a delay between the heating being switched on and warming up the rooms.

This period of time is termed lag (see Figure 3.4.4). Similarly, when the room temperature is reached, the heater is switched off but the temperature continues to rise a little before it starts to cool down once again. This process of overshooting and undershooting is known as hunting. Hunting and lag are evident in most control systems where a feedback element exists.

Uses of control systems

Much use is made of feedback in control systems for positional control within machinery. Complicated electronic circuits are used to monitor speed and rotational movement and provide signals back to motors to either increase, decrease speed or stop. Computer-controlled machinery makes extensive use of such systems but because of the speed of processing there is no lag.

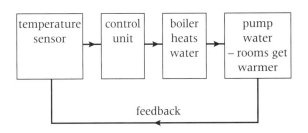

Figure 3.4.3 Block diagram of central heating system

> ### Task
>
> A washing machine needs a control system that takes into account several different factors:
>
> - door (open or closed)
> - water temperature and level
> - which program has been selected
> - drum speed and cycle.
>
> A number of these factors are decided when you select your working programme.
>
> Produce a block diagram for a washing machine and identify the various input/output components needed to make it perform successfully.

2. Energy sources

Energy is all around us. We cannot touch it, we cannot see it, although we can see and feel its effects. It can exist in many forms and it can also be changed from one form to another. A car uses petrol as its energy source in a chemical form. Following combustion, it is changed into a useful output in the form of kinetic energy as the car is made to travel. There is, however, always waste when any process is used to convert energy and in the example of the car, heat and fumes are given off.

All energy originates from the sun with direct light and heat being the obvious ones. Coal formed from decayed plant life and vegetation that grew as a result of sunlight. Water evaporated from the sea would not fall as rain without the sun, to run into rivers where the movement can be harnessed.

Energy can be obtained from:

- direct sunlight
- nuclear and fossil fuel
- movement from water and air.

Energy can be broken down into two groups:

- Capital – those that once they have been used cannot be replaced such as gas, oil and coal.
- Income – those that continue to be available and will not run out such as solar and tidal power.

The principles of generating renewable energy

Wave

Waves are formed by winds blowing across the surface of oceans and tidal patterns. They have enormous power that causes havoc and destruction during severe storms. It is though quite difficult to harness this power.

Where it is harnessed, floating rafts are connected together that bob up and down as the waves roll over the water's surface. This mechanical movement is converted into electricity.

Tidal

Tides happen as a result of gravitational pull of the sun and the moon. Occurring twice a day, there is an enormous source of energy in terms of movement available to be harnessed. In certain areas of the British Isles, the tidal levels are quite varied but in parts of the River Severn and the Bristol Channel it can be up to 15 metres.

Tidal movements can be harnessed in two ways: by the water flowing through channels that have turbine blades, or by the changing volumes of water filling and emptying huge basins which again carry turbine blades.

The flowing water in both of these cases creates a rotational movement of the turbine blades that are in turn connected to electrical generators.

Geothermal

As you drill a few miles into the earth's surface, temperatures start to rise. However, in places like Iceland and New Zealand hot spots are much closer to the surface and hot springs form naturally. Deep holes are drilled into rock formations which are much warmer than those on the earth's surface and water is pumped down into one hole and extracted through another providing hot water that can be added into the mains hot water supply.

Solar

Direct solar energy can be harnessed in several ways: solar panels, cells or furnaces. Solar panels are used in domestic situations to heat water. The panels are normally placed on the roof of the house facing in a southerly direction. It is estimated that solar panels on the roof of an average house could generate 50 per cent of the hot water demands for that household. The major drawback with this method is that the most solar energy is available in the summer when household demands are at their lowest.

Solar cells are also known as photovoltaic cells and they convert sunlight directly into electricity. They are very expensive and for this reason they are not used widely. However, they are used for satellites and spacecraft to provide power while in space. Solar furnaces make use of strong sunlight and concave mirrors to concentrate the rays. Extremely high temperatures can be reached at the focal point of the mirror and these can be used to heat water or even to cook with.

Nuclear

Uranium is used to produce heat energy in nuclear fission reactors. Uranium exists in various **isotopes** but uranium-235 is split in the reactor and produces heat energy that is in turn used to heat water to provide steam to drive turbines and generators. One kilogram of uranium can produce as much energy as one million kilograms of coal. The major problem, however, is that the waste produced from the reaction is very harmful and continues to be so for hundreds of years. Its disposal has caused major problems and this is why so many environmental groups oppose its use.

Fossil fuels

Coal

Coal is a fuel, which is burnt in power stations to generate steam to drive turbines and generators. It is also still burnt in some houses to provide heat and hot water. Coal has taken millions of years to form from the decomposition of plants and vegetation. As these dried out and eventually became covered by rock and sand, they became compressed to form a rock-like substance. With movement in the earth's surface the material became folded and buried deep underground. Extraction of coal often involves digging deep channels to gain access, but in other places around the world, coal is close to the surface and can be open-cast mined.

There are environmental implications associated with the mining and extraction of coal as well as with the burning of it as this causes acid rain because of the sulphur dioxide given off as a gas.

Oil

In a similar way to coal and gas, oil was formed millions of years ago in shallow water around land masses. The sea bed became littered with the dead remains of sea life and plants and these became covered with sand and rocks as the land mass was slowly eroded. As they became compacted, they decomposed to become oil and gas. Depending on the rock type, they either bubbled through porous rock or became trapped in large volumes under non-porous rock.

The oil wells were tapped by drilling into them and extracting the valuable material. The costs of extraction and further exploration are enormous but the financial rewards are huge for the companies involved in the exploration and extraction of oil.

The oil is pumped back to refineries on land where it is processed and split into petrol, paraffin, diesel and further cracked to produce a wider range of oils, plastics and fertilisers. The residue – bitumen – is used on roads and in some protective waterproof paints and sealants.

Some estimates predict that oil will run out within 20 years. This presents many problems in that cars will no longer be able to run on petrol and new ways will need to be found of producing many of the plastics that are derived from oil.

Gas

Gas is found along with oil trapped in pockets and requires little cleaning and processing before it is burnt in power stations or in homes for heating and hot water. As with oil, estimates predict that natural gas will run out in about 20–30 years.

Table 3.4.1 *Energy comparison table*

	Advantages	Disadvantages
Tidal	• free and available • occurs throughout the day on a regular basis	• could restrict passage of ships in rivers
Geothermal	• generates hot water free from underground sources	• restricted to certain global areas
Solar	• huge amounts of energy available • generates electricity via solar cells	• cost of solar cells • biggest demand in winter when heat from the sun is at its lowest
Nuclear	• small amount generates huge amount	• disposal of harmful waste materials
Coal	• relatively cheap and available	• emissions when burnt • running out • dangers when mining
Oil	• wide range of uses from by products	• emissions when burnt • price • running out
Gas	• efficient and effective method used in domestic environment	• running out • dangers from explosion

Tasks

1 Explain what you understand to be the difference between income and capital energy.

2 There is a theory among certain groups that income energies should be used in preference to capital sources. Why is this? Explain your answer with examples.

3 What are the implications of building large tidal barriers across rivers?

3. Levers and linkages

Levers

A **lever** can be defined as a rigid rod that pivots about a fixed axis called the fulcrum. Levers can be used to generate small output movements from large input movements as can be seen when using a screwdriver to prise open a tin of paint.

Conversely, small inputs can be used to generate large movements in output such as a toggle clamp. Levers are sometimes not so obvious in their use unlike crowbars and tyre levers. Bike brakes, door handles, scissors and nutcrackers are all forms of levers and they can be classified into three different groups or classes. Each class has the fulcrum, effort and load in a different position (see Figure 3.4.6).

Class 1 and 2 levers

In most situations you will find levers configured as Class 1 or 2 levers. This is simply because they provide a **mechanical advantage** (MA) that means you can move large loads by using just a small effort.

The mechanical advantage is easily calculated and is done simply by comparing the load with the effort.

Taking the example of the wheelbarrow shown in Figure 3.4.6b, with a load of 400N and effort of 100N, the mechanical advantage can easily be calculated as follows:

$$MA = \frac{Load}{Effort} = \frac{400}{100} = \frac{4}{1} \text{ or 4:1 or 4}$$

The mechanical advantage of any mechanism can be calculated in this way. The larger the number, the greater the mechanical advantage.

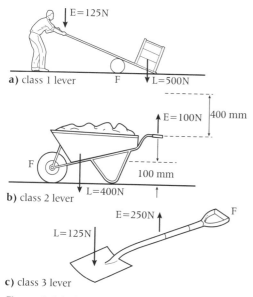

a) class 1 lever

b) class 2 lever

c) class 3 lever

Figure 3.4.6 *Classes of levers*

Task

Calculate the MA of a crowbar if the load is 500N and the effort is 125N.

Class 3 levers

Class 3 levers are not used in situations where large loads are involved because they have a mechanical advantage of less than 1. This can be demonstrated in Figure 3.4.6c where an effort of 250N is required to move a load of 125N:

$$MA = \frac{Load}{Effort} = \frac{125}{250} = \frac{1}{2} = 1:2 = 0.5$$

If you refer back to the example of the wheelbarrow in Figure 3.4.6b, it would appear that it is quite easy to move large loads with ease. This is not strictly the case. You are having to move the effort a far greater distance than the load. If you compare the two distances this gives the **velocity ratio (VR)**. Using the same example from Figure 3.4.6b:

$$VR = \frac{Distance\ moved\ by\ effort}{Distance\ moved\ by\ load} = \frac{400}{100} = \frac{4}{1} \text{ or 4:1.}$$

This shows that to move a load four times greater than the effort, you have to move the effort four times the distance.

Efficiency

The **efficiency** of a mechanism is a comparison of what you put in against what you get out. In reality, efficiency is never 100 per cent. Levers bend and belts rub and twist making them less efficient.

The efficiency of a mechanism can be calculated using the formula:

$$Efficiency = \frac{MA}{VR} \times 100\%.$$

For the example illustrated in Figure 3.4.7 where the MA = 3 and the VR = 4:

$$Efficiency = \frac{3}{4} \times 100\% = 75\%.$$

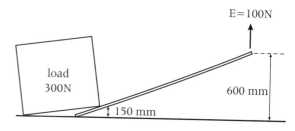

Figure 3.4.7 *Heavy box being lifted by a lever about a fulcrum*

Linkages

Linkages are often used to change the direction of motion within a component or system. The most basic form is the reverse motion linkage which reverses the input direction. By carefully considering the position of the fulcrum point, the output motion can be amplified by making the pivot point off-centre. Although this will effect the input and output force as well as the movement, the prime concern in any mechanism is the motion. If an output motion is required in the same direction as the input, an extra pivoted arm and linkage are required. This type of linkage is known as a push-pull linkage and it is pictured in Figure 3.4.8.

Linkages based on a parallelogram are used to move two or more parts together or to keep linkages parallel to each other as they move. The opposite sides of the linkage always stay parallel. This type of linkage is used on cantilever toolboxes, safety gates on lifts and on a pantograph drawing instrument that is used to enlarge or reduce drawings manually.

Bell cranks

The bell crank lever is a class 1 lever with the load and effort being at right angles to each other. The input motion is transmitted through 90 degrees to give an output motion which makes it ideal for getting motion around corners providing sufficient clearance is given for the rotating parts.

Toggles

Toggle clamps are used to obtain a large force to lock things into position. They are quick to operate and can be locked into position with one hand.

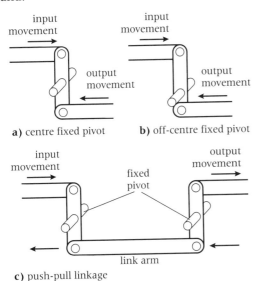

a) centre fixed pivot **b)** off-centre fixed pivot

c) push-pull linkage

Figure 3.4.8 Various linkages

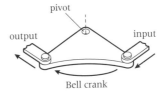

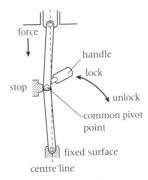

Toggle clamp in locked position

Figure 3.4.9 A bell crank and toggle clamp mechanism

They are used extensively in industry for holding and locking work in position while it is being worked upon. In schools/colleges they are used to hold work on the drilling machine and sheet plastic on the vacuum forming and blow moulding machines.

The toggle mechanism consists of two linkages both attached to a common pivot. One of the ends is connected to a fixed surface and the second lever is configured to move in a straight line only. With the application of an effort on the common pivot point, the toggle mechanism is pushed out until the levers lock when they are in a straight line or just over-centre and the clamping force is at its maximum. This toggle principle can be seen in Figure 3.4.9. An example of the use of toggle clamps is a child's collapsible buggy, where they fix the buggy in the open position and also keep the rain hood down.

Tasks

1 Identify and sketch at least ten household products that make use of the lever principles. Make a note of whether they are class 1, 2 or 3 levers and indicate the relative positions of the L, E and F.
2 A lemon juicer, uses a 50N force to squeeze juice from the lemon using only a 10N effort. The effort moves a distance of 80 mm and the load moves 20 mm. Calculate the mechanical advantage, the velocity ratio and efficiency.

4. Gear systems

A gear wheel is a basic mechanism that when coupled together with other gears can transmit rotary motion and force and change the direction of motion. Each gear has a shaft passing through its centre and the gear is fastened on to the shaft in one of several ways using:

- keys and keyways
- cotter pins
- splines
- grub screws.

When gears are brought together their teeth mesh and they closely interlock. Most gears are made with the contacting forces in the form of an involute curve (see Figure 3.4.10a). An involute is the locus of a point on a string as it is unwrapped from around a cylinder. This shape gives rise to the correct rolling action when the

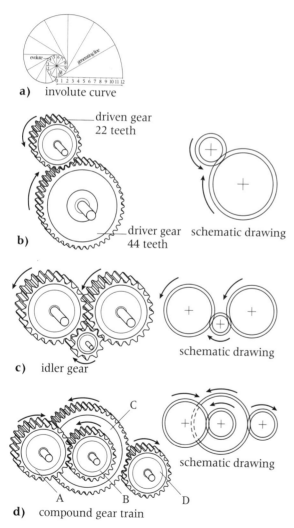

a) involute curve

b) driven gear 22 teeth · driver gear 44 teeth · schematic drawing

c) idler gear · schematic drawing

d) compound gear train · schematic drawing

Figure 3.4.10 *Gear forms and configurations*

teeth mesh and the path along which they mesh is known as the line of action. A number of gears fixed together on parallel shafts is termed a **gear train**.

Velocity ratio

The shafts will turn in opposite directions and if the gears are of different sizes, at different speeds. The difference in their relative speeds is known as the velocity ratio (VR). This is also sometimes known as the gear ratio and can be calculated by:

$$VR = \frac{\text{No. of teeth on driven gear}}{\text{No. of teeth on driver gear}}.$$

Using the example illustrated in Figure 3.4.10b, the velocity ratio is:

$$VR = \frac{22}{44} = \frac{1}{2} = 1:2.$$

This means that for every revolution of the driver, the driven rotates twice in the opposite direction. To get both to turn in the same direction however, a third gear needs to be introduced and this is known as the idler gear (see Figure 3.4.10c). The idler gear has no direct bearing on the overall velocity ratio of the gear train, it simply ensures that the driven and driver rotate in the same direction irrespective of its size.

We also need to consider the relative speed of the gears or the shaft velocities. It is quite easy to see that if two gears meshing each have 15 teeth, then in one revolution of the driver, 15 teeth will mesh with 15 teeth on the driven. If the driver gear rotates at 300 revolutions per minute (rpm), the driven must also rotate at 300 rpm.

If, however, we refer to Figure 3.4.10b again and the driver wheel is rotating at 400 rpm, the driven wheel must rotate at 800 rpm in the opposite direction since the teeth need to mesh in the ratio of 44/22 = 2:1, since one revolution of the driver needs two revolutions of the driven. From this example it can be seen that:

$$\frac{\text{Velocity of driven}}{\text{Velocity of driver}} = \frac{\text{No. of teeth on driver gear}}{\text{No. of teeth on driven gear}}.$$

If the driver gear is rotating at 400 rpm, then the driven gear must rotate at:

$$400 \times \frac{44}{22} \text{ rpm} = 400 \times 2 = 800 \text{ rpm}.$$

Although there is an increase in rotational velocity, there is, however, a decrease of rotational force which is known as torque.

Tasks

1 Driver gear A is rotating at 600 rpm with 15 teeth. It meshes with gear B with 60 teeth. What is:

   • the gear ratio
   • the velocity of shaft B?

2 Given the details as illustrated in Figure 3.4.10c, prove that the idler gear has no impact on the overall velocity ratio.

Compound gear trains

A compound gear train consists of several pairs of gears meshing together. Compound gear trains are used where large speed changes, either up or down, are required. In Figure 3.4.10d two pairs of gears are involved. To be able to work out the total velocity ratio, it is essential to know the velocity ratio of each pair.

In this example the two are:

VR1 = 3:1
VR2 = 8:1
Total VR = VR1 × VR2 = 3:1 × 8:1 = 24:1.

Tasks

In an identical configuration to the compound gear train shown in Figure 3.4.10d calculate:

1 the gear ratio, given the sizes of the gears in 2
2 the velocity ratio of gear A given that gear A has 40 teeth, gear B has 20 teeth, gear C has 60 teeth and gear D has 20 teeth. Driver gear D rotates at 360 rpm.

Bevel gears

It is sometimes necessary to transmit motion and forces through 90 degrees.

Bevel gears use shafts at 90 degrees to each other and therefore allow the rotary motion to be moved through a right angle (see Figure 3.4.11a). By using two gears of the same size and teeth number, there would be no reduction or increase in speed and the VR would remain the same. If, however, the meshing gears each have a different number of teeth then speed changes can be achieved as in the case of the hand drill. The driver wheel, known as the crown wheel, is the larger gear and the rotating shaft which holds the drill bit is a smaller gear. This means that the drill bit will rotate faster, therefore making drilling easier.

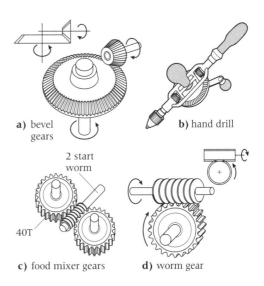

a) bevel gears **b)** hand drill

2 start worm

40T

c) food mixer gears **d)** worm gear

Figure 3.4.11 Bevel and worm gears

Worm gears

Another way of converting rotary motion through 90 degrees is with the use of a worm gear and it is also possible to make large reductions in speed using this method. The worm gear resembles a screw thread fixed to the driven shaft and is at right angles to the driver shaft and worm wheel (see Figure 3.4.11d). The worm gear itself should be considered as having one tooth only since it is wrapped around a cylinder and this is what gives rise to the large speed reductions.

Using the example illustrated in Figure 3.4.11d, the VR can be calculated in the same way for any gear system:

$$VR = \frac{\text{No. of teeth on driven}}{\text{No. of teeth on driver}} = \frac{40}{1} = 40 \text{ or } 40:1.$$

Worm gears are widely used in industry because they can be used to achieve large reductions in velocity in a relatively compact space. Worm gears are also used in a variety of household appliances. In a food mixer for example, where the two whisks mesh together in opposing directions, one worm gear is used between two spur gears as illustrated in Figure 3.4.11c. Here the velocity ratio is:

$$VR = \frac{50}{2} = 25:1.$$

Task

An electric motor is running at 1800 rpm and an output is required at 90 degrees to the motor shaft at 60 rpm. Sketch details of a gear system that could be used with an indication of the size of the gears to be used.

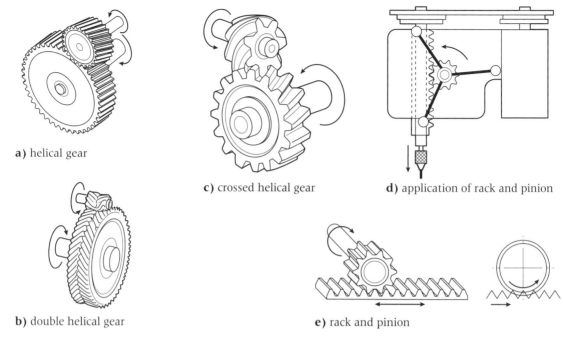

a) helical gear

c) crossed helical gear

d) application of rack and pinion

b) double helical gear

e) rack and pinion

Figure 3.4.12 Helical gears

Helical gears

The teeth on a helical gear are cut in the form of a helix on a cylindrical surface (see Figure 3.4.12a). Helical gears are quieter and more efficient than normal spur gears due to the gradual engagement of the teeth resulting from their shape. The overall effect results in a smoother transfer of load from tooth to tooth and it also allows more power to be transmitted with less noise.

Where large forces are transmitted, double helical gears are used as illustrated in Figure 3.4.12b. Two gears with opposite hand helices are mounted together on a shaft, sometimes with a small gap between. Similarly, the meshing gear is also a double helical gear. These gears are known as herring-bone gears. Helical gears are often used in gearboxes where smooth, quiet, efficient transfers are essential. Helical gears can also be used to change drive direction through 90 degrees by angling the teeth even more as shown in Figure 3.4.12c.

Rack and pinion systems

Rack and pinion systems are used to change rotary motion into linear motion or vice versa. This type of system is used on a pillar drilling machine to bring the drill down on to the work by rotating the hand wheel (see Figure 3.4.12d). The rack part of the system is a straight bar with teeth which mesh with the teeth on the pinion wheel. As the rack moves in a straight line the pinion rotates (see Figure 3.4.12e). As with the

profile of the teeth of a wheel being formed on an involute, if the rack teeth are of the same formation, they will be straight-sided.

Steering systems in cars are based on a rack and pinion with the track rods attached to each end of the steering rack and the pinion attached to the end of the steering column.

Tasks

1 Given the compound gear train shown below, calculate the velocity of shaft C where shaft A is rotating at 240 rpm.

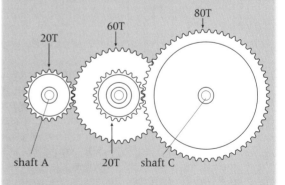

80T

60T

20T

shaft A

20T

shaft C

2 Dismantle an old electrical product such as a power drill or a food mixer. Carry out a careful analysis of the gear mechanisms inside looking at the specific types of gear and how they have been used.

5. Resistors

Resistors are the most commonly used components in electric circuits and they are used to control the amount of **current** flowing in a circuit. Resistors are classified by three factors:

- a resistance value in ohms (Ω)
- a tolerance
- power rating in watts.

Each of these factors must be considered when choosing a resistor for a particular situation.

As components, they obey Ohm's law, which means that the amount of current that passes through them is fixed by the **voltage** differential between their ends, and this can be represented by the formula:

$$R = \frac{V}{I}$$

where
V is voltage across the resistor
I is the current passing through it
R is the resistance of the resistor.

Consider the following situation as illustrated in Figure 3.4.13a.

A resistor with a value of 100Ω is connected between 5 volts (V) and 0 volts. To calculate the current flowing through it:

$$R = \frac{V}{I}$$

where
V = 5V
R = 100Ω.

Therefore $I = \frac{V}{R} = \frac{5}{100} = 0.05$ amps (A).

It is common practice to measure current in milliamps (mA) since essentially we only deal with very small currents. Therefore the resistor has a current of 50mA flowing through. Similarly, resistance values tend to be quoted in kilohms (kΩ) where 1 kilohm is 1000 ohms:

1000 ohms = 1kΩ
1/1000th amp = 1mA.

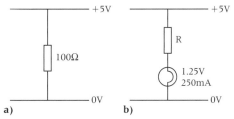

Figure 3.4.13 *Controlling current with resistors*

Resistors can also be used to control and restrict the amount of current flowing through a particular part of a circuit.

For example, Figure 3.4.13b shows a resistor in series with a bulb. The bulb is rated at 1.25V, 250mA. We need to calculate the value of resistor that will give us a current of 250mA.

The bulb requires 1.25V to operate, therefore the voltage across the resistor will be 5 – 1.25 = 3.75V. Using Ohm's law we can calculate the resistance:

$$R = \frac{V}{I}$$

where
V = 3.75
I = 250mA.

Therefore $R = \frac{3.75}{250} = 15\Omega$.

So a 15Ω resistor will restrict the current to 250mA. Unfortunately, resistors are not manufactured to precise values or indeed to every possible value. Preferred values are manufactured only and these fall into two different series: E12 and E24 – these lists can be found in any electronic components catalogue.

Tolerance bands

All resistors have a tolerance limit and this is denoted by a gold or silver band which can be found on one end of the resistor. If a 1kΩ resistor had a gold band on it, then the upper resistance value would be 1kΩ + 5 per cent (1050Ω) and the lower limit would be 1KΩ –5 per cent (950Ω):

- Gold band = +/–5 per cent.
- Silver band = +/–10 per cent.

Task

How much current would flow through a 33kΩ resistor if it were connected between a 5V supply and 0V?

Notice that by increasing the size of the resistor the current flowing through it has been reduced. The size of resistor is controlling the amount of current flowing between the supply voltage and zero volts.

Tasks

1 If you use a 27kΩ resistor, what is the greatest and least resistance it could have?
2 If the resistor value in Figure 3.4.13b was calculated to be 20Ω and you only had the E12 series of resistors available, what value resistor would you use, 18Ω or 22Ω? Justify your choice by calculation, stating what would happen to the bulb when the smaller resistor was used.

Power ratings

When a current passes through a resistor it heats up and since this cannot be avoided, great care must be taken to ensure that the correct power rating of a resistor is used to get rid of the heat without taking up too much space.

The amount of heat generated in a resistor is calculated by:

$$W = VI$$

where

W is the heat generated per second measured in milliwatts (mW)

V is the voltage dropped across the resistor measured in volts (V) and

I is the current which goes through it measured in milliamps (mA).

Again, consider the example in Figure 3.4.13b; the amount of heat generated through the resistor would be:

$$W = VI$$
$$= 3.75 \times 250\text{mA}$$
$$= 938\text{mW}.$$

Resistors are supplied in the following power ratings: 250mW, 500mW, 1000mW and 2000mW.

In the example above, if a 250mW resistor was used, it would soon overheat and burn out; conversely a 2000mW resistor would be too bulky and expensive. For this example a 1000mW would be ideal although it would still get a little warm.

Variable resistors (rheostats)

A resistor has a fixed resistance but a variable resistor can be made from a **potentiometer**. The potentiometer can be used in two different configurations. It can be used as a rheostat to control the current in a circuit as shown in Figure 3.4.14a. In this situation, only two of the three contacts are needed, the wiper and one end. The rotating wiper increases or decreases the resistance and subsequently varies the current.

The potentiometer can also be used to act as a **potential divider** to obtain any voltage from the maximum supply voltage down to zero volts. In this case all three tags are used with the outside two being connected to the supply rails.

Variable resistors are used as controls in radios for volume and tuning. They are available in either rotary or linear track and the smaller values are made with carbon tracks and the larger values from wire wound tracks. A smaller version, presets, is available and needs to be adjusted with a small screwdriver.

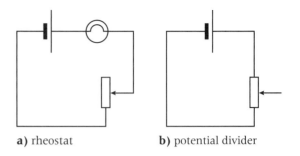

a) rheostat   **b)** potential divider

Figure 3.4.14 *Variable resistor set as a rheostat and a potential divider*

Colour coding

Resistance values range from single figure values up to tens of millions of ohms. Their value can be identified by the series of coloured rings running around their body. The most common type of resistor is likely to have four coloured rings on it as shown in Figure 3.4.15.

To identify the value of a resistor it should be viewed with the tolerance band on the right. The first two bands represent a number between 10 and 99 in accordance with the colours below, and the third band represents the number of zeros which need to be put on the end of the number to get the final resistance value. For example, a resistor whose bands are blue, grey, red and silver would have the value of 6.8kΩ: blue and grey giving the number 68 and red, two zeros, making the total 6800Ω or 6.8kΩ with a tolerance of +/–10 per cent.

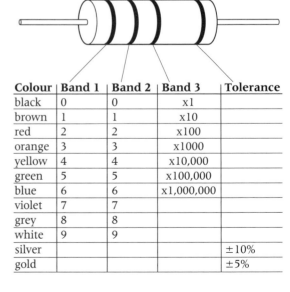

Colour	Band 1	Band 2	Band 3	Tolerance
black	0	0	x1	
brown	1	1	x10	
red	2	2	x100	
orange	3	3	x1000	
yellow	4	4	x10,000	
green	5	5	x100,000	
blue	6	6	x1,000,000	
violet	7	7		
grey	8	8		
white	9	9		
silver				±10%
gold				±5%

Figure 3.4.15 *Resistor colour code*

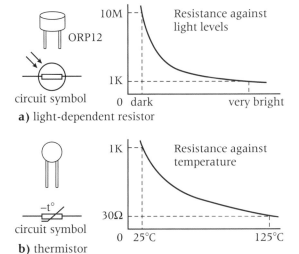

Figure 3.4.16 *Light-dependent resistor and thermistor*

Resistors also exist in a number of other forms. The two most common forms are the **light-dependent resistor (LDR)** and **thermistor** (see Figure 3.4.16).

Light-dependent resistor

Cadmium sulphate is a semiconductor transducer whose resistance decreases as the light intensity falling on it increases. This occurs as a result of the light energy setting free electrons from the atoms within the semiconductor material which increases its conductivity, hence reducing its resistance.

The most popular form of LDR is the ORP12 which has a cadmium sulphate cell mounted inside a clear resin block with two soldering leads. Like the majority of resistors it is a non-polarised device and therefore it does not matter which way around it is attached in the circuit.

In total darkness the LDR has a resistance of about 10MΩ but when exposed to a bright light its resistance falls to about 1kΩ.

Point to remember

Dark – high resistance, approximately 10MΩ.
Bright light – low resistance, approximately 1kΩ.

In practical applications LDRs are used in light-sensing circuits such as street lamps or external house lights turning on at a certain level of light intensity. In order to achieve this degree of sensitivity, the LDRs are placed into a potential divider to generate outputs that can be monitored and acted upon. Potential dividers are dealt with on the next page.

Thermistors

A thermistor or thermal resistor is also a semiconductor transducer whose resistance changes rapidly when its temperature changes. Generally, most thermistors are negative temperature coefficient (ntc) and as they get hotter their resistance decreases. This type of thermistor is normally made from oxides of nickel and copper. They are extensively used for temperature measurement and control being heated either externally via the environment in which they are placed, or by the amount of current flowing through them. As the resistance changes, the current and voltage through them changes and again when fixed in a potential divider they provide significant voltage swings which can be further processed.

With positive temperature coefficient (ptc) the resistance increases as the temperature increases. This type of thermistor is based on barium titanate. It is used as a sensor to prevent damage in a circuit which may be exposed to a large temperature rise such as an overloaded electric motor. The working characteristics vary from type to type although suppliers state the resistance of the thermistor at two known temperatures. It is a good idea to set up a small practical experiment to record resistance and temperature and to plot a graph of resistance against temperature like the one in Figure 3.4.16b. Values can then be taken off at certain temperatures and voltage and current levels calculated.

Tasks

1 a) Set up an experiment to measure the resistance of an ntc thermistor at a range of temperatures between 100°C and 0°C.

   b) Plot a graph of your results similar to the one in Figure 3.4.16b.

2 If the thermistor was connected to a 9v supply, calculate the current flowing through it at:

   a) 0°C
   b) 50°C
   c) 100°C.

6. Potential divider

Resistors have many uses and as well as controlling current they can be used to control the voltage at a point in a circuit. In order to do this, two resistors need to be connected in series and this allows us by using different valued resistors to divide the potential at the supply rails into a smaller voltage. Before you can consider how the voltage is split you need to know how resistors behave when connected in series (see Figure 3.4.17).

The value of the voltage at V_{out} depends upon the ratio of R1 to R2 in the voltage divider. Obviously, if R1 = R2, then you would expect the voltage at V_{out} to be half of the supply voltage. If, however, the values are not equal, then the voltage output will be between the supply voltage and zero volts. When two resistors are connected in series, as shown in Figure 3.4.17, the total resistance is given by:

Rs = R1 + R2.

Therefore, if R1 = 2.2kΩ and R2 = 3.3kΩ
Rs = 2.2kΩ + 3.3kΩ = 5.5kΩ.

This now enables us to calculate the current flowing through the resistors, and since V = IR:

I = V/R = 5/5.5kΩ = 0.91mA.

Using this, we can now work out the voltage dropped across R1 since we know the resistance value and the current flowing through it:

$$V = IR = 0.91mA \times 2.2kΩ$$
$$= 2.0V$$

If 2.0 volts are dropped across R1 the output at V_{out} must be:

$$V_{out} = V_s - \text{voltage drop across R1}$$
$$= 5 - 2 = 3V.$$

This means that in this very simple circuit, we have been able to divide the supply potential in

the ratio of R1:R2 which in this case is 2.2:3.3 or 2:3, and since R1 is the smaller resistance, less voltage is dropped across it. To prove that we end up at zero volts on the bottom supply rail we can calculate the voltage drop across R2:

$$V = IR = 0.91mA \times 3.3kΩ$$
$$= 3V.$$

Since we now have 3 volts at V_{out} and 3 volts are dropped across R2, we end up at zero volts.

In a similar fashion, a voltage of 4 volts is required at V_{out}, given a voltage supply of 9 volts. We can calculate values of resistors that will give us V_{out} given a current of 2mA:

$$R_s = V/I = 9/2mA = 4.5kΩ$$

If 2 volts are required at V_{out}, then the voltage drop across R1 will be:

V across R1 = $V_s - V_{out}$ = 9 − 2 = 7V.

Given a current of 2mA across R1:

$$R1 = \frac{V}{I} = \frac{7}{2} = 3.5kΩ.$$

Since R_s = R1 + R2
R2 = R_s − R1 = 4.5kΩ − 3.5kΩ.
Therefore R_s = 1kΩ.

Since it is not possible to buy a 3.5kΩ resistor, a 3.3kΩ is the nearest preferred value and we therefore arrive at:

R1 = 1kΩ and R2 = 3.3kΩ.

Task
Given the values of R1 and R2 in the table below, calculate for each set of values:

a) total resistance in series
b) the current flowing through the arrangement
c) the voltage at V_{out} given a supply voltage of +9V.

R1	R2
2.2kΩ	2.2kΩ
10kΩ	4.7kΩ
4.7kΩ	2.2kΩ
6.8kΩ	820Ω
10MΩ	10kΩ
10k Ω	33Ω

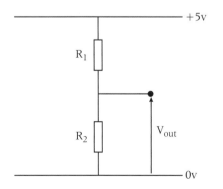

Figure 3.4.17 *Two resistors connected in series*

Adjustable sensing inputs

Adjustable sensing inputs can be made by using LDRs and thermistors in potential dividers. As their resistance fluctuates depending on either changing temperatures or light levels, when connected into potential dividers, V_{out} will also change:

- In Figure 3.4.18a where an LDR is in series with a 10kΩ resistor in bright daylight, the LDR will have a low resistance in the order of

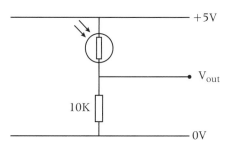

a) light-sensing potential divider

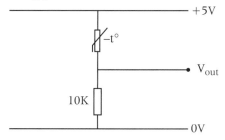

b) temperature-sensing potential divider

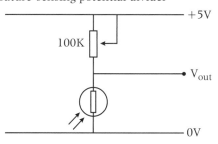

c) light-sensing potential divider

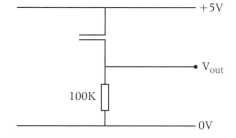

d) moisture-sensing potential divider

Figure 3.4.18 Potential dividers

1kΩ. This means that only a small voltage drop will occur across the LDR since R2 is about ten times greater than R1, the LDR. Therefore about 1/10th of V_s will be dropped across the LDR, making V_{out} approximately 9/10th of V_s, about 4.5 volts. As the light intensity falls to being very dark, the resistance of the LDR rises to about 10MΩ and the ratio between R1 and R2 about 1000:1 which means that the whole of the voltage supply will be dropped across the LDR and V_{out} will be zero volts. In this configuration then, a voltage swing of 4.5 volts can be achieved at V_{out}.

- Similarly, in Figure 3.4.18b where a thermistor is used in place of an LDR, voltage swings at V_{out} can be achieved as a result of changes in temperature. In Figure 3.4.18c the LDR has been moved into the position of R2 and a variable resistor has replaced the fixed resistor. In this example, when in bright light, V_{out} is at approximately 0.05 volts and when in the dark, V_{out} is approximately 4.95 volts. This voltage that occurs as a result of covering the LDR is sufficient to cause a transistor to turn on a bulb (this will be examined later in the unit).

- The significance of using a variable resistor in place of a fixed resistor is that the system could be used in varying light levels and the variable resistor can change the sensitivity of the system or the balance of the system in terms of the output voltage.

- The circuit in Figure 3.4.18d can be used to detect water or moisture in soil or damp walls. The contacts are simply a pair of stiff prongs made from metal and held fairly close together. In air, the resistance is large and so V_{out} is low. Once the contacts are placed in water their resistance falls to well below 100 kΩ and so V_{out} gets pulled up to about +5V.

Task

Given the circuit diagram in Figure 3.4.18b, and the data below concerning the thermistor, calculate V_{out} at both temperatures.

Temperature	Resistance
0°C	1kΩ
100°C	30Ω

7. Diodes

A **diode** is an electronic device that allows current to flow easily in one direction but not in the other(see Figure 3.4.19a). A diode has two leads, an anode and a cathode. The cathode can be identified by a band at one end and it is at this end where the current leaves the diode when forward biased. Forward bias is the conventional way in which a diode is used, i.e. to allow a current to flow through it from anode to cathode. Diodes are available in different formats and made from a variety of materials such as silicon and germanium. Diodes are put to many uses in electronics and some of them are listed below:

- light-emitting diodes
- zeneer diodes (voltage regulators)
- protective devices
- rectification of devices.

Light-emitting diodes

Light emitting diodes (LEDs) are output transducers which emit light when current passes through them (see Figure 3.4.19b). They are made from different types of crystal that are encapsulated in translucent plastic. In comparison to conventional bulbs they last much longer and require less current in operation, and so they do not get hot.

An LED operates in the same way as all diodes and only lets current pass through it in one direction, from the anode to the cathode. When looking at an LED the cathode can be identified as the short lead or by the flat edge on the circumference of the LED rim. LEDs need about 2 volts in order to emit light and therefore a protective resistor should always be connected in series with them.

Figure 3.4.19c clearly demonstrates that once 2 volts have been exceeded the current rises rapidly causing the LED to emit light. It should also be noted that LEDs will not survive if the current exceeds 50mA or a reverse bias voltage of more than 5V is applied. A reverse bias voltage means that you try to make a current flow from the cathode to the anode. Although no current will flow through it, the LED will break down at around 5V.

A suitable value resistor must be connected to protect the LED, as we have already discussed, but how large should the resistor be? Given the circuit diagram in Figure 3.4.19d where the voltage supply is 5 volts and the LED is rated at 2 volts, 5mA we can calculate the value of the resistor needed.

Using $R = \dfrac{V}{I}$

where
V = 5 − 2 = 3V
I = 5mA

$$R = \frac{3}{5mA} = 600\Omega.$$

The nearest preferred value is 560Ω. Although this is below the calculated value, it means the current flowing through the LED would be a little higher than the rated 5mA but not sufficient enough to cause any damage. It is also worth considering the power rating at this stage:

W = VI

where
V = 3 volts
I = 5mA
W = 3 × 5mA = 15mW

and therefore a 250mW rated resistor could be used.

Task
Calculate what value resistor should be used to protect an LED rated at 2V, 10mA running from a 12-volt supply.

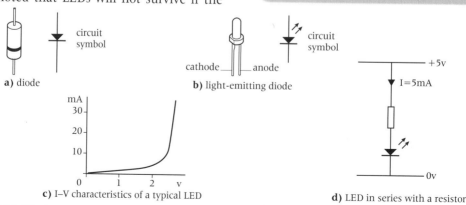

a) diode

cathode — anode

b) light-emitting diode

circuit symbol

circuit symbol

+5v
I=5mA

0v

c) I–V characteristics of a typical LED

d) LED in series with a resistor

Figure 3.4.19 *Diodes*

Protection devices

Diodes are used in some circuits as protective devices and they are always used where relays appear. A relay contains an electromagnet and when turned off, a large voltage known as a back **electromotive force (emf)** is produced. The changing magnetic field induces a voltage in the coil and this causes a current to flow backwards. The faster the relay is switched on and off and the magnetic field changes, the larger the back emf generated across the ends of the coil in the relay. This back emf can cause damage to transistors in circuits and therefore whenever a relay is used, a diode is placed across the coil of the relay. The diode allows the back emf, which is in the opposite direction to the battery voltage, to pass through it rather than to pass through and damage any transistors (see Figure 3.4.20).

Rectification using diodes

There are two stages needed to convert an AC signal into a DC one. They are **rectification** and smoothing. We shall only consider the rectification part here and this process can be achieved by using diodes.

There are two types of rectification:

- half wave
- full wave.

Half wave rectifier

A half wave rectifier is essentially a voltage divider that contains a diode and a resistor as shown in Figure 3.4.21a. When the input is positive the diode will be forward biased, therefore having a low resistance, which means that V_{out} will be virtually the same as V_{in}. Conversely when V_{in} is negative, the diode will be reversed biased, therefore having a large resistance making V_{out} zero volts since it will be

pulled up by the resistor R. The result of this action gives an output whose wave formation is half of that of the input, hence the term half wave rectification. In order to make use of this output, it needs to be smoothed so that the level of V_{out} remains more constant. This is achieved by putting a **capacitor** across the output terminals as shown in Figure 3.4.21b. The action of the capacitor being charged and discharged has smoothed V_{out} to make it more constant although there is still a degree of ripple.

Full wave rectifier

In full wave rectification four diodes are configured as shown in Figure 3.4.21d. When the input voltage is positive a current takes the path of A, D_2, R_L, D_3, B and when negative, B, D_4, R_L, D_1, A giving a full wave output. Again, it needs to be smoothed with a capacitor across the output as in Figure 3.4.21b. In the case of full wave rectification the capacitor is charged twice as often as in half wave rectification and therefore there is even less ripple from full wave rectification.

This is a popular method of converting an alternating current into a direct current and it is made all the cheaper by buying the four diodes already configured in one package known as a bridge rectifier.

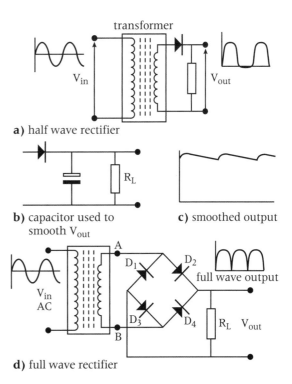

a) half wave rectifier

b) capacitor used to smooth V_{out}

c) smoothed output

d) full wave rectifier

Fig 3.4.21 Half and full wave rectifiers

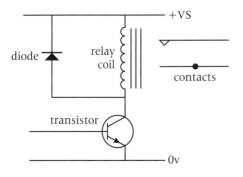

Figure 3.4.20 Diode used to protect a transistor driving a relay

8. Capacitors

A capacitor can be used to store an electric charge in a circuit. The larger the capacitor used, the larger the charge it can store.

Essentially, a capacitor consists of two metal plates with an insulating material between them which is a dielectric material. Different types of material can be used as the insulating material such as paper, ceramics, polyester, mica and polystyrene.

As the two leads of a capacitor are connected to a battery the capacitor starts to store a charge. The voltage across the capacitor creates a surplus of electrons on one plate and a deficiency on the other. The collection of electrons on the one side gives that plate a negative charge while the deficient plate has a positive charge. This process is said to be the charging process and the capacitor becomes fully charged when the voltage across the plates is the same as the supply voltage.

Capacitance

This charge-storing ability is termed its capacitance (C). Capacitance is measured in farads (F) but 1 farad is a large unit of capacitance and it is more common to use microfarads (μF) which are 1/1000000th of a farad. There are also smaller units of capacitance:

- Microfarad = 1×10^{-6} farads.
- Nanofarad = 1×10^{-9} farads.
- Picofarad = 1×10^{-12} farads.

Once fully charged the capacitor stays charged until it is discharged or the voltage leaks and the level of charge returns to its initial state.

The amount of charge that a capacitor can hold, C, can be calculated by:

$$C = \frac{Q}{V}$$

where
Q = change in coulombs (C)
C = capacitance in farads (F)
V = voltage in volts (V).

Working voltage

Capacitors are classified by two factors: their capacitance and working voltage. The working voltage is the maximum voltage that can be connected across it. If this voltage is exceeded, the capacitor will break down. It is quite usual for even small capacitors to have high working voltages of up to 250V. Small capacitors would be regarded as 1.0μF and below and these are generally non-polarised in that they can be connected into a circuit any way around. As the value of the capacitor increases above 1.0μF it is normal to use electrolytic capacitors and these are shaped in a tube or can.

Electrolytic capacitors

Electrolytic capacitors are polarised and therefore they must be inserted and connected into the circuit in the correct orientation (see Figure 3.4.22). They work in this fashion because an oxide is formed by electrolytic action when in use.

The positive terminal of the capacitor must be inserted towards the positive terminal of the battery in the circuit and capacitors are marked with a positive sign (+ve) at the necked end of the casing. The circuit diagram for an electrolytic capacitor is also marked with a positive (+ve) and can also be identified by an open bar on the symbol.

Tasks

1 Put the following capacitors in descending order (largest to smallest):
   10nF, 10μF, 10pF, 100μF, 100pF.
2 A 10V supply is used to charge a 1μF capacitor. How much charge can it store?
3 A charge Q is needed for 0.56C from a 12V supply. What value capacitor should be used?

Example

How much charge can be stored on a 1000μf capacitor if it is charged up by a 9-volt battery?

Using $C = \dfrac{Q}{V}$

$Q = CV$
$\quad = 1000\mu f \times 9$
$\quad = 0.009C.$

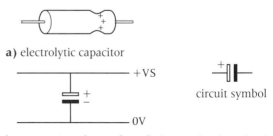

a) electrolytic capacitor

b) connections for an electrolytic capacitor in a circuit

Figure 3.4.22 *The capacitor*

Capacitor/resistor networks

Many systems and products make use of time delays or timed sequences in a control process. A timing device may be used to keep lights on for a certain period of time while, for example, you get from the garage into the house. They may also be used in the kitchen to alert you that a certain cooking time has elapsed.

A very simple way to create a **time delay circuit** is to connect a resistor and capacitor together in series. When a capacitor is charging up the voltage rises to a maximum of the supply voltage V_S. The time taken for the capacitor to charge to two-thirds of the maximum voltage is called the time constant. When a capacitor and resistor are connected together in series the product of the two gives us the time constant:

$$t = CR$$

where
t is time in seconds (S)
C is capacitance in farads (F)
R is resistance in ohms (Ω).

In this combination it takes about five time constants for the capacitor to reach the supply voltage (see Figure 3.4.23) .

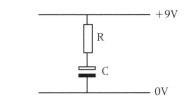

a) RC network

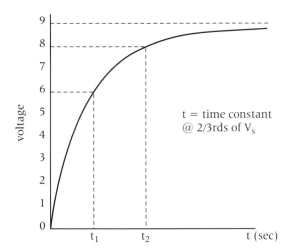

b) voltage against time

Figure 3.4.23 *Resistor/capacitor network*

Example 1

Given the basic circuit in Figure 3.4.23a, where R = 100kΩ and C = 100μF, calculate the time constant.

Time constant t = CR
$$= 100\mu F \times 100k\Omega$$
$$= 10 \text{ seconds.}$$

Example 2

With the same circuit set up as in Figure 3.4.23a, calculate the value of resistor needed to give a time constant of one second given a capacitor of 1000μF.

If t = CR, then R $= \dfrac{t}{C}$

$$= \dfrac{1}{1000\mu F}$$

$$= 1k\Omega.$$

If the fixed resistor was replaced with a variable resistor, then it could be adjusted to give a variety of time delays and if calibrated it can easily be used to give a fixed incremental range of time delays.

Tasks

1 If a 100μF capacitor was used in series with a 1MΩ variable resistor, how long will it be before it reaches its time constant in minutes?
2 Construct a circuit on breadboard or veroboard similar to that in Figure 3.4.23a with a 9-volt supply. Use a resistor of 1MΩ and a capacitor of 100μF. Make sure that you connect up the capacitor the correct way around with the positive (+ve) terminal towards the positive supply rail. Connect a voltmeter across the capacitor, turn on the power supply and record the voltage every five seconds in a table similar to the one below for at least six minutes:

Time (secs)	Voltage (V)
5	
10	

Plot a graph of time against voltage and mark on it the time constant, the time it takes to reach two-thirds of the supply voltage, i.e. 6 volts. Compare the actual time taken to reach the time constant with the calculated value and explain your findings.

9. Transistors

Silicon as a material is a semi-conductor and depending upon how it is used, it can be an insulator or a conductor. Without such a material microelectronics would not exist since there would be no **transistors** or integrated circuits (ICs) that may contain many thousands of tiny slices of silicon.

A transistor is a three-terminal device which may be used either as an electronic switch or as an amplifier. Whereas non-amplifying components such as resistors, capacitors and diodes are said to be 'passive' components, transistors are 'active' components. There are hundreds of different types of transistors available either as discrete components or in ICs. Each has its own identification code and performance specification. Some of the more common types of transistor are listed in Table 3.4.1.

Table 3.4.1 Common types of transistor

Type	Gain	IC maximum
BC108	200–800	100mA
BFY51	40	1A
ZTX300	50–300	500mA
2N3055	20–70	15A

There are two basic types of transistor:
- the bipolar or junction transistor
- the unipolar or field effect transistor (FET).

Here we only consider the first type since FETs are covered in Unit 4 Section B Option 3.

The bipolar or junction transistor

The three terminals on the transistor are base, emitter and collector and it is essential that each leg is connected to the correct section in the circuit (see Figure 3.4.24).

The base of the transistor must always be connected via a protective resistor to the main circuit. If too much current is allowed to flow into the transistor it will be damaged and burn out. The base of the transistor is the pin which basically senses any change or increase in voltage from the other parts of the circuit. It only takes a small voltage in the order of 0.6 volts to switch the transistor on and this voltage is known as the threshold voltage and it is the point at which the transistor becomes a conductor rather than an insulator.

It is crucial that any transistor chosen must have suitable properties for the specific application in respect of gain and power.

Transistor gain

Transistors can be used as electrical switches but they can also be used as amplifiers. In Figure 3.4.24b the current flowing into the base of the transistor I_B is smaller than the current flowing from the collector to the emitter, I_C.

The gain of a transistor is derived from the ratio of I_C to I_B and it varies significantly from type to type. The gain of a BC108 varies from 200 to 800 and it is not very precise since it is a cheap transistor. In contrast, a BFY51 is a little more expensive but has a much more accurate gain band.

In this instance where a small current is used to turn on a large current we say that the input signal has been amplified and has become a large output current.

In summary then, we can say that until the base-emitter junction is forward biased by about 0.6V for a silicon-based transistor, a small base current I_B flows and turns on a larger current I_C. This amplification factor can be defined by:

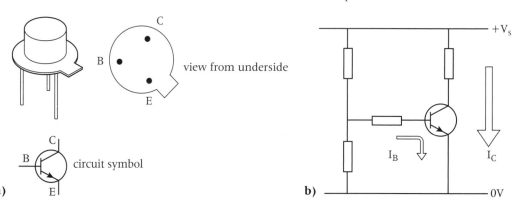

Figure 3.4.24 The transistor

$$h_{FE} = \frac{I_C}{I_B}.$$

It should also be noted that:

$$I_E = I_B + I_C.$$

The gain is normally calculated when a transistor is saturated which means that the collector has the same voltage as the emitter.

Example

Calculate the gain of a transistor given that I_B = 0.05mA and I_C = 4.95mA and calculate I_E.

$$\text{Gain} = \frac{I_C}{I_B} = \frac{4.95\text{mA}}{0.05\text{mA}} = 99$$

$$I_E = I_B + I_C = 4.95\text{mA} + 0.05\text{mA}$$

$$I_E = 5.0\text{mA}$$

Transistor power

In choosing a transistor very careful consideration also needs to be given to the power of the transistor and this is obviously linked to the maximum current that I_C can take. Again, this data is supplied for each type of transistor in a manufacturer's guidebook. Ultimately, the choice comes down to a degree of compromise between the gain and I_{CMAX}.

Example

The transistor in Figure 3.4.25 is fully saturated.

1 What is the value of V_{out}?
2 Calculate the current through R_L.
3 If the gain is 100 calculate I_B.
4 What is the voltage drop across R_B?
5 How big should V_{in} be?

Answers:
a) If the transistor is saturated, V_{out} = 0 volts.
b) Since V = IR, $I = \frac{V}{R} = \frac{5}{2.5\text{k}\Omega}$
   Therefore I = 2mA.
c) Gain $= \frac{I_C}{I_B}$. Therefore $I_B = \frac{I_C}{\text{gain}}$.

   $$I_B = \frac{2\text{mA}}{100} = 0.02\text{mA}$$
d) Since V = IR, V = 0.02mA × 100kΩ
   V = 2 volts
e) As V_{BE} must be 0.6 volts to turn on
   V_{IN} = 2 + 0.6 = 2.06 volts

Designing with transistors

By linking together some basic building blocks such as inputs using LDR and thermistors, and a control element using a transistor and outputs such as bulbs, buzzers, motors and LEDs, we can create some useful sensing circuits such as those illustrated in Figure 3.4.26. You should now be able to understand how they work and follow the events through.

Tasks

1 Describe in detail what each of the two circuits in Figure 3.4.26 do and how they work.
2 Given the diagram in Figure 3.4.25 calculate:
   a) the value of R_L if the current is 10mA
   b) I_B if the gain is 150
   c) the voltage drop across R_B if it is valued at 22kΩ.

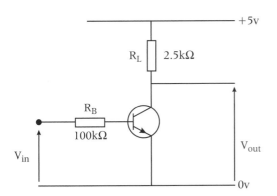

Figure 3.4.25 *Example of a transistor*

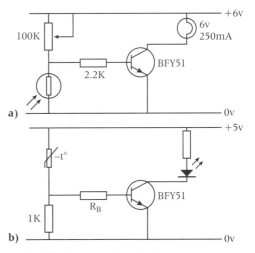

Figure 3.4.26 *Two sensing circuits*

10. Relays

A **relay** contains an electromagnet that can be used to separate two circuits (see Figure 3.4.27). The control part of the circuit such as a transistor is used to energise the coil within the relay and switches the contacts that are electronically isolated from the coil to complete a secondary circuit.

Relays are used to create a secondary circuit where the output required needs either its own supply voltage that may be different from that of the primary sensing circuit, or where the current required is too big for the transistor to handle.

There are many different types of relay available and they are rated according to:

- coil voltage
- coil resistance.

When the control current flows through the coil, a soft iron core becomes magnetised and attracts a soft iron armature. As the armature rocks on its pivot it either opens or closes and the electrical contacts are opened or closed. This action can be clearly seen in the cross-sectioned view of the relay in Figure 3.4.27c.

The current required to operate a relay is called the pull in current and the drop out current is that when the relay just stops working.

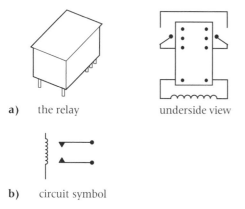

a)   the relay   underside view

b)   circuit symbol

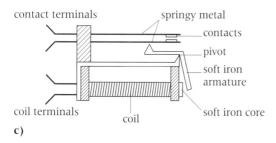

c)

Figure 3.4.27 *The relay*

Example

A relay is rated at an operating voltage of 12V with a coil resistance of 285Ω. Calculate the pull in current.

Since $V = IR$, $I = \dfrac{V}{R}$

$= \dfrac{12}{285}$

$I = 42\text{mA}.$

It is therefore now possible to calculate values for resistors to be used in the control part of the circuit to protect the relay and the transistor from being damaged. As already discussed in the section on diodes, when the relay is de-energised a voltage in the region of up to 200 volts can be generated as a back emf across the relay and through the transistor. It is always necessary therefore to put a diode across the coil connections.

Relays are also made with different numbers of contact switches. Single and double pole relays mean that one or more separate circuits can be controlled. Double pole switched relays can also be made to latch (stay on) once the initial coil current has dropped out.

Relays can also be obtained in either a normally closed (NC) or normally open (NO) state. Once the coil current is pulled in the state of the relay contacts are reversed.

Task

You have been approached to design a circuit that will turn on a fan whenever the temperature rises above a certain level. The fan is rated at 24V, 500mA.

1 Draw a circuit diagram of your system.
2 Describe how the system will work.

11. Circuit testing

A **multimeter** is an essential tool in every electrician's tool box and it is a vital piece of equipment for use in electronics work in school/college. A modern digital multimeter will test and measure:

- current
- voltage, both AC and DC
- resistance
- continuity.

Current

The movement of electrons through a conductor is an electric current and it can be measured with a multimeter. Since current flows through all components in a circuit, it is essential that the current is measured in series which means having to make a break in the circuit. The positive terminal from the meter must be connected to the positive side or terminal of the supply. The correct way to measure the current is illustrated in Figure 3.4.28a.

Voltage

The potential difference of a circuit or of points around a circuit is measured in volts. To measure the potential difference, whether it be AC or DC, the meter should be connected in parallel with the component or spot and the correct procedure is illustrated in Fig 3.4.28b. It is necessary depending upon the exact type of multimeter being used that either DC or AC is selected as a function when measuring voltage. The reading that is obtained when measuring a voltage is the difference between those two points at which the reading was taken.

Resistance

Resistance can also be measured using a multimeter but when measuring any component's resistance it is essential that it be disconnected from any part of the circuit. If this is not the case, then the circuit generally will affect the reading indicated.

Normally, the component will simply be held against or between the two leads and a measurement taken (see Figure 3.4.28c).

Continuity testing

A continuity test will simply indicate via an audible warning device whether there is a break in a wire, track or fuse. The multimeter contains a battery and when switched into this mode, it passes a small current between the two contacts. If, for example, you want to determine whether a fuse has blown or not, once isolated from the plug, a continuity test can be used. If the fuse has blown, then the current will not be able to complete the circuit and the audible alarm will not sound. However, if it is intact, the circuit will be complete and the device will sound.

Whether using an analogue or digital multimeter it is essential that the correct selections are made for the required function. The test leads should be inserted into the correct positions marked with (+) positive, (–) negative or com. (common) and VΩ for resistance. Every meter is different and so you must make yourself familiar with the type that you have available in your school/college.

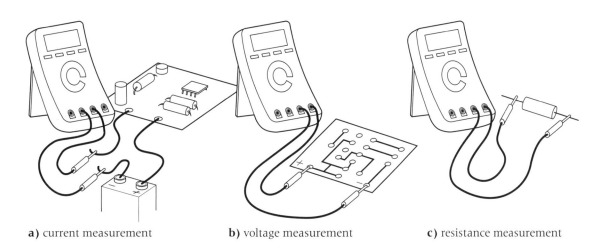

a) current measurement   **b)** voltage measurement   **c)** resistance measurement

Figure 3.4.28 *The multimeter*

Exam preparation

You will need to revise all the topics in this unit, so that you can apply your knowledge and understanding to the exam questions. In preparation for your exam, it is a good idea to make brief notes about different topics, such as 'Gear Systems'. Use subheadings, bullet point lists, sketches and diagrams where appropriate. A single side of A4 should be used for each of the headings from the Specification.

It is very important to learn exam skills. You should also have weekly practice in learning technical terms and formulae and in answering exam-type questions. When you need to answer any questions you should:

- read the question carefully and pick out the key points that need answering
- always show your working in calculations so you can gain marks for applying formulae, even if your final answer is incorrect
- match your answer to the marks available, e.g., for two marks you should give two good points that address the question
- always give examples and justify statements with reasons, saying how or why the statement is true.

Practice exam questions

1 Energy falls into two categories, income and capital. Explain briefly how energy is derived from:
a) oil
b) coal
c) solar system
d) waves
e) geothermal. (15)

2 a) Illustrate using appropriate sketches and examples a class 1, 2, and 3 lever. (6)
b) A class 1 lever is used with an effort of 250N to move a load of 750N. Calculate the mechanical advantage. (3)
c) The lever has to move a distance of 500 mm to lift the load 100 mm. What is the velocity ratio? (3)
d) Calculate the overall efficiency of the mechanism. (3)

3 A driven gear A has 15 teeth that mesh with a second gear B that has 60 teeth. On the same shaft as gear B, another gear C has 10 teeth. This meshes with gear D that has 50 teeth. Calculate:
a) the total gear ratio (9)
b) the overall rpm if the driven gear A rotates at 1200 rpm. (6)

4 a) Sketch a characteristic graph of light levels against resistance for an LDR. (5)
b) Given the circuit diagram below and that in very bright light the LDR has a resistance of about 1MΩ, calculate:
i) the current flowing through both resistors (5)
ii) the voltage at V_{out}. (5)

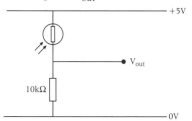

5 A capacitor rated at 12v, 470nF is charged from a 9V supply.
a) State how much charge can be stored in the capacitor. (3)
b) The capacitor is now connected in series with a 560kΩ resistor. Calculate the time constant (t) for this circuit. (3)
c) Sketch a graph of time against voltage for this circuit with appropriate indicators on the axis. (5)
d) It was decided that the time constant needed to be variable. Explain how this could be achieved and draw a suitable circuit diagram. (4)

Part 3

UNIT 4A Materials, components and systems (R401)

Summary of expectations

1. What to expect
Unit 4 is divided into two sections:

- Section A Materials, components and systems
- Section B consists of three options, of which you must study the same option that you studied at AS level.

Section A is compulsory and builds on the knowledge and understanding of materials, components and systems that you gained in Unit 3.

2. How will it be assessed?
The work that you do in this unit will be externally assessed through Section A of the Unit 4 examination paper.

You are advised to spend **45 minutes** on this section of the paper.

3. What will be assessed?
The following list summarises the topics covered in Section A and what will be examined:

- Selection of materials:
  - the relationship between characteristics, properties and materials choice.
- New technologies and the creation of new materials:
  - the creation and use by industry of modern and smart materials
  - the impact of modern technology and biotechnology on the development of new materials and processes
  - the recycling of materials

  - modification of the properties of materials.
- Values issues:
  - the impact of values issues on product design, development and manufacture
  - responsibilities of 'developed' countries in relation to production and the environment.

You should apply your knowledge and understanding of materials, components and systems to your Unit 5 coursework.

4. How to be successful in this unit
To be successful in this unit you will need to:

- have a clear understanding of the topics covered in Unit 4A
- apply your knowledge and understanding to a given situation or context
- organise your answers clearly and coherently, using specialist technical terms where appropriate
- use clear sketches where appropriate to illustrate your answers
- write clear and logical answers to the examination questions, using correct spelling, punctuation and grammar.

5. How much is it worth?
This unit, with the option, is worth 15 per cent of the full Advanced GCE.

Unit 4 + option	Weighting
A2 level (full GCE)	15%

177

1. Selection of materials

Everyone who is involved with either designing new products or improving existing products must have an understanding and working knowledge of materials in order to be able to select, process and finish the materials.

- A car designer strives to produce aerodynamic, efficient machines that are aesthetically pleasing with improved fuel economy and reduced emissions.
- An aircraft designer must try to balance the weight of the plane with the requirements that are set out with respect to strength, temperature fluctuations and the repeated stresses and strains imposed upon the structure when taking off, landing, in turbulence or adverse weather conditions.

Materials choice

When choosing any material for a specific application, full consideration must be given to the material, its working properties, the relevant manufacturing processes that can be used, appropriate finishes and dimensional accuracy. Cost is also important in the selection process since it has a significant bearing on the purchase price of the raw material, subsequent processing methods in manufacture and the retail price of the product. If any one of these variables were to be changed it would affect many of the others and may ultimately end up making the material unsuitable for its task. It is therefore essential that designers or engineers fully understand the working constraints and limitations of the material that they are considering using.

> As a designer, you need to consider the choice of material very carefully in your coursework project and the earlier that you can do this the better. You also need to consider the manufacturing processes that are going to be used since they will play a significant part in the project's cost-effectiveness.

When trying to make associations between materials, processes and available components a designer should be aware of the differences in terms of availability and different manufacturing processes. For example, consideration could be given to the production of sections in aluminium and plastic by extrusion compared to rolling and drawing in the production of steel sections. This would enable a designer to have some understanding of how those materials may behave or in what forms they may be available.

The relationship between characteristics, properties and materials choice

In the early stages of designing, a general overview is taken about what can be achieved with a material, whereas in the later stages a much more detailed analysis is needed when specifying manufacture. The selection of appropriate materials and manufacturing processes is quite a complex issue, with one influencing the other. Materials choice has become more difficult in recent years due to the rapid growth in the availability of new materials. For example, in addition to the more familiar woods and rubbers available, there is an ever-increasing range of new materials in the form of alloys, ceramics and complicated composites. Production engineers have also continued to develop and refine manufacturing processes and procedures. With the widespread use and availability of computers, the control of machines and processes has meant that new demands are now able to be met with increased precision and lower overheads in terms of a human workforce.

The prime concern remains that of the relationship between materials and processes and the final form of the product. In order to examine this relationship, it is useful to compare several products that fulfil the same function but are made from a range of different materials.

Manufacturing inevitably involves a production process which is in direct response to materials, people and money. Before we go on to consider the relationship between properties, characteristics and materials choice in relation to a series of products, it is worth reviewing the various levels of production, whether it be a one-off diamond ring or the continuous flow production of electrical wire. The level of production is one of the most important aspects in determining why a product is the way that it is.

> ## Task
> What are the materials' limits and manufacturing processes of the materials that you are considering using for your coursework project for Unit 5?

Levels of production

The level of production can be categorised in the following three areas.

One-off production

This is where a single item is required, often in response to an individual customer's need or requirements. It may be a stadium for the World Cup finals or a wedding dress or a very specialised piece of equipment for a disabled person. As a result of this level of production the associated cost tends to be much higher because of the materials used, labour required, skills, design and production costs, since only one is being made. This presents in some cases, such as the piece of equipment needed for a disabled person, a conflict of interests as to whether the project is financially viable. The project may be rejected on the grounds of cost and investment of time. The social issues in terms of providing a better quality of life should also be considered.

Batch production

This level of production makes products in specified quantities. They can be made in one production run of up to 1000 items, or just ten items depending upon the scale of the project. This level of production does have the advantage of freeing up machines once a batch has been completed so that with new tooling it can be used to make other products. If a batch of the original product is required by the customer, the original tools can be re-set once again. This level of production is generally capable of responding very quickly to customer demands and once in production the batch size can easily be increased or decreased. Workers who operate this type of machinery are likely to be more skilled because of the versatility of the machines and tools. One disadvantage of batch production is that serious problems may arise if appropriate planning is not carried out.

High-volume production

Large quantities of products are produced, sometimes on a 24-hour basis of continuous production. The machinery is highly specialised, and therefore expensive, but the variety of products manufactured is kept low. This results in minimal changes to tooling and setting costs which take time and money. Most of the operations that take place are repetitive and components are assembled on assembly lines. In some cases robots are used to assemble products and this eliminates any risk of incorrect assembly or complacency by human labour where it can become very tedious working on repetitive tasks.

> **Task**
> Compare and contrast the labour implications and the tooling costs involved in the production of plastic disposable pens and a wheelchair.

A comparison of how costs change as the level of production is increased is shown in Figure 4.1.1.

Case study 1: chair design

The chair is an example of how designers have made statements concerning their personal design philosophy through the look, construction and materials used in the chair. In the examples selected it is worth considering the date each chair was designed and constructed, the materials used and the manufacturing technologies and processes available at that time.

It can be seen what influence the material has had on each of the designers in terms of the form of the product, but obviously manufacturing processes have been exploited, in some cases in order to achieve the desired outcome.

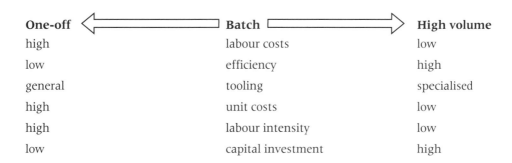

One-off		Batch		High volume
high		labour costs		low
low		efficiency		high
general		tooling		specialised
high		unit costs		low
high		labour intensity		low
low		capital investment		high

Figure 4.1.1 *A comparison of how costs change as the level of production increases*

Figure 4.1.2 Mass-produced wood chair designed by Michael Thonet, 1902–3

Figure 4.1.3 The Wassily chair, made of tubular steel, designed by Marcel Breuer, 1925

Michael Thonet

Michael Thonet was very successful at mass producing chairs. At the time, 1902–3, the process of steam bending solid wood was revolutionary. He mass produced the individual components and stored them ready for assembly at a later stage. The limitations of the material have been fully exploited both by being able to bend and also as a structural member since the chair has been reduced to its simplest form (see Figure 4.1.2). There is a fine balance in this example of the development of mass-produced standard components and the aesthetic qualities of the timber even though it has been largely manufactured by machines.

Marcel Breuer

The B3 chair from 1925 later became more widely known as the Wassily chair (see Figure 4.1.3). The designer Marcel Breuer was an architect who had graduated from the Bauhaus, a German art school. The basic philosophy of the Bauhaus was to create products that avoided historical styling, and that used modern industrial materials. The products were to be designed using just the basic elements and were not to be over decorated.

The Wassily chair has many of the characteristics of the Bauhaus principles. It has been stripped down to its basic structural geometric form and it has been widely recognised as one of the first and finest examples of modern tubular steel furniture.

Tubular steel is a material that is widely available today at relatively low costs. It is now manufactured by either rolling it and drawing it through a series of ever-decreasing sized dies, in which case it is seamless, or it can be rolled from a sheet and electronically resistance welded (ERW). Once degreased, it is capable of taking a variety of surface treatments such as plating, dip coating and spray painting. Structurally, tubular steel can be regarded as being very stiff with respect to torsional forces and reasonably strong when subjected to bending forces.

The combination of resistance to bending and torsional forces make steel an ideal choice of material for this application. The simple geometric construction has meant that the manufacturing processes required to make it have been kept to a minimum. Simple angle bends are easy to achieve on a pipe bending vice in the workshop, however in industry the frames would be produced on a larger scale, and different techniques are used. The pipes are internally filled with oil under pressure to stop them from caving in when bent, and an example like this would be fixed into a jig and then subjected to movement provided by hydraulic rams.

Task

Discuss the properties of the materials used in the manufacture of both Thonet's chair and the Wassily chair.

Gerald Summer

Gerald Summer's lounge chair of 1933–4 was specifically designed for use in the tropics (see Figure 4.1.4). Maintenance and deterioration were uppermost in his mind when he designed it. The humidity would affect the dimensional stability of any natural timbers used. Any joints used could open and subsequently result in failure of the product.

Plywood, which is a manufactured board, has excellent properties with respect to dimensional stability. It also has great strength due to the nature in which the alternate layers have been bonded together at right angles to each other. Various grades are also available in that some types are more resistant to moisture and are therefore even more suited to this type of environment. What is quite extraordinary about the chair is that it has been manufactured from a single sheet of plywood. With cuts in the appropriate places, the rear legs and arm rests have all been able to be formed without the addition of extra components. Therefore, all possibility of joints having to be cut have been eliminated.

More conventionally perhaps today, this sort of structure would be manufactured by sticking much thinner sheets together with decorative veneers on the outside surfaces over a former. This process is known as laminating and it is used as an alternative to steam bending to shape timbers. The life expectancy of Summer's chair has been greatly extended as a result of him using these materials in this way. It is an excellent example of where the designer has fully considered the environment in which the product is to be used.

Verner Panton

When Verner Panton designed his stacking chair he was given the credit of having created the first, single-piece plastic chair (see Figure 4.1.5).

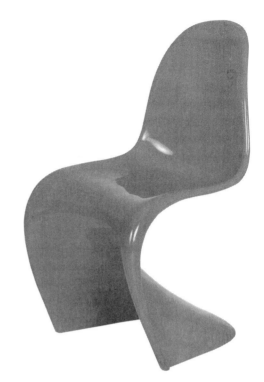

Figure 4.1.5 Stacking chair made of plastic, designed by Verner Panton, 1960

The plastic is formed in such a way that a cantilever-type structure is created, which makes it structurally sound in terms of taking the weight of the person sitting on it.

Although the original versions were produced in 1960, it was not until some seven years later that the technical difficulties had been resolved and the chair was put into production. The availability of bright colours in a glossy finish are trademark signs of a plastic product. Plastics generally require little surface finishing and because of the nature of the material once plasticised, it can be injected or blown into the most complex shapes. Panton fully exploited the materials to create an icon of design in the 1960s.

Jasper Morrison

The Thinking Man's Chair is by Jasper Morrison (see Figure 4.1.6). He is a new designer who has emerged in Britain since the 1980s. He very much believes in and considers the importance of design in relation to the look, manufacturing processes and costs of the product. His chair is constructed from spray-painted tubular steel and flat steel for the backrest and seat. The flowing gentle shape and curve of the seat are in contrast to what appear to be very cold and heavy engineering materials. The materials used possess great properties as far as strength is concerned and they can be easily joined by brazing or welding. Jigs would have been used to ensure that all pieces

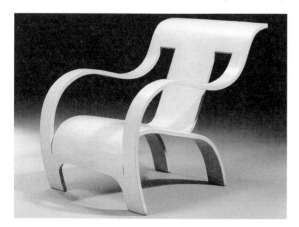

Figure 4.1.4 Plywood lounge chair designed by Gerald Summer, 1933–4

Figure 4.1.6 *Thinking Man's Chair made of tubular steel and flat steel, designed in 1987 by Jasper Morrison*

were held in the correct place before any joining took place. The chosen finish would be easily and quickly applied to leave a hard-wearing surface requiring little or no maintenance, in contrast to how the tubular steel was used by Breuer when it was chrome plated. Both finishes have a particular function in that mild steel has to be treated to avoid surface corrosion.

In summary

The general overview that needs to be taken by the designer of any product is represented in Figure 4.1.7 which looks at the interaction needed between the material choice, design implications and manufacturing processes.

Task

Items of furniture can be manufactured as one-offs or as high-volume components from either single materials – wood, metal or plastics – or in any combination of these. The manufacturing processes, however, govern the limits the material can be put through.

Choose two contrasting pieces of furniture and analyse the materials used and the manufacturing processes in relation to the shape and form of the piece.

Case study 2: the design and manufacture of window frames

The wear and deterioration of materials is a critical factor when choosing materials that will have to withstand the natural elements. Windows have many functions, from letting in light to being able to see out. They are also required to keep the heat in and the cold out. We do not, however, want to have to keep repairing them and maintaining their appearance. If we do neglect them we run the risk of letting the window frame become rotten. Then they become inefficient in terms of insulation properties and large parts may need to be replaced.

As manufacturing processes and materials technology advanced, window frames improved in terms of their resistance to wear and deterioration. Window frames are now widely made from the three basic raw materials: wood, metal and plastic. Obviously, due to the nature of the materials and their working properties

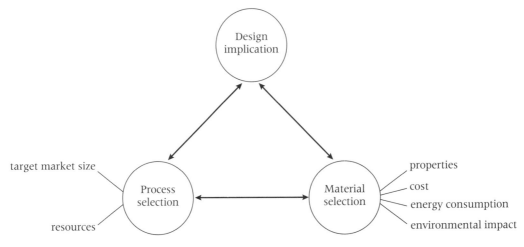

Figure 4.1.7 *An overview of the relationship between manufacturing processes, design implications and the choice of material*

and characteristics, they are made using differing processes. One other major advancement in the window industry has been the advent of double-glazing and the benefits that it has brought the consumer in respect of heat and noise insulation.

Wooden frames

Wooden sections are prepared in long lengths on either spindle moulders or rebating saws. These sections are prepared irrespective of the final size of window since the sections are standard throughout.

Window sills are prepared with a tapered front edge so that water can run off rather than allowing it to collect on a flat surface and to penetrate the material. A special half round profile is also machined underneath the front edge to prevent any water running back to penetrate the joint between the frame and the wall. The remaining sections are prepared to allow the glass to be fitted into rebates to be fixed by either putty or wooden beads and a flexible waterproof sealant.

The frames are joined at the corners using traditional construction techniques such as mortice and tenons and any adhesives used need to be of the waterproof type such as animal glues, cascamite or waterproof PVA.

Frames are typically made from softwoods which then have to undergo various stages of painting – primer, undercoat and a top gloss coat. Careful preparation of the surface is essential when the windows need repainting. It is recommended that windows of this type should be repainted externally every three years and in doing so, the painted surface should be rubbed down or burnt off back to the original

Figure 4.1.8 *A rotten wooden frame that has been neglected*

wood. If the paint is allowed to flake off and the wood is exposed, then rain and frost will eventually penetrate the wood and the timber will eventually rot away (see Figure 4.1.8). It can be a false economy not to maintain the frames properly since if the wood becomes rotten the whole piece or window will need to be replaced. Hardwood frames tend to be stained or treated with some sort of preservative to act as a barrier to water.

In terms of relative costs wooden frames are the cheapest type, with hardwood frames being more expensive than softwood ones. A manufacturer would normally produce a range of windows in a particular style that included a variety of standard sizes. It is, however, possible for certain window manufacturers to be able to produce a one-off to fit a particular sized opening because they would be handmade as a one-off, but this type of service is more expensive than purchasing stock-sized windows.

Metal frames

Steel frames The mild steel type were extensively used in the 1960s and are now quite rare. The sections are hot rolled in the steel mills and subsequently welded together to make strong rigid frames. The glass must be held in with putty and the hinges are an integral part of the frame. Unprotected steel will soon start to oxidise on the surface and corrode if left unprotected. To combat this the steel is galvanised, which involves dipping the fluxed steel components into a bath of molten zinc at 450°C. If the surface becomes damaged at any point, the zinc will corrode and not the steel since zinc is higher in the electrochemical series than steel.

If the steel is to be painted a special type of paint has to be used that will adhere to and not react with the galvanised surface. The window sills tend not to be an integral part of the frame but are often built with specially shaped bricks or tiles cemented in at an angle so as to allow the water to run off (see Figure 4.1.9).

Aluminium frames Steel window frames were superseded by aluminium frames with the sections being produced by extrusion. Essentially, extrusion is similar to squeezing toothpaste from a tube. Metals, however, need to be extruded hot with aluminium between 450°C and 500°C. The material is forced under pressure through a die which has the required cross-section cut in. The aluminium sections are welded together at the corners. All the hinging parts and locking mechanisms are made from plated steel due to the forces being exerted upon them.

Figure 4.1.9 Metal window frame

Figure 4.1.10 UPVC window frame

Aluminium is a material that requires no surface treatment or finishing other than to be polished. It can be anodised but this is mainly for decoration purposes rather than for protection and therefore production costs could be reduced. As with the steel windows though, a hardwood frame was typically used with a wooden sill and this would be fixed in to the opening and the aluminium frame subsequently fixed to it. Although the window needs no maintenance the frame itself does, so there are still minimal requirements to keep it in good condition. However, the price of windows produced in this fashion tends to be more expensive than timber windows due to the raw material cost and availability.

Plastic window frames The major advances in the production of windows came with the advent of UPVC (unplasticised vinyl chloride) (see Figure 4.1.10). This is a lightweight material that can be easily extruded and as a result of its properties and characteristics, it requires no maintenance whatsoever. The extrusion of thermoplastic material can be regarded in principle as a continuous injection moulding process. The plastic material can be extruded into endless cross-section shapes and uniform sections. In order to produce a continuous feed of plasticised material through the die, a feed screw such as an archimedian screw is used rather than the piston-type ram used when extruding metals.

Granules and any additional agents are fed into the hopper and gradually wound into the feed screw. The heater is generally contained within the screw itself with a temperature gradient along its length. As the feed screw rotates the plastic material is fed nearer to the die and as it becomes hotter and more plasticised it gets forced through a restrictive die (see Figure 4.1.11).

There is naturally some shrinkage and contraction once the shape cools and production engineers have to make allowances for this

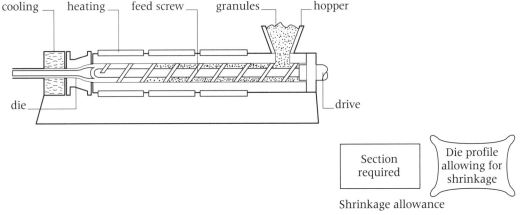

Figure 4.1.11 The process of extrusion

when they produce the dies (see Figure 4.1.11). As the newly extruded shape leaves the die, it is still in a semi plasticised state and therefore it needs to be cooled quickly either by a shot of air, a spray of fine mist or in a water bath.

The one exception to this is UPVC, the type of material used for the windows, since it is a rigid plastic. The profiles for the frames and sills are all cut to length and held in jigs so that they can be welded. The whole frame and any individual opening sections are totally waterproof and resistant to any wear or deterioration. The only maintenance that is required is simply to wash the UPVC. They are totally free from maintenance in respect of any surface treatment.

The glass panels are held by snap-in beads with gasket seals to make them draught proof and to enhance general security. As with any other type of window, UPVC windows are produced in standard sizes but they can be batched up easily or made as one-offs when used as replacement windows in an older house. Naturally though, they are the most expensive type, perhaps because they are maintenance free and therefore require no further servicing.

Tasks

1 Draw up a table like the one below and summarise the details concerning windows into the various categories:

   a) overall quality
   b) manufacturing processes for preparing the materials
   c) construction techniques used in the production of the frames
   d) wear and deterioration
   e) maintenance.

	Metal frames	Wooden frames	Plastic frames
Overall quality			

2 With regard to 'life costs' which is the best type of window frame to install? Explain your answer.
3 Builders have to make a compromise on which type of window they can afford to install into their new houses. Detail the advantages and disadvantages of all the window types discussed in this section for both the builder and the house purchaser.

Case study 3: kettles

Kettles are good examples of how materials have changed and brought about new developments in manufacturing technologies (see Figure 4.1.12). The Victorian kettle made from cast iron pushed the material to its limit as a hollow product at the time. As a metal it would naturally have the required thermal conductive properties where it could be heated over a fire or on a range. The kettle would require careful handling with gloves or some insulating material because the handle would also get very hot.

As materials became more readily available, copper replaced cast iron kettles. Copper kettles could be fabricated by soldering or formed from a single piece or spun. The spouts would be made from a single piece and soldered into place. Copper has a much higher coefficient of thermal conductivity than cast iron and so makes it much more efficient in terms of the amount of energy required to heat the water inside. Great care still needs to be taken though, since the handle gets even hotter due to the thermal conductivity of the copper.

With the advent of plastics and injection moulding it became possible to mass produce components quickly and cheaply. Plastics are an ideal material for use in kettles since they are excellent insulators of both heat and electricity. Due to new manufacturing processes, new and improved shapes were designed with enhanced ergonomic performance. It also became possible to build in new features such as water-level indicators.

Designers such as Philip Starck and Alessi challenged the concepts of shape and form in the 1990s with the 'Hot Bertaa' aluminium kettle and the 'Graves kettle' respectively. These have become modern-day icons of design and yet they still retain the basic function of the kettle – that of heating water.

Task

Working in small groups, consider the following aspects of kettle design:

- How will kettles develop in the future?
- What will customers want?
- Are there any new technologies that can be incorporated?
- Produce some concept sketches for a new kettle.

Present your thoughts to the others in your class in a formal presentation.

Copper kettle

Victorian cast iron kettle

Plastic injection-moulded kettle, 1990s

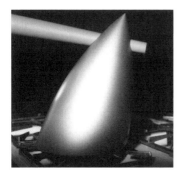

'Hot Bertaa' aluminium kettle, designed by Philippe Starck, 1991

'Graves kettle' produced for Alessi

Figure 4.1.12 *Kettles through history depicting how materials have allowed designers to challenge both shape and form*

Life costs

The cost of a product can be expressed in many ways and it has to take account of many factors. Even before a product takes its place on the high street shelves, the cost of research and development has to be met and inevitably recouped in the final price. Advertising costs, production, packaging and distribution also have to be considered and added into the price paid by the consumer.

The cost implication, however, far outreaches the ticket price that is displayed on the product. Certain products and materials have hidden costs attached with regard to life costs and the various implications associated with them.

Environmental costs

The production of almost everything requires materials that affect the environment in one way or another. For example:

- the depletion of our forests for timbers that take hundreds of years to replace
- the extraction of metals and ores from the earth's surface which requires mining and open-cast mining
- the exploration of oil for the production of polymers.

These natural resources are all being used at ever-increasing rates and we are not able to replace them at anywhere near the same rate. In fact, as far as oil is concerned we are not able to replace it at all. Forests can be managed and to a certain extent we are able to replenish stocks. It does, however, take considerable time for a tree to reach maturity before it can be felled and converted into useful timber.

The amount of energy needed to produce products through their manufacture also needs to be considered. The production of steel and any subsequent processing requires an enormous amount of energy to heat it up to temperatures in excess of 1200°C. The casting of aluminium and alloys requires high temperatures, as do forging and any related heat treatment processing needed to change or enhance the mechanical properties. The environmental cost also must be considered since emissions from factories have to be monitored and treated as appropriate. Emissions can take the form of gases and vapours as well as miscible oils and solvents which need to be treated as industrial effluent.

The deforestation of areas has led to soil erosion in certain parts of the world and the land has now become infertile as the rains and storms have washed away the top soil. This has led not only to environmental damage but also to economic downturn for those timber-producing regions which can no longer work the land to generate income.

Finally, the disposal of the product must be considered when it reaches the end of its effective working use. The designer should have regard for how it can be recycled or how parts can be disposed of. In 1992 an environmental scheme was established to monitor, assess and encourage manufacturers to make products that cause less damage to the environment. It provides consumers with information which allows them to make better-informed decisions about the products they buy.

2. New technologies and the creation of new materials

The creation and use by industry of modern and smart materials

Tinted glass

Special glass that darkens when exposed to light from the visible and ultraviolet spectrum and fades again in the dark is known as **photochromic glass**. This photochromic property is reversible and it can undergo thousands of cycles without any change in its performance. The glass is made in the normal way as described in Unit 3 but with the addition of sub-microscopic particles of silver-halide. When used in the photographic development process silver halide will decompose. When these particles are trapped inside the glass they can neither decompose nor diffuse. The reaction with ultraviolet light causes a chemical change and the glass changes colour. This type of light-reactive glass is used in some glasses whose lenses change automatically to block out ultraviolet light and to protect the eyes.

In the same way that glasses change colour, welding masks and goggles now use the same technology to protect the eyes from the arc when welding. Conventional welding masks have very dark lenses but they do cause problems when trying to set up and position ready for welding to take place. New welding goggles and masks now have clear lenses that automatically darken when welding commences.

Solar panels

The developed countries of the world currently use a disproportionately large share of the world's energy consumption even though the whole planet is feeling the effect of the emissions and global warming. More consideration needs to be given to alternative methods of producing and generating energy.

It is estimated that in terms of energy demand, the sun is providing 2000 times more energy than the current demand, even allowing for the heat that is absorbed by the sea and lost to moving air around the planet. Greater efforts need to be made to harness this energy to relieve the pressure and demands on the capital resources. In terms of the generation of electricity, the **photovoltaic cell** is one method of doing so.

The development of the photovoltaic cell can be charted back to the early 1870s when a British scientist discovered that selenium was sensitive to light. The real breakthrough did not come until the 1950s when silicon was discovered to be sensitive to light and that a substantial voltage was generated when certain impurities were added to it. By 1954 the first solar cell had been developed but it was only assessed to be about 6 per cent efficient.

The actual cell itself consists of a p-n semiconductor junction where the p-type layer is thin enough to allow light to reach the junction. The p-type material and side acts as the positive terminal and the n-type acts as the negative terminal. When connected into a circuit, current flows through it where the energy source is the light from the sun. The voltage available depends on the materials used to make the junction, the intensity of the light falling upon it and the current drawn. A silicon-based cell in full sunlight will generate a voltage of about 0.45v and a maximum current of about 35mA for each square centimetre of cell. The silicon cell is still only operating at about 10 per cent efficiency, only 10 per cent of the light falling upon it is changed into electrical energy, whereas gallium arsenide operates at about 20 per cent.

Figure 4.1.13 *Solar panels in use to harness the sun's energy*

When connected in series-parallel, cells can be used to power satellites and space vehicles, and in developing countries they have been used to provide power for health care and in oceans for marine buoys. Figure 4.1.13 shows **solar panels** on the roof of a house.

Thermo-ceramics

Without refractory materials, such as **thermo-ceramics**, it would not have been possible to contain certain metals at the very high temperatures at which they melt.

Advanced ceramics have a structure which gives them great hardness and stability at very high temperatures. Silicon nitride is an example of an advanced ceramic, and although it is somewhat brittle it is now being used for turbine blades and turbo-charge units for the automotive industry.

Silicon nitride and silicon carbide can withstand very high temperatures and they are under development for future use in the internal combustion engine. By combing thermo-ceramics and metal powders to form cermets, even better insulation properties can be gained. The operating temperature within a diesel engine can be increased to 1100°C making it 50 per cent more efficient overall.

Thermo-ceramics and cermets are made by sintering finely powdered oxides. They are then compacted under high pressure at high temperatures.

Shape memory alloys

During the late 1970s metallurgists discovered **shape memory alloys**. When made into components these alloys can be plastically deformed at a certain temperature. They will retain their shape while held at this temperature. When the temperature is removed the component reverts to

its original shape. It was later discovered that by processing alloys in certain ways some alloys could be 'trained' to show memory where the components demonstrated total reversibility on heating and cooling.

Early applications saw shape memory alloys used in greenhouse window openers. They consist of a coil spring of copper-zinc-aluminium alloy which opens and closes the window on a hinge in response to the changes in ambient temperature. A more recent development has seen shape memory alloys used as thermally activated fasteners for use as electrical cable fasteners and hydraulic pipe connectors. The connectors are prepared by making them expand, normally by chilling them, and then placing them over the area to be joined and heating them making the shape memory alloy return to its original shape.

Shape memory properties occur in several alloys including nickel-titanium, gold-cadmium and iron-nickel-cobalt-titanium with the most common of these being nickel-titanium, called nitinol.

The cycle of being able to straighten and bend when heated can be repeated millions of times. The heat needed to make the shape memory alloy move is generally provided by passing an electrical current through it. Because shape memory alloys have a relatively high electrical resistance heating it in this way is an appropriate method.

Common shape memory alloy wires are available in a range of different diameters from 5 mm to 5/1000ths of a millimetre. Nitinol has been developed to 'remember' that it has a shorter length when it is heated above its transition temperature which is between 70 and 80°C.

Liquid crystal displays

Liquid crystal displays (LCDs) are used as numerical and alpha-numerical indicators and displays. As they require much smaller currents they have replaced LED (Light Emitting Diode) displays because they prolong the life of batteries by using microamperes rather than milliamperes.

Liquid crystals are organic, carbon-based compounds, which exhibit both liquid and solid characteristics. When a cell, containing a liquid crystal, has a voltage applied across its terminals, and on which light falls, it appears to go 'dark'. This is caused by the molecular rearrangement within the liquid crystal. A liquid crystal display has a pattern of conducting electrodes which is capable of displaying the numbers 0 to 9 via a seven-segment display. The numbers are made to appear on the LCD by applying a voltage to certain segments which go dark in relation to the silvered background.

Tasks

1 It has been suggested that shape memory alloys are to be fitted into bras and trouser creases. Discuss what the designers are trying to achieve here and how would the temperatures be controlled.

2 Discuss some of the advantages and disadvantages of using photovoltaic cells to generate electricity.

Task

Many piezo-electric transducers are used in greetings cards. Analyse such a card by considering the following:

- how the transducer is activated
- the voltage that is generated across it
- the commercial availability of such transducers.

Piezo-electric actuators

Piezo-electric actuators work in two ways; they either produce movement in response to an applied voltage or they produce a voltage in response to an applied pressure. Piezo-electric actuators are used in greetings cards that play tunes when opened. They produce a sound from an electrical signal as a result of the card being opened (see Figure 4.1.14).

When piezo-electric transducers are used as sensors they are capable of picking up small signals which can then be amplified and processed. They are used in a wide variety of applications including burglar alarms. The transducer produces a voltage in response to a loud sound, such as a breaking window, or to a movement such as treading on a mat or stair tread.

The transducers are made from minerals, ceramics or polymers. The piezo-electric film is bonded to a base material once coated with a metallic film and contacts are then attached. In some cases amplifier circuits are built in to the whole transducer but in most examples they are left like the examples in Figure 4.1.14.

The voltage generated as a result of the material being deformed is sufficient enough to light an LED as shown in Figure 4.1.14.

Smart composite materials

'Smart materials' is a term that has been applied to a broad range of materials whose physical properties can be varied by an input. These materials are now being used to replace devices and components that once had separate sensing and actuation components. A single smart material has reduced the overall size and complexity of the device. Smart materials have opened up enormous developments for new sensors, actuators and structural components. Smart materials can be subdivided into various groups and probably the best known of these are the piezo-electrics. These devices (see below) produce a small shape change when a small voltage is applied and because of the response times they are being utilised in high frequency devices such as ultra-sound generators and audio speakers.

Shape memory alloys constitute another group of smart materials (see above). These alloys return to their original shape after they have been plastically deformed. Large forces can be generated as the material returns to its original shape. For example, an alloy of nickel and titanium (nitinol) in a wire form 0.01" OD is capable of generating 10N as it changes its length by 5 per cent of its original length. Other smart materials include the following:

polymer transducer

disc type

symbol for piezo-electric transducer

Figure 4.1.14 Piezo-electric actuators in use in a musical greetings card

- Piezo-electric ceramics. These materials expand and contract in response to an applied voltage. They are being considered as replacements for the large heavy iron wound speaker drivers which would reduce weight and the overall size and bulk.
- Electrorheological and magnetorheological fluids. These special fluids can change their viscosity within milliseconds when placed in an electric or magnetic field. The automotive industries are carrying out research on these fluids to ascertain their suitability and application for use in suspension systems and engine mounts.
- Optical fibres. Fibre optics allow light to flow along it since the glass used has a high refractive index. This technology makes it possible for light to be transmitted over 200 km. The advantage of glass fibres over copper conductors in telecommunications is the small diameter of the glass fibres and their greater load carrying capacity. They are now extensively used in telecommunications systems, computer networking and in surgery where they can be inserted into the body for exploration purposes. Currently, fibre optics are being used by the US space agency NASA to measure the strain in composite materials where the fibres are embedded into the composite material. When a fibre optic breaks due to failure of the material around it, the light signal fed through it becomes interrupted indicating failure.

Composites

In general, reinforced plastics are best suited for large structural items such as boat hulls and storage tanks. The first reinforced plastics were made with glass fibre strands as the reinforcing material and this is still the most common kind today. Glass reinforced plastic (GRP) is available in several forms: a loosely woven fabric, a string of filaments wound together, a matting of short fibres, or loose short strands.

More recently, we have seen the advent of carbon fibres and they are basically used in the same format as glass fibres. They are, however, much stronger composites and are used in the aerospace industry, for making some sports equipment and for body armour and protection. Composites based on carbon fibres or with a special polymer, Kevlar™, have excellent protective applications and are used by the police and military for bullet-proof vests and helmets. The added advantage is that great weight reductions have also been achieved making the vests up to 3 kg lighter and helmets 1 kg lighter.

The carbon fibre strands are held in a matrix in a similar fashion to GRP. Once the liquid resin has been applied it is cured or hardened around the fibres. The polymerisation reaction that follows converts the resin into a rigid cross-linked thermoset solid. The chemical reaction is started by the addition of a catalyst or hardener and in some cases an accelerator is used to control the speed of the reaction.

Pigments, fillers and other additives are also used where necessary to change the colour or to increase buoyancy, for example. Polyester resin and epoxy resin are most commonly used as the matrix material in composite fibre structures. Polyester resins are used with GRP in the production of boat hulls because they are much cheaper than epoxy resins. In the production of storage tanks and pipework, epoxy resins are used because of their excellent resistance to chemical attack.

Large products such as boat hulls have traditionally been produced by hand lay up which is a relatively laborious method. The process has undergone some mechanisation recently. The basic and simplest method of making a reinforced structure is by laying sheets of matting over a wooden mould and wetting it with resin. Additional layers are added with resin to build up extra thickness where required. The production method of boats and car body panels is now more automated and when produced with carbon fibres, they are lighter and mechanically stronger.

One method now in use is illustrated in Figure 4.1.15, which shows a mixture of fibres and resin sprayed on to a mould. A continuous spool of fibres is wound off a drum and mixed in a spray gun with the resin, catalyst and hardener and sprayed on to the mould. The process is obviously much quicker but great care is needed to ensure that an even application of material is made across the whole mould, avoiding building up excessive thickness in one area.

Task

Chris Boardman rode a bike with a single-piece frame made from carbon fibre to win an Olympic Gold medal. Detail the benefits that he would have gained from this type of bike frame compared to the more conventional and traditional metal-framed bikes.

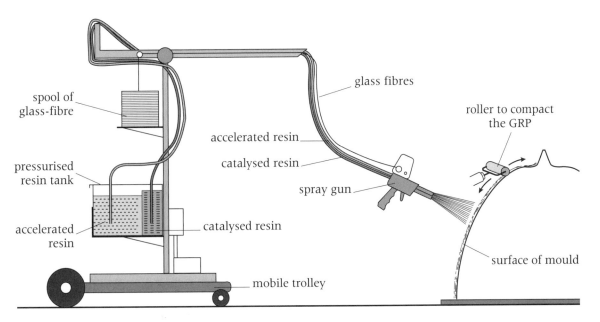

Figure 4.1.15 *Spraying system used to spray fibres on to a mould*

New materials used in the computer and electronics industry

Semiconductors are a special type of material that have an electrical resistance which changes with temperature, i.e. they conduct electricity better as the temperature rises. The resistivity falls as the temperature rises. Semiconductors include both compounds and elements. Perhaps the most common type of element is silicon.

Silicon is the second most abundant and widely distributed of all the elements after oxygen. It is estimated that about 28 per cent of the earth's crust is made up from silicon. It does not occur in a free elemental state but it is found in the form of silicon oxides, such as quartz, sand, rock or in complex silicates such as felspar. Silicon is used in the steel industry as an alloying element but its main use is in the computer technology industry. In particular, it is used in the manufacture of silicon chips and other electronic components such as transistors and diodes. It is also used in the manufacture of glass, enamels, cement and porcelain.

Like other semiconductors, silicon behaves as an electrical insulator or conductor depending upon the temperature. At absolute zero, the material is an electrical conductor. When heat is applied to a piece of silicon, some of the electrons gain enough energy to jump from a valence band to a conduction band. The movement of these electrons can carry charge through the material when a potential difference is applied across it. The higher the temperature becomes, the more electrons jump across the bands, and the resistance falls making it an electrical conductor.

The production of integrated circuits (ICs) involves cutting single crystals of silicon into thin wafers. The surface of each wafer is then coated with a photosensitive polymer so that it can be etched by exposing light to predetermined areas. Several masks of different layouts are needed in order to construct the integrated circuit. As the accuracy of the photolithography (the process used to transfer the patterns) has improved, accuracy has improved to within less than one micrometre. Due to the individual devices being so small, the integrated circuits are produced on a larger wafer up to 20 cm in diameter that can contain up to one thousand million circuit elements (see Figure 4.1.16).

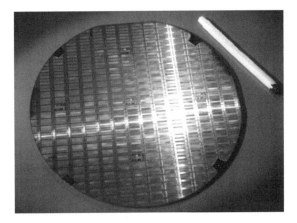

Figure 4.1.16 *Silicon wafer containing many smaller ICs*

Computers have their entire central processing unit (CPU) made from a single integrated circuit containing more than a million transistors. The same computers also require memory chips and their capacity has increased and continues to increase at an ever-increasing rate.

Task

Silicon has led to rapid developments in the world of technology. Produce a time-line over the past ten years looking at some of the developing technologies and products that you have been exposed to such as CD players, increasing computer power and laptops, and more recent developments such as DVDs and MP3 players.

Impact of modern technology and biotechnology on the development of new materials and processes

Genetic engineering in relation to woods

Recent developments in science and technology have given rise to a whole new culture of genetically modified foods, plants, materials and animals.

Biotechnology is now at the forefront in the production of new materials and research and experimentation into genetically engineered and modified timber is growing rapidly.

Genes are currently being investigated with a view to providing quicker growing trees. This would enable forests to be managed more efficiently in terms of replacing trees at the same rate at which they are cut down. The new trees planted would therefore reach maturity much quicker in terms of the useful bulk of timber that can be obtained from it.

Investigations are also taking place as to how wood can be engineered to be more resistant to wear, rot and animal infestation. Obviously, there are benefits to be had in relation to these improvements. What though are the implications beyond this as a result of timber not rotting? At the moment, timber can be left to rot naturally as the elements attack and break the timber down. If it was not for this decaying and decomposing timber millions of years ago we would have no coal or oil today. If timber does not rot, then maybe it will have to be burnt to be disposed of. The consequences of burning the timber will result in emissions from the burning process being left to damage the ozone layer and to cause acid rain.

Paper

One major area of development as far as genetically engineered timber is concerned is in the production of paper. The process of making paper is an environmentally damaging one which involves the use of some very toxic chemicals. The chemicals have to be used to remove the lignin from the wood pulp. Lignin is a natural tough polymer-like material that gives the tree its strength and rigidity. In the USA, scientists have discovered a way of reducing the natural lignin content that also produces trees that grow faster. It is thought that this will lead to the reduction of toxic chemicals used in the paper making industry. It is also predicted to return more wood per square kilometre resulting in commercial and environmental benefits.

There are sometimes unforeseen benefits to be had when experimenting on this level. The same scientists when working on aspen trees, the trees traditionally used for pulp production, made some remarkable discoveries. As they peeled back the bark from the saplings, they found that the timber was not its usual whitish colour. The timber was in fact a salmon reddish colour. The only problem was that each sapling exposed was slightly different in colour and some in fact were spotted in appearance. Its use is now being considered beyond that of pulp and paper production. It is not inconceivable to think that we may end up with coloured timbers being used in furniture, panelling or even external cladding that would require no maintenance.

The scientists involved in this work are now considering the study of these aspens in a natural environment. As with any work of this nature, however, they are having to apply to the United States Department of Agriculture for a licence to do so.

Task

What benefits might the impact of genetically engineered timber bring to the following?

- pests and timber infestations
- for use in the construction of outside furniture
- for the long-term future of a managed timber supply.

Environmentally friendly plastics

A plastic is basically any material that can be heated and moulded so that it retains its shape once it cools. Today, a wide variety of plastics exist as polymers and resins. Synthetic plastics are derived from oil and hydro-carbons form the basic building blocks. The carbon-based molecules bond together through a chemical reaction and the bonds made determine the physical properties and characteristics.

One disadvantage of plastics generally has been the issue of how they are disposed of.

Recent advances in biotechnology and bioengineering have seen the development of **environmentally friendly plastics**. In fact, it was some 60 years ago that saw the creation of the world's first biodegradable polymer, Biopol (see Figure 4.1.17). Much has been made of the need to create plastics by other means than from petrochemicals. This led to the development of fibres such as nylon from petrochemicals and PVC.

Biopol has the advantages of synthetic polymers and those of natural polymers. It is biodegradable, can be produced in bulk and the raw materials are quite readily available. Scientists discovered that a natural polymer produced from food stuffs could be mass produced by fermentation. Once the polymer had been extracted it was substituted into the production process to produce plastic products. The major advantage of the 'plastic' once it had reached its end of life was that it could be disposed of by biodegradation.

'Green' credit cards made from Biopol have now started to find their way into the market place as a genuine replacement for some of the 20 million credit cards in circulation today.

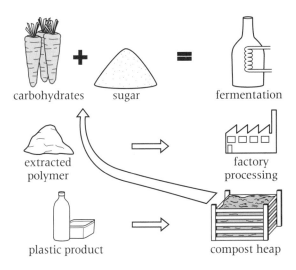

Figure 4.1.17 *The production of Biopol*

Task

Discuss the environmental benefits in terms of recycling plastics that materials such as Biopol have brought.

The recycling of materials

Once the function of a product has been performed or it reaches the end of its useful working life, it has to be disposed of. This is becoming a prominent issue that society is having to face. In Germany, for instance, the supplier and manufacturer are responsible for the return and disposal or recycling of the packaging such as any expanded polystyrene and cardboard. The consumers have to return the packaging to the store where it is then collected and managed by external waste handling companies.

It is difficult to recover materials from certain products for a number of reasons with the most significant being how the materials are used and widely spread within a product. Sometimes base metals have been plated, sprayed or even galvanised using large quantities of zinc, tin and even silver and gold. It is very difficult to recover those materials commercially with the exception of the more precious types.

One of the most complicated pieces of engineering and manufacturing which combines a multitude of components and materials is the motor car. Recently, there has been pressure on the automotive industries to consider future manufacturing implications with regard to recycling and the reuse of materials and components. Companies such as Rover and BMW have pledged to make this a key consideration for all future designs. Rover has set up an auditing system that documents what the car and its various components are made up from in order to make the recycling easier. It is also considering how to reduce the complexity and variety of materials used so that it becomes commercially possible to recover a greater amount of the car's material.

The UK government has set some very tough targets for the automotive and recycling industries to achieve. The average proportion of car parts by weight that has been declared as waste for disposal by shredding has to be decreased to 15 per cent by 2002 and to 5 per cent by 2015. Any materials that are disposed of rather than recycled also have to be included within this figure. Companies involved in the dismantling of cars should reuse components and fluids such as brake fluids as far as is technically and economically viable. Nonrecyclable parts will need to be disposed of properly or they will need to be passed on to a certified disposal company.

The basic materials used in the manufacture of cars (see Figure 4.1.18) are:

- steel
- aluminium
- glass
- rubber
- plastics.

Other materials are used in solders and plating but in quantities which are too small to justify their recovery economically. Laminated glass is used in windscreens and the rear windows as well as for the headlights. Laminated glass is difficult to recycle due to its laminar structure as is the glass used for headlights since they tend to be made as sealed units and therefore they are combined with many other materials. In each case, the glass is ground up into fine particles where foreign bodies can be removed by various sorting methods and the remaining glass cullet is sent off for recycling where it is simply introduced into the furnace and remelted.

It is currently estimated that some two billion tyres are scrapped every year and although some are used as planters in the garden, most are burnt or recycled. Some, however, are re-treaded where the worn tread is stripped off and fresh rubber is moulded on to form a new tread. Re-treaded tyres have to undergo some tough tests to ensure that they are safe to use before they can be sold.

Plastics are widely used and they present enormous problems in terms of recycling. They are used in textiles coverings for seats, foam in the seats, switches, dashboards and most of the interior trims. It is estimated that about one tenth of the weight of a car is plastic and it is very difficult to sort, separate and recycle any of it because of the wide variety of plastics used. If any of the plastics are recycled they have to be separated into their various forms. They are then shredded into tiny pieces, melted and fed into an extrusion machine where the output is chopped into small pellets to be used again in the production of new products, such as garden hose pipes. It goes without saying that the only type of plastics which can undergo this recycling process are thermoplastics.

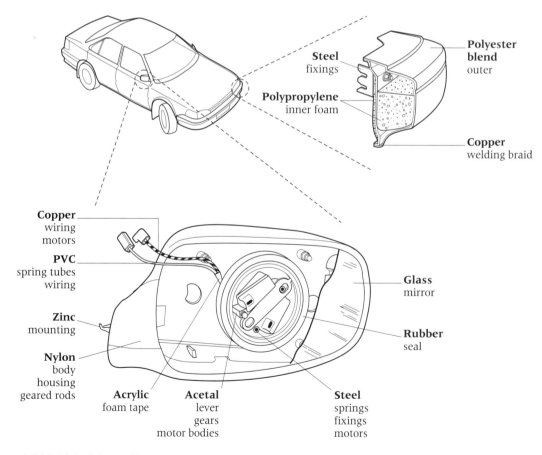

Figure 4.1.18 *Materials used in a car*

Aluminium is used for engine blocks or in the form of alloys for wheels. These large items can be easily removed for recycling but smaller parts can be separated out once the remaining parts have been shredded. The reclaimed aluminium is taken back to the foundry where it is introduced into the furnace and melted down to make 'new' aluminium.

Steel is the world's most recycled material and that used in the production of cars is no exception. The majority of recycled steel is used in the construction industry and large engineering structures. Car bodies and chassis are cut into shreds and chopped up and passed over a magnetic separator. The ferrous metals are held in the magnetic field and the non-ferrous metals are deflected into a separate container. The shredded steel is then introduced back into the furnace in the production of new steel. This recycling process of metals, be it aluminium or steel, makes enormous savings in terms of energy consumption compared to the making of steel from new.

The overall impact of recycling at this level has enormous benefits:

- by reducing the demand on valuable resources
- by reducing the amount of energy consumed in the production of the car
- by reducing the overall environmental impact.

Tasks

1 Choose a household product such as a washing machine or a fridge. Describe how parts of it could be recycled.
2 Discuss some ways in which the general public can be encouraged to undertake more recycling.

Modification of properties of materials

Metals

An alloy is a combination of one metal with one or more other metals and in some cases, non-metals. Steel is an alloy of iron with carbon; brass is an alloy of copper and zinc. There are thousands of alloys in existence but they are strictly controlled by the International Standards Organisation (ISO) and similar bodies. There are very stringent guidelines and specifications laid down that dictate the maximum and minimum limits of composition and the mechanical and physical properties required by each.

An average car may contain as many as ten different alloys, including:

- mild steel for the body panels
- heat-treated steel alloys for gears
- cast iron or aluminium alloys for the engine block
- lead alloys used in the battery, etc.

Alloys are prepared by mixing two or more metals in the molten state where they dissolve in each other before they are paired into ingots. Generally, the major metal is melted first and the minor is then dissolved into it.

The iron carbon alloy has been covered in some detail in Unit 3 but it is worth considering a few of the details once again. Iron as a pure metal is very soft and ductile, and carbon is very brittle. Yet when the two are combined they form a metal that exhibits none of the properties that the two original ingredients possessed.

As would be expected, the ratio in which the two materials are combined also affects the mechanical and physical properties of the new material.

Figure 4.1.19 gives an indication of how the increase in the percentage of carbon affects the hardness of steel. It should be noted, however, that as a direct result of increase in hardness, the ductility (the ability to be drawn out) is decreased.

Engineers have to make compromises at times by having to balance how the increase in one property decreases another. Other properties can also be further enhanced by alloying. Resistance to corrosion can be increased by the introduction of chromium into the alloy mix.

A material's properties can also be modified by heat treatment. The basic processes are hardening, tempering, annealing and normalising. A basic summary is given in Table 4.1.1 of the main processes.

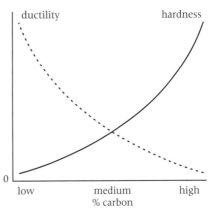

Figure 4.1.19 *The effect of carbon content on hardness and ductility*

Table 4.1.1 Heat treatment processes

Process	Description
Hardening	The hardness, resistance to indentation and abrasion can be increased in steels with a carbon content of 0.4 per cent or greater. The process involves heating the steel to just above its upper critical temperature and holding it there while it soaks before it is quenched in water. (Other types of hardening will be looked at later in some detail.)
Tempering	After the material has been hardened it is very brittle, and to remove this property it must be tempered. This involves heating the material to a certain temperature depending upon its eventual use before it is quenched in water.
Annealing	As the structure of the metal is deformed by cold working, it becomes harder. To restore its original grain structure, heat is applied to the piece which allows the strain to be dissipated throughout. Annealing takes place at relatively low temperatures.
Normalising	This process is confined to steel and it is used to refine the grain structure after a component has been forged or work hardened.

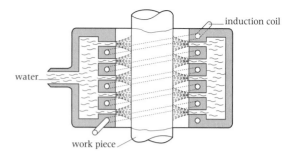

Figure 4.1.20 Induction hardening

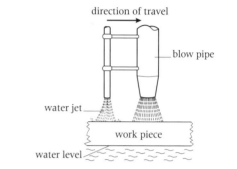

Figure 4.1.21 Flame hardening

Work hardening

If you were to take a thin piece of metal, such as a paper clip, and bend it backwards and forwards, it would eventually break. However, there are two noticeable changes that occur before fracture; the metal becomes harder to bend and it gets hot: we say that this metal has been work hardened.

Many manufacturing processes rely upon this change. Prior to processing, mild steel is ductile allowing it to be pressed easily in large dies, resulting in components whose strength has been increased slightly by work hardening.

Age hardening

Age hardening of materials was discovered by accident. In an attempt to improve the strength of cartridge cases made from aluminium, a German research metallurgist created an aluminium alloy containing 3.5 per cent copper and 0.5 per cent magnesium. The initial result of heating and quenching the metal was not successful. He returned several days later to discover that the hardness had increased due to its age. Special alloys have now been created specifically for their age hardening properties.

The hardening of metals can be achieved in many different ways. It is not possible to harden by conventional means carbon steels with less than 0.4 per cent carbon content. This does not mean, however, that they cannot be hardened in any other way.

Case hardening

Case hardening is a process that is used to form a hard skin around the outside of a component. The metal has to be heated to a cherry red colour before it is dipped into a carbon powder and allowed to cool. The process needs to be repeated two or three times before it is finally heated and quenched in water. This type of hardening is used on axles where only the surface is subjected to wear, but a soft case needs to be retained that is capable of withstanding the shock and sudden impact.

Induction hardening

Induction hardening also creates a similar pattern with a hard outside and a soft core (see Figure 4.1.20). Again, axles and shafts are hardened in this way.

An induction coil is used to heat a localised area of the work piece. As it is made to move up, as the work rotates, it is followed by water jets which cool the work rapidly. This results in just the outer surface of the axle being hardened.

Flame hardening

A similar process, flame hardening, is used on flat surfaces and complex profiles (see Figure 4.1.21). The surface is again heated to a temperature above its upper critical temperature, normally by an oxy-acetylene torch, and it is followed immediately by a water cooling jet. Both flame and induction hardening can only be used on steels that have more than 0.4 per cent carbon content.

Sintering

Materials that have very high melting points are often processed by sintering. Sintering is a process associated with powder metallurgy and it is an economic way of shaping materials with minimal waste. Metal powders are mixed in the proportions required to form alloys, for example copper and tin to make bronze. Graphite and lubricating oils can also be added at this stage before they are compacted and sintered to form bronze bushes. The graphite and oils make them ideal as oil retaining bushes for use in washing machines and vacuum cleaners where they can be expected to last for the entire duration of the product's lifespan.

The actual process of sintering gives the powdered mixture its strength by heating and fusing the particles together.

Plastics

It seems somewhat strange to be thinking how plastics can be changed and modified but it is possible. In the same way that separate metals can be alloyed, separate monomers can be altered. Two or more monomers can be combined to form a new material and this process is known as **co-polymerisation** (see Figure 4.1.22), and the new material is known as a copolymer. An example of this would be a mixture of vinyl chloride and vinyl acetate. The combined copolymer is known as polyvinyl chloride acetate and is shown in Figure 4.1.22.

Cross-linking is another way of increasing strength. In the vinyl chloride monomer, one atom of hydrogen has been removed and replaced by an atom of chlorine. The new links have formed up to create a new polymer, poly-vinyl chloride (PVC), as shown in Figure 4.1.22.

Additives can also be used to increase the mechanical properties of plastics. Plasticisers are added as liquids to improve the flow of plastics when being used in moulding processes. They also lower the softening temperature and generally make them less brittle.

Fillers and **foamants** are added into plastics in an attempt to reduce bulk and overall costs because they are less expensive than polymers. They improve strength by reducing brittleness which also makes them more resistant to impact from shock loading.

One of the early problems with plastics in general was their inability to resist deterioration and exposure to ultra-violet light. The addition of stabilisers has made them more resistant to ultra-violet light and they no longer yellow or become transparent when exposed for long periods.

Tasks

1 Produce an information sheet on one side of A4 paper only for a GCSE student who needs to revise the basics of heat treatment.
2 Why is it sometimes necessary for certain components to have a hard surface on the outside but to retain a softer central core?

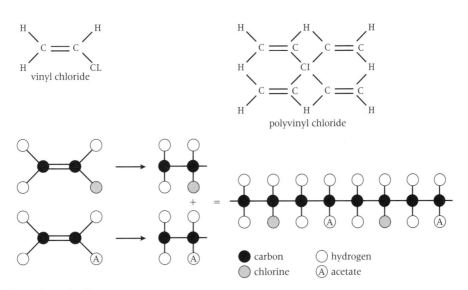

Figure 4.1.22 Co-polymerisation

Woods

Seasoning

Natural air seasoning is the traditional method of removing the excess moisture from newly felled trees. Although it is a very cheap system to operate it is very dependent upon the weather conditions. The timber slabs are stacked with sticks between them allowing free air to circulate. This results in the evaporation of moisture, but this method has two major disadvantages:

* It is slow and inaccurate, taking on average one year to season 25 mm of slab thickness.
* The moisture content can only be reduced to that of the surrounding atmosphere (15–18 per cent).

Kiln seasoning, however, results in a much quicker, more reliable method. This time, however, with the timber stacked with sticks between, it is placed into a sealed chamber. Steam is then pumped into the chamber and is absorbed into the timber. The pressure and humidity is then drawn out by an extractor fan before the temperature is raised and hot air is circulated. Very careful monitoring and recording takes place in order to attain the precise moisture content level.

Moisture content can be calculated using the following formula:

Percentage of moisture content =

$$\frac{\text{Initial weight} - \text{Dry weight}}{\text{Dry weight}} \times 100$$

Overheating can result in a form of a case-hardened timber which is brittle on the outside. Kiln seasoning has a number of advantages:

* It only takes between one and two weeks per 25 mm of slab thickness.
* Less space is required since the process is quicker.

* There is improved turnover of stock.
* It kills insects and bugs in the process.
* Accurate moisture content can be achieved.

Laminating

The development of plywood was an important process that improved the physical properties of timber. Plywood is made from thin layers of wood, veneers, about 1.5 mm thick, called laminates. They are stuck together with an odd number of layers, but with the grain of each layer running at right angles to the last. This means that the two outside layers have their grain running in the same direction.

The interlocking structure gives plywood its high uniform strength, good dimensional stability and resistance to splitting. It is also available with a variety of external facing veneers and it can be made with waterproof adhesives which means it can be used externally.

These veneers or laminates can also be stuck together over formers to produce curved shaped forms. This process is known as **laminating** and since different shapes can be formed, the strength of the material can be further enhanced by the shapes into which the material is formed.

Other types of manufactured boards are also available that possess qualities of strength: block board, lamin board and batten board all use the laminating, joining together approach to increase the overall strength (see Figure 4.1.23). These three boards are also clad on their external surfaces with thin laminates for decoration and strength reasons.

Particle boards such as hard board, chip board and medium density fibreboard (MDF) also exhibit properties of strength although they are made in a different way. Again, they can all be prepared so that they are waterproof and can be used externally. In particular, due to its uniform structure, MDF is particularly strong as well as having an excellent surface which is capable of taking a variety of finishes.

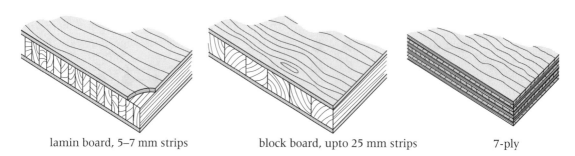

lamin board, 5–7 mm strips   block board, upto 25 mm strips   7-ply

Figure 4.1.23 *Laminated forms of manufactured sheet timber*

3. Values issues

Value judgements are made each and every day of our lives and, as designers, we make evaluative judgements when making and taking decisions about what we should pursue and develop or cast aside.

'Is it worth doing?' Most companies will invest enormous amounts of money into research and development to gauge consumer interest and demand. They will proceed with a project purely on its commercial viability. Design projects also come to fruition because of people's needs. They may well be genuine needs such as a stair lift for someone who has arthritis in his or her legs or they may be market-led needs, for example mobile telephones.

Impact of values issues

Case study: designing for the market

Every need is a value judgement, if only for that person. Not all needs though will ever be met because of the economic and commercial viability for the required product.

An example of the decisions that have to be made and the implications considered is the situation faced by a company that designs and manufactures motorised wheelchairs. The views of physiotherapists and engineers who had been working closely on developing prototypes at hospital level were taken into consideration. They had produced a series of one-offs where chairs had been individually moulded around the patient. The chair is a means of providing physical support that could eliminate the chance of the medical condition becoming worse.

At this point, a company specialising in the design and manufacture of motorised wheelchairs was contacted. From its point of view the problem was to develop a solution that could be mass produced rather than made as one-offs. Although the company was a multimillion-pound concern, it needed to ensure that the product was commercially viable.

The base, controls and drive mechanism already existed but the company had to redesign the seat so that it could be mass produced. The marketing manager was concerned with 'Will it make a profit?'. The marketing manager worked hard trying to assess and generate sales by canvassing opinions from patients and specialists alike. 'What are you prepared to pay?' was the question asked of the potential customers.

The product was developed to a final prototype stage and fully tested. It was regarded as a success by the potential customers but after significant investment of time and resources,

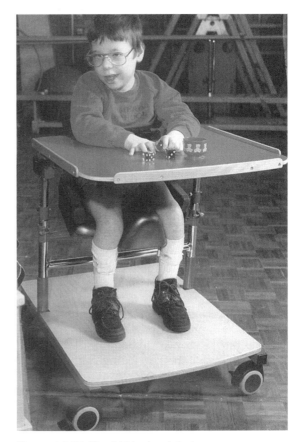

Figure 4.1.24 The SAM wheelchair

the company decided to shelve the product because it could not guarantee commercial viability. The sales that it had predicted fell well below what the company considered to be acceptable levels. Although the company felt a sense of priority and value about the product in that it improved people's quality of life, it was ultimately concerned about its profit levels.

If private money is not invested, should government provide funds to allow this sort of product to be manufactured? Sometimes company profits are put before the genuine needs of some people.

As a result, the SAM (seating and mobility system) wheelchair has been redesigned and relaunched by the company. The design maintains the same principles as the first using the same seat. This supports the body in a forward leaning position to align body posture for users with spinal deformities (see Figure 4.1.24).

The modification of the design comes from adding a motor to allow the user mobility and directional control through a joystick. The base material has been changed to plastic to ensure that any moving parts are covered. The cost of the wheelchair is, therefore, higher but in doing so it has become a more commercially viable product by offering a wider range of uses and possibilities.

Responsibilities of developed countries

The classification of whether a country is developed or developing is generally based on how well it matches a number of criteria based on socio-economic factors. These measures are normally related directly or indirectly to technology and, until quite recently, their specific manufacturing technologies.

The terminology used suggests that all developing countries have positive aspirations to one day becoming a developed country like those that are so deemed to be developed today. As a result of the requirements to meet the qualifying criteria to become a developed nation there is increased pressure to acquire these manufacturing technologies as a symbol of status.

In many ways the developing countries have already had a taste of the status as a result of the export/import markets and so they have had increased accessibility of the products associated with success. The technology and the source of origin is an important value in terms of its worth. However, the value of a technology must always be considered in relation to the product, the environment and social responsibilities. It would take a lot to convince anyone that companies are in business for no other reason than to make money for their owners or shareholders.

There are some very stringent conditions which have to be met as far as financial controls are concerned. However, there are not many controls to protect against environmental damage. Certain measures have been taken such as the banning of CFCs (chlorofluorocarbons) that damage the ozone layer. There is a move within some countries and industries to consider how they can meet the requirements and demands of the customer at the same time as conserving resources.

Developed countries have a responsibility to consider the environmental impacts like the waste and by-products generated as a result of manufacturing processes, the disposal of a product when it reaches the end of its useful life or the pollution created as a result of the energy required in the manufacturing processes.

Design and manufacture should take into account wherever possible the need for:

- more effective and efficient use of materials, and the reuse and recycling of waste materials and products
- reducing the impact on the environment from the products and processes used in their manufacture
- safer disposal of waste
- more efficient use of energy and natural resources
- increased use of sustainable resources such as timber from managed forests.

It is the case with any design decision and solution, that an optimum is looked for and balance drawn between the cost and benefit. Balancing the needs against the impact to the environment is becoming increasingly more difficult for manufacturers as they strive to develop new products and processes. Life cycle assessment (LCA) is a technique now widely used to assess and evaluate the impact of the product from its conception and realisation through to its disposal once it has reached its working end. Designers are now having to consider how parts can be reused, recycled or replaced and maintained so that the product can be serviced rather than simply thrown away.

Tasks

Consider the situation discussed in the case study 'Designing for the market'. List the advantages and disadvantages of the project from the point of view of:

- the customer
- the physiotherapist and
- the managing director of the company.

Exam preparation

You will need to revise all the topics in this unit, so that you can apply your knowledge and understanding to the exam questions. In preparation for your exam, it is a good idea to make brief notes about different topics, such as 'The impact of modern technology and biotechnology on the development of new materials and processes'. Use subheadings or bullet point lists and diagrams where appropriate. A single side of A4 should be used for each of the headings from the Specification.

It is very important to learn exam skills. You should also have weekly practice in learning technical terms and formulae and in answering exam-type questions. When you need to answer any questions you should:

- read the question carefully and pick out the key points that need answering
- match your answer to the marks available, e.g., for two marks you should give two good points that address the question
- always give examples and justify statements with reasons, saying how or why the statement is true.

Practice exam questions

1 Solar power can be harnessed in many ways.
   a) Describe how photovoltaic cells can be used to harness solar power. (3)
   b) Explain the disadvantages of this method of harnessing solar power. (2)

2 a) Window frames can be made in a variety of materials such as timber, aluminium and PVC. Select *two* of the following and explain how they affect the choice of material:
   - material limitations
   - wear and deterioration
   - maintenance. (4)
   b) Describe one disadvantage to the environment of manufacturing the window frames from aluminium. (2)

3 The recycling of materials is an important way of reducing landfill. List five separate component parts of a motor car and explain how they can be recycled or reused. (5)

4 The properties of metals can be modified by heat treatment.
   a) Give an example of one heat treatment process. (1)
   b) Explain how one heat treatment process can modify the properties of metal. (4)

5 a) Explain what is meant by the term 'seasoning'. (1)
   b) Describe using notes and diagrams two methods of seasoning timber. (4)

6 A designer must consider resistance to deterioration when selecting materials for a frame for a children's outdoor swing.
   a) Identify two different materials that could be used for the frame. (2)
   b) Describe the surface finish you would apply to the frame. (3)

7 a) State one way in which biotechnology can reduce the amount of plastic being dumped in landfill sites. (1)
   b) Explain two advantages of the genetic engineering of timbers. (4)

8 Identify the factors a designer might take into account when selecting materials for the frame of a greenhouse. (5)

9 Carbon fibres are now widely used in the manufacture of products such as:
   - tennis rackets
   - skis
   - golf clubs
   - protective body armour.
   Choose one of the products listed above and explain three benefits of using carbon fibre for that product. (6)

Design and technology in society (R402)

Summary of expectations

1. What to expect

Design and technology in society is one of the three options offered in section B of Unit 4. You must study the same option that you studied at AS level.

2. How will it be assessed?

The work that you do in this option will be externally assessed through Section B of the Unit 4 examination paper. The questions will be common across all three materials areas in product Design. You can therefore answer questions with reference to **either**:

- a Resistant Materials Technology product such as a carbon fibre racing bike;
- a Graphics with Materials Technology product such as a 'green' credit card;
- **or** a Textiles Technology product such as a Kevlar bullet proof vest.

You are advised to **spend 45 minutes** on this section of the paper.

3. What will be assessed?

The following list summarises the topics covered in this option and what will be examined.

- Economics and production:
  - economic factors in the production of one-off, batch and mass-produced products.
- Consumer interests:
  - systems and organisations that provide guidance, discrimination and approval
  - the purpose of British, European and International Standards relating to quality, safety and testing
  - relevant legislation on the rights of the consumer when purchasing goods.

- Advertising and marketing:
  - advertising and the role of the design agency in communicating between manufacturers and consumers
  - the role of the media in marketing products
  - market research techniques
  - the basic principles of marketing and associated concepts.
- Conservation and resources:
  - environmental implications of the industrial age
  - management of waste, the disposal of products and pollution control.

4. How to be successful in this unit

To be successful in this unit you will need to:

- have a clear understanding of the topics covered in this option
- apply your knowledge and understanding to a given situation or context
- organise your answers clearly and coherently, using specialist technical terms where appropriate
- use clear sketches where appropriate to illustrate your answers
- write clear and logical answers to the examination questions, using correct spelling, punctuation and grammar.

There may be an opportunity to demonstrate your knowledge and understanding of design and technology in society in your Unit 5 coursework.

5. How much is it worth?

This option, with section A, is worth 15 per cent of the full Advanced GCE.

Unit 4 + option	Weighting
A2 level (full GCE)	15 %

1. Economics and production

Figure 4.2.1 shows the UK's manufacturing sectors.

Economic factors in the production of one-off, batch and mass-produced products

The sequence of activities required to turn raw materials into finished products for the consumer is called the **production chain**. It is the aim of all manufacturing companies to undertake such activities in the most cost-effective manner. The purpose of this is to maximise profit.

The economic factors that combine in order to produce profit include:

- variable costs
  - the costs of production, such as materials, services, labour, energy and packaging
- fixed costs
  - related to design and marketing, administration, maintenance, management, rent and rates, storage, lighting and heating, transport costs, depreciation of plant and equipment.

In order to remain profitable, a manufacturing company must calculate accurately its total costs and set a suitable selling price. This calculation must allow for variable costs, fixed costs and a realistic profit.

The production chain

The production chain includes the following:

- The primary sector is concerned with the extraction of natural resources such as mining and quarrying.

- The secondary sector is concerned with the processing of primary raw materials and the manufacture of products. Although this sector supplies a large proportion of exports from developed countries (such as those of western Europe and the USA), it employs a decreasing proportion of the workforce, as changes in technology and the global economy occur.

- The tertiary sector industries provide a service and include employment in education, retailing, advertising, marketing, banking and finance. This sector employs the most people in developed countries.

In your design and technology course you are mostly concerned with the secondary and tertiary sectors. When you design and manufacture a coursework product, your main concern should be product viability in terms of its cost of manufacture and market potential. For any industry in the secondary sector, however, product viability relates to market potential and profit. Product viability is essential to its very existence and to the employment of that industry's workforce.

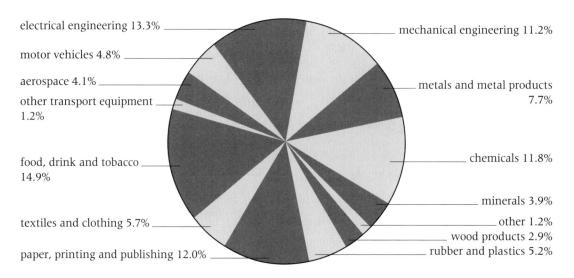

electrical engineering 13.3%

motor vehicles 4.8%

aerospace 4.1%

other transport equipment 1.2%

food, drink and tobacco 14.9%

textiles and clothing 5.7%

paper, printing and publishing 12.0%

mechanical engineering 11.2%

metals and metal products 7.7%

chemicals 11.8%

minerals 3.9%

other 1.2%

wood products 2.9%

rubber and plastics 5.2%

Figure 4.2.1 *Different sectors of manufacturing are located in every region of the country. The sectors of manufacturing that use resistant materials include 'engineering and allied industries', which is the largest group*

Productivity and labour costs

A company's productivity is a measurement of the efficiency with which it turns raw materials (production inputs) into products (manufactured outputs). The most common measure of productivity is output per worker, which has a direct effect on labour costs per unit of production. The higher the productivity, the lower the labour costs per unit of production and therefore the higher the potential profit. Table 4.2.1 compares the weekly wage, output per worker and labour cost per unit of production for two companies. It shows how an efficient company with high output per worker can keep labour costs per unit of production low.

Table 4.2.1 *Comparison of productivity*

	Weekly wage	Output per worker	Labour cost per unit of production
Efficient	£280	40.0	£7
Less efficient company	£250	25.0	£10

Labour costs are linked to the type and length of any production process. For example, a washing machine made from mild steel sheet will have sharp edges where the steel has been cut to size. In order to produce a good quality product these sharp edges will need to be removed or covered. Introducing an additional process such as this will increase labour costs and therefore increase the cost of the product.

Scale of production

Within the economies of the developed countries of the west and Asia, there is a responsibility for all the functions of a company, including manufacturing, to be profitable. For example, in many large companies:

- different internal departments are 'customers' to other internal departments within the same company
- each department has a budget and has to work within this budget or make a profit.

In manufacturing companies the level or scale of production is an extremely important factor for profitability, because it influences the process of manufacture, where the product is manufactured, the choice of products available on the market and their resulting selling price.

One-off products

One-off or custom-made products need to use materials, tools and equipment that are available or that can be resourced fairly easily. They are often less efficient to manufacture, because they may use different or 'specialised' materials and processes. One-off products are usually much more expensive to buy, since materials and labour costs are higher, but they do provide 'individual' or made-to-measure products, such as hand-made kitchen units.

Mass production and the development of new products

On the other hand, mass production has revolutionised the choice and availability of a range of relatively inexpensive products:

- It is increasingly difficult for a company to remain in profit without developing new products, even when existing ones are selling well. Consumer demand can be very fickle and sales of even a best-selling product tail off in time, as new or different competing models come on the market.
- The cost of developing new products is high. It includes initial manufacturing setting up costs such as the factory and its layout and the cost of the workforce.
- New products may require changes in production, which are often difficult to achieve due to the high levels of investment required.
- The development of new production methods needs long-tem planning and may need to overlap with existing production, in order to keep the company running and in profit.
- There is a constant need to reduce the time-to-market of new products. The most successful companies produce the right product at the right time, in the right quantity and at the right cost – one that the market will see as providing the right image as well as being 'value for money'.

Task

Select two similar products, such as a hand-made storage unit and a mass-produced flat pack. For the two products compare the following:
- the type of materials and components used
- the number and estimated length of assembly processes
- the selling price.

Sources, availability and costs of materials

The cost of materials depends on the type and quantity of materials required and their availability. As a general rule, it is a question of supply and demand, so that materials in short supply cost more. Different scales of production also result in different levels of costing. Materials costs are generally lower in high volume production than in one-off manufacture. All product manufacturers require a reliable and continuous supply of raw materials at an economic price to enable profit to be made.

Softwoods and hardwoods

Most softwood is grown in the colder regions of northern Europe and North America. Careful management of these forests enables the control of supply and demand. As conifers are relatively fast-growing and produce straight trunks, they are economic to produce, with little waste. Softwoods are therefore relatively inexpensive. They are used extensively for building construction and joinery. Waste softwood is used in the manufacture of manufactured board and paper.

Hardwoods are slower growing and therefore more expensive than softwoods. They come from broad-leaved deciduous trees, growing in the temperate climates of Europe, Japan and New Zealand. The hardwoods grown in the tropical climates of Central and South America, Africa and Asia are mainly evergreen. These grow all year round and reach maturity earlier, so they are cheaper than the northern hemisphere hardwoods. They are used for furniture, kitchen utensils, flooring, toys, etc.

Manufactured board

The UK is one of the least wooded areas of Europe and has to import almost 90 per cent of its timber needs. Manufactured board is usually supplied debarked, in board form, ready for further processing. Importing the timber in board form is more cost-effective than importing raw timber. There is less waste from processing and manufactured board can travel faster in freight container ships rather than in bulk cargo ships.

Plywood and blockboard are more expensive than medium density fibreboard (MDF) because they are made from better quality timber.

- Plywood is made from European or American birch and meranti from South East Asia.
- Blockboard is made from birch and pine. Birch is used for the facing because it is more durable. The core is made from European or American pine.
- MDF is less expensive than plywood or blockboard because it is made from small section or thinned timber and reconstituted wood.

Manufactured board is made in high volume and is widely used in self assembly furniture, shop fittings and flooring.

Task
Using suppliers' catalogues or the Internet, investigate the cost of softwoods, hardwoods and manufactured board. Explain why there are variations in the cost of different standard sizes.

Metals

Metal ores form about a quarter of the weight of the Earth's crust; the most common ores being aluminium, followed by iron. These metals are relatively inexpensive. They have no particular pattern of distribution around the world, but some countries have larger deposits than others.

Iron and steel account for almost 95 per cent of the total tonnage of all metal production. Ships, trains, cars, trucks, bridges and buildings and thousands of other products depend on the strength, flexibility and toughness of steel.

Sources of ore

- The main sources of iron ore are Europe, North America and Australia. Iron ore has a high metal content and is easily available, so the price of steel is relatively low. Over-production and fierce competition have led to the loss of steel making in some countries.
- Aluminium ore (bauxite) is mainly found in the southern hemisphere. Bauxite is easily accessible, so aluminium is cheaper to make than steel.
- Copper ore is found in the USA, Canada and Chile. The comparative rarity of copper makes it much more expensive than iron ore or bauxite.

Metals in common use, such as iron and aluminium are easily available and the supply problems associated with timber do not normally occur. Lower metal production costs are often achieved by smelting ore close to its source. This reduces transport costs and may make use of lower labour costs.

The importance of oil

Crude oil is an important commodity because it supplies much of the world's energy needs. It is also the principle raw material for making plastics and polymers, without which modern society could not long continue to flourish.

Unfortunately, oil is rarely found where it is needed. The largest oil-producing countries are not themselves major consumers and they are therefore able to export much of their oil. These countries are part of the Organisation of Petroleum Exporting Countries (OPEC), a cartel which sets output quotas in order to control crude oil prices. The members of OPEC are the Middle East, South America, Africa and Asia, but not the USA, the Russian Federation or European oil producers such as the UK. In the 1970s, OPEC controlled 90 per cent of the world's supply of crude oil exports. The resulting high price of oil that OPEC maintained then allowed more expensive fields such as the North Sea and Alaska to be brought into production (see Figure 4.2.2). Oil costs continue to fluctuate, depending on the control of its supply. This can result in higher petrol, energy and raw materials prices worldwide.

Plastics

Most thermoplastic and thermosetting plastics are derived from crude oil so are easily available. In many industries traditional materials such as wood or metal are replaced by inexpensive plastics, which often use fewer processes, as products can be made in one piece. For example polyester (PET) bottles are safer, lighter and cheaper to produce than ones made from glass.

- Thermoplastics are available in sheet or rod form for processing into products, or as granules for injection moulding. Acrylic, polythene, polystyrene, polypropylene and polyester are widely used for a whole range of domestic products.
- The thermosetting plastic epoxy resin is used in adhesives, surfboards and motorbike helmets.

Cost of materials

As we have seen, the cost of timber, manufactured board, metals and plastics is related to their sources and availability. The following can be said about most raw materials:

- materials in short supply or in great demand cost more
- materials that are difficult to process cost more
- materials that come from isolated sources have to be transported further so cost more.

Advantages of economies of scale of production

Economies of scale are factors that cause average costs to be lower in high-volume production than in one-off production (see Figure 4.2.3). The unit price is lower because inputs can be utilised more efficiently. Economies of scale in high-volume production are brought about by:

- specialisation – the work processes are divided up between a workforce with specific skills that match the job
- the spread of fixed costs of equipment between more units of production
- bulk buying of raw materials at lower unit costs
- lower cost of capital charged by providers of finance
- the concentration of an industry in one area – attracting a pool of labour that can be trained to have specialist skills
- a large group of companies in one area – attracting a large network of suppliers whose costs are lower, because of their own economies of scale.

Figure 4.2.2 *Offshore oilfields currently produce about a quarter of the world's crude oil. Great technological skill has been required to design platforms that are stable enough to allow drilling to take place and resilient enough to withstand the harsh conditions of wind and waves*

Task

Devise a checklist that will make your own production more cost-effective. Think about the range of materials, components and processes you might use.

Figure 4.2.3 *One-off products are more expensive to produce, such as this cap and necklace, by Val Hunt. They are made from beer cans, which are annealed, woven, pleated, frilled or curled to produce exciting and creative products*

The relationship between design, planning and production costs

> **SIGNPOST**
> 'Efficient manufacture and profit'
> Unit 3B1 page 111

In order to remain profitable, manufacturers must accurately calculate their total costs and set a suitable product selling price. Target production costs are established from the design stage and checked against existing or similar products. This is done so that the design team can make sound decisions early in the design task.

All costs in a manufacturing company are initiated in the design phase. It is in the manufacturing stage that the major costs are incurred. It is often said therefore that designing for manufacture (DFM) is directly related to designing for cost. The main aims of DFM are:

- to minimise component and assembly costs
- to minimise product development cycles
- to enable higher quality products to be made.

The cost of quality

> **SIGNPOST**
> 'Aesthetics, quality and value for money'
> Unit 3B1 page 113

Manufacturing a competitive product based on a balance between quality and cost is the aim of all companies. The costs of quality are no different from any other costs, because like the cost of design, production, marketing and maintenance,

they can be budgeted for, measured and analysed. There are three types of quality costs:

- the costs of getting it wrong
- the costs checking it is right
- the costs of making it right first time.

The costs of getting it wrong

There are two ways to get it wrong: **internal failure costs** and **external failure costs**.

Internal failure costs occur when products fail to reach the designed quality standards and are detected before being sold to the consumer. They include costs relating to:

- scrap products that cannot be repaired, used or sold
- reworking or correcting faults
- re-inspecting repaired or reworked products
- products that do not meet specifications but are sold as 'seconds'
- any activities caused by errors, poor organisation or the wrong materials.

External failure costs occur when products fail to reach the designed quality standards and are not detected until after being sold to the customer. They include costs relating to:

- repair and servicing
- replacing products under guarantee
- servicing customer complaints
- the investigation of rejected products
- product liability legislation and change of contract
- the impact on the company reputation and image – relating to future potential sales.

The costs of checking it is right

These costs are related to checking:

- materials, processes, products and services against specifications
- that the quality system is working well
- the accuracy of equipment.

The costs of making it right first time

There is one way to get it right: **prevention costs**. These are related to the design, implementation and maintenance of a quality system. Prevention costs are planned and incurred before production and include those relating to:

- setting quality requirements and developing specifications for materials, processes, finished products and services
- quality planning and checking against agreed specifications
- the creation of and conformance to a quality assurance system
- the design, development or purchase of equipment to aid quality checking

- developing training programmes for employees
- the management of quality

Costing a product

Costing is the process of producing an accurate price for a product which will make it saleable and create a profit (see Figure 4.2.4). Setting the selling price too high may reduce sales below a profitable margin, while setting it too low won't allow a profit even if vast numbers are sold. Checks against a competitor's product are often used to establish the potential price range of a new product because they can give an idea of what the market can stand.

Products are sometimes said to have a value, a price and a cost:

- Manufacturers want the income from selling the finished products, rather than keeping them in stock, so for them the product value is always lower than the selling price.
- On the other hand, consumers want the product more than the selling price, as they see the product value as being higher than the selling price.

The total cost of a product takes account of the following:

- **Variable costs** (also known as direct costs) – the actual costs of making a product, such as materials, services, labour, energy and packaging. Variable costs vary with the number of products made. The more products that are made, the greater the variable costs of materials. Variable costs may account for around 50–65 per cent of the total product selling price (SP).
- **Fixed costs** (also known as indirect or overhead costs) – the costs, for example, of design and marketing, administration, maintenance, management, rent and rates, storage, lighting and heating, transport costs, depreciation of plant and equipment. Fixed costs are not directly related to the number of products made, so they remain the same for one product or hundreds. A company's accountants will establish a way to divide up fixed costs between the various product lines made by a company, so that each product carries its share. Marketing and selling costs often account for 15–20 per cent of the total SP.
- **Profit** – the amount left of the SP after all costs have been paid. Profit is referred to as gross or net. The gross profit is calculated by deducting variable plus fixed costs from the revenue from sales. Net profit is gross profit minus tax. Net profit is used to pay dividends to shareholders, bonuses to employees and for reinvestment in new machinery or in new product development.

The break-even point

In order to cover the cost of manufacture, enough products need to be sold at a high enough price. Calculating this requirement is called 'break-even analysis'. The starting point for working out the break-even point is the relationship between fixed costs, overhead costs and the selling price. For example, if the selling price of a lawnmower is £120, how many would need to be sold to cover manufacturing costs and break even? The following formula can be used to work out the break-even point:

$$\text{Break-even point} = \frac{\text{Fixed costs}}{\text{Selling price} - \text{variable costs}}.$$

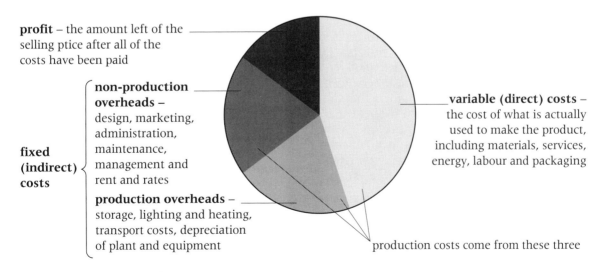

profit – the amount left of the selling ptice after all of the costs have been paid

non-production overheads – design, marketing, administration, maintenance, management and rent and rates

fixed (indirect) costs

production overheads – storage, lighting and heating, transport costs, depreciation of plant and equipment

variable (direct) costs – the cost of what is actually used to make the product, including materials, services, energy, labour and packaging

production costs come from these three

Figure 4.2.4 What's in a price?

Suppose the variable costs of making a lawnmower are £72 and it sells for £120. If the fixed cost of making the lawnmowers is £12,000, what is the break-even point?

$$\text{Break-even point} = \frac{12,000}{120 - 72} = 250$$

So 250 lawn mowers need to be sold to reach the break-even point. Any lawn mowers sold over 250 would make a profit for the company.

Tasks

1 The variable costs for making a cordless drill are £49 and it sells for £85. If the fixed cost of making the drills is £8,500 work out the break-even point.
2 Explain the difference between gross and net profit.

The material and manufacturing potential for a given design solution

When manufacturers calculate the potential selling costs of a product, they have to take into account more than just manufacturing costs. Consumer expectations of the value of the product play an important part. This will depend on two things: what customers perceive as value for money and what the competition is offering.

As can be seen from Figure 4.2.5, the forces acting on pricing decisions are complex. The perceived value of a product is reflected in the likelihood of customers continuing to buy a

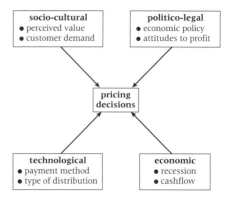

Figure 4.2.5 *The forces acting on pricing decisions*

product in the face of a price increase. This is the pattern for products like food items or services like heating. Unless they become prohibitively expensive, we continue buying them. For non-essential purchases such as a second car, demand can drop when they become more expensive. Other forces acting on price include the economic and political climate – how high are taxes, is there a recession, is there full employment?

Task

Some say that there is no direct connection between the product cost and the selling price. In the same way that materials in short supply cost more, the manufacturer of a popular product in limited supply can add a large mark-up to the price. Give examples of products that prove or disprove this theory.

2. Consumer interests

The relationship between manufacturers as producers and consumers as buyers is important. Manufacturers want their products to sell well and make a profit. Consumers want to buy high-quality, attractive products that are reliable, easy to maintain, safe to use and that provide value for money at a price they can afford. A manufacturer's success in producing goods that meet consumer requirements relies on keeping consumer needs and values at the heart of the business.

Systems and organisations that provide guidance, discrimination and approval

Most large companies use market research to establish consumer needs, values and tastes.

They must also take into account consumers' statutory rights when buying products. These rights are enforced and regulated by a wide range of legislation relating to consumer protection and fair trading. There are many systems and organisations that provide guidance, discrimination and approval for consumers. These include:

- the Institute of Trading Standards Administration
- British, European and International Standards organisations
- consumer 'watchdog' organisations.

Consumer 'watchdog' organisations

These days consumers are much more aware of new products. One reason for this developing consumer awareness is the profusion of 'style' sections in newspapers and magazines. Products ranging from kettles to cameras are regularly featured and their desirability and value for money evaluated.

Consumer 'watchdog' organisations and specialist magazines also provide guidance, discrimination and approval for new products (see Figure 4.2.6). These organisations are independent of product manufacturers and provide objective reviewing and testing of products. One such organisation is the Consumers Association, which publishes the magazine *Which?*. This provides reports about product testing and 'best buys'. It has a website, found at www.which.co.uk, which provides a range of information, such as an overview of its activities, 'headlines' for daily consumer news and links to electronic newspapers.

Other groups that provide consumer support include television and radio programmes, many of which give information and guidance on consumer rights. Consumer advice and support is also available from the Citizens Advice Bureau (CAB).

Task

Investigate the work of two different consumer organisations. Compare their roles and the range of products they evaluate. For each organisation explain how their product reviews:

- help or hinder product manufacturers
- guide consumer choice.

DIGITAL CAMERAS		Canon Digital Ixus 400	Canon PowerShot G3	Casio Exilim EX-Z3	Fujifilm FinePix F 410 Zoom	Fujifilm FinePix M 603 Zoom	Kodak EasyShare LS 633 Zoom	Konica Digital Revio KD-500Z	Kyocera Finecam S5	Minolta Dimage F300	Minox DC 3311	Nikon Coolpix 31
SPECIFICATION												
Price (£)	1▷	450	600	350	296	350	300	450	350	430	350	280
Largest image size in pixels		2,272x1,704	2,272x1,704	2,048x1,536	2,816x2,120	2,832x2,128	2,032x1,524	2,592x1,944	2,560x1,920	2,560x1,920	2,048x1,536	2,048x1,53
Effective megapixels	2▷	4.0	4.0	3.2	3.1	3.1	3.3	5.0	5.0	5.0	3.1	3.2
Zoom range	3▷	36-108	35-140	35-105	38-114	38-76	37-111	39-117	35-105	38-114	32-96	38-115
Size (hxwxd) (cm)		6x9.5x3.1	8x13x7.5	6x9.5x2.4	7x9x3.5	9.5x7x4	6x12x4	6x10x3.5	6x9.5x4	6x11.5x4	8x11.5x7.5	7x9x4.5
Weight (g)	4▷	231	525	147	199	288	240	229	198	239	349	219
Number of batteries required		1	1	1	1	1	1	1	1	1	4	2
Supplied with rechargeable batteries	5▷	✓	✓	✓	✓	✓	✓	✓	✓			✓
Supplied with battery charger	5▷	✓	✓	✓	✓	✓	✓	✓	✓			✓
Software included	6▷	Zoom Browser EX, ArcSoft photo suite	Zoom Browser EX, Adobe Photoshop	Photo Loader	Finepix Viewer	Finepix Viewer	Kodak Easy-Share software	none supplied	ArcSoft photo suite	Dimage Image Viewer	MGI PhotoSuite, Photo Vista	Nikon View, Adobe Photoshop Elements
FEATURES												
Manual focus setting	7▷	✓	✓	✓					✓	✓	✓	
Short video recording	8▷	✓	✓	✓	✓	✓	✓	✓	✓	✓		✓
Sound recording	8▷	✓	✓		✓	✓	✓	✓	✓	✓		
MEMORY												
Camera's internal memory (Mb)	9▷	0	0	10	0	0	16	2	0	0	8	0
Memory card supplied (Mb)		32	32	0	16	16	0	16	16	64	0	16
Compatible memory cards	10▷	CF I	CF I or II	SD or MMC	xD	xD or CF II	SD or MMC	SD or MS	SD or MMC	SD	CF I	CF I
Image quality settings	11▷	12	13	12	4	5	4	8	8	16	6	4
PERFORMANCE												
Shutter delay on auto focus (sec)	12▷	0.9	1.4	0.5	0.5	0.7	0.7	1.1	1.2	1.5	2.5	0.7
Flash		☆	★	○	☆	☆	☆	☆	○	☆	○	☆
Battery life		○	★	☆	★	○	★	☆	○	◕	★	★
Time to download pics to PC		☆	★	★	★	★	◕	◕	○	★	☆	★
Focusing	13▷	☆	☆	☆	○	☆	☆	☆	○	☆	☆	☆
Close-up rating	14▷	◕	☆	★	★	☆	☆	★	★	★	★	☆
Time between shots	15▷	★	★	☆	★	☆	★	★	★	★	○	★
Overall picture quality		☆	☆	○	○	☆	○	☆	○	☆	○	☆
Overall ease of use		☆	○	☆	☆	○	○	○	○	○	○	☆
TOTAL TEST SCORE (%)		64	62	51	58	59	56	56	55	60	48	63

Figure 4.2.6 Products are regularly reviewed in consumer magazines

The purpose of British, European and International Standards relating to quality, safety and testing

SIGNPOST
'British and International Standards'
Unit 3B1 page 120

European and International Standards organisations set national and international standards, testing procedures and quality assurance processes to make sure that manufacturers make products that fulfil the safety and quality needs of their customers and the environment. Most standards are set at the request of industry or to implement legislation. Manufacturers of upholstered furniture, for example, have to conform to established fire safety standards. The test procedures for checking fire safety have to comply with British Standards (BS) guidelines and must be carried out under controlled conditions.

Any product that meets a British Standard can apply for and be awarded a 'Kitemark'. This shows potential customers that the product has met the required standard and that the manufacturer has a quality system in place to ensure that every product is made to exactly the same standard.

The relationship between standards, testing procedures, quality assurance, manufacturers and consumers

Common to all commercial product manufacture is the need to produce a quality product. For manufacturers, incorporating quality management systems into the design and manufacture of products is therefore important. ISO 9000 is an internationally agreed set of standards for the development and operation of a **quality management system** (QMS). ISO 9001 and 9002 are the mandatory parts of the ISO 9000 series. They specify the clauses manufacturers have to comply with in order to achieve registration to the standard. A QMS involves a structured approach to ensure that customers end up with a product or service that meets agreed standards.

Quality management systems

All industrial quality management systems use structured procedures to manage the quality of the designing and making process. The following designing and making procedures illustrate the kind of quality management process that industry adopts and uses:

- Explore the intended use of the product, identify and evaluate existing products, consider the needs of the client.
- Produce a design brief and specification.
- Use research, questionnaires and product analysis.
- Produce a range of appropriate solutions.
- Refer back to the specification.
- Refer to existing products. Use models to test aspects of the design.
- Check with the client. Use models to check that the product meets the design brief and specification.
- Plan manufacture and understand the need for safe working practices.
- Manufacture the product to the specification.
- Critically evaluate the product in relation to the specification and the client. Undertake detailed product testing and reach conclusions. Produce proposals for further development, modifications or improvements.

You will probably be familiar with many of the procedures outlined above, because they are very similar to ones you use in your coursework.

Task
Compare the designing and making procedures listed above with the ones you used in your most recent project. Comment on any similarities and differences you find.

Applying standards

Risk assessment

In any product manufacturing situation, hazards must be controlled. A hazard is a source of potential harm or damage or a situation with potential harm or damage. Hazard control incorporates the manufacture of a product and its safe use by the consumer. As part of the Health and Safety at Work Act 1974 risk assessment is a legal requirement for all manufacturers in the UK. Its use is a fundamental part of any quality management system. The main purpose of the Health and Safety at Work Act is to control risks and to enable decisions to be made about the level of existing risk control. Figure 4.2.7 shows how a risk assessment may be planned.

A risk has two elements:

- the possibility that a hazard might occur
- the consequences of the hazard having taken place.

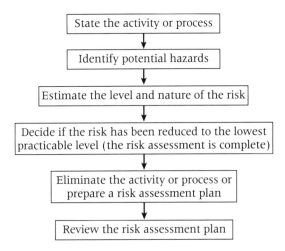

Figure 4.2.7 How a risk assessment is planned

Ergonomics

SIGNPOST
'Anthropometrics and ergonomics'
Unit 3B1 page 118

Ergonomics is the application of scientific data to design problems. This means applying the characteristics of human users to the design of a product – in other words matching the product to the user. In order to do this, data about the size and shape of the human body is required – this branch of ergonomics is called anthropometrics.

Anthropometric data must take into account the greatest possible number of users. This data exists in the form of charts, which provide measurements for the 90 per cent of the population that fall between the fifth and the ninety-fifth percentiles (see Figure 4.2.8). Consumer products ranging from tools to storage units are generally easier, safer and more efficiently used if anthropometric data is used in their design.

Relevant legislation on the rights of the consumer when purchasing goods

Consumers are protected by a body of law called 'statutory rights'. This sets out what consumers should *reasonably* expect when buying products. The body of law includes legislation such as the Sale of Goods Act 1979,

the Supply of Goods and Services Act 1982 and the Sale and Supply of Goods to Consumers Regulations 2002.

Statutory rights protect consumers' 'reasonable expectations' when buying products in a shop, market, on the doorstep, by mail order, through direct response TV, leaflets, magazines and newspaper advertisements or on the Internet. In fact, it does not matter where or how goods are bought, consumers' statutory rights remain the same.

Statutory rights

As a consumer you expect any product that you buy to look and perform satisfactorily. In order to meet the Sale of Goods Act 1979 products must satisfy the following conditions:

- They must be 'as described', 'of satisfactory quality' and fit for any purpose which the

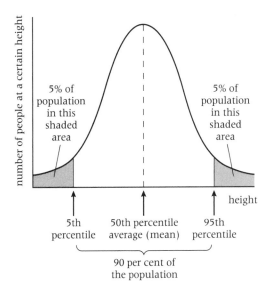

Figure 4.2.8 Anthropometric data uses measurements representative of 90 per cent of the population (the fifth to ninety-fifth percentile).

consumer *makes known* to the retailer. For example, if you are told a computer game will work on your particular machine it must do so, or you have good reason to complain.

- Products are of satisfactory quality if they reach the standard that a reasonable person would consider satisfactory, taking into account their price and how they are described. For example, if a product is described as being scratch proof and scratches appear during reasonable use, you have good reason to complain.
- Satisfactory quality covers fitness for purpose, appearance and finish, freedom from minor defects, durability and safety.

Under the Sale of Goods Act 1979 it is the *retailer*, not the manufacturer who is responsible. If a product is not of satisfactory quality the buyer is entitled, within a reasonable time, to return the product and get a refund. In order to build customer loyalty, many retailers exchange products that consumers decide are the wrong size, fit or colour, as long as there is proof of purchase.

Sale goods

The Sale of Goods Act 1979 still applies to sale goods, so notices that say 'no refunds on sale goods' are illegal and local authorities can prosecute traders who display them. However, you are not entitled to a refund on a sale item if you were told about some fault before purchase, did not see the fault, damaged the product yourself, bought the item by mistake or changed your mind about it.

The Sale and Supply of Goods to Consumers Regulations 2002

The Sale and Supply of Goods to Consumers Regulations 2002 became law in March 2003. It ensures that consumers enjoy a minimum level of protection when they buy goods from any country within the European Community. The new legislation states that:

- every consumer has the right to a repair or replacement for faulty goods
- if the consumer requests a repair or replacement, then for the first six months after purchase it will be for the retailer to prove that the product was not faulty when sold
- after six months and until the end of six years, it is up to the consumer to prove that the goods were faulty when sold. This does not mean, however, that a product has to last for six years as the life expectancy of products will vary.

Task

Before you buy

Choose two mid-price products that you recently bought. For each product answer the following questions:

- Did you think through buying it?
- Is it what you really wanted?
- How much did you want to pay?
- How did you pay – cash, credit or a different way?
- Did you shop around?
- Did you compare prices?
- Did you ask about after-sales service?
- Could it have been delivered?
- Was it an impulse buy?
- Did you buy it from a trader who is fair?

Write a report on the two products, summarising the above points. Compare your report with a colleague.

If things go wrong

If a product is not of a satisfactory quality when you buy it or when you try it out, you can reject it and get your money back.

- You need not accept a replacement, a free repair or a credit note.
- If you do agree to a repair, you can still claim your money back if the repair turns out to be unsatisfactory.
- Be careful if you accept a credit note as there may be restrictions on its use.
- You do not lose the right to reject a product by signing a delivery note.

If you have used the product for more than a trial and it goes wrong or is of unsatisfactory quality, you cannot reject it, but can claim reasonable compensation. This can be for loss in value of the product and for any harm caused by its use. Reasonable compensation is often repair, replacement or a price reduction.

If the product was faulty when you bought it and if it is reasonable for it to last that long, you can claim compensation for up to six years after purchase. If you bought the product on credit or with a credit card, you may also have rights against the credit company.

If you need to complain about a faulty product, you should quickly return to the shop, state the problem and how you want it dealt with. If the response is not satisfactory, write to the shop head office with details of the problem and a copy of your receipt. If you have lost the receipt use other evidence, such as a credit card or bank statement.

Help in solving problems

Sometimes consumers need advice and guidance on everyday shopping problems. Local authority Trading Standards Officers enforce and advise on a wide range of legislation relating to consumer protection and deal with problems and complaints. Details of local Trading Standards departments can be found on the Trading Standards website: www.tradingstandards.gov.uk.

> ### Tasks
> **Making a complaint**
> Sometimes a product does not perform as expected and a complaint must be made. Imagine you have recently bought a portable DVD player that fails to work properly. Describe the actions you would take to complain about the product:
>
> **a)** in person
> **b)** by telephone
> **c)** in writing.

3. Advertising and marketing

Advertising and the role of the design agency in communicating between manufacturers and consumers

Advertising is any type of media communication that informs and influences existing or potential customers. The cost of advertising is a major marketing expense and in spite of all the money that is spent on it no one really knows what really makes it work!

Many large companies employ advertising agencies to run their advertising campaigns. Successful campaigns sell products and they are often the ones that we as consumers remember. There are said to be two approaches to advertising – hard sell and soft sell.

Hard sell

A hard sell advertisement has a simple and direct message about the benefits of a product. It projects a product's **unique selling proposition (USP)**; its unique features and advantages over a competitor's product. Hard sell works best with functional products such as computer equipment e.g., in a recent campaign a company grinds to a halt because it does not use IBM computers.

Soft sell

On the other hand, soft sell advertisements promote a product's image, with which consumers can identify. This approach takes for granted the benefits of the product and focuses on creating positive emotional associations with the product. Soft sell is often used to create brand loyalty and is successfully associated with frequently bought items like detergent.

> ### Task
> Find one hard sell and one soft sell advertisement in a newspaper or magazine.
> **a)** Devise a list of changes that would make the hard sell softer and the soft sell harder.
> **b)** Explain how your changes would make the advertisements still appeal to the same target market groups.

Successful advertising campaigns

Successful advertising campaigns are often associated with brands. For example, the Black & Decker cordless Quattro VP 2000, a multi-functional power tool, was launched into a highly competitive market in 1998. Different heads can be plugged into a Power Handle to convert it into a drill, screwdriver, sander or saw.

The product marketing used traditional marketing techniques and promotions were clearly aimed at developing new DIY market opportunities by satisfying the needs of first-time buyers in this market. The unique selling proposition (USP) for the Quattro was that it was sold as a one-kit box, with no need to buy extra attachments and the rechargeable batteries made the tool ready for use when needed.

Advertising standards

The Advertising Standards Authority (ASA) regulates all British advertising in non-broadcast media. The code has three basic points which state that advertisements should:

* be legal, decent, honest and truthful
* show responsibility to the consumer and to society
* follow business principles of 'fair' competition.

The role of the media in marketing products

The main aim of marketing through the media is to influence customers' buying decisions, to help sell more products and promote a good public image for a company. Paid-for media options include:

* the press – newspapers, magazines and direct mail
* broadcast media – television and radio
* cinema
* outdoor – posters and sports grounds
* electronic – direct e-mail and the Internet.

An important source of information when choosing an advertising medium is a large-scale regular survey called the Target Group Index (TGI). This researches the consumption patterns of a representative sample of consumers – asking questions about the products they buy and use, what they watch, read and listen to. Subscribing to this survey allows a marketing organisation to match its target market with the media it uses most.

Table 4.2.2 is a guide to the strengths and weaknesses of the major types of media.

Table 4.2.2 Strengths and weaknesses of the major types of media

Strengths	Weaknesses
Television (around 33% of UK advertising expenditure) • High audiences, but spread over channels • Excellent for showing product in use	• Short time span of commercials is limiting • High wastage – viewers not in target market
Newspapers, magazines (around 60% of UK advertising expenditure) • Can target the market with detailed info • Can get direct response (reply coupon)	• Can have a low impact on consumers • Timing may not match marketing campaign
Radio (around 2-3% of UK advertising expenditure) • Accurate geographical targeting • Low cost and speedy	• Low numbers compared to other media • Listen to it in the background to other tasks
Posters (around 4% of UK advertising expenditure) • More than 100,000 billboards available • Relatively cheap	• Seen as low impact/ complicated to buy • Subject to damage and defacement

Task

1 Collect a variety of advertisements from magazines and newspapers. For each advertisement explain:
   * the image given about the product – is it luxury or bottom end of the market or something in between?
   * the target market, relating to demographics and lifestyle
   * any 'hidden ' messages about the product – the use of emotions, concern, fear, compassion, persuasion, politics
   * any 'values' attached to the product
   * if it is hard sell or soft sell
   * if the product is advertised in other media or is part of wider campaign. If so, do any other adverts differ? How?

2 You need to promote your coursework product to the consumers in your target market group.
   a) Describe the features and characteristics of your product.
   b) Describe the buying behaviour and lifestyle of your target market group.
   c) Choose two different media for an advertising campaign and explain why each is appropriate for your product.
   d) Explain how an Internet marketing campaign could help you reach your target market.

Market research techniques

Questions such as 'Who are my customers?' and 'What are their needs?' must be answered before any decision is made about what to make, what to charge, how to promote it and how to distribute it. In order to find answers to such questions, it is necessary to undertake marketing research. This involves the use of market research techniques to identify:

* the nature, size and preferences of current and potential target market groups and sub-groups (called **market segments**)
* the buying behaviour of the target market group

- the competition – and its strengths and weaknesses (this includes pricing and marketing policies)
- the required characteristics of new products – matching these to target market needs (this information is also used to improve existing products and to identify 'gaps' in the market)
- the effect price changes might have on demand – how sales would be affected by a price increase, how the price compares to that of a competitor, the price to set for a new product
- trends in design, colour, demographics, employment, interest rates and inflation.

Conducting marketing research

Marketing research comes from two types of sources:

- Primary sources provide original research, from things like internal company data, questionnaires and surveys.
- Secondary sources provide published information from things like trade publications, commercial reports, government statistics, computer databases. Other sources of secondary research include the media and the Internet.

When conducting primary research to find out, for example, about the size and buying behaviour of a target market group, two types of data can be collected: quantitative and qualitative.

Quantitative research

This kind of research often uses a survey to collect data about *how many* people hold similar views or display particular characteristics. Normally, the information is collected from a small proportion (a 'sample') of a target market group. The views of the whole target market group are then based on the responses from the sample.

Qualitative research

This kind of research collects data about *how* people think and feel about issues or *why* they take certain decisions. Qualitative research explores consumer behaviour and is conducted among a few individuals. It is often used to plan further quantitative research to see if the views of a few are representative of the whole target market group.

Surveys

A survey is a way of collecting quantitative data, often about behaviour, attitudes and opinions of a sample in a target market group. The most effective way to conduct a survey is to follow a series of key activities.

Task

There are four main types of surveys; interview, telephone, mail and self-completion surveys. They all have benefits and disadvantages. Some of the benefits are listed in the table below. For each of the four survey types, list and explain the disadvantages of using that particular method.

Table 4.2.3 *Benefits of different survey types*

Survey type	Benefits
Interview	The most reliable way to get data using a questionnaire. Questions can be clarified by the interviewer.
Telephone	Quick and inexpensive if the questionnaire is short.
Mail	Usually very inexpensive (no interviewer or phone costs). Can use longer questionnaires to reach a wide population
Self-completion surveys	The least expensive. Can distribute questionnaires to a captive audience on trains and planes.

Questionnaires

The design of any questionnaire is critical in order to get the kind of answers that allow decisions to be made. Always test a questionnaire before using it. In general, shorter questionnaires are usually better than long ones. The wording of questions is important too. They should be:

- relevant – only include questions that target the information required
- clear – avoid long words, jargon and technical terms;questions must be easy to understand
- inoffensive – take care with questions about age, social class, salary, ethnicity, so as not to cause offence (use these types of question at the end)
- brief – short questions of less than 20 words
- precise – each question should tackle one topic at a time
- impartial – avoid 'leading' questions that influence the answer.

Types of questions

- Open-ended questions, such as 'What is your opinion of the C5 car?', allow very wide and ambiguous answers that may not be useful.

- Closed questions provide a limited number of optional answers to choose from. They are easier to answer and are often used in surveys. Avoid offering two options such as yes/no because they are of limited use.

Multiple-choice questions offer a range of different types (see Figure 4.2.9).

Task

You are designing a folding stool for young people going camping. Draw up a questionnaire to find out their requirements.

Product analysis

SIGNPOST
'Developing product analysis skills'
Unit 1 page 13

As we have seen in Unit 1, product analysis is an important tool for the designer. It enables the analysis of a competitor's product and the development of specifications for new products.

Tasks

Planning a shop report
A shop report can involve:

- window shopping
- going into shops and stores to look for trends, themes, styling and colour ideas
- going to art galleries and museums to look for ideas and design information.

Plan a shop report on interior domestic lighting. Use your research to match the design, style and price of desk lights to the potential customer. Sketch the products and record the materials and components used.

Figure 4.2.9 Multiple-choice questions from a questionnaire on kettles

What is your age? (tick one only)
Under 18 ☐   18–64 ☐   65 or over ☐
Which types of kettles do you prefer? (tick as many as apply)
Jug ☐   Stainless steel ☐   Patterned ☐
Where did you buy your kettle?
Supermarket ☐   DIY store ☐
Department store ☐   Mail order ☐
Don't know ☐
Other (please specify) ——————————

Test marketing (test selling)

The purpose of **test marketing** is to find out potential problems with a new product before its full-scale marketing. It is done under real market conditions to find out customer and retailer reactions to the product – who are the buyers? how often do they buy? This enables forecasts to be made of future sales and profitability and enables production planning to take place.

Marketing research case study – taking risks

The risk of not doing any research is high, because it can mean making the wrong decisions. Imagine that a company is thinking about adding a new product to its range, but is put off by the high cost of research. The company has the option of launching the product on the market and risking failure rather than funding research costs. A product failure could undermine the reputation of the company and its existing products. Should it decide to undertake the costly research or risk launching the product?

The case study below illustrates the importance of undertaking marketing research when developing new products. It tells the story of the Sinclair C5 car.

The C5 car

The image of the one-seater, three-wheeler C5 came somewhere between a car and a bicycle (see Figure 4.2.10). It was developed as a result of two circumstances – the abolishment of tax on electric vehicles in 1980 and legislation allowing anyone over the age of 14 to drive an electrically assisted cycle without

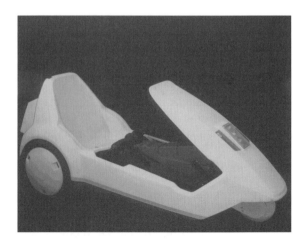

Figure 4.2.10 Many consumers thought that the C5 was a 'fun' car, rather than a serious form of transport

a helmet or insurance (would this be allowed today?)

Developing the car

Sir Clive Sinclair had already achieved technological success with his executive pocket calculator and pocket TV. He openly admitted that he did not believe in marketing research because he did not think it worked for new products. How could the demand for an innovative product be assessed when nothing like it already existed? Sinclair predicted sales of 100,000 C5 cars a year and planned to start production in the autumn of 1984. Any research that was done was mainly connected with product development. At the same time 63 families from urban and suburban areas were asked to try out the prototype car. They were also asked how much they thought the car would cost and estimates ranged from £1,000 to £2,500. The final product price was set at £399 and the car was to be sold by mail order.

The C5 is launched

There was no test marketing of the car and it was launched in January 1985 at Alexandra Palace in north London. The timing and venue couldn't have been worse! Alexandra Palace is set in a hilly area and it had been snowing. Journalists were invited to go for a test drive through the snow-covered, hilly grounds of 'Ally Pally'. The journalists that did test drive the car were concerned about its road-worthiness under such conditions. But worse was to come! The Consumers Association tested the C5 and produced the following criticisms:

- On the road, the C5 was the same height as the bumpers of other cars – this made it difficult to see and increased the chance of accidents.
- The C5's low height meant that exhaust fumes, spray from rain and dazzle from the headlights of other cars were in the direct line of vision of the C5 driver.
- The C5's headlight beam was not strong enough, the horn was too quiet and mirrors and indicators were optional extras.
- There was no reverse gear, so drivers had to get out of the C5 to move it backwards.
- The top speed of the car was 15 mph – this caused problems even where the speed limit was 30 mph.
- The C5 only went for 15 miles on a fully charged battery, not the 20 miles as was planned.
- Drivers had to pedal on hills, because the motor kept cutting out.

In addition to this, the car had been tested only on a test track, rather than in heavy traffic, and accident testing had been simulated. After only three months, production was cut back by 90 per cent. Production was stopped within six months, after only 14,000 cars had been produced. Could it have been that the marketing was wrong? Many consumers thought that the C5 was a 'fun' car, rather than a serious form of transport to rival the moped.

Task

Read the C5 case study and then answer the following questions:

a) Describe your reactions to this case study. Do you think it humorous or tragic? Justify your answer.

b) Describe what went wrong with the C5 design and development. Explain how market research could have resulted in a different outcome. Describe what this outcome might have been.

c) List the main types of research you think should have been done. Explain why this research could have been helpful.

d) Produce annotated sketches to describe any changes that could have been made to improve the design of the car. Develop these ideas into a new car design.

e) Describe the characteristics of the intended users of your new car design.

The marketing research process

There are three key stages in the marketing research process. These are planning, implementation and interpretation.

Planning

Identify a clear reason and purpose for marketing research. This reason usually relates to a problem, an issue or opportunity for design. Once the reason is found (often in the form of a design brief), it is used as a starting point for research – what data needs to be found out and how to collect it.

Implementation

There are many ways of collecting data, depending on the research plan and what needs to be found out. Surveys and questionnaires can be useful, but can sometimes be expensive. Always think about alternatives.

Interpretation

The information that is created when data is collected should be interpreted in relation to the design problem. All findings should be used to influence decision making.

Tasks

Planning marketing research

Read the marketing research process above.

a) Choose a target market group for the C5 car.

b) Write a design brief to include purpose of the car, what it should do and the range of potential users.

c) Draw up a marketing research plan, that includes planning, implementation and interpretation.

The basic principles of marketing and associated concepts

SIGNPOST
'Design and marketing' Unit 3B1 page 111

Marketing involves anticipating and satisfying consumer needs while ensuring a company remains profitable. The main objectives of marketing include:

- generating profit
- developing sales
- increasing market share
- diversifying into new markets.

In order to do this companies must create opportunities for meeting customer needs, for managing change within design and production and for promoting a corporate image. The main method of achieving this is through a marketing plan.

Marketing plan

A good sales and marketing plan involves developing a competitive edge through providing reliable, high-quality products at a price customers can afford, combined with the image they want the product to give them. This is sometimes called lifestyle marketing.

The basic structure of a product marketing plan includes:

- background and situation analysis, including **SWOT** (product strengths, weaknesses, opportunities and threats from competition) and **PEST** (political, economic, social and technological issues)
- information on markets, customers and competitors
- a plan for action and advertising strategies
- planning marketing costs
- time planning – the best time to market the product to an achievable timetable
- a plan for monitoring the marketing.

Target market groups

Companies supply their goods to customers. A market consists of all the customers of all the companies and organisations supplying a specific product, for example the car market or the domestic lighting market. As a result of undertaking marketing research, some companies decide that they cannot possibly supply all the potential customers in their markets – maybe the market is very large, geographically scattered, maybe the competition is strong or customer needs too varied. In this case companies have to decide which types of customers to aim for and then to target their products at them – at a selected part of the market (known as the market segment). The process of identifying market segments and developing products for it is called target marketing.

Consumer demand and market pull

Customers in a market demand or 'pull' products and services to satisfy their needs. The job of the marketing department is to maximise the demand for its own company's products. Existing customers must be satisfied with these products and not be tempted to buy from other suppliers. At the same time the customers of other suppliers need to be persuaded to change their product brand loyalty. Further to this, potential new customers need to be attracted, in order to expand the company's market share.

Task

Identify three products which you think have been developed as a result of market demand. Identify the characteristics of these products.

Lifestyle marketing

Lifestyle is used as a basis for target marketing. Different lifestyles have been identified by investigating the geographic and demographic characteristics of the population. People with similar demographic characteristics often live in similar types of houses and have similar lifestyles. For example, young professional people living in towns and cities and who are either working or studying to improve their lifestyle form one group. They tend to be young, highly educated, live in high-status areas and have a high level of mobility. This group may then be broken down into further types, such as well-off town and city areas, singles and young working couples, furnished flats and bedsits, younger single people.

Lifestyle marketing is the targeting of these potential market groups and matching their needs with products. Market research identifies the buying behaviour, taste and lifestyle of these potential customers. This establishes the amount of money they have to spend, their age group and which products they like to buy. New products can then be developed to match their needs.

Brand loyalty

Branding is a key marketing tool for many manufacturers. A 'brand' is a marketing identity for a generic product that sets it apart from its competitors. The brand name protects and promotes the identity of the product, so that it cannot be copied by competitors. Typical brand names include 'Hoover' or 'Dyson'. A branded product usually has additional features or added value over and above other generic products – something that makes the product 'special' in the eyes of consumers.

Advantages of branding for the customer

For the customer, buying branded products provides an expected and reliable level of quality. Brand names also give consumers benchmarks when making their own purchasing decisions. For example, some people might use the AppleMac personal computer (see Figure 3.2.1 in Unit 3B1 on page 96) as a reference brand against which other computers are compared. The status and image of a strong brand and brand loyalty can therefore be powerful influences over which products consumers buy (see Figure 4.2.11). For consumers, the benefit of knowing which brands provide certain reliable or good quality products can also save time when deciding which product to buy.

Figure 4.2.11 *Strong brands promote brand loyalty amongst consumers*

Competitive edge and product proliferation

If there are several companies producing a wide range of similar products for the same customers with similar needs, the only criterion upon which customers can base their buying decision is price. In theory the most expensive products would not sell, but this is rarely the case – since most customers are not aware of every product and price on the market.

To ensure that their products have a successful market share, many manufacturers try to make their products different from a competitor's. This involves creating unique features for the product in order to give it a 'competitive edge'. For example, some manufacturers might offer 'special' features or different levels of quality. Different price levels can then be set – these are often based on the value that customers might put on these features or qualities.

Task

Compare the cost and design features of a branded product with the cost and design features of a similar 'own brand' product. Explain how the unique features of the branded product give it a competitive edge over the own brand.

Task

Investigate the design features of a range of branded hand tools sold in your local DIY store. Explain how this product range promotes a brand image and why it might be attractive to the target market.

Price range and pricing strategy

Price is one of the most important aspects of marketing because a product's price affects profit, the volume of products manufactured, the share of the market and the image of the product. We've probably all heard the term 'cheap and nasty'!

Task

Market share and promotional gifts

1 The aim of marketing departments and advertising companies is to increase the market share of brands and products. Research has shown that in advertising success breeds success. Increasing the market share of an already successful product or brand is easier than for a less successful or less well-known brand. Try to explain the reasons for this.

2 Direct marketing often includes mailshots with free 'gifts' or samples, often with a coupon that provides money off for the next purchase. Explain why you agree or disagree with this kind of marketing.

The key to successful pricing is the attractiveness of the price to the customers. The concept of price, value and quality are difficult to separate. How much we are prepared to pay for a product depends on how much we value it. The justification for a higher price may depend on the following:

- a product's extra features, characteristics or innovative design
- the perceived quality of the product
- the increased reputation of the product brought about by advertising and promotion
- the possibility of paying by credit, which justifies a higher final price
- the guarantee of a specific delivery date and easy access to the product through mail order or the Internet.

Distribution

The distribution of products covers a variety of operations. They make the product available to the maximum numbers of target customers at the lowest cost. The way that technology and communications have changed in the past few years has had an enormous impact on the distribution of products and the way we shop.

Task

List three ways that consumers shop these days in comparison with shopping in the 1970s. Explain the main factors that have brought about these changes in shopping.

4. Conservation and resources

Environmental implications of the industrial age

One of the greatest problems relating to the industrial age is the consumption of non-renewable, finite resources which will eventually be exhausted (see Figure 4.2.12). Recognition of this problem leads to an understanding of the need for conservation and the better management of resources. It also needs to lead to a better understanding of the meaning of 'design' and the **'purchase-attraction'** culture.

The future – designing where less is more

There are a number of questions relating to product design that need to be answered. For example:

Figure 4.2.12 *Open cast mining is now used to obtain the bulk of most minerals, although the environmental damage is severe*

- What will be the aims of product design in the future?
- How can we manage the changes necessary to our technological-industrial society to make life on earth bearable in the future?

One of the greatest problems for product designers of the future will be how to design with the environment in mind. Previous sections of this unit discussed mass production and the marketing of products. We saw that the aim for most manufacturers is to sell as many products as they can in order to make a profit. Designers now and in the future will need to decide if this is an ethical way forward.

Influencing the future

The key question is how design can influence the environmental safety of products and how it can contribute to a reduction in the number of products made.

At present we have what is called a 'purchase-attraction' culture, which results in the proliferation of products that we see in the market place today. In the future this may have to make way for a culture that supports long-term use and the conservation of resources. Changing the purchase-attraction culture could be achieved by:

- changing our attitude to products from purchase-attraction to their long-term use and usefulness
- developing products that would not be bought, but that remain the property of the manufacturer
- paying for the use of the product and its maintenance
- returning products to the manufacturer to be serviced, repaired, recycled and reused.

It is the task of all of us, including designers and technologists, to find starting points for changes to our purchase-attraction culture in order to ensure the future of the planet. Good design has an ethical and moral value – something that you have been asked to take account of, for example, when drawing up a design specification. Industrial production is becoming an increasing problem, with the production of more and more products. This is placing an enormous burden on the environment.

Tasks

1 Explain what is meant by the term a 'purchase-attraction' culture.
2 Put forward arguments for and against mass production and the marketing of products.

Conservation

Conservation is concerned with the protection of the natural and the manufactured world for future use. In urban areas, for example, buildings may be protected because of their historic interest. In rural areas, plant species, animal habitats and landscapes may all be protected.

Resource management

Conservation is also concerned with the sensible management of resources and a reduction in the rate of consumption of non-renewable resources, such as coal, oil, natural gas, ores and minerals. The aim of conservation is to achieve sustainable development. The 1987 Brundtland Report, *Our Common Future* (World Commission on Environment and Development), defined sustainable development as:

'development that meets the needs of the present, without compromising the ability of future generations to meet their own needs'.

Efficient management of resources includes:

- using less wasteful mining and quarrying methods
- making more efficient use of energy in manufacturing
- reducing fuel consumption in motor vehicles
- using cavity and roof insulation in buildings
- using low-energy light bulbs.

The use of non-renewable raw materials and fossil fuels during the manufacturing process

SIGNPOST
'Environmental costs' Unit 4A page 186

Many modern products are made from non-renewable resources such as metals and plastics. The electrical energy used in their manufacture comes from coal, gas, oil or nuclear power. The management of these finite resources will increasingly become the responsibility of us all. Existing British, European and international legislation already places demands upon companies to design and manufacture products with the environment in mind. In this respect, product designers need to consider:

- reducing the amount of materials used in a product
- using efficient manufacturing processes that save energy and prevent waste
- reusing waste materials within the same manufacturing process

Figure 4.2.13 *Glass is one of the most cost-effective materials to recycle*

- recycling waste in a different manufacturing process (see Figure 4.2.13)
- designing for easy product maintenance, so that parts can be replaced, without the need to dispose of the whole product at the end of its useful life
- designing the product so that the whole or parts of it can be reused or recycled.

Task
We are all responsible when it comes to the environment. Explain your views on the following issues:

a) The need for manufacturers continually to produce new products.

b) The use of lifestyle marketing to encourage consumerism.

c) Buying cheaper, short-lifetime products rather than more expensive but more durable ones.

d) Throwing away products because they are old fashioned or out of date.

e) Recycling or reusing products.

Renewable sources of energy, energy conservation and the use of efficient manufacturing processes

Renewable resources are those that flow naturally in nature or that are living things which can be regrown and used again (see Table 4.2.4). These include the wind, tides, waves, water power, solar energy, geothermal, biomass, ocean thermal energy and forests (see Figure 4.2.14).

Table 4.2.4 *Renewable energy sources*

Renewable energy source	Process	Advantages	Disadvantages
Wind	Power of wind turns turbines	Developed commercially Produces low-cost power	High set-up cost Contributes small proportion of total energy needs Wind farms sometimes seen as unsightly
Tides	Reversible turbine blades harness the tides in both directions	Occurs throughout the day on a regular basis Reliable and non-polluting Potential for large-scale energy production	Very high set-up cost Could restrict the passage of ships Could cause flooding of estuary borders, which might damage wildlife
Water	Running water turns turbines and generates hydro-electric power	Clean and 80–90% efficient	High set-up cost Suitable sites are generally remote from markets Contributes small proportion of total energy needs of an industrial society
Solar	Hot water and electricity generated via solar cells	Huge amounts of energy available. Could generate 50% of hot water for a typical house Relatively inexpensive to set up	Cost of solar cells Biggest demand in winter when heat from sun is at its lowest
Geothermal	Deep holes in earth's crust produce steam to generate electricity	Provides domestic power and hot water	Only really cost-effective where earth's crust is thin, e.g. New Zealand, Iceland
Biomass	Burning of wood, plant matter and waste generates heat	Produces low-cost power	Environmental pollution Potential for deforestation

Figure 4.2.14 *Several large wind farms have been built in Europe and the USA, principally at windy coastal sites*

Forests are renewable as long as they are not used faster than they can be replaced. In recent years, the indiscriminate destruction of the world's rainforest has led to a severe shortage of tropical hardwoods, such as Jelutong from Southeast Asia. In order to conserve valuable renewable resources such as these, manufacturers are encouraged to use only those woods grown on plantations or in managed forests.

Tasks

1 Explain your views on the use of renewable energy when compared to using coal, oil or gas.
2 Describe the benefits and disadvantages of renewable energy in relation to set-up costs, accessibility, production processes and environmental impact.

The use of efficient manufacturing processes

Even the most industrially advanced economies still depend on a continual supply of basic manufactured goods. This production will continue to require large amounts of raw materials and energy. Product manufacturers can contribute to sustainable development and to reducing costs by using more efficient manufacturing processes. This can often be achieved through redesigning an existing product.

Reducing costs and environmental impact through the redesign of an existing product

Fulleon Ltd is a leading European supplier of elements for fire alarm systems including bells, electronic sirens, flashing beacons and break-glass call points. Fulleon decided to improve the competitiveness of its break-glass call point product by simplifying the manufacturing process. The existing call point product uses injection moulding to manufacture the call point plastic casings and other components. The new design has:

- reduced the number of components by 35 per cent
- reduced plastic consumption by 27 per cent
- rounded corners and edges on some mouldings to reduce the time taken for moulding
- fewer components and easier snap-fit assembly to reduce assembly time by 35 per cent.

The average cost of materials has fallen by 11 per cent, assembly costs by 34 per cent and the average unit cost has fallen by 21 per cent. The saving in manufacturing costs amounts to £92,650 per year and the payback period has been just over a year.

The environmental benefits associated with the redesigned product include:

- reduced raw material consumption
- reduced energy use (machines run for less time)
- reduced transport costs for materials and products
- less waste at the end of the product's life.

Tasks

1 Identify a product that you think is badly designed. Give reasons for your choice.
2 Using annotated diagrams, explain how the product could be redesigned to improve the efficiency of its manufacture.

New technology and environmentally friendly manufacturing processes

SIGNPOST
'New materials, processes and technology'
Unit 3B1 page 107

Redesigning a product is one way of achieving efficiency in manufacturing. For many companies this also improves their

Figure 4.2.15 *The Envirowise logo*

environmental performance and helps them to increase profits.

Since 1994 one organisation that has been helping UK companies to do just this is Envirowise (see Figure 4.2.15). This is a joint initiative of the Department of Trade and Industry (DTI) and the Department for Environment, Food and Rural Affairs (defra). Envirowise aims to help manufacturing companies improve their environmental performance and increase their competitiveness.

The main themes of the Envirowise programme are waste minimisation and cost-effective **cleaner technology**:

- Waste minimisation often generates significant cost savings, through the use of simple no-cost or low-cost measures.
- Cleaner technology is the use of equipment or techniques that produce less waste or emissions than conventional methods. It reduces the consumption of raw materials, water and energy and lowers costs for waste treatment and disposal.

Using waste minimisation to reduce scrap

Apollo Sports Technologies Ltd manufactures a range of shafts for golf club manufacturers worldwide. The company joined the Envirowise project to get specialist help for improving its complex engineering process.

Golf club shafts are manufactured using a four-stage, cold-drawing process. To draw a steel tube, a 'tag' of reduced diameter is formed at one end. The tag is cut off and scrapped several times during processing. The elongated steel tube is cut into lengths and formed into the final shaft by 'step tapering'. The shafts are then heat treated, straightened, polished and chrome plated, before being dispatched to the customer.

A review of operations showed that more than 70 per cent of the scrap metal from the manufacture was generated during the cold-drawing process. The waste minimisation team investigated reducing the tag size, the number of tags used and the length of off-cuts produced. Implementation of the most suitable waste minimisation options resulted in a reduction of scrap metal of 64 tonnes per year. This saved the

company £50,000 a year in reduced raw materials costs, without the need to invest in new equipment.

Cleaner technology using improved techniques

A good example of the development of cleaner technology is a new vapour boron technique for protecting timber and board from fungal and insect attack. Existing treatment methods use liquid preservative with either organic solvents or water as a base:

- Water-based preservatives can swell and distort and the timber needs to be dried before use.
- Organic solvents produce volatile organic compounds (VOC) emissions which need expensive pollution-control equipment.

The new vapour boron technique delivers a timber preservative, boric acid, into the timber fibres (see Figure 4.2.16). Trimethylborate – an azeotrope with methanol – hydrolyses on contact with the moisture in the timber and deposits the boric acid preservative while

Figure 4.2.16 *Manufacturing speciality golf club shafts*

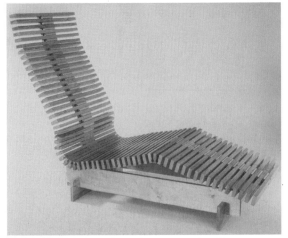

Figure 4.2.17 *Avad contemporary furniture*

enabling methanol to be recovered. The benefits of this process include:

- it is a fast, effective, economical process
- no drying of timber is required before use
- the virtual elimination of VOC emissions.

Cleaner design

Cleaner design is aimed at reducing the overall environmental impact of a product from 'cradle to grave'. It uses life-cycle assessment (LCA) to evaluate each stage of the product life-cycle from raw materials to end-of-life.

Table 4.2.5 *Cleaner design using LCA*

Raw materials	Reduce materials use. Use materials with less environmental impact.
Manufacture	Use fewer energy resources. Produce less pollution and waste.
Distribution	Reduce the impacts of distribution.
Use	Use fewer energy resources. Cause less pollution. Optimise functionality and product life.
End-of-life	Make re-use and recycling easier. Reduce the environmental impact of disposal.

Case study: Avad contemporary furniture

Avad is a small company that manufactures high-quality contemporary furniture. It makes effective use of resources by:

- using sustainably managed hardwood
- developing sustainable construction methods, such as joints that require no adhesives or additional fixing materials.

This has resulted in production savings, minimal use of non-sustainable materials,

increased product life and the possibility of greater material re-use at end-of-life. These cleaner design features have helped increase demand for Avad's contemporary, environmentally sustainable products.

The importance of using sustainable technology

In the previous sections you have been introduced to different aspects of manufacturing that relate to the environment: using cleaner design and cleaner technology. These are both aspects of what is known as 'sustainable development'. This concept puts forward the idea that the environment should be seen as an asset, a stock of available wealth. If each generation spends this wealth without investing in the future, then the world will one day run out of resources. The concept of sustainable development includes a number of key concepts:

- that priority should be given to the essential needs of the world's poor
- meeting essential needs for jobs, energy, water and sanitation
- ensuring a sustainable level of population
- conserving and enhancing the resource base
- bringing together the environment and economics in decision making
- making industrial development more inclusive.

Sustainable development is a problem for the whole world and many countries are involved in trying to develop policies which support it. In the UK, for example, many government programmes are involved, such as Envirowise. Bio-Wise is another government initiative that supports and advises companies and organisations on developing sustainable practices that make use of biotechnology.

For more information on both initiatives, visit the Envirowise website on www.envirowise.gov.uk and the Bio-Wise website on www.biowise.org.uk.

Information about biotechnology can be found in the next section.

Tasks

1 Discuss the importance of using sustainable practices when manufacturing products. Include references to raw materials and manufacturing processes.
2 Explain how you could adapt sustainable technology to your own manufacturing.
3 Research further examples of good practice in manufacturing, using the Internet, CD-ROMs or libraries.

Management of waste, the disposal of products and pollution control

SIGNPOST
'Life cycle assessment'
Unit 4B1 page 200

As we saw from the Envirowise Programme, waste minimisation often generates important cost savings, through the use of simple changes to manufacturing processes. There are three key approaches to reducing waste:

- reduce the amount of materials used in manufacture
- reuse materials in the same manufacturing process where possible
- recycle materials in a different manufacturing process if possible.

Reducing materials use

The possibility of reducing the amount of materials used to manufacture products is often found in processes that involve cutting and stamping shapes from sheet materials. For example, in can manufacture careful calculations must be made to limit the amount of aluminium used for making the circular tops of the cans. There are two ways of arranging the can top on a rectangular sheet, as shown in Figure 4.2.18. In (a) the tops are in a square formation, each sitting in its own square of aluminium. In (b) the tops are in a triangular formation, which is the closest that they can be packed together. When the scrap for each is worked out (a) is found to produce a staggering 21.4 per cent scrap, while (b) works out at only 9.3 per cent scrap. Clearly the placement of the can tops on the aluminium sheet will have an enormous impact on the amount of aluminium required to manufacture the cans.

The disposal of products and pollution control

The disposal of products when they have reached the end of their useful life is a major problem. Around 90 per cent of household rubbish in the UK is buried in landfill, five per cent is incinerated and only five per cent is recycled. One of the best options for products is, firstly, to create the need for fewer of them to be made and, secondly, to design for recycling.

For the disposal of industrial waste a simple solution is 'skip and tip' into either landfill or the sewers. Disposal by landfill is currently inexpensive and popular, but legislation is expected to enforce change. Pollution control is

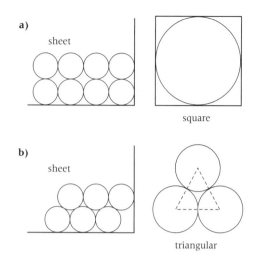

Figure 4.2.18 *Reducing the amount of aluminium required to make aluminium can tops depends on how they are arranged on the aluminium sheet*

the responsibility of a variety of agencies which enforce the 1990 Environmental Protection Act (EPA). This Act introduced wide-ranging legislation with tight controls on the discharge of waste into air, water and land in the UK. It also reinforced the policy of 'polluter pays'. The aim of this policy is to restrict potentially harmful materials from entering the environment and to place greater responsibility on those generating, handling and treating wastes. Legislation is strictly enforced so that any company or organisation that causes pollution can be fined huge sums.

Tasks
Discuss the impact of the policy 'polluter pays' on product manufacture. Relate your discussion to one product type, such as PET bottles. Explain how product pricing might be affected.

Impact of biotechnology on manufacture

Biotechnology is the use of biological processes which make use of living proteins, called **enzymes**, to create industrial products and processes. These enzymes are the same kind that help us digest food, compost garden rubbish and clean clothes. The use of yeast in making bread and wine was one of the first examples of the use of biotechnology. Technologists also developed enzymes that could be added to detergents to improve their cleaning properties, resulting in 'biological' washing powders.

Biotechnology is being used in an increasing number of industries to provide efficient and ecologically sound solutions to environmental problems. Current applications of environmental biotechnology include: the treatment of industrial air emissions; **aerobic** and **anaerobic** treatment and reed beds to treat industrial effluent; composting to treat domestic, industrial and agricultural organic waste; and **bioremediation** techniques to clean up contaminated land. Not only are many companies using biotechnology to increase their competitiveness, but they are using it to meet strict new environmental legislation and to improve their competitive edge.

Compared with more traditional methods, biotechnology can often produce better, faster, cleaner, cheaper and more efficient ways of doing things. One example, in the engineering industry, is the treatment of waste cutting fluids.

Treating waste cutting fluids

In the engineering industry, many companies use cutting fluids to cool and lubricate components while they are machined. After being used for a time, the fluids becomes contaminated with bacteria. This makes them go 'off' and become useless. Every year around half a million tonnes of used cutting fluids and oily wastes are disposed of – mainly to landfill, sewers and incinerators.

Biotechnology is being used to solve this problem (see Figure 4.2.19). The cutting fluids are passed through an anaerobic treatment tank to digest the oil. Any remaining contaminants are passed through an ultrafiltration system to extract any remaining contaminants. The result is purified water, which is reused. This biotechnology process gives the following benefits:

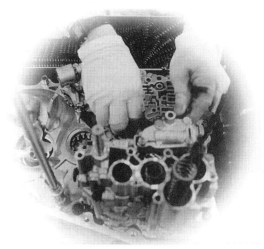

Figure 4.2.19 *Biotechnology can be used in the treatment of cutting fluids used to cool and lubricate components while they are machined*

- All types of cutting fluids can be treated.
- Water and effluent disposal costs are reduced.
- Site health and safety is improved.
- Costs related to handling and disposal of contaminated wastes are removed.

Turning waste wood dust into garden compost

The UK furniture and timber industries generate around three million tonnes of waste wood dust each year. Wood dust is a serious health hazard and requires costly disposal to landfill.

A recent biotechnology project demonstrated how to turn waste wood dust into garden compost. The main difficulty in this process is the lacquers, sealers and solvents left in the dust after furniture manufacture. Adding microbes that feed on these substances overcomes this problem. Hardwood, softwood, wood chips and MDF dust can all be composted using a computer programmable system. This controls variables such as temperature, oxygen and airflow to produce uniform, clean compost.

This environmentally-friendly composting system will not only cut the costs of disposal by landfill but will provide furniture manufacturers with a saleable product.

The advantages and disadvantages of recycling materials

> **SIGNPOST**
> **Environmentally friendly processes**
> **Unit 3B1 page 108**

The advantages for the environment of recycling are numerous. Recycling conserves non-renewable resources, reduces energy consumption and greenhouse gas emissions, reduces pollution and the dependency on raw materials.

For manufacturers the advantages of recycling are cost related, with metal, glass and paper being the most cost-effective materials to recycle:

- Scrap non-ferrous metals are sorted into different grades for recycling, due to their relatively high commercial value.
- Steel and cast iron are graded by size, due to their lower commercial value.
- Items made of glass, rubber and plastics are more difficult to sort and have a much lower value than metals.
- Plastics, paper and glass recycling are growing industries.

Scrap materials from the manufacturing process are the most valuable because their

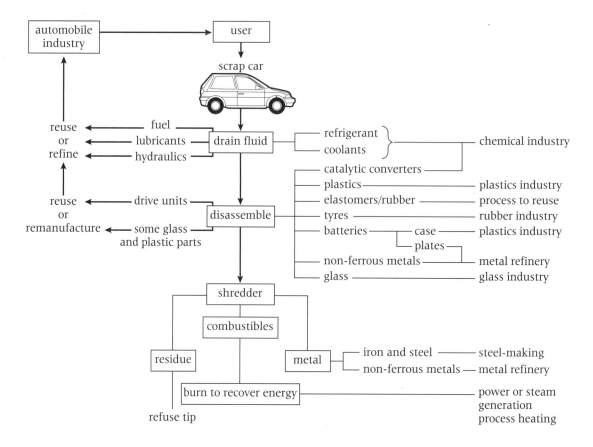

Figure 4.2.20 *The concept of car recycling*

materials content is known and they are easily available. The disadvantage of recycling scrap from old products is that the chemical or physical make-up of their materials is often very complex, so for some products recycling is too expensive or impossible. The result is that 'old' scrap from products has a lower commercial value.

Design for recycling

Under proposed European regulations, manufacturers may have to recycle electrical and electronic parts rather than disposing of them by landfill or incinerating them. By 2006 customers may be able to return electrical goods to stores for recycling. This will have a major impact on the way that products are designed.

With this in mind British engineers have developed a mobile phone that falls apart when heated, so that the component parts can be recycled. The phone is made from **shape memory polymers**, plastics that revert to their original form when heated. Different components of the phone will change shape at different temperatures, allowing them to fall off at different times, when they pass along a conveyor belt. The reusable parts can be recycled. The phones will only fall apart under extreme temperatures – so they will be safe if left in the car in the sun!

Recycling cars

Design for recycling is also a growing feature of the automobile industry. It is expected to result in a major new industry, that of car disassembly and recycling. The potential is enormous. A small family car weighs approximately 1000 kg and its average life is about 10 years. With over 20 million new registrations annually in Europe alone, that represents 20 million tons of component materials becoming available for recycling every year.

The problem with recycling cars is that they are made up of many different materials and components, each with a specific function. The potential is for 98 per cent of ferrous metal, 90 per cent of non-ferrous metal and other materials like glass and rubber to be recycled from a small family car.

In order to recycle a scrap car, all the different materials need to be recycled. Figure 4.2.20 shows the concept of car recycling.

Exam preparation

You will need to revise all the topics in this unit, so that you can apply your knowledge and understanding to the exam questions. Some questions may ask you to give answers related to a product example. If you cut out and save newspaper and magazine articles about products, it will help keep you up-to-date with the latest information.

In preparation for your exam it is a good idea to make brief notes about different topics, such as 'Relevant legislation on the rights of the consumer when purchasing products'. Use sub-headings or bullet point lists and diagrams where appropriate. A single side of A4 should be used for each heading from the Specification.

It is very important to learn exam skills. You should have weekly practice in learning technical terms and in answering exam-type questions. When you answer any question you should:

- read the question carefully and pick out the key points that need answering
- match your answer to the marks available, e.g. for two marks, you should give two good points that address the question
- always give examples and justify statements with reasons, saying how or why the statement is true.

Practice exam questions

1 a) Economic factors need to be taken into account when manufacturing products. Explain three of the following terms:
   - production chain
   - primary sector
   - secondary sector
   - tertiary sector. (6)
   b) Describe how productivity is measured and its impact on profitability. (4)
   c) Explain the issues a company needs to consider when developing a new product range. (5)

2 a) Explain why hardwoods are more costly than softwoods. (4)
   b) Outline the factors that cause costs to be lower in high volume production. (5)
   c) Explain the cost of making a product 'right first time'. (6)

3 a) Outline what is meant by a 'quality management system'. (5)
   b) Describe the following terms:
   - risk assessment
   - hazard. (4)
   c) Explain what is meant by the term 'statutory rights'. (6)

4 a) Explain two of the following terms:
   - quantitative research
   - qualitative research
   - surveys. (4)
   b) Product development starts with the identification of a need. Discuss the factors that must be identified before product development can begin. (6)
   c) Advertising is used to inform and influence potential consumers. Describe the characteristics of soft sell advertising used to promote everyday products. (5)

5 a) Describe the basic structure of a marketing plan. (5)
   b) Discuss two of the following terms:
   - target market group
   - market pull
   - brand loyalty. (6)
   c) Explain how and why a manufacturer might attempt to give a product a 'competitive edge'. (4)

6 a) Describe three ways in which efficient management of resources could be achieved. (6)

b) Renewable sources of energy include tides, geothermal and biomass. Explain which of these sources of energy would be most suitable for an environmentally conscious company to use. (3)

c) Explain, using an example for each, the difference between cleaner design and cleaner technology. (6)

4 B2 CAD/CAM (R403)

Summary of expectations

1. What to expect
CAD/CAM is one of the three options offered in Section B of Unit 4. You must study the same option that you studied at AS level.

2. How will it be assessed?
The work that you do in this option will be externally assessed through Section B of the Unit 4 examination paper. The questions will be common across all three materials areas in product Design. You can therefore answer questions with reference to **either**:

- a Resistant Materials Technology product such as a robotic arm;
- a Graphics with Materials Technology product such as a toy robot;
- **or** a Textiles Technology product such as a 3D knitted jumper.

You are advised to **spend 45 minutes** on this section of the paper.

3. What will be assessed?
The following list summarises the topics covered in this option and what will be examined.

- Computer-Aided Design, Manufacture and Testing (CADMAT):
  - Computer-Integrated Manufacture (CIM)
  - Flexible Manufacturing Systems (FMS).

- Robotics:
  - the industrial application of robotics/control technology and the development of automated processes
  - complex automated systems using artificial intelligence (AI) and new technology

  - the use of block flow diagrams and flow process diagrams for representing simple and complex production systems
  - the advantages and disadvantages of automation.

- Uses of information and communications technology (ICT) in the manufacture of products:
  - the impact and advantages/disadvantages of ICT within the total manufacturing process.

4. How to be successful in this unit
To be successful in this unit you will need to:

- have a clear understanding of the topics covered in this option
- apply your knowledge and understanding to a given situation or context
- organise your answers clearly and coherently, using specialist technical terms where appropriate
- use clear sketches where appropriate to illustrate your answers
- write clear and logical answers to the examination questions, using correct spelling, punctuation and grammar.

There may be an opportunity to demonstrate your knowledge and understanding of CAD/CAM in your Unit 5 coursework. However, simply because you are studying this option, you do not have to integrate this type of technology into your coursework project.

5. How much is it worth?
This option, with Section A, is worth 15 per cent of the full Advanced GCE.

Unit 4 + option	Weighting
A2 level (full GCE)	15%

1. Computer-Aided Design, Manufacture and Testing (CADMAT)

CADMAT

Systems that fully integrate the use of computers at every level and stage in the manufacturing process can be described as CADMAT systems. Unit 3 looked at the benefits of CAD and the advantages that CAM brings and you were introduced to the wider role that computers now play in manufacturing. In addition to their application in CAD/CAM, computers are also used extensively for decision making within CADMAT in a variety of ways, including:

- information control through the gathering, storage, retrieval, and organisation of data, information and knowledge
- simulations in which 'models' are used to help to provide answers to 'What if?' questions; for example 'What would be the consequences if we changed to a flexible manufacturing system compared with our present sequential system of manufacturing?'
- narrowing the field of choices available using number-based and other analytical methods; for example graphs can be used for analytical and mathematical purposes rather than simply as visual aids to explain data

- production process and management techniques to control or 'run' some parts of a manufacturing operation – this could include the routine scheduling of maintenance or minimising the effects of machine **downtime** when cutting tools have to be replaced.

As with all systems the efficiency of a CADMAT system is determined by the effectiveness of many interrelated sub-systems. A failure in any of the input, processing or output sub-systems leads to production lines that malfunction or operate below capacity. As an example, one of the key areas in any of these systems is the quality, accuracy and speed of processing the relevant electronic data. The handling and processing of data is usually constrained within clearly defined but interrelated operating procedures and operations. The relationship is described in a systems diagram (see Figure 4.3.1).

Product data management (PDM)

Product data management (PDM) is a complete (holistic) data management system that aims to integrate all aspects of manufacturing from product modelling to the management of

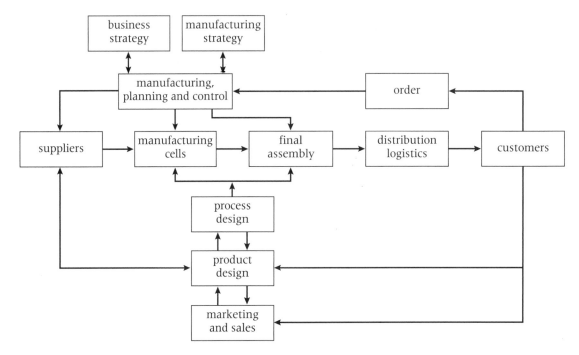

Figure 4.3.1 A system flow chart – integrated manufacturing

business processes. Online order tracking is an example of the potential power of PDM because of the advances in information and communications technology (ICT), particularly in the area of **telematics**. This new technology will allow a product to be managed electronically from receipt of the customer order. The product will be tracked from development into manufacturing, on through delivery to after-sales support via real-time feedback from telematic reporting systems.

Production data from a manufacturing plant or a volume production line can be simultaneously merged with other data such as product demand and financial figures. This means that raw materials and components for the production line are bought in as required. As a result, financial efficiency improves as the size of the stock inventory and its storage space reduces. Reduced business overheads equals increased profitability. This type of approach is known as 'just in time'.

Just in time

Just in time (JIT) is a management philosophy which is applied in businesses around the globe. It was first developed in the 1960s by Taiichi Ohno within Toyota's car manufacturing plants in Japan as a means of meeting consumer orders with the minimum of delay, to the required level of quality and in the right quantity. It has also come to mean producing with minimum waste. Waste here is taken in a general sense to include such things as time and resources as well as raw materials (see JIT manufacturing below). JIT is achieved by applying a strategy of computer-aided inventory management in which raw materials, components or part assemblies are delivered from the 'supplier' just before they are needed in each stage of the manufacturing process.

JIT 'suppliers' and 'customers'

A 'supplier' can either be the organisation that provides the original raw materials, components or stock needed for the product, or it can be the previous stage of the manufacturing process (downstream).

A 'customer' can either be the purchaser of the final product, or it can be another stage of the manufacturing process further along the production line (upstream).

JIT manufacturing

This is a systems approach to developing and operating all the processes in a manufacturing system. JIT has been found to be so effective that it increases productivity, work performance and product quality, while saving costs. Information flow through the system is vital to

its success, and advances in computer-based applications have further enhanced its effectiveness. Before discussing the specific elements of JIT, it is useful to identify the underlying principles:

- JIT is a continuous operation, not a one-off event, and workers are responsible for the quality of their individual output.
- There has to be synchronisation (matching) or balance between operations so that all production occurs at a common rate.
- Simple is considered to be better, so that a continuous effort is made to improve (**Kaizen**) by operating with fewer resources (time, personnel and equipment) and in less-complicated ways such as employing foolproof (**poka-yoke**) tools, jigs and fixtures to prevent mistakes.
- It is necessary to concentrate on fundamentals and remove anything that does not add value to the product.
- Factory layouts should be product led so that less time is spent moving materials and parts.

Waste caused by the following should be eliminated:

- overproduction and making to stock rather than to order
- too much waiting time between processes and product distribution
- transporting materials, components and sub-assemblies
- processing methods that are not integrated
- an unnecessarily large inventory
- defects that are not identified early enough.

The key features of JIT workplace organisation

The control systems for JIT are the most visible manifestation of the JIT approach but there are other important features:

- Operational set-up times are reduced, increasing flexibility and the capacity to produce smaller batches more cost effectively.
- There is a multi-skilled workforce that is capable of operating multiple processes leading to greater productivity, flexibility and increased job satisfaction.
- Production rates are either levelled or varied, as appropriate, to smooth the flow of products through the factory.
- **Kanban** is a control technique that is used to 'pull' products and components through the manufacturing process. The Kanban controls production rates and the flow of materials by using computer applications to calculate exactly the right quantity of resources (components, sub-assemblies or purchased

parts) required. The computer will then schedule operations so that the resources are exactly at the right place at precisely the right time.

- **Jidoka (autonomation)** is about looking for opportunities to provide machines that have the capability to regulate their own operation or automatically shut down if there is a problem on the production lines. This allows workers in a JIT environment to do something more productive than 'machine-minding'.
- Andon (trouble lights) are used to signal processing problems and the need for corrective action.

Task

Research what role computers played in manufacturing operations in the 1960s compared with now. Write a short report explaining what it was like then and how advances in ICT since then have supported the further development of modern manufacturing systems.

Computer-Integrated Manufacture (CIM)

In Unit 3 we saw that to achieve full CIM, all aspects of a company's operations must be integrated so that they can share the same information and communicate with one another. A CIM system uses computers to

integrate the processing of production and business information with manufacturing operations in order to create cooperative and smoothly running production lines. The tasks performed within CIM will include:

- the design of components
- planning the most effective production sequences and workflow
- controlling the operations of machines
- performing business functions such as ordering of stock and materials and customer invoicing.

On automated production lines computers will control the methods for transferring materials and components to the required points on the assembly lines, the numerically controlled (NC) machines or the robots used for fabricating or assembling components and, as we shall see later, quality and inspection systems. The various computers and microprocessors automate the processes of monitoring and provide information (feedback) to a 'host' computer that informs operators about the state of the system. Figure 4.3.2 shows a typical CIM layout.

Flexible Manufacturing Systems (FMS)

In the late 1960s all the leading Japanese manufacturers moved towards the flexible factory as a new source of competitive advantage. With increasing global competition and the creation of open markets, consumers are demanding

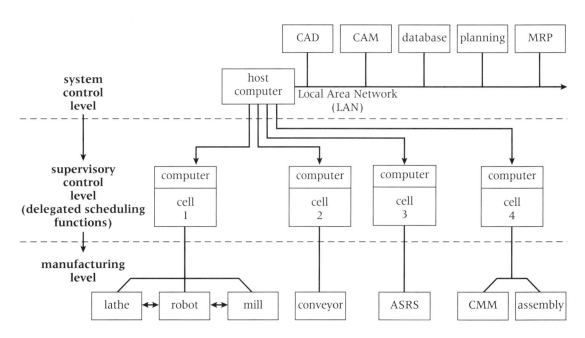

Figure 4.3.2 *A typical CIM layout*

increased product diversity and regular product updating beyond cosmetic changes. This, in turn, is influencing manufacturers to invest in more flexible plant and equipment. A piece of flexible equipment is one that has the ability to perform multiple processing tasks on a wide range of products; for example CNC machining centres for machining a variety of parts, or robots for material handling. The introduction of machinery that can operate flexibly enables manufacturers to explore various processing sequences that might be available through alternative configurations of plant and equipment.

Process-based or product-based manufacturing cells?

In all modular or cell manufacturing systems – sometimes referred to as group technology – machinery is organised so that related products can be manufactured or processed in a continuous flow. In modular layout, computers play an important role in controlling equipment, material and workflow. The product flows smoothly from start to finish, parts do not sit waiting to be worked on and do not travel long distances from one part of the factory to another. This can be contrasted to a typical production system, where machines are grouped by their function, for instance a 'bank' of milling machines or lathes, and products move from function to function from one end of a manufacturing facility to another and back again. This results in long waiting times between procedures.

Creative and technical design: computer-aided engineering

Computer-aided engineering (CAE) can be part of a CAD application or it can form a 'stand-alone' system that can analyse engineering designs, often simulating a design under a variety of conditions to see if it actually works.

Consider, for example, the design of the body of a mobile phone. A CAD modelling system provides the surface modelling tools to design the ergonomic body for the appliance with all the necessary controls and displays. The CAE system will allow the solid representation of the design to be converted into a thin shelled case that can be made from a plastic material. The model would be 'cut' in half and all the bosses, ribs and flanges required to mould the case can be added. On the CAM side, CAE enhances the design of the moulds with pieces that are not symmetrical or that have irregular boundaries. The CAE functions can create and check the numerically controlled (NC) tool path needed to create the complex injection mould that would be needed.

Modelling and testing

With increased bandwidth now a reality in communications technology there will be significant progress in developing fully integrated CADCAM software so that CAD models can be sent to manufacturing directly from the PC desktop. In Unit 3 we looked at the range of CAD modelling techniques that have been developed to help designers to represent their ideas, and there is an increasing range of specialist modelling techniques that combine CAD and CAM techniques to produce 3D models, such as Rapid Prototyping (RPT).

RPT is a rapidly growing area of CAD modelling first developed in the 1990s. RPT works on the principle of building up layers of a material whose physical shapes are representations of electronic 'slices' taken through a digital model. In simple terms digital data is used to create a 3D physical object. It is sometimes called layered object modelling (LOM). There are now many RPT technologies either in use commercially or under development. Using these technologies, the manufacturing time for complex products or prototypes is measured in hours instead of days.

Task

Using an Internet search engine of your choice, investigate the emerging technology of RPT and compile a short illustrated report showing its application in CADMAT.

Virtual Reality Modelling Language

3D virtual product modelling is an emerging technique, looked at on pages 135–6 in Unit 3B2. Virtual Reality Modelling Language (VRML) further extends the power of product modelling as a design tool. It is a specification for displaying 3D objects on the Internet. It is the 3D equivalent of HTML. Files written in VRML have a *wrl* extension (short for world); HTML files have the extension *html*. The VRML script produces a virtual world or 'hyperspace' on the computer display screen. The viewer 'moves' through the world or around an object by pressing computer keys or using another input device to turn left, right, up or down, or go forwards or backwards. This technology is still in the early stages of development; the first VRML standards were set only in 1995. It will become a powerful tool for the computer-based modelling of products (see Figure 4.3.3).

Figure 4.3.3 *3D virtual modelling of a CIM system*

Production planning

Production planning is one area where computational aids can be used to good effect. The range of scheduling software applications that is available is testimony to the many different planning approaches used in manufacturing. The term 'finite capacity scheduling' describes a processing schedule that is based on the overall manufacturing capacity available. By contrast, infinite capacity schedules use the customers' order due date as an end stop. The aim is to complete the order by working back from the due date using the available capacity.

Time – the strategic weapon for competitiveness

Modern manufacturers regard time and responsiveness as strategic weapons; to them time is the equivalent of money or increased productivity. They focus on reducing 'non-value-adding' time rather than trying to make people or machines work harder or faster on value-adding activities. The ways that leading companies use computers to manage time – in production, in new product development, in sales and in distribution – represent the most powerful new sources of competitive advantage. Today's new-generation companies compete with flexible manufacturing and rapid response systems, expanding variety and increasing innovation. A company that has a time-based strategy is a more powerful competitor than one with a traditional strategy based on low wages, lower scales of production or a narrow product focus. These older, cost-based strategies require managers to do whatever is necessary to drive down costs. This could involve moving production centres to a low-wage country, building new facilities by consolidating, in effect closing down, old plants to gain economies of scale, or focusing operations down to the most

economic activities. These tactics reduce costs but at the expense of responsiveness.

In contrast, time-based strategies based on the principles of flexible manufacturing and rapid response systems need factories that are close to the customers. They serve to provide fast responses rather than low costs and control. The whole process is coordinated via computer databases and software applications that provide a range of scheduling functions.

Master Production Schedule

The Master Production Schedule (MPS) is a top-down scheduling system that sets the quantity of each product to be completed in each week or **time bucket** over a short-range **planning horizon**. It is derived from known demand, forecasts and the amount of product to be made for stock. The planning assumption is that there is always sufficient manufacturing capacity available. For this reason, this method is sometimes called 'infinite capacity scheduling'.

Other computer-aided scheduling functions

Resource scheduling is a finite scheduling function that concentrates on the resources that are required for converting raw materials into finished goods. Other scheduling functions may include the entering and invoicing of sales orders (sales order processing), stock recording and cost accounting. These functions combine to provide a powerful integrated database for the company. The only real problem with these applications is related to the accuracy of the data that is input into the database – inaccurate data causes cumulative problems as products move through the processing stages.

Types of computer-based scheduling

- Electronic scheduling board. The simplest scheduler is the electronic scheduling board, which imitates the old-fashioned card-based loading boards used to sequence machining operations. The advantage of this computer-based system is that it calculates times automatically and warns the production staff of any attempt to load two jobs on to the same machine.
- Order-based scheduling. In order-based scheduling the computer schedules tasks based on order priority. The sequencing and delivery of individual component parts and resources is determined by the overall priority of the order for which the parts are destined. It is a distinct improvement on infinite capacity schedulers but its biggest drawback is that it allows gaps to appear in resources. Some schedulers allow the process to be repeated to try to reduce gaps before it is put into practice in order to reduce production

times but this computerised rescheduling can be a very time consuming process.

- Constraint-based schedulers. With the constraint-based schedulers the aim is to locate potential bottlenecks in a production line and ensure that they are always well provided by synchronising the flow through the MPS.
- Discrete event simulation. This simulation loads all the required resources at a chosen point on the production line. When all processing problems and queues are resolved at that point it moves on to the next point on the line. Because the simulation moves from one set of processing events to the next, there are far fewer gaps in the schedules and consequently production lines are far more stable.

Control of equipment, processes, quality and safety

Materials Requirements Planning

Materials Requirements Planning (MRP) is a planning tool geared specifically to assembly operations. The aim is to allow each manufacturing unit to tell its supplier what parts it requires and when it requires them. The supplier may be the upstream process within the plant or an outside supplier. The software determines how many parts or particular components are required based on the number of finished products required. MRP is classed as a top-down approach to scheduling.

Kanbans

We saw earlier in this unit that a Kanban system is a means to achieve just-in-time production. It is also a practical example of the concept of time-based management. It works on the basis that each process on a production line only 'pulls' the number and type of components that the process requires, at just the right time. The timing mechanism used is a Kanban card that is usually a physical card produced from a computer-based scheduling system, but other visual devices can be used. Two kinds of Kanban cards are mainly used:

- Withdrawal Kanban specifies the kind and quantity of product which a manufacturing process should withdraw from a preceding process.
- Production-ordering Kanban specifies the kind and quantity of product that the preceding process must produce. The production ordering Kanban is often called a 'production Kanban'.

Task
Research and report on how Kanbans actually control operations on a production line. Why are they so effective?

Approaches to Total Quality (TQ)

Total Quality Control (TQC) is the system that Japan has developed to implement Kaizen or continuing improvement for the complete life cycle of a product, both within the function of the product and within the system to develop, support, and retire the product. **Total Quality Management (TQM)** is the US version of how to implement quality systems for the same purposes. What both systems have in common is that they are 'purpose driven', they involve comprehensive change and both are long-term processes.

Implementation of TQ systems

Computers are used during all three stages in the development of TQ, ranging from supporting training through providing interactive learning methods to computer-aided statistical tools and methods. The three stages are:

1 awareness raising – to recognise the need for TQ and learning its basic principles
2 empowerment – learning the methods of TQ and developing skills in practising them
3 alignment – harmonising the business and TQ goals with the manufacturing practices of the company.

TQC and TQM tools

In a manufacturing system thinking tools are equally as important as the physical tools we use to make things. Thinking tools enhance the way we plan to do things. In the context of TQC or TQM there are several types of intellectual tool, including the use of computer-aided systems, to improve all aspects of manufacturing quality. They allow tasks to be completed effectively, eliminate failure and assist in the exchange and dissemination of information. In general, computer-based tools can be classed under the following functions:

- management
- product planning
- quality functions
- statistical process control (SPC).

Computer-aided SPC

There are several graphically based statistical methods for representing and analysing processes, events and the effects of an action. They can all be produced or drawn with the aid of computer software.

- The Pareto Principle suggests that most effects come from relatively few causes. In quantitative terms, 80 per cent of the problems come from 20 per cent of the causes (machines, raw materials, operators, etc.); therefore effort aimed at the right 20 per cent can solve 80 per cent of the problems. Pareto charts can be used to compare 'before and after' situations which allow managers to decide where to apply the initial effort for maximum effect (see Figure 4.3.4).

- A scatter plot is effectively a line graph with no line – the intersections between the two data sets are plotted but no attempt is made to physically draw a line. They are used to define the area of relationship between two variables and to predict the behaviour of a specified characteristic (see Figure 4.3.5).
- Control charts are used for production processes (see Figure 4.3.6). Upper and lower production limits are calculated for a particular process and sampled measures are regularly plotted about a central line between the two sets of limits. The plotted line corresponds to the stability and trend of the process. Control action can be taken based on trends over time rather than when an individual variation occurs. This prevents over-correction on the production line.

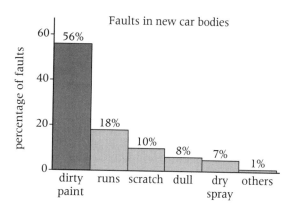

Figure 4.3.4 *A Pareto chart identifies the most important areas to concentrate on*

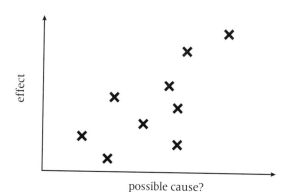

Figure 4.3.5 *A scatter plot/graph could be used to show how production (effect) varies with causes: longer working hours; reworking time to correct problems; inspection time*

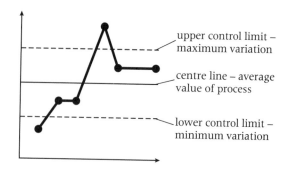

Figure 4.3.6 *A control chart – any point outside the limit is considered abnormal and requires investigation*

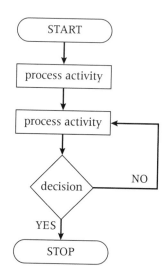

Figure 4.3.7 *A flow chart – used to show the movement of people, materials, paperwork or information and processes*

- Flow charts use pictures, symbols or text coupled with lines and arrows to show direction of flow (see Figure 4.3.7). They enable the modelling of processes, problems or opportunities and critical decision points.
- Cause and effect, fishbone or Ishikawa diagrams provide a method for analysing processes by relating causes and effects to provide a sequential view of a process or operation (see Figure 4.3.8).
- A histogram, or bar graph, provides a graphic summary of the variation in a set of data, and when used to analyse data it is easier to see patterns that would otherwise be difficult to see in a table of numbers (see Figure 4.3.9).
- A check sheet is an adaptable data recording form used for collecting quantitative or qualitative repetitive data during production.
- Checklists are used under operational conditions to ensure that all important steps or actions have been taken to guarantee

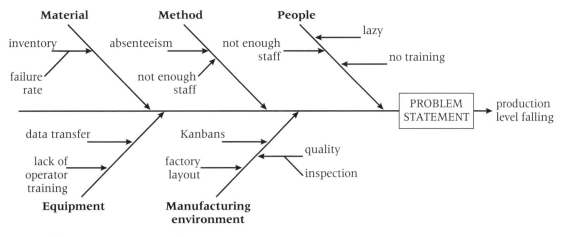

Figure 4.3.8 *A cause and effect diagram*

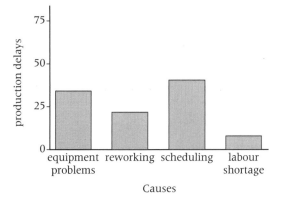

Figure 4.3.9 *A bar graph – an analytical tool to compare outputs, percentages or activities*

suitable quality. As a management tool, they are generally used to check that all aspects of a situation have been taken into account before action or decision making.

Task

In 1976, Japanese manufacturers proposed the following additional 'tools' for use in statistical process/quality control systems:

- relations diagram (problem solving tool)
- affinity diagram (KJ method); systematic diagram (tree diagram)
- matrix diagram
- matrix data analysis
- process decision program chart (PDPC)
- arrow diagram.

Use an Internet search engine of your choice to investigate what each of these terms means. Compile a table to show what they are used for and the role that computers play in each.

Inspecting quality

Despite the progress in designing for quality and incorporating quality into manufacturing processes, inspection still remains a necessary component of most quality programmes. The cost of defects escalates as material moves through the supply chain from the supplier, through manufacturing and finally to the customer. To produce each component piece exactly to a fixed dimension every time would increase the costs of manufacture so much that the product would be uneconomic to make. This means that the actual machined dimension will often be different from the nominal dimension. This is generally acceptable providing the errors lie within given limits that are defined by the **tolerances** on the drawing. In general, there will be dimensional errors in any machined work piece that need to be determined by **metrology**. There are two main types of dimensional measurement in the manufacturing process:

- Post-process measurement involves making measurements after the part has been produced. If the dimensions are not within the given tolerance zone, a correction can be made to the CNC program before the next part passes through the machine tool. The typical measuring tools used are gauges, micrometers, Vernier calipers, profile projectors, lasers and coordinate measurement machines (CMMs).
- In on-process measurement, parts are measured while they are on the machine tool. This is essential when the manufactured parts are large or material cost is high or there is a long production 'cycle time'. In these and other cases, on-process measurement is required to improve productivity levels and reduce the cost of failure. Currently, inspection

is part of the continuous quality improvement programme adopted by many companies that seeks to achieve zero defects from processes. This zero-defect approach can be incorporated into computer-based inspection models because each part in an assembly operation can be modelled separately to determine the number of inspection stages and where they will be most effective.

Task

Here is an example of how the inspection process for a CD player might be modelled in three stages:

Stage 1 is the sampling inspection of the quality of incoming raw materials, sub-assemblies and components.

Stage 2 involves functional inspections at different predetermined points in the product assembly process.

Stage 3 is a 25 per cent quality assurance audit that tests the function of completed products.

Using a product that you have already made or are planning to make

- identify where you could plan an inspection stage
- compile a flow chart showing the main stages in your production process and where inspections will take place
- explain what you will test and how you will test it.

Coordinate measurement machine (CMM)

Traditional measuring instruments, such as micrometers, Vernier calipers and height gauges, can provide mechanical solutions for the measurement of dimensions such as length, height, inside and outside diameters as well as other attributes such as flatness. A CMM combines these inspection and measurement functions in one versatile instrument that can also be fully automated, linked to a CAD system and integrated into an FMS. CMMs offer a flexible cost-effective means of quality control through accurate part and component inspection. CMMs can check the dimensional and geometric accuracy of everything from small engine blocks to sheet metal parts and circuit boards. Examples of a large and a small CMM are shown in Figure 4.3.10.

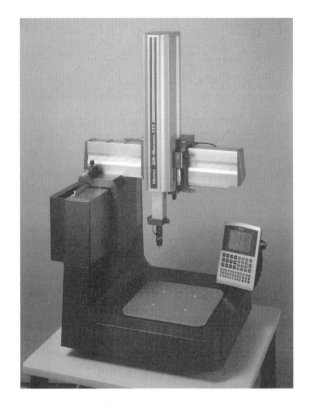

Figure 4.3.10 *CMMs are characterised by their structural and dimensional stability that is provided by rigid frames and features such as thermally stable ceramic measuring tables, guides and high precision bearings on all moving parts*

Computer-aided inspection of 3D parts

There are several software applications that integrate inspection with 3D CMMs and inspection arms. Typical of these applications is PowerINSPECT™ produced by a US company, Delcam. It allows users to inspect complex machined parts and compare them with the original CAD model and to produce customised reports in tabular, graphical and pictorial formats to highlight discrepancies. There is also the facility to view the original CAD model as a wireframe on which the measured points are displayed so that flaws can be seen at a glance.

Typical applications for inspection software will be the inspection of prototypes, batch parts, moulds, tools, patterns and master models.

Scanning measurements using laser light

The object to be measured interrupts the beam and produces a time-dependent shadow. This shadow is electrically detected by a receiver and converted into dimensional readings by a microprocessor-based control unit. The data can then be analysed and displayed against the dimensions specified in the original CAD model.

Control of complex manufacturing processes; integrated and concurrent manufacturing

Computer integrated manufacturing

Integrated systems of manufacturing use computers for describing designs and production processes in a variety of ways including CAD and CAM product modelling. As we saw in Unit 3B2, CAD modelling will describe both the geometry and the functional aspects of a product. Computers are also used to describe the factory model that will include the layout of plant and equipment, machining capacity and product scheduling. Computers are used to model workflow through the manufacturing cell.

Controlling workflow

The term 'workflow' describes the tasks required to produce a final product. Project management software allows a manufacturer to define different workflows for different types of jobs and coordinate production cells in an overall MPS. For example, in a design environment a CAD file might be automatically routed from the designer to a production engineer to purchasing for comment or action. At each stage in the workflow, one individual or group is responsible for a specific task such as ensuring the right materials are in the right place when required. Once the task is complete the workflow software ensures that the individuals responsible for the next task are notified and receive the data they need to execute their stage of the process.

Parts recognition systems

Computer-controlled visual recognition systems can recognise parts and components to ensure they are distributed to where they are needed. They can also be used to identify where the part is in the production process. Data communication tags (bar codes) attached to stock pallets or individual assemblies are used in electronic identification systems. These tags can be read by a sensor mounted to either an automated storage/retrieval system (ASRS) or on a conveyor belt. Typically, the sensor used to read the bar codes is a laser scanner. This is because it is suited to applications requiring high reading performance, small size and low cost. A digital pre-processor receives and decodes the signal into data that can be read and analysed by a computer. This data is then transmitted to the 'supervising' computer controlling the production line. The development of these systems has improved the operational effectiveness of manufacturing systems based on the concurrent model.

Sequential or concurrent manufacturing systems?

The design of an effective and marketable product is dependent on the input from a wide range of specialists and the efficiency of the chosen manufacturing system. Sequential manufacturing systems employ a linear or 'over the wall' or function-based approach to design and processing tasks. The product passes through a series of discrete self-contained stages in different departments. Ideas are then thrown 'over the wall' for consideration by the next department. At each stage of the process there has to be verification that what is being planned is possible. If it is possible, the product moves on to the next stage; if not, it is referred back to one of the previous stages. This system is slow to respond to change, has longer lead times and is often characterised by low product quality because of the separation of design and manufacturing functions and costly design and redesign loops.

The key feature of concurrent or simultaneous manufacturing is the team-based approach to project management so that the right people get together at the right time to identify and resolve design problems. There are several approaches to project or team-based manufacturing but all of them employ ICT, TQM and milestone planning as project management tools in order to develop and produce quality products in a shorter period of time.

Sequential and concurrent manufacturing are compared in Figure 4.3.12.

Quality decisions = quality products

The concurrent engineering approach is intended to cause manufacturers to consider all elements of the product life cycle from conception through to disposal, including quality, cost, schedule and user requirements. One of the key objectives of concurrent manufacturing is to make all the right

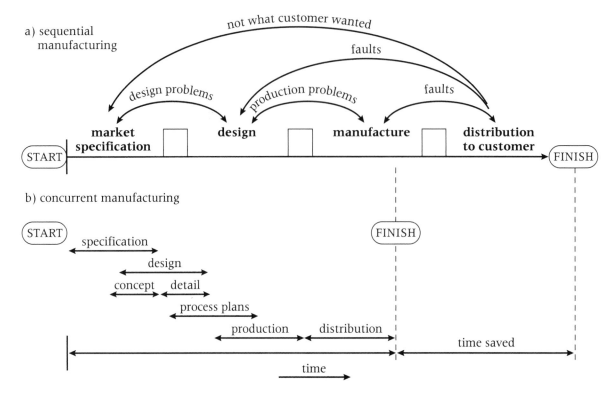

Figure 4.3.12 *A comparison of sequential and concurrent manufacturing. The latter reduces time to market*

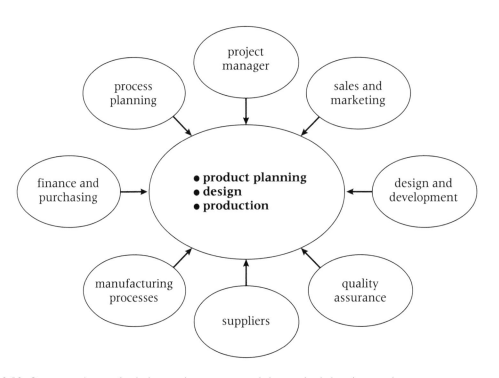

Figure 4.3.13 *Concurrent manufacturing – a team approach to product development*

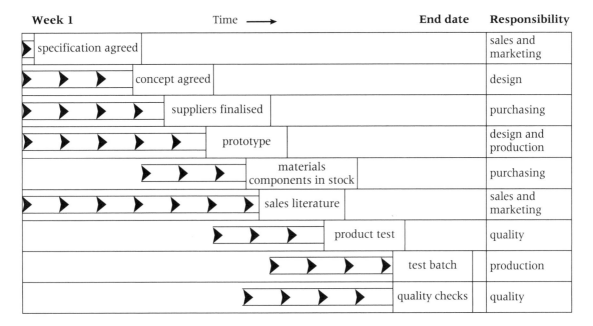

Week 1	Time ⟶		End date	Responsibility
▶ specification agreed				sales and marketing
▶ ▶ ▶ concept agreed				design
▶ ▶ ▶ ▶ suppliers finalised				purchasing
▶ ▶ ▶ ▶ ▶ prototype				design and production
▶ ▶ ▶ materials components in stock				purchasing
▶ ▶ ▶ ▶ ▶ ▶ sales literature				sales and marketing
▶ ▶ ▶ product test				quality
▶ ▶ ▶ ▶ test batch				production
▶ ▶ ▶ ▶ quality checks				quality

Figure 4.3.14 *A milestone plan for a typical manufactured product*

decisions from the start of the product development cycle. This will enable fast, efficient and cost-effective manufacture of both new and existing products. Achieving high quality means setting the right 'quality indicators' to evaluate both the design and the intended processing methods. Total quality approaches make quality the responsibility of everyone in an organisation, not just the quality control or inspection departments.

We saw above that TQ is a culture of continuously improving the manufacturing system. For example, representatives from the production areas will be able to comment on a design and whether or not it can be manufactured using available equipment (design for manufacture – DFM). This discussion will anticipate manufacturing problems that the designer may not be aware of, and it also allows solutions to the problems to be developed and shared more rapidly. Computers are becoming increasingly useful in DFM as companies create **'expert systems'** or databases of best practice procedures such as online help files.

Many companies also involve their suppliers at an early stage in the product development cycle. The linkage between suppliers and manufacturers is known as a value chain. To achieve the maximum value from these chains means information has to flow efficiently and quickly between the partners. Increasingly, this communication takes place electronically through Electronic Data Interchange (EDI) systems, which we shall look at in more detail later in this unit. Using these communications

systems suppliers can comment on factors such as component or material supply constraints to avoid the company using parts that are difficult to source or about to be discontinued. The organisation of a typical product development team is shown in Figure 4.3.13.

Milestone planning
Different members of a team will take responsibility for ensuring that the product deadlines or 'milestones' are met, but everybody takes part in regular, often weekly, product review meetings. Milestone planning has also been shown to be effective in reducing the 'lead-in times' for new products. This is particularly important in market sectors such as electronics, especially mobile phones, where the pace of technological change is so great that product life cycles are getting shorter. Figure 4.3.14 shows a milestone plan.

Task
1 Select a product that you are familiar with and try to identify the people who might have been in the product development team.
2 What are the benefits of using a concurrent manufacturing system to produce this product in comparison with a sequential manufacturing system?
3 Explain why the use of ICT is such an important feature in concurrent manufacturing systems.

2. Robotics

Electronic or computer control systems are used in many areas within the manufacturing operation and associated business processes. Modern control systems support continuous operation and allow many processes to run either concurrently, sequentially or in combination. They help to maintain the quality of products and help to reduce waste caused by production processes that malfunction. They also play a vital role in creating safe and secure working environments. The systems are designed to shut down to a fail-safe state in case of an accident or a situation that is potentially harmful to anyone.

The industrial application of robotics/control technology and the development of automated processes

Automation is a term describing the automatic operation and self-correcting control of machinery or production processes by devices that make decisions and take action without the interference of a human operator. Robotics is a specific field of automation concerned with the design and construction of self-controlling machines or robots. In operational use CNC and automated NC machines either move a cutting tool or move the work piece in relation to one another. Robots can move or manipulate a greater number of objects through a wider range of linear and more complex motions. They can also sense and react to the environments they are working in.

The first operator-guided robotic manipulating devices were developed in the 1940s for use in the radioactive conditions surrounding the development of atomic and hydrogen bombs during World War II. The first industrial robots developed in the late 1950s and early 1960s included sensors and other simple feedback devices. The use of robots peaked in the 1990s with the development of new manufacturing systems such as CIM and FMS (see Figure 4.3.15). The next generation of manufacturing robots will have sensory feedback systems that are more sophisticated and possess a degree of **artificial intelligence** (AI).

Control systems

The common factor in all automated processes, including the use of robots, is that they require a control system. Control systems regulate, check, verify or restrain actions. Automatic or robotic manufacturing systems are able to sense and control how processes are operating by combining sub-systems of electrical, electronic, mechanical and pneumatic devices (see Figure 4.3.16). All these devices produce performance data that may need to be monitored by instrumentation systems. Instrumentation systems provide data in the form of either visual displays or electronic signals that indicate how effectively the manufacturing sub-systems are operating, both individually and in relation to one another in the overall system. Because of their ability to store, select, record and present data, computers and microprocessors such as programmable logic controllers (PLCs) are widely used to direct and control actions and process operations.

The application of robotic devices

Robotics is one branch of artificial intelligence concerned with developing devices that can move and react more effectively and efficiently to sensory inputs such as sound, sight and touch when processing, moving or handling components. Robots play an increasingly significant role in the development of industrial automation and CAM. Manufacturing robots are computer-controlled machine tools that can be programmed to perform any of a number of often high-precision functions such as electric arc welding or picking and placing electronic components on a circuit board. Their ability to make consistent repeated motions mean that robots are also used effectively for loading and unloading materials into a CNC or automated machine in a flexible manufacturing system.

Figure 4.3.15 *A manufacturing robot*

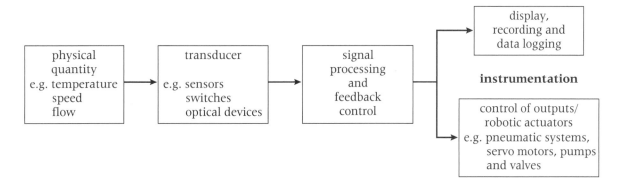

Figure 4.3.16 *A simple systems model can represent a manufacturing control system*

Computer or microprocessor controlled systems are also used to automate processes such as the selecting of stock and carrying it to the materials processing areas. The same systems are used for removing finished components to a holding area for onward processing.

The Zanussi factory producing washing machines in Italy is one of the most efficient automated production facilities in Europe. It uses an automated, driverless, pallet system to deliver parts and collect finished items from the different manufacturing cells within the factory.

Robots in hostile environments
Robots are also used in special manufacturing situations that would be dangerous for humans, for example in handling toxic wastes in nuclear reprocessing plants. Robots can also

perform repetitive, uncomfortable, tiring, or monotonous tasks, and can do them with greater speed and accuracy than can human beings (see Figure 4.3.17). Two of the most common tasks associated with robots are the spot welding and spray painting of car bodies, both of which have been shown to damage the health of human operators. Robots are being used in space on the Space Shuttle (see Figure 4.3.18) and on the assembly of devices such as the Hubble telescope and the International Space Station.

The use of robots in automated manufacturing cells
The operation of CNC machines and robots are combined effectively to create a flexible manufacturing or machining cell. In the automated machining cell in Figure 4.3.19 on page 248, the system will allow the production of a part that requires both milling and turning.

Limitations on the use of robots
Robots cannot be used in all manufacturing or product assembly situations. The greater the complexity of the operation, the greater the number of interactions and calculations that need to be carried out before an action can be taken. This inevitably slows down the robot's speed of action and increased manufacturing time leads to a reduction in operating profits. Sensing, control and AI technologies are continually evolving and there will be significant increases in the processing power of computers in the future, so we can say with certainty that the range and complexity of tasks that can be performed by manufacturing robots will increase. In the short term, designers are looking to design for robot assembly, which is a fundamental shift in design thinking.

Figure 4.3.17 *A computer-operated robot cutting holes in oil drill mandrels*

Figure 4.3.18 *The loading bay on the Space Shuttle showing the Canadian Robot Arm in use by astronauts*

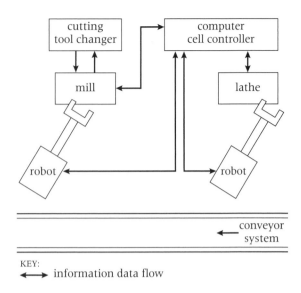

KEY: ⟷ information data flow

Figure 4.3.19 *An automated machining cell*

Task

Here is an extract from a manufacturer's specification for a robot product:

'The FK series is our flagship line of fully featured 3 to 5 axis traverse robots. AC Brushless Servo drive systems are used on all axes as standard. Pneumatic and AC variable frequency drive systems are also available to our customers who want a lower cost alternative for less demanding applications. Vertical (Z) axis strokes range from 6 mm to 25 mm and payloads from 5 kg to 70 kg to fit every need. The FK traverse robots are engineered to handle all types of applications including parts removal, insert loading, palletising and secondary equipment loading.'

Research each of the design features and functions mentioned, using sources such as the Internet. Then explain, with the aid of diagrams if necessary, what each means.

Automatic storage and retrieval systems

Raw materials and finished products can be automatically retrieved and stored by a system that is managed by a host computer. Automatic storage and retrieval systems (ASRS) range from the simple magazine loading of materials and components, to a completely automated system based on the use of pallets. All parts and assemblies are transported by the ASRS so that material is supplied to the manufacturing system at the required time for processing

orders. Component or pallet transfer from the ASRS to the machines can be accomplished using either a conveyor or an automated guided vehicle (AGV).

An AGV is an unmanned vehicle that carries components or sub-assemblies automatically along a pre-programmed path. AGVs use different navigational systems. One of the simplest is a photo-sensor operated system that 'reads' strips of reflective tape that can be easily altered if the layout of a production line changes. In more sophisticated systems, computer programs select the AGV's destination and control how the AGV performs its functions, such as lifting material on to a conveyor, along its route. The logistics and timing of all of these operations are scheduled from the Master Production Schedule discussed above.

The construction of an ASRS

An ASRS consists of horizontal or vertical storage racks containing pallets that are accessed by robots with built-in computers that can operate along the X, Y and Z axes of the storage bay (see Figure 4.3.20). Different systems employ different ways of moving the robot through the storage racks, one of the most common being to mount the robot on a gantry. The robot has a device that accurately locates to guides on the underside of the pallet which keeps it stable when the robot is in motion. The robot is configured by computer software to remove a pallet from the storage bay and place it on to a conveyor or AGV ready for transportation to the first manufacturing operation. On completion of the manufacturing

Figure 4.3.20 *ASRS system made by Stöklin in use in a warehouse for selection and retrieval of stocks*

process a command is sent from the computer controlling that manufacturing cell to tell the robot to collect the pallet and replace it in the appropriate rack on the ASRS. The robot's built-in computer stores all the necessary programs and positioning data, including the location coordinates of the individual storage bays.

Complex automated systems using artificial intelligence

Artificial intelligence (AI) was a term defined by John McCarthy at the Massachusetts Institute of Technology (MIT) in 1956. It describes the branch of computer science concerned with developing computers that think and act like humans. AI is a broad area of development covering a wide range of different fields, including engineering, ranging from 'machine vision' to 'expert' systems. The common thread that links research in this area is the creation of devices that can 'think'. Computers are not yet able to fully simulate human behaviour in manufacturing environments, but this is a major research area in manufacturing and it is only a matter of time because there have already been significant developments in the use of AI in other areas. In 1997 an IBM super-computer called Deep Blue defeated the world chess champion.

What is a thinking machine?

In order to 'think' it must be necessary to possess intelligence and knowledge. Intelligent behaviours may consist of solving complex problems or making generalisations and constructing relationships. To do these things requires perception and understanding of what has been perceived. Intelligent systems should be able to consider large amounts of information simultaneously and process them faster in order to make rational, logical or expert judgements. Perhaps the best way to gauge the intelligence of a machine is British computer scientist Alan Turing's test. He stated that a computer would deserve to be called intelligent if it could deceive a human into believing that it was human.

Knowledge-based or expert systems

A knowledge base stores the knowledge related to a particular area or domain. Expert systems in which computers are programmed to make decisions in real-life situations already exist to help human experts in several domains including engineering, but they are very expensive to produce and are helpful only in special situations or in hostile working environments like working in space. Expert systems are designed by knowledge engineers who study how experts make decisions. They identify the 'rules' that the expert has used and translate them into terms that a computer can understand.

Application of AI in design and manufacture

In Unit 3B2 we saw that CAD systems already provide a quick and efficient means of representing the technical form of a product. Present systems currently provide limited design information or advice to inform the decision making part of the design process. CAD/CAM software readily generates sets of manufacturing instructions, but a designer receives limited information from the software to decide whether the designed part is capable of being manufactured economically. At present, these types of decision are reached by combining and applying the experience and expertise of the whole product development team.

Applying design or production rules

It is possible to represent some knowledge in the form of a set of facts or rules. In electronics, for instance, there are the IF and THEN statements which can be combined with logic gate truth tables – when designing an electronic system, IF a set of conditions is true, THEN a conclusion can be made or an action can be taken. In a warning system, for example, if two inputs are true, then an audible alarm will sound. If two inputs are both true and an audible warning is required, then logic dictates that you would use an AND gate.

> **Task**
>
> Suggest a set of rules for choosing a logic gate for a control system to keep the temperature of heated plastic in a production process within specified limits.

AI areas currently under research and development

Because of the pressure to develop more responsive systems, considerable research and development time is focusing on developing manufacturing systems that fully integrate the use of CAD modelling, artificial intelligence, ICT and knowledge-based databases. These areas include:

- neural networks
- voice recognition systems
- natural language processing (NLP).

Neural networks

A neural network is a type of artificial intelligence that differs significantly from the domain-based knowledge systems described above. In practice, it is a computer system modelled on how the human brain and nervous system operate. Traditionally, computers are digital – they only manipulate zeros and ones. In a neural network, intelligence is simulated by attempting to adapt to changing conditions by reproducing the types of processing connections (neurons) that occur in the human brain. Neural networks are particularly effective for predicting events when they have a large database of examples to draw on. They are proving successful in a number of areas such as voice recognition and natural language processing (NLP). There has been research in this area since the 1950s but the lack of sufficient processing power and the cost of computing systems restricted developments. In relation to manufacturing, research in this area is gathering pace and it will affect the development of automated intelligent systems such as those needed for diagnosing faults in products and operating systems

Voice recognition systems

These are computer systems that can recognise spoken words. At present a computer can take dictation but is unable to understand what is being said. Until recently, because of their operating limitations and high cost, voice recognition systems have been used only in special situations as an alternative to computer keyboards. They find uses in situations such as working in space or other hostile environments when using a keyboard is impracticable or when an operator is disabled. In the future these systems will allow an operator to talk directly to an expert system for guidance or instruction. Increases in computing power mean that the costs of these systems will decrease and performance will improve, so that in the future speech recognition systems will be used more widely.

Natural language processing

If successfully developed, NLP will allow computers to understand human languages. This offers the greatest potential rewards because it would allow people to interact with computers without needing any specialised knowledge. You could simply walk up to a computer and talk to it. Unfortunately, programming computers to understand natural languages has proved to be more difficult than originally thought. Some rudimentary translation systems that translate from one human language to another are in existence, but they are not nearly as good as human translators

Representing simple and complex production systems graphically

Block flow diagrams

Systems thinking and design are evident all around us in the manufactured world. For example, an audio system can contain many different components and devices that can be configured to operate in a variety of ways. In the natural world we can sometimes make sense of it by applying systems thinking, as when we talk about a weather system. Systems diagrams have been developed to explain how the parts or activities that make up a system are organised and related to one another. They explain the processes that change an input into an output (see Figure 4.3.21).

There is a set of drawing conventions for representing what the blocks that make up a block flow diagram do (see Figure 4.3.22).

Flow process diagrams

All systems, whatever they do, contain sub-systems that perform the functions or processes required to achieve the required output. Complex processing within a manufacturing system can be modelled by breaking down the system into a collection of sub-systems each with their own input and output. In terms of automating a production line it may also be necessary to treat each processing sub-system as a complete system in its own right in order to

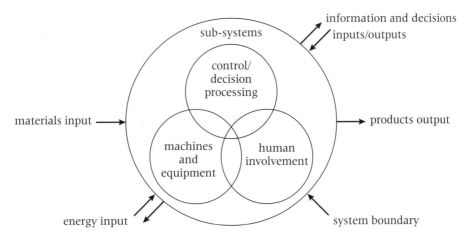

Figure 4.3.21 A system has a boundary that defines the limit of the system

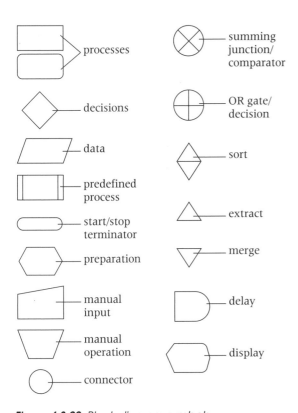

Figure 4.3.22 Block diagram symbols

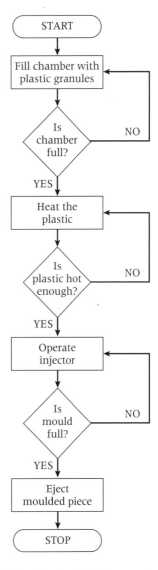

determine the input processes that are needed before the sub-system can perform its output function in the Master Production Schedule (see Figure 4.3.23).

Open- and closed-loop control systems

A system operating open-loop control has no feedback and will continue without interference from the controlled system. This is a major disadvantage in an automated process, as we

Figure 4.3.23 A simplified material processing system and its sub-systems for injection moulding

shall see later. A system operating closed-loop control can have either positive feedback or negative feedback in which information is fed back and combined with the input signal in order to modify the output signal.

Positive and negative feedback

In an automated process positive feedback would result in the system becoming unstable because an increase in the output leads to an increase in the input which creates an increase in the output and so the loop starts again. Negative feedback is often used in automated control processes because it works to change the input in such a way that the output is decreased to provide stable operating conditions. It is a system used throughout manufacturing, for example in the use of the Kanban that controls the flow of work on a production line.

Error signals

In any system with feedback, the difference between the input signal and the feedback signal is called the error signal. The size of the error signal determines how much the system output will need to be changed. When the system is in a near-stable state the error signal will be nearly zero. In a high-volume industry, for instance, an error signal will be generated when there is a difference between the projected sales figures and the actual sales figures. If the sales are higher than expected this will generate a positive error and signal the need to increase production levels. A negative error signal is generated when sales fall to a predetermined level lower than those projected, which signals the need to reduce production.

Hunting

Hunting in a system occurs when the system cannot reach a stable state. In the case described above, if the production level is overcorrected it will swing the error signal from positive to negative or vice versa, so the system is continually searching to set the right production levels, which results in waste or problems delivering goods on time.

Lag

In any large-scale system or automated process it will take time for the system as a whole to respond to the feedback signals it is getting. If a faulty batch of products has got out into the distribution chain it will not be noticed until customers or the outlets selling the product notify the company of the problem. This time delay before the system is able to respond is known as lag and it is a common feature in closed-loop control systems. The ways in which manufacturers and others are using ICT to improve the speed of communications at all levels of its business processes will be discussed later. The measures being taken to reduce lag include **Electronic Data Interchange** and improved 'real-time' sales data from Electronic Point of Sales (EPOS) information systems.

Task

For each of the following, hunting and lag, suggest where they might occur and what their effects might be in an automated production process that you have studied. What steps can be taken to minimise their effects in the system?

Automated systems using closed-loop control

Open-loop control systems have a major disadvantage when it comes to controlling devices such as motors on a conveyor belt. If the motor is put under too great a load its speed decreases, and it may stop completely with disastrous effect such as overheating. The alternative is a closed-loop system in which negative feedback is used to provide proportional control of the motor speed. Any difference between the required motor speed and its actual speed produces an error signal that is fed back to the speed controller in order to stabilise the conveyor system by adjusting the speed of the motor. Figure 4.3.24 shows open- and closed-loop control of an electric motor.

Sequential control

Robotic and automated processes often use sequential control programs in which a series of actions take place one after another. For instance, on an automated material loading system on a CNC machine each action depends on the previous one being carried out. If the system has not 'sensed' that the material blank to be loaded is in place the machine will not operate. It will wait until the sensor sends it the required information signal to pick up the blank.

Logical control of automated and robotic systems

Combinational logic is used in situations where a series of conditions have to be met before an operation can take place. There are a number of conventional logic gates that you should be familiar with such as the AND/OR/NAND gates. PLCs can also perform similar operations. Figure 4.3.25 is an example of how it could be applied in the operation of a CNC machine.

a) open-loop motor control

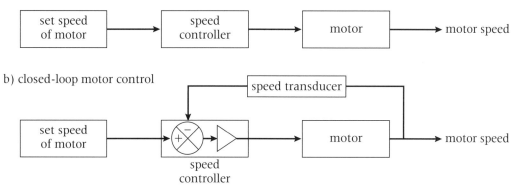

b) closed-loop motor control

Figure 4.3.24 *Open- and closed-loop control of a motor*

Fuzzy logic systems

Fuzzy logic was developed in the 1960s and it recognises more than the simple 'true' and 'false' values such as those used in electronic systems design based on zeros and ones. With fuzzy logic, propositions can be represented with degrees of truthfulness and falsehood. For example, the statement 'Today is sunny' might be 100 per cent true if there are no clouds, 80 per cent true if there are a few clouds, 50 per cent true if it's hazy and 0 per cent true if it rains all day. Fuzzy logic allows conditions such as rather warm or pretty cold to be formulated mathematically and processed by computers in an attempt to apply a more human-like way of thinking. Fuzzy logic has proved to be particularly useful in expert systems, other artificial intelligence applications, database retrieval and engineering.

Fuzzy control

Fuzzy controllers are the most important applications of fuzzy theory. They work rather differently from conventional controllers. Expert knowledge is used instead of equations to describe a system. This knowledge can be expressed in a very natural way using linguistic variables, which are described by fuzzy sets. A fuzzy set is a collection of objects or entities without clear boundaries.

Fuzzy control is useful:
- for very complex processes, when there is no simple mathematical model
- for nonlinear processes
- if the processing of (linguistically formulated) expert knowledge is to be performed.

Fuzzy control is less useful if:
- conventional control theory provides a satisfactory answer to the control problem
- an easily solvable and adequate mathematical model already exists
- the problem is not solvable.

Robot configurations

Robots can be configured to move and work in different ways as shown below. They can operate as manipulators (see Figure 4.3.26) or they can be designed to provide a load-carrying function. The final configuration is the work volume (see Figure 4.3.27). This is the area in which the end effector of the robot can be operated.

Representing degrees of freedom in a robotic system

In Unit 3B2 you studied the way that CNC tools generate a toolpath. The type of movements that a robot can provide are similar – point-to-point motion, contouring or continuous path (linear, arcs or combination moves).

The end effector on a robot arm can be positioned to give five or six degrees of freedom within the work volume – three linear and three rotational – as shown in the jointed or

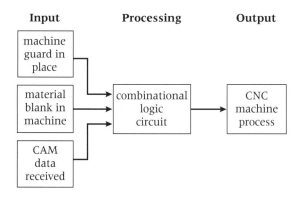

Figure 4.3.25 *All three inputs have to be 'on' for the CNC machine to operate*

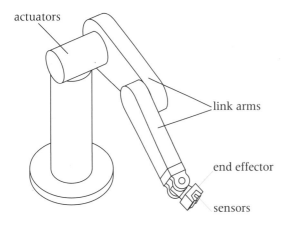

Figure 4.3.26 *The parts of a robot arm*

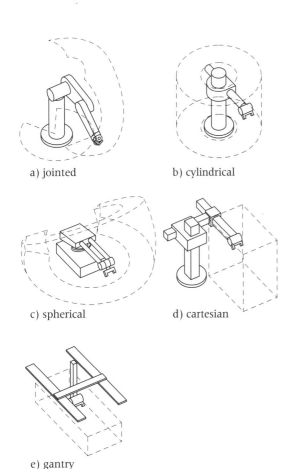

a) jointed

b) cylindrical

c) spherical

d) cartesian

e) gantry

Figure 4.3.27 *Robot configurations and work volumes*

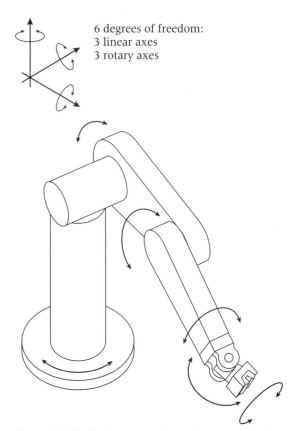

6 degrees of freedom:
3 linear axes
3 rotary axes

Figure 4.3.28 *Six degrees of freedom on a robotic arm*

Task

Various types of robotic movement are described above. Using diagrams to support your answer, explain how they can be applied in an automated production process.

Methods of providing feedback in an automated process

All the electronic switching and control circuits used in an automated process have three stages: input, processing and output. Sensors and switches are input transducers used to provide feedback information in an automated system. **Transducers** allow electronic circuits to **interface** with the physical world (see Figure 4.3.29). Depending on how they operate they provide either an analogue or a digital signal. An analogue signal is produced from a transducer device such as a heat sensor used in a plastics production process. As the temperature increases, the signal that is produced increases; as it falls, the signal falls. The analogue signal is continuously varying but it

articulated robot in Figure 4.3.28. Generally, three degrees of freedom are provided by the main operating mechanism and the other two or three by the end effector, depending on how it is configured.

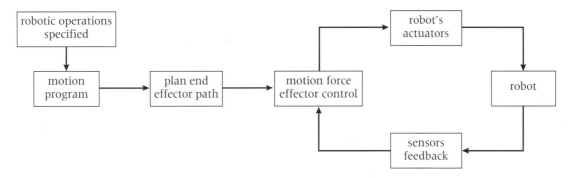

Figure 4.3.29 *Sensing and control in robotic motion*

is being used to switch the heater on or off which is a digital operation (on or off). An analogue signal also has to be converted into a digital signal in order to be processed by a computer-based control system as all computers operate in a digital way using zeros and ones. This analogue to digital (A/D) conversion is a critical process for providing feedback in computer or microprocessor control applications.

The advantages and disadvantages of automation and its impact on employment, both local and global

The pressure for automated manufacturing

In many large manufacturing organisations the main focus of research and development is on improving the ability of all their production operations to respond to unpredictable disturbances and increasing change on a global scale. Global competition forces companies to compete on all fronts in terms of cost, quality, delivery, flexibility, innovation and service.

Traditionally, the performance of all production systems, including those that are automated, has been assessed in terms of their output under steady-state operating conditions. However, greater product variety, smaller batch sizes and frequent new product introductions, coupled with tighter delivery requirements, are becoming the norm. This means that manufacturers have to devise and develop automated operations that are capable of performing consistently under continually changing or disturbed conditions. Disturbances may be external to a production process (for example sudden changes in demand for the product, variations in raw material supply) or internal (for example machine breakdowns). Automated production will play an increasing part in production

responsive strategies. We saw in Unit 3 that a characteristic of these approaches is the negative impact it has on local and global employment patterns.

Advantages of automated manufacturing

- The quality and reliability of the output is improved.
- There is a high level of value-added because of the removal of labour costs.
- There is increased productivity as automated systems can work continuously.
- There is a shorter pay-back time on the capital invested in an automated production line.
- Reduced employment and overhead costs accompany a change to automated production.
- It offers a more flexible and predictable system because labour-intensive processes are removed.

The impact of automation on patterns of employment

The people working in an automated manufacturing environment have to be able to operate in a more flexible way than ever before. This requires education, training and the development of new ICT skills such as the handling and interpretation of production data. In the UK there is a chronic shortage of people willing to enter engineering and to train for work in highly automated environments. The people who do want to work in this sector need a much wider range of basic skills and the capability to transfer existing skills and knowledge into new situations. Workers in an automated manufacturing cell have to be capable of handling and responding to conditions on several.different machines simultaneously. To do this they have to be adaptable individuals who are capable and willing to work as multi-function operators.

3. Uses of ICT in the manufacture of products

Electronic communications

E-manufacturing

The term electronic manufacturing or e-manufacturing has been developed to reflect the fact that ICT has dramatically changed the way that manufacturing is organised and managed. ICT is now having an impact from the boardroom, throughout the business, and out into the supply and distribution chains (see Figure 4.3.30). This is made possible by the development of more technologically efficient and more cost-effective methods of electronic communications and information handling.

Beyond e-mail

ICT is improving the reach and the range of communications channels. The reach refers to the level of communication that is possible with other users across a communications network, and the range refers to the types of interaction that can take place. Electronic mail (e-mail) operating within a company has a low level of reach and range when it is used for messaging or sending files to an individual or a work group. When business or manufacturing data can be shared by anyone, anywhere, irrespective of the computer's operating system, the basic building block for an effective integrated manufacturing system with extended reach and range is in place. There are many elements that need to be in place to achieve complete Electronic Data Interchange.

Electronic Data Interchange

Computers talk to one another across networks. Electronic Data Interchange (EDI), sometimes referred to as paperless trading, involves the transfer of data between computers using local area or global networks such as a **LAN** or the Internet. As more companies connect to the Internet, EDI is becoming increasingly important as an easy mechanism for companies to buy, sell and trade goods as well as share

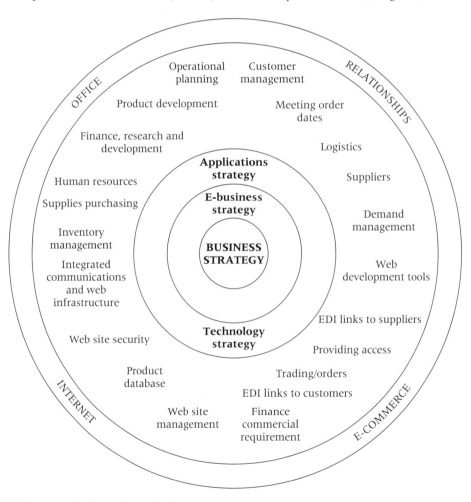

Figure 4.3.30 The organisation of an e-business

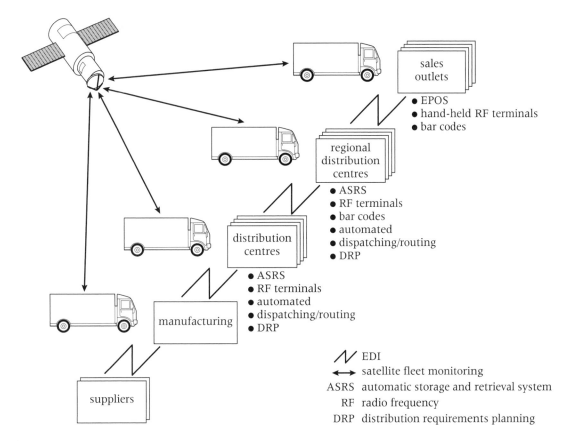

Figure 4.3.31 *The future uses of EDI in the total manufacturing process*

information. Originally developed in the 1980s, EDI was used to support traditional business operations such as processing orders and invoices. As ICT continues to improve, EDI is used to implement new manufacturing strategies or to make existing strategies such as just in time and Kanban more effective (see Figure 4.3.31).

Electronic Data Exchange

The development of EDI into a means of exchanging technological data about all aspects of a product is well under way. CAD/CAM Data Interchange (CDI) refers to the process of exchanging product design and manufacturing data. Electronic Data Exchange (EDE) describes systems in which EDI and CDI are combined to provide an effective automated data transfer system over a network of computers. There are various networks available for manufacturers to use.

Integrated Services Data Network

Integrated Services Data Network (ISDN) is an international communications standard for sending voice, video and data over digital telephone lines. The speed with which data can be transmitted from one device to another is the

data transfer rate or throughput. ISDN provides high-speed data transfer rates, which is why it is so useful to manufacturers who need to transfer large data files like CAD drawings. ISDN lines provide more than three times the throughput rate provided by today's fastest **modems**.

Local Area Networks

In a manufacturing situation, Local Area Networks (LANs) are used in a variety of ways; for example to communicate manufacturing data from the design office directly to the CNC manufacturing tools, usually over relatively short distances. LANs are usually set up using equipment and software that best meets the manufacturer's individual needs, but this restricts communications to the internal company networks and they are in effect a closed system.

Wide Area Networks

Many large manufacturing companies have processing and business centres all over the world and require more open methods of data transfer. Wide Area Networks (WANs) can provide this. Most WANs connect to an existing digital telephone system and follow a set of agreed standards and protocols to ensure compatibility across the different computer systems. For some companies WANs are too restrictive, so they are looking to use the global network provided by the Internet and the world wide web.

Intranets and extranets

An intranet is an Internet-based communications and data exchange system. An intranet web site looks and acts just like any other web site, but there is a '**firewall**' surrounding it that prevents unauthorised access into the site. Intranets are used by manufacturers in the same way as everybody else uses the Internet – to share information and expertise – but they are much less expensive for a company to set up and manage compared with a private network (WAN) using dedicated equipment, software and protocols.

Only people who are members of a company or organisation can use intranets but an extranet provides various levels of access to partners outside the company. Extranets are an increasingly popular means for business partners in different companies to share and exchange information in a secure way. Access to intranets or extranets is possible only if a person has a valid username and password. The user's 'identity' will also determine which parts of the network he or she can view.

The Internet and the world wide web

The World Wide Web is a global network of Internet servers that support specially formatted documents written in a language called **HTML** (Hypertext Mark-up Language) that supports links to other documents, as well as to graphics, audio and video files. This means you can jump from one document to another simply by clicking on hot spots or links known as **hyperlinks**. Not all Internet servers are part of the World Wide Web (see intranet and extranet above). There are several applications called **web browsers** that make it easy to access the World Wide Web. Two of the most popular are Netscape Navigator and Microsoft's Internet Explorer.

Task

Effective use of the Internet to find information is where most people run into trouble as hours can be wasted in visiting inappropriate web sites. Using a web browser and search engine of your choice, produce a list of links for a range of consumer products in your chosen materials area. Present your links as a reference source to be shared with other people who are studying design and technology.

Advantages of using the Internet and the Web

The Internet is becoming an invaluable tool for designers and manufacturers. It provides:

- an easily and cheaply accessible means of sharing ideas
- a vast and growing body of knowledge and information (sometimes not correct though!)
- a medium to communicate with potential customers, current customers and other manufacturers
- a readily accessible, online source of reference and design data on areas as diverse as material specifications, marketing trends and catalogues of parts and components.

Disadvantages of using the Internet

Industrial espionage is a real problem in a paper-rich environment, but there is no guarantee that Internet systems are any more secure. Security can be improved by data encryption techniques. Passwords can be used to allow access rights to certain areas, but there is always the risk that sensitive commercial information can be intercepted electronically. The more that security measures are built into the data management system the more difficult it becomes to use.

Videoconferencing

Computers, telecommunications and video technologies have revolutionised the way people live in the world today. Videoconferencing (VC) integrates these three technologies to enhance communications and speed up the decision making process in a business. VC happens between two or more participants at different sites by using computer networks to transmit audio and video data. Various forms of VC organisation are used:

- Desktop video conferencing (DTVC) or point-to-point (two-person) VC systems work like a video telephone. Each participant has a video camera, microphone and speakers mounted on to a standard desktop computer equipped with a sound card. As the two participants speak to one another their voices are carried over the network and delivered to the other's speakers, and whatever images appear in front of the video camera appear in a window on the other participant's monitor.
- Multi-point VC allows three or more participants to sit in a 'virtual' conference room and communicate as if they were sitting right next to each other.

Until the mid-1990s, the cost of the hardware made videoconferencing too expensive for most manufacturers, but that situation is changing rapidly. Videoconferencing is a rapidly growing segment of ICT as hardware costs continue to fall.

Benefits of videoconferencing for manufacturers

Videoconferencing allows people to communicate face to face without the tremendous cost of accommodation and travel and time spent away from the office and home. VC can be used in many applications, including the following:

- Marketing presentations. Marketers and manufacturers may not operate in the same country. When a new product is to be launched at a trade show or directly to the public, it is important to know how the product will be presented to persuade people to buy it. VC provides the opportunity to see the presentations as they develop and enables instant opinions on their effectiveness.
- Corporate training. If there is something employees all over the world need to know it may be much faster and cheaper to train them using videoconferencing.
- Remote diagnostics. Experts in a particular process may work in one office but the problem requiring their immediate expertise might occur half-way around the world. VC allows the experts the opportunity to solve the problem without travelling from the office. Production downtime is reduced and the expert and the other employees can get back to whatever it was they were originally doing without wasting time.

Problems in implementing VC in manufacturing

The biggest problem with videoconferencing has been the **compatibility** issue. There are several different manufacturers, each using their own 'standards' for the hardware and software that make videoconferencing work. A standard has been approved by the International Telecommunication Union (ITU). This defines how audiovisual conferencing data is to be transmitted across networks. In theory, this should enable users to participate in the same conference although they might be using different videoconferencing applications. In the UK, Denford Ltd has already developed a system called Remote Manufacturing that uses videoconferencing for educational purposes (see below).

How does DTVC work?

The popularity of videoconferencing has increased dramatically over the past few years owing to the increased availability of low-cost add-on DTVC products. A typical DTVC consists of a board that digitises and compresses a video signal. This signal is decompressed at the receiving station where it is reconstructed to resemble the original information. Compressing and decompressing DTVC information is accomplished using a CODEC (*Compression–Dec*ompression) system. This is done with hardware or software. The more information that can be compressed, the larger and smoother the video images are at the receiving end. A basic DTVC system produced by Denford Ltd for use in school/college situations is shown in Figure 4.3.32.

Setting up a DTVC link

The miniature video camera attached to a computer display is only suitable for face-to-face meetings as it has a narrow field of view and a relatively short depth of focus. For larger groups a conventional camcorder mounted on a tripod can be set up to allow individuals within the group to talk without the need to be constantly moving to and from the computer.

A microphone and loudspeakers are also part of a DTVC system, allowing two-way conversations to occur. The microphone and the soundboard on the computer allow the speaker's voice to be digitised and compressed. A good microphone can pick up more than one voice, but if several microphones are to be used they need to be controlled by a suitable sound 'mixer'.

Figure 4.3.32 *Denford has identified the potential of videoconferencing as an educational tool by incorporating the vital dimension of data sharing to allow staff and students to open notebooks, documents, drawing files and work together discussing problems and jointly solving them*

An external amplifier and speakers can be added to the 'Line Out' connection (available on most audio boards) to broadcast to larger groups.

The compressed audio and video signals are sent over a communication line to the other computer. Originally intended for voice only, standard telephone lines do not handle video signals very well. Because video contains much more information than audio, it requires a much larger **bandwidth** (a larger information carrying capability) to handle this complex signal. A limited bandwidth causes several problems for VC, including:

- 'choppy' video pictures that cause delays in the movement of an object so that it appears jerky
- lack of synchronisation when voices are heard but the mouth isn't moving.
- low-resolution and poor quality or 'noisy' images that are fuzzy and difficult to see.

Many manufacturers are installing ISDN lines for VC since they can handle a tremendous amount of information ensuring a smooth, 'noise-free' video signal. Two-channel ISDN lines allow simultaneous file transfers. After a design meeting ends, the design information which has just been reviewed needs to be sent to a regional office. This electronic file can be transferred either after the videoconference meeting has ended or, if a two-channel ISDN line is in use, it can be sent in the background on one channel while sight and sound information is still being exchanged on the other channel.

Remote manufacturing of components using videoconferencing

ICT provides the opportunity for expertise and expensive equipment to be made available to a number of schools, colleges and universities from one central location. Denford Ltd has pioneered the educational use of CAD/CAM via videoconferencing in the UK, enabling staff and students to manufacture parts at a distance in real time using industry standard equipment and software.

Task

Earlier in this unit and in Unit 3 we saw that computers are playing a much greater role in the whole life cycle of a product. Using examples from your chosen materials area, list and describe how a manufacturer might use the various computer networks and information systems that have been considered.

The steps involved in remote manufacturing through videoconferencing

(see Figure 4.3.33)

Step 1. The student creates a design on CAD/CAM software on a PC (stand-alone or networked).

Step 2. The student and teacher participate in a live video conference with the Remote Manufacturing Centre or the Denford on-demand facility.

Step 3. The student's design is downloaded to the Remote Manufacturing Centre where it is discussed and amendments made, where necessary.

Step 4. The Remote Manufacturing Centre creates the CNC file containing the student's design.

Step 5. The student's design is manufactured on a CNC machine while he or she views via the remote video camera.

Step 6. The finished component is evaluated, shown to the student on the VC and then posted back to the school/college.

Source: Denford Ltd

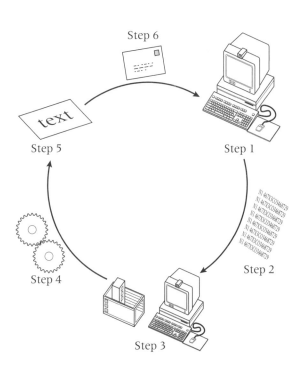

Figure 4.3.33 *The steps involved in remote manufacturing through videoconferencing*

Electronic whiteboards

Electronic whiteboards
This is a relatively new communications technology that has a growing place in a manufacturing context alongside DTVC. The electronic whiteboard, sometimes called a 'smart board', integrates the simplicity of a whiteboard with the power of a computer, becoming an interactive, flexible tool for use in presentations, video conferences, training sessions and many other applications (see Figure 4.3.34). Simply touching the board allows access to:

- a sensitive writing surface with a scanner and a thermal printer for producing hard copy
- high-quality data and video images such as animated 3D virtual products
- live or stored information from the Internet
- live video stream from a camera or video recorder
- an automatic way of recording a video conference, making it available for later reference
- software to store notes and drawings into a computer file so they can be e-mailed to colleagues, printed or pasted into other applications
- other computer applications such as spreadsheets and databases.

Electronic information handling and 'agile' manufacturing

An agile manufacturer recognises the uncertainty that change brings and puts mechanisms in place to deal with it. The organisation moves from being manufacturing-driven to customer-driven, and it realises that customers won't pay a premium for product quality: quality is always assumed. Agile manufacturers work in partnerships with customers and suppliers, and understand that the so-called 'soft' business information processes are important to the entire manufacturing process. In an agile manufacturing environment, information is the primary enabling resource and ICT is the enabling technology. In order to find out what the customer needs and wants, manufacturers set up a range of computer-based systems for collecting market information.

Computer-Aided Market Analysis (CAMA)
Market research is a term that describes the collection and analysis of data about consumers, market niches and the effectiveness of marketing programmes. Market analysis focuses on the collection, analysis and the application of research data to predict the future of a particular market (trends). The analytical process will include the examination and evaluation of relevant information (data) in order to select the best course of action from the possible business options. The analysis can be undertaken 'in-house' by the manufacturers themselves or through specialist market research agencies or consultancy firms who will provide tailor-made or customised data sets related to specific companies, customers or markets. The analysis of business data and market trends generates a vast flow of information and data that is now most efficiently managed in a computerised relational database. Such a database can be interrogated in various ways depending on the type of analysis required:

- A qualitative analysis will tell a company who is buying the products and why, or what customers like or dislike about a product and its after-sales support.
- A quantitative analysis will provide facts and figures such as where the products are being bought and when, or a comparative analysis of the company's financial ratios over time.
- A trend analysis will tell a company what is happening in a particular sector of a market and put the company's performance into a local, regional, pan-European or global context.
- Market timing is about attempting to predict future market directions, usually by examining recent product volume or economic data, and investing resources based on those predictions.
- In situations of high product volumes, existing customer information can be profiled

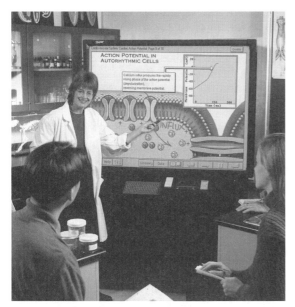

Figure 4.3.34 *Electronic whiteboard*

against lifestyle surveys and demographic data to give a detailed picture of the company's ideal customer.

Benefits of CAMA

In a modern e-business environment, a manufacturer needs access to up-to-date research, in-depth product and market analysis and industry-specific expertise to make the best ICT-led decisions in relation to the core business goals. Using advanced computer-based marketing tools and expertise will help a manufacturer to:

- convert data into actionable information with which to make sound marketing and planning decisions
- calculate demand for products and services more accurately and set the right sales targets
- identify markets and find out where potential customers are shopping
- employ a marketing technique – market segmentation – that targets a group of customers with specific characteristics
- launch new products more effectively by focused strategies such as regional or mini product launches rather than whole country product 'roll outs'.

CAMA applied to manufacturing practice

CAMA provides research data for the people concerned with formulating e-business strategies in manufacturing industries. The data not only informs supply chain planning; it is used also to direct or inform the development of manufacturing strategies such as automation and related control technologies or plant layouts. As a manufacturer moves into an ICT-based model of the manufacturing process it must identify its core business strategy, devise an e-business strategy and develop a design and technology strategy.

The use of computers in an integrated design environment

An effective product design that satisfies functional requirements and can be manufactured easily requires vast amounts of 'expert' knowledge. Integrated IT-based systems already exist where design features can be generated by CAD software and then checked for ease of manufacture (design for manufacture – DFM) and for ease of assembly (design for assembly – DFA) by a knowledge-based expert system. With the increased volume of design information generated by computer-based systems, designers now have to analyse and evaluate large data sets of design constraints to find a design specification that satisfies those constraints.

Computer-Aided Specification of Products (CASP)

A design specification is a document which explores and explains the internal design of a given component or sub-system. It should be sufficiently detailed to permit the manufacturing phase to proceed without significant reworking resulting from flawed or missing design details. Intelligent design systems and expert databases are being developed to support all aspects of the design process from CASP to CADMAT.

Intelligent design systems

There will be three distinct classifications of information within the intelligent design system database: CAD data, a design 'catalogue' and a knowledge database The CAD data contains specific information about the physical characteristics of each component part being designed. The design catalogue is a reference source that contains data such as the cost, weight and strength characteristics of the standard parts and fasteners that are available to the manufacturer. The knowledge database contains 'rules' about design and manufacturing methods. These automated and intelligent design environments when fully developed will enable a designer to perform and manage complex automated design tasks including decision making. One of the major benefits to follow from these developments is that when a designer moves on to another area of specialism or to a manufacturing competitor his or her 'expert' design knowledge remains available and readily accessible because it has been incorporated into the intelligent design system and the expert databases.

Task

Using the knowledge you have gained from making different things in your chosen materials area, devise a list of six design and manufacturing rules that you have applied. The rule can be written as an If/Then statement. For example, 'If the product case were to be injection moulded, then the plastic material would be in the thermosetting category.'

Automated stock control

Earlier in this unit, we looked at the benefits that arise out of applying the just-in-time (JIT) philosophy. A characteristic of JIT is that product variety increases as the range of processing systems decreases and waste is reduced by a variety of means including automated stock control systems. These ensure the size of the inventory is optimised but available on demand when and where it is needed. These automated stock control systems support the move from batch to continuous flow production. They are also an advantage in the process of line balancing, which is a scheduling technique that reduces waiting times caused by unbalanced production times.

Production scheduling and production logistics

Computer-based scheduling and logistics systems ensure that a production plan is implemented and that production is 'smoothed' so that small variations in supply and demand are managed without causing problems. This is achieved by spreading the product mix and the quantities of each produced evenly over each day in a month. Different manufacturers have different planning horizons that determine when the detailed production plan is produced; typically, it is one month in advance. The advantage of these computer-based scheduling and logistics applications is that:

- they are flexible and easily adapted if the product mix or quantity required is changed at short notice
- they minimise work in progress and reduce the inventory
- they maintain balance between the stations on a production line
- they raise productivity levels.

Quick Response Manufacturing

Quick Response Manufacturing (QRM) focuses on reducing product lead times and the production of small batches. It provides a better 'time to market'. Real-time reprogramming of manufacturing is a production management tool that offers high-volume, rapid-turnover manufacturers the potential for enormous savings in both time to market and increased business efficiency. The ability to re-programme automatically both manufacturing and business processes in response to market pressures is on the horizon. Stock levels will be constantly re-evaluated as demand patterns change. The demand patterns also affect capacity planning

and so the relevant individual within the business would be automatically alerted. The impact that a change to the business or a manufacturing process may have will be immediately available for review from anywhere in the world. The change to real-time re-programming also presents the possibility for disastrous levels of confusion unless the information flow is carefully managed with an appropriate product data management system (PDMS) based on highly integrated knowledge bases.

Production control

Mechanical methods for measuring and inspection

These methods usually employ a probe that is in mechanical contact with the work piece and connected to a microprocessor (see Figure 4.3.35). For the measuring process, the probe is moved towards the work piece and it is deflected by the contact that is made. The coordinate value of the point of the touch makes it possible to calculate the dimension, provided the starting position of the probe is known. This probe method is employed in coordinate measurement machines (CMMs).

Figure 4.3.35 *Three axis displacement probe*

Advantages of using a computer-aided CMM

Depending on the sophistication of the machine and the software support, the advantages will include the following:

- Different types of inspection processes are supported through the use of different probes and sensors including touch, trigger, analogue contact, non-contact and vision systems.
- The data produced from the probe transducers can be processed electronically through interfacing devices into computer-based software packages such as Delcam's PowerINSPECT™.
- 'Offline' programming and control of manual or automated CNC-based measuring systems is possible, linked to the original CAD model and the manufacturing process.
- Free-form positioning of the probes provides the flexibility to select any inspection point on the surface.

The principal advantages of optical methods of measuring and inspecting parts

- There is no need for direct mechanical contact between the sensor and the object.
- The distance from the object to be measured to the sensor can be large.
- The response time is limited only by the electronics used in the sensor.

Advantages of all computer-aided inspection methods

- They provide ongoing quality throughout manufacture.
- They optimise inspection time.
- Errors are identified and analysed early, which reduces costs.
- The problem of 3D inspection at a production stage is made easier.
- The software can generate reports that are fully compliant with **ISO9000**.
- The applications can export inspection information in the form of Initial Graphics Exchange Specification (IGES) data for use in other applications.

Visual monitoring of quality

Earlier in this unit, you learned that visual inspection is important in monitoring quality. It enables manufacturers to:

- detect parts that are incorrectly manufactured
- detect parts that are not in the right position for further processing
- make measurements of material/components/ assemblies in process
- identify material/components/assembly errors in process.

Inspection has always been incorporated into the manufacturing process. However, this often amounted only to the selection of a random sample of finished components; if any errors are detected at this late stage, machining and processing has already been carried out and rectification is not only costly but may not be possible. This results in high scrap rates and wasted machining time. To help alleviate this problem, 100 per cent piece-by-piece inspection can be carried out using a low-cost 'intelligent camera' connected to a computer and monitor, which will improve quality at minimal cost. Other benefits of computer-based visual control systems include:

- monitoring work in progress (WIP)
- inventory tracking in automated stock control systems
- component identification.

Task

Consider a product you are familiar with and list six critical dimensions that contribute to its functionality. For instance, on a CD player with a loading tray, the dimensions of the tray are critical if the CD is to be loaded correctly. For each of the identified dimensions on your chosen product, describe what inspection or measurement techniques might be employed during manufacturing.

Product marketing, distribution and retailing

Electronic point of sale

Information is at the centre of any business; used properly it ensures the business stays one step ahead. We saw earlier in this unit that time to market is an important driver in the move to concurrent engineering. Manufacturers in the high-volume sectors of industry can gain an advantage over their competitors by employing ICT such as electronic point of sale (EPOS) to supply and deliver their products and services faster. ICT applications also support QRM in low-volume manufacturing operations by reducing the time between the placing of an order and the receipt of the product. Electronic information is collected and recorded at the point of sale (POS) by a range of peripheral devices such as fixed or hand-held bar code readers. Each product that is sold has a unique bar code attached to it that electronically identifies it. Manufacturers collect this sales information automatically or at scheduled times during the day such as close of business. In addition, the two-way information flow can include financial data, e-mails and price updates.

EPOS and the associated management software provides manufacturers with:

- a full and immediate account of the financial transactions involving the company's products
- the data needed to undertake a sales/profit margin analysis as it can be exported into financial management software such as spreadsheets
- the means to monitor the performance and popularity of all product lines, which is particularly important in high-volume situations as it allows the company to react quickly to demand fluctuations and be able to deal with surges in demand by being notified of them immediately
- accurate information for identifying buying trends when making marketing decisions rather than relying on guesswork
- a full and responsive stock control system by providing real-time stock updates for product sales, transfers between retail outlets, goods received, etc.
- a system to ensure that sufficient stock is available to meet customer needs without overstocking and tying up capital (this is known as a continuous product replenishment system CPR).

Figure 4.3.36 shows how a manufacturer uses a communications network to keep in touch with customers, suppliers and distribution centres.

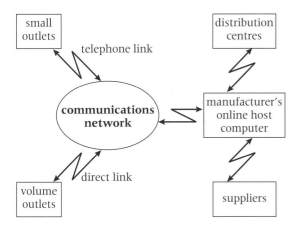

Figure 4.3.36 *Manufacturer's communication links with distribution centres, suppliers and retail outlets*

Using ICT effectively for the business processes in manufacturing

Throughout this unit we have considered how ICT is being employed to improve profitability and product quality on the production side of manufacturing. CAD/CAM technologies and the use of robotics lead to new ways of organising manufacturing. As we have seen, ICT can also be used to speed up business processes such as invoicing and stock control, but this on its own will not necessarily increase productivity. One of the key benefits that increased use of ICT brings is in better integration. This means that manufacturers have to change not only their manufacturing processes but also the way that they do business outside the company.

Internet marketing

Entering the Internet Market in order to create e-business is also a major strategic decision for a manufacturer. It generally means an almost total restructuring of the internal and external business processes as well as their supply chains and their relationships with customers. For many manufacturers this redesign of the business process presents a bigger challenge than the change to automated production systems or other ICT-based manufacturing processes.

The lure of the Internet

For many companies the rush to the Internet and the development of web sites was ill-conceived and badly thought out. Many businesses invested heavily in terms of time and money merely to put their existing product catalogues out on the world wide web to little commercial effect other than an electronic presence 'out there'. There was no underpinning business strategy and customers were able to do little more than browse the catalogue electronically. If they wanted to contact the company it had to be by conventional means such as phone or fax. Some companies added e-mail addresses in recognition of a need to communicate interactively. Using the Internet to market a business is more than that.

The importance of interactive 3D products on the Web

The move towards interactive 3D virtual products in marketing and sales on the Web is a natural extension of modern marketing and sales operations. Manufacturers are now faced with shortening product life cycles, increasing product complexity and tightening global competition, so they must ensure that customers understand their products better. This could mean providing ways of allowing a customer to configure the product for their own needs. One of the essential areas for Web development is the provision of interactive 3D products. 3D product images provide more information than conventional pictures, and they offer the potential for online product trials. At the time of writing we are at the start of this process with the introduction of virtual car showrooms where customers can benefit not only from reduced prices but 'customise' their cars to meet their own requirements.

Benefits of Internet marketing

- Instant global reach, access into new markets and an increased customer base.
- Faster processes and transactions resulting in efficiency savings and reduced overhead costs.
- Detailed knowledge of user preferences and better electronic documentation leading to improved customer service through better product and after-sales support.
- Access to designs that can be relatively easily customised.
- Reduced time to market.
- A better company image and an increased profile worldwide.

The future use of ICT in manufacturing

Advances in ICT will provide manufacturing with the benefits of faster access and response times as well as facilities for instant viewing of a product. As desktop PC-based systems grow ever more powerful, anyone with access rights within a company will be able to view the progress of a product at any time in its life cycle from anywhere in the world. For example, if there is a problem, such as a component failure on an aircraft, it could be evaluated by the design engineer responsible or any other concerned party within the company at the same time. Further developments in mobile communications (third generation technologies) as well as in data compression and satellite technologies will allow access to the company from anywhere in the world. This will revolutionise the business process in areas such as post-sales support and the on-site analysis and solving of problems.

The development of knowledge ware

Manufacturing is also beginning to see the development of 'knowledge ware' or expert databases that are targeted directly at the design process. These databases will provide a comprehensive electronic library instantly accessible via the Web by any designer with the relevant access levels and a desktop PC. So those areas of complex designs that previously might have caused severe problems for the designer such as product specific planning can be started by the designer before the consultation with the production specialists within the product development team. A company's business processes will also benefit from the development of readily available 'knowledge ware' that are databases of best practice procedures. This process has already begun with the development of more detailed 'solution-led' help files in business and project management software.

More customised products, more ICT

The streamlining of product development within manufacturing will continue. Eventually, customers will be allowed direct access to the design process and product specification via the Internet. The use of safety-based expert systems and AI will block the customer's interference in areas where safety is critical. As customers become involved in specifying their own products or solutions, it creates a new pressure on manufacturing. As an example, component stock levels will be difficult to predict and after-sales support of customised products is made more difficult.

There is clear economic pressure in all aspects of a manufacturing business to develop and refine their ICT solutions. We have seen that ICT provides the means to integrate both product and business data into the coherent information flow that is needed to ensure survival in a global economy.

Task

Explain how the development of new communications technologies is changing the way that manufacturing companies do business. Use examples of products from your chosen materials area to illustrate your points.

Exam preparation

You will need to revise all the topics in this unit, so that you can apply your knowledge and understanding to the exam questions.

In preparation for your exam it is a good idea to make brief notes about different topics, such as 'Production scheduling and production logistics'. Use sub-headings or bullet point lists and diagrams where appropriate. A single side of A4 should be used for each heading from the Specification.

It is very important to learn exam skills. You should have weekly practice in learning technical terms and in answering exam-type questions. When you answer any question you should:

- read the question carefully and pick out the key points that need answering
- match your answer to the marks available, e.g. for two marks, you should give two good points that address the question
- always give examples and justify statements with reasons, saying how or why the statement is true.

Practice exam questions

1 a) Explain the following terms related to the use of computers in manufacturing:
   (i) CADMAT   (6)
   (ii) product data management (PDM).   (3)
   b) Describe what is meant by a manufacturing cell.   (6)
   c) Explain why computer-aided engineering is important when developing a product.   (6)

2 a) Describe the meaning of three of the following terms related to production planning:
   - master production schedule
   - resource scheduling
   - order-based scheduling
   - materials requirements planning.   (9)
   b) Describe the importance of inspecting quality when manufacturing products.   (6)

3 a) Explain the difference between automation and robotics.   (8)
   b) Outline the limitations on the use of robots in product assembly.   (3)
   c) Describe two of the following terms:
   - automatic storage and retrieval system
   - artificial intelligence
   - fuzzy logic system.   (4)

4 a) Explain three of the following terms related to electronic communications:
   - electronic data interchange
   - local area network
   - global network
   - integrated services data network.   (6)
   b) Discuss the benefits for manufacturers of using video-conferencing.   (4)
   c) Explain how desktop video conferencing works.   (5)

5 a) Explain the meaning of quick response manufacturing.   (4)
   b) Describe the advantages of using computer-aided inspection methods for production
      control.   (5)
   c) Discuss the issues related to Internet marketing.   (6)

UNIT 4 B3 Mechanisms, energy and electronics (R404)

Summary of expectations

1. What to expect

Mechanisms, energy and electronics is one of the three options offered in Section B of Unit 4. You must study the same option that you studied at AS level.

2. How will it be assessed?

The work that you do in this option will be assessed through Section B of the Unit 4 examination paper. You are advised to spend **45 minutes** on this section of the paper.

3. What will be assessed?

The following list summarises the topics covered in this option and what will be examined:

- pulleys and sprockets
- shafts and couplings
- cams and followers
- conversion of motion
- brakes
- clutches
- screwthreads
- transistors
- thyristors
- logic
- circuit construction.

4. How to be successful in this unit

To be successful in this unit you will need to:

- have a clear understanding of the topics covered in this option
- apply your knowledge and understanding to a given situation or context
- organise your answers clearly and coherently, using specialist technical terms where appropriate
- use clear sketches where appropriate to illustrate your answers
- write clear and logical answers to the examination questions, using correct spelling, punctuation and grammar.

There may be an opportunity to demonstrate your knowledge and understanding of mechanisms, energy and electronics in your Unit 5 coursework. However, simply because you are studying this option, you do not have to integrate this type of technology into your coursework project.

5. How much is it worth?

This option, with Section A, is worth 15 per cent of the full GCE Advanced GCE.

Unit 4 + option	Weighting
A2 level (full GCE)	15%

1. Pulleys and sprockets

Pulleys

Pulleys have been in use for thousands of years where people have needed to lift weights that could not be raised because they were too heavy. As a result, lifting machines and devices were developed that have a large mechanical advantage to raise the heavy loads more easily.

Pulleys are also used in the transfer of motion, be it rotary to rotary or rotary to linear. For example, the rotary motion of a stepper motor in a plotting machine is turned into a linear movement where the pen moves across the paper with the aid of a belt. Pulleys are also a means by which the speed can be changed either up or down. The pillar drilling machine is a good example of this, where two sets of pulleys are set against each other, one on the motor driving the system and the second attached to the chuck, the output. By positioning the belts between the two sets of pulleys, the rotational speed of the chuck can be either increased or decreased. A motor and pulley system is shown in Figure 4.4.1a.

Belts

All **transmission systems** essentially transmit rotation from one shaft to another by means of a flexible belt running on pulleys or by a chain and **sprocket**. There are, however, a range of belts and pulleys available to choose from.

Flat belts

Flat belts, as their name suggests, are flat and they can be made from different materials: woven fabric, leather or reinforced neoprene rubber. If the **shafts** and pulleys are not perfectly aligned, the belts are prone to slipping off. To overcome this the belts are sometimes made slightly tapered or they have a camber. One advantage of flat belts is that they can be twisted to transmit the motion through a right angle or cross over completely to give a change of rotational direction.

V belts

The V belt, however, has a number of advantages over a flat belt. As a result of its wedged shape it can transmit up to three times the power that a flat belt can. It is also much less likely to slip because of its shape since it is being pulled into the pulley that has a similar cross-section profile and so the frictional forces are much greater. The risk of slippage is further reduced because the belts are normally made from rubber with nylon chords embedded in them. V belts are most commonly used for electric motor drives and car fan belts. V belts are still, however, prone to slipping, causing the driven shaft to rotate slower than intended, and this is sometimes seen in motor cars when they overheat because the fan belt is slipping.

Toothed belts

Toothed belts are used when it is critical for the driving pulley to stay in sequence with the driven pulley. Special toothed pulleys also have to be used and the belt and pulley seemingly mesh together like gears or a chain and sprocket (see Figure 4.4.1b). The timing of the valves as they open and close in a car engine is controlled via a toothed belt, as are very accurate graphic plotters.

Coned pulley

A coned pulley and belt is capable of handling variable speeds or giving a variable output speed. The speed is controlled by moving the pulleys together or further apart. As the distance changes the belt moves up or down the cone-shaped pulley accordingly. To prevent the belt slipping the pulleys have radial teeth and the inside of the belt has mating grooves.

Sprocket and chain

A sprocket and chain found on a bicycle is used to transmit rotary motion from the pedals to the rear wheel. A sprocket is the toothed wheel on which the chain runs (see Figure 4.4.1c). Bicycles and motorbikes use this method of transmission because of its strength and positive location that removes any chance of slipping. One of the major disadvantages, however, is the maintenance factor and any chain must be kept well oiled if rusting is to be avoided.

Changing speeds

As with any pulley or chain and sprocket transmission system, speed changes are made by using different-sized pulleys or sprockets. By comparing the size of the two pulleys or sprockets the velocity ratio of the system can be calculated.

Using the example in Figure 4.4.1a, the velocity ratio can be calculated by:

$$\text{Velocity ratio} = \frac{\text{Driven pulley diameter}}{\text{Driver pulley diameter}}$$

$$= \frac{40}{160} = \frac{1}{4} \text{ or } 1:4.$$

That is to say that for every rotation of the driver the driven rotates four times. The output is four times bigger than the input.

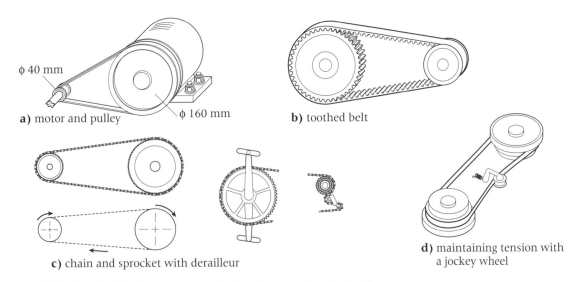

a) motor and pulley

φ 40 mm

φ 160 mm

b) toothed belt

c) chain and sprocket with derailleur

d) maintaining tension with a jockey wheel

Figure 4.4.1 *Toothed belt, chain and sprocket, jockey wheel and derailleur*

Maintaining tension in drive belts

Whatever kind of transmission system is used, whether it be a pulley system with a V belt or a chain and sprocket, it is essential for efficient and smooth running that it be tensioned correctly. If a belt is too loose it may slip or come off the pulleys and if it is too tight it will apply bending forces to the pulley shafts. In most systems it is possible to adjust the tension of the belt by having adjustable pulleys. Once the correct tension is achieved, the pulleys are locked in position and this method can normally be found on some pillar drilling machines and milling machines in schools/colleges.

Another method of achieving and maintaining the correct tension in a belt is to use a jockey wheel. A jockey wheel is a small pulley that is held against the moving pulley and is kept there by the action of a spring (see Figure 4.4.1d). If the belt stretches and its length increases, the jockey wheel will adjust its position and continue to tension the belt to the appropriate level.

A similar method is used to tension the chain on a bicycle. A derailleur gear is fixed on to the rear wheel and the chain is made to run through it. The derailleur gear acts as a spring loaded jockey wheel and it keeps the chain under constant tension (see Figure 4.4.1c). In the same way that the chain needs to be kept oiled, it is essential that the derailleur is kept well oiled too.

Tasks

1 Draw up a table and list the relative merits and drawbacks of each of the following types of belt:

   a) flat
   b) V belts
   c) toothed belts.
2 Compare the advantages and disadvantages of a pulley system and a chain and sprocket system.

2. Shafts and couplings

How aligned and non-aligned shafts can be coupled

A major problem that is encountered in many rotary systems is that of how to connect two rotating shafts together. It is quite simple if the shafts are 'aligned', i.e. they are on the same centre line. It is more difficult if they are 'non-aligned' shafts, i.e. they do not share a common centre line. A **coupling** is a joint that is used to connect shafts together while still enabling

motion and torque to be transmitted. There are a number of ways to connect aligned shafts together and they are:

- solid bolted flange coupling
- muff coupling
- compression coupling.

Flange couplings

A bolted flange consists of two flange plates that are bolted together either side of the

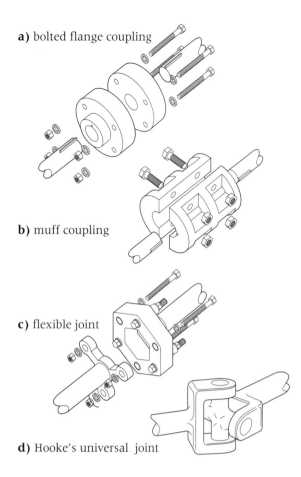

a) bolted flange coupling

b) muff coupling

c) flexible joint

d) Hooke's universal joint

Figure 4.4.2 *Shaft couplings*

joining shafts (see Figure 4.4.2a). The shafts must have a positive locating point that holds them to the flange plate. Once the two halves have been accurately aligned the two flange plates are bolted together.

Muff coupling

A muff coupling works in a similar way but the sleeves fit longitudinally along the shaft with one half keyed into the shafts. The two halves are then bolted together (see Figure 4.4.2b).

Compression coupling

A compression coupling consists of a split double conical sleeve that fits tightly over the shafts and which is then compressed on to the shafts as they are bolted together. This type of connection is friction based and does not rely on keys and keyways. The prime advantage of this method is that it can be easily assembled and disassembled without interfering with the shafts.

Flexible joints

Flexible joints need to be used where the shafts are not in perfect alignment. They can also be used to dampen vibrations or shocks that a shaft

may be subjected to. Most joints are constructed from a disc of rubberised material sandwiched between two 'spiders' (see Figure 4.4.2c).

The elastic properties of the rubber compensate for the variation in angle between the two non-aligned shafts. This type of coupling is relatively cheap and requires no lubrication.

The rubber does, however, perish and hardens over a period of time. The maximum angle at which the coupling can operate over is small and it is not very good at transmitting high torque. This type of flexible coupling, however, is used in the steering column on most motor cars.

Universal joints

Where shafts are more than just a few degrees out a universal joint is often used. It can be used to transmit motion through angles of up to 20 degrees and the most basic of universal joints, the Hooke's type is shown in Figure 4.4.2d. A yoke is fixed to the end of each rotating shaft which pivots on a central 'spider'.

One problem associated with universal joints is that because the two shafts are at different angles to each other, the output shaft does not run at a constant speed as it normally speeds up and slows down. In order to overcome this problem universal joints are normally used in pairs, but if this is to work properly the driven and driver shafts must be at the same angle to the intermediate connecting shaft and the yokes of the two joints must be in line with each other.

If the required angle is greater than 20 degrees, then a constant velocity joint has to be used. Irrespective of the angle or speed, the output will follow the input speed. This type of coupling is used extensively in front-wheel drive cars to connect the drive shafts from the engine to the wheels.

Fixing wheels and couplings to shafts

All pulleys, gears and cams have to be fitted to shafts, as do couplings whether they are of the aligned or non-aligned type. It is critical that they are held firmly since in use there are normally forces trying to separate them as they rotate. Some of the more common methods of fixing them together are shown in Figure 4.4.3.

Keys and keyways

Keys and keyways provide a very secure method of fixing wheels and pulleys to shafts. A keyway is a single groove that is cut into the shaft on a milling machine. In some instances the keyway is cut in a localised point but it is sometimes

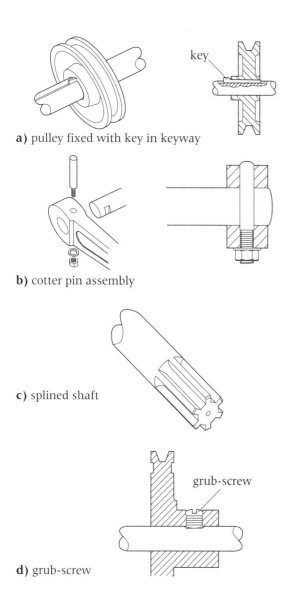

a) pulley fixed with key in keyway

b) cotter pin assembly

c) splined shaft

grub-screw

d) grub-screw

Figure 4.4.3 *Shaft fixings*

more economical to cut the keyway over the entire length of the shaft. Any amount of additional pulleys can be added or moved at a later stage without too much disruption.

The key consists of a rectangular section of material that is slightly tapered with chamfered edges. Because they are subjected to large stresses and they must withstand resistance to shear forces, the keys are normally made of high tensile steel or steel alloys. A corresponding slot also needs to be cut in the pulley and when the two grooves line up, the key is firmly tapped into place.

Cotter pins

Cotter pins are another method of fixing and holding shafts. They are commonly used on bicycles to hold the pedal to the crankshaft. A cotter pin is tapered and either rectangular or tapered in cross-section and it is very useful when loads are under an axial force. The cotter pins are inserted and tapped lightly into place and they can be easily removed by tapping from the underside. In some cases, the cotter pin has a threaded section and is held in place by a washer and nut.

Splined shafts

A splined shaft is used in situations where the pulley or wheel may need to move longitudinally along the shaft when in use. It obviously still needs to be stopped from rotating independently on the shaft and the splines around the shaft restrict this from happening. They do, however, allow the lateral movement of the pulley along the shaft.

Grub-screws

Grub-screws are most frequently used where little force is involved. An extra flange is produced on the pulley and a small threaded hole is machined into this section. The grub screw is inserted here and is screwed down to bear on to the shaft. The holding effect can be increased by producing a small flat on the shaft which increases the surface area available on which the grub screw can grip. Sometimes a second grub screw is placed behind the initial one to stop it from working loose by vibration.

3. Cams and followers

Cams

A cam is a mechanism which is used to change an input rotary or oscillating motion into either reciprocating or oscillating output motion. A follower is held against the cam, either under its own weight or by a spring, and as the cam rotates, the follower as its name suggests, follows the profile of the cam. The way in which the follower moves is entirely dependent upon the nature and profile of the cam.

Some basic geometry of the cam is illustrated in Figure 4.4.4 and the critical aspects have been identified.

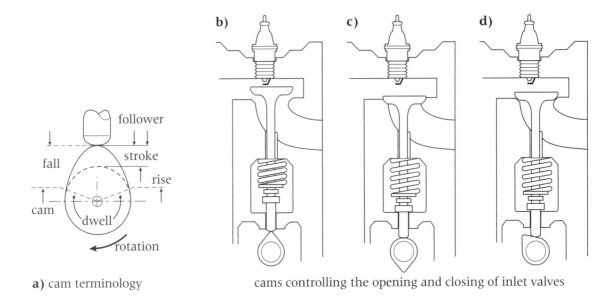

a) cam terminology   cams controlling the opening and closing of inlet valves

Figure 4.4.4 *The motion of a cam and follower*

The motion of a cam and follower

Let us consider the pear-shaped cam illustrated in Figure 4.4.4b where it is being used to control a valve. The valve in this case is the follower and it will move as the cam rotates. By analysing the geometry of the cam profile you can see that there will be periods of time when the follower does not move because the cam is in a dwell period. This is because the distance from the centre of rotation to the edge profile during this period is constant; it is part of a concentric circle. As the cam continues to rotate the follower rises until it reaches its maximum point of deflection. This distance, the distance between the extreme point on the cam and that of the radius of the dwell period, is termed the stroke. It is the distance the follower travels between the rise and the fall of the cam in any one rotation.

If this is now applied to the valve control mechanism in Figure 4.4.4b–d we can see how the valve is controlled by the rotating cam. When the cam is in its upright position as depicted in Figure 4.4.4b, the valve is fully lifted from its seat and the cam is said to be at the top of its stroke. As the cam rotates another 180 degrees, the follower has fallen to its lowest position and is now fully at rest on its seating and the cam is in its dwell period. On further rotation of 135 degrees the cam is now in the rise period and the follower has just started to be lifted by the cam.

This arrangement of valves opening and closing due to the rotation of a small cam happens

thousands of times a minute as a motor-car engine ticks over at idle. A number of cams are fixed on to a small camshaft with each cam being slightly offset. Each individual cam controls a valve with two valves to each cylinder within the engine. The movement of the valves controls the fuel/air mixture entering the combustion chamber and the exhaust gases leaving it.

Task
Cams need to be fixed to the rotating shaft just like a pulley. Draw and label two different methods of fixing a cam to a shaft.

Pear-shaped cams
The type of cam used to control the opening and closing of the inlet and exhaust valves in an engine are pear-shaped cams. With pear-shaped cams, the dwell period is quite long and normally accounts for more than half of the cycle during which time there is no movement of the follower. The rise-and-fall times of the cam are identical due to the symmetrical shape of the cam, but the overall distance that the follower moves depends upon the stroke of the cam. The cam illustrated in Figure 4.4.4a is a typical profile for a pear-shaped cam.

Circular (eccentric) cams
A circular cam is the simplest form of cam and is known as an 'eccentric' cam because it is a circular disc fitted to a driving shaft off centre.

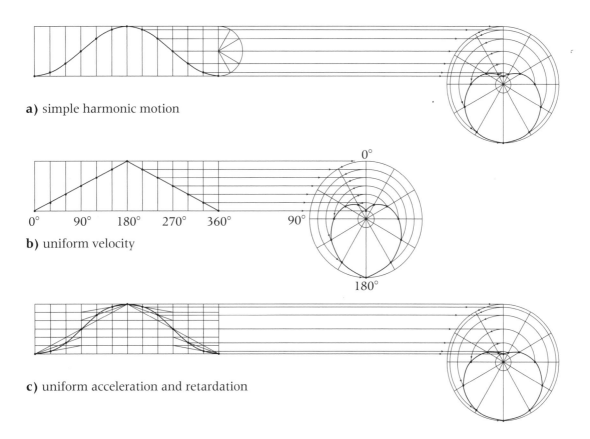

a) simple harmonic motion

b) uniform velocity

c) uniform acceleration and retardation

Fig 4.4.5 *Cam performance*

This cam gives a very smooth rise and fall of the follower and this continuous movement is known as simple harmonic motion (see Figure 4.4.5a). The output motion can also be described as having constant acceleration and retardation. Due to this output motion, eccentric cams are used in mechanical fuel pumps to move the diaphragm up and down to pump fuel into the engine.

Heart-shaped cams

Another type of continuous motion is generated by the heart-shaped cam (see Figure 4.4.5b). In this case the acceleration and retardation is constant. The heart-shaped cam is symmetrical and it is frequently used on bobbin-winding mechanisms such as fishing reels. Similar mechanisms are used in industry to wind wire, cable and threads on to reels or drums. By carefully constructing the geometric path that the follower takes, the output characteristics can be plotted and analysed in terms of acceleration, retardation and maximum distance travelled. Alternatively, it is possible to draw the path you want the follower to take and then generate the

profile of the cam needed to be able to produce that motion.

Uniform acceleration/retardation cams

The cam in Figure 4.4.5c has been constructed to give uniform acceleration and retardation. It has been constructed by plotting the apex, the midpoints and the base. The remaining four quarters are divided equally. The curve is generated by the intersection of these points as shown and the cam profile is shown.

Followers

If a disc is cut to produce a cam with a suitable contour and fixed to a shaft as it rotates it will lift a follower. Followers are available in a range of profiles and great care must be taken when choosing a suitable follower to match the profile of the cam. Followers can be flat, knife-edged, point or roller-based and they can be fixed in line with the centre of the cam or offset. The follower is normally held against the cam under its own weight or by a spring. Details about followers are given in Table 4.4.1.

Table 4.4.1 Types of followers

Type	Profile	Description
Flat		Lots of friction Cannot follow hollow contours
Knife		Provides the most accurate conversion of movement Can be used to follow hollow contours
Point		Rapid wear of point Accurate following of the profile Can follow hollows
Roller		Least friction Cannot be used to follow hollow contours More expensive

Key points for cams and followers

- Rotary cams convert a rotary motion into a reciprocating or oscillating motion.
- The profile of the cam controls the distance the follower moves. The rate at which it moves is dependent upon the rotational velocity of the cam!
- The choice of follower is critical and it depends upon the profile of the cam being used.

Tasks

Cams can be used to convert rotary motion into reciprocating motion.

1 Using annotated sketches, describe how a constant velocity can be achieved with a cam and give an example of where it might be used.
2 Sketch a performance graph for a pear-shaped cam and state the different periods of the graph.

4. Conversion of motion

Crankshafts, cranks and sliders, rack and pinion and cams and followers are all mechanisms that are used to convert rotary motion. There are four types of motion that we must consider and they are rotary, oscillating, linear and reciprocating (see Table 4.4.2).

Crank and slider mechanism

A crank could be described as a simple handle attached to a shaft to make the lift or moving of an object easier. Torque is a rotational force and the torque applied to a shaft is the product of the applied force and the distance from the axis. When a number of cranks are put on to the same shaft it is known as a crankshaft.

A child's go-cart or pedal car uses a crank-shaft to convert the torque generated by the child pedalling to a rotary motion which drives the go-cart forward in a linear motion. A crank-shaft in a car engine converts reciprocating motion from the pistons within the cylinder

Table 4.4.2 Types of motion

Type	Description
Rotary	Rotary motion is probably the most common form of motion. Rotary motion is a circular type of motion like the movement of hands of a clock and the wheels on a car.
Oscillating	Oscillating motion is a swinging backwards and forwards movement in an arc like the pendulum of a grandfather clock.
Linear	Something that travels in a straight line in one direction is said to have linear motion, like a pencil moving along a ruler on a page.
Reciprocating	Reciprocating motion is when an object moves backwards and forwards in a straight line like a piston inside a cylinder block.

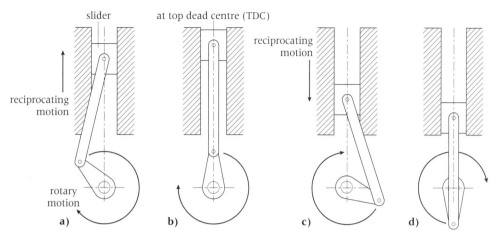

Figure 4.4.6 *Crank and slider mechanism*

block into rotary motion via the connecting rods to provide the necessary output to drive the car forward.

A compressor makes use of the conversion of rotary motion into reciprocating motion by a crank and slider. An electric motor is used to make a piston reciprocate within a cylinder block that has a chamber controlled by one inlet and one outlet valve. As the piston reciprocates it draws air in on the downward stroke and expels it through a one-way valve into a receiver tank on the upward stroke.

When the piston/slider reaches the top of its motion it is at its top dead centre and the velocity of the piston at this point is zero. When the piston is at the lower point of its motion it is bottom dead centre and again the velocity is zero. The distance that the piston moves between top and bottom dead centre is called the stroke. The motion of a crank and slider mechanism is shown in Figure 4.4.6.

Crank and slider mechanisms are used extensively in the testing of materials and products due to their continuous reciprocating motion. They can be set up with wire brushes or abrasives attached to the end of the slider or connecting rod and when a weight is applied and the motor turned on, the piece under test

will be abraded. Alternatively, the connecting rod could be quite easily attached to a kitchen door or drawer to test how the hinges or drawer runners stand up to repeated use (see Figure 4.4.7). This type of testing enables companies to see how sturdy their products are and helps them to be able to offer guarantees in terms of use. Quite often, a counting device such as an electromagnetic counter is used to count the number of cycles that the door has been opened and closed.

Rack and pinion

A rack and pinion mechanism is used to convert rotary motion into linear motion or linear into rotary motion. A spur gear known as the pinion meshes with a rack whose gear teeth are set in a straight line. This conversion of motion can be made to occur in one of two ways:

- If the pinion rotates about a fixed centre, the rack moves in a straight line.
- If the rack is made to move in a straight line, the pinion rotates about a fixed centre.

When the pinion is turned, the movement of the rack is governed by the number of teeth per metre on the rack, and the number of teeth on the pinion.

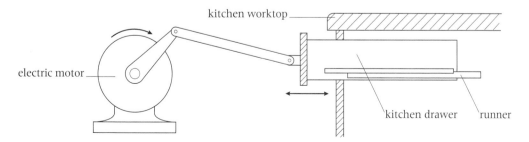

Figure 4.4.7 *Crank and slider set up to pull and push in a kitchen drawer to test the runner mechanism*

Example

A rack has 150 teeth per metre and it meshes with a pinion that has 30 teeth. Calculate how far the rack moves if the pinion makes one revolution.

If the pinion makes one revolution, 30 teeth on the pinion will have meshed with the rack. Since there are 150 teeth per metre, the distance moved is:

$$\frac{30}{150} \times 1 \text{ metre} = \frac{3}{15} = \frac{1}{5}$$

$$= 1/5\text{th of a metre} = 200 \text{ mm.}$$

Therefore for every revolution of the pinion the rack is made to move 200 mm.

Ratchet mechanisms

A ratchet and pawl device allows rotation in one direction only and prevents rotation in the opposite direction. The ratchet part of the device is a wheel with saw-shaped teeth cut around its circumference and the pawl is a single saw-tooth-shaped device held against the ratchet, normally by a spring (see Figure 4.4.8a).

A ratchet wheel will also arrest motion when fixed to a shaft and winding drum as shown in Figure 4.4.8b. As the cable is wound on to the drum using the crank handle, the ratchet rotates and the pawl is held under tension by a retaining spring. As each tooth passes, the pawl is sprung back into position. Should the crank handle be released the pawl will restrict the shaft from rotating in an anticlockwise direction even if the cable remains in tension.

Cams

We have already taken a close look at cams of the rotary form. There are, however, many other forms of cams that are available either as flat cams, box cams and cylindrical cams.

If the edge of a flat plate is shaped the profile can be used to guide the follower and will generate a reciprocating motion. The same is to be said of the box cam which has a profile cut into its flat surface and the cylindrical cam which has a channel cut around its circumference. These types of cams, which can be seen in Figure 4.4.8c–e, are often used to control the tool path of machines when cutting identical components.

Tasks

1 Sketch a common profile of any cam with an appropriate follower and state a specific example of its use.
2 A rack has 240 teeth per metre and meshes with a pinion that has 60 teeth (Figure 4.4.8f). Calculate how many revolutions are needed to make the rack move 750 mm.

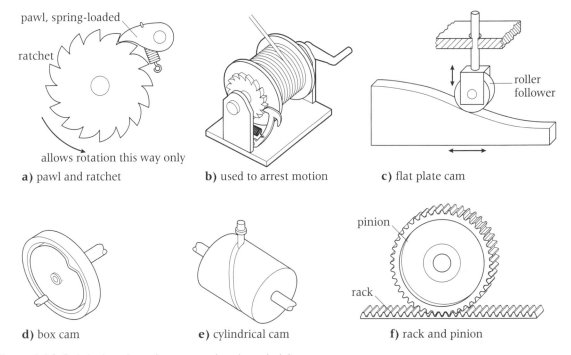

a) pawl and ratchet   b) used to arrest motion   c) flat plate cam

d) box cam   e) cylindrical cam   f) rack and pinion

Figure 4.4.8 *Ratchet and pawl, cams and rack and pinion*

5. Brakes

Types of brakes

Designers and engineers are very careful to consider how friction may be eliminated in their designs. However, at certain times friction between contacting surfaces is of prime importance and this is certainly the case as far as brakes are concerned. Friction enables brake linings to transmit forces to the wheels and tyres to grip the road.

A car moving along the road has kinetic energy and this must be converted into another form of energy if the car is to be brought to rest carefully and safely. The rate at which the energy is converted determines how quickly the car can stop. Most **braking systems** convert this kinetic energy into heat and in an efficient braking system the heat is dissipated by air flowing over the brake. The brakes on a Formula One racing car can be seen at times to glow red due to the heat being generated by the braking forces. If the brake gets too hot it becomes less efficient and if this happens it can be dangerous.

How one material slips against another is known as the co-efficient of friction. The smaller the number, the less friction that exists between the two materials and this is shown in Table 4.4.3.

The two important comparisons to look at in Table 4.4.3 are metal on ice and rubber on tarmac. From these data, it is clear to understand why ice-skates have steel blades and how important in terms of grip the co-efficient

Table 4.4.3 *Approximate co-efficient of friction between a range of materials*

Material 1	Material 2	Approximate co-efficient of friction
Metal	Metal	0.20
Metal	Hardwood	0.60
Leather	Metal	0.40
Rubber	Tarmac	0.90
Rubber	Metal	0.40
Metal	Ice	0.02
Teflon – a non-stick coating used for saucepans	Steel	0.04

of friction is between rubber and tarmac, a typical road surface. The two basic types of car brakes are drum brakes and disc brakes. Each type uses a friction pad or shoe to press against a rotating disc or wheel (see Figure 4.4.9).

Hydraulically and mechanically operated braking systems

Most cars have two types of brake operating system, hydraulic and mechanical. The majority of cars have disc brakes at the front and drum brakes on the rear. The reason for this is due to the fact that the weight of the car is transferred forward when the car brakes. As a result of this, greater breaking power is needed on the front

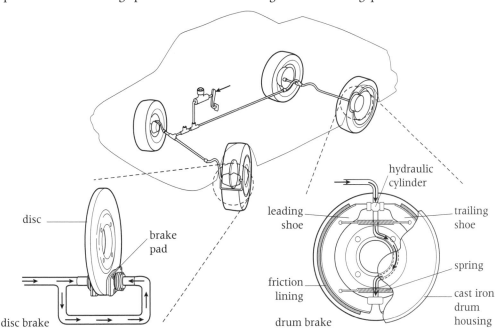

Figure 4.4.9 *Drum and disc brakes*

brakes in comparison with the back brakes. Disc brakes are more efficient than drum brakes because they have a larger surface area and the air is allowed to flow around the disc to dissipate the heat quickly.

Disc brakes

Disc brakes consist of a metal disc attached to the hub or axle of the rotating wheel. When the brake is applied by pushing the pedal down, a brake caliper is made to grip the rotating disc. The hydraulic system used in motor vehicles uses a cast iron disc sandwiched between the two brake pads which are made from an asbestos-based material. On some larger vehicles, the braking system is enhanced by a servo unit to increase the pressure of the fluid that compresses the brake pads.

Drum brakes

Drum brakes are not very efficient at dissipating heat but they are suitable for use on the back wheels of motor cars because they are required to take less of the braking force.

The two shoes are placed on the inside of the rotating wheel hub and each shoe has an asbestos-based friction lining bonded or riveted to it. As the brake pedal is depressed, the shoes are forced out by a cam and the lining is expanded and comes into contact with the cast iron housing and the rotational speed is decreased. Rotation of the drum housing has the tendency to pull the left-hand shoe harder into contact and the right-hand disc off the drum. This means that the left-hand disc, the leading shoe, wears quicker, and the right-hand disc, the trailing shoe drum, has less effect and less wear. The major advantage of drum brakes on the rear is that they can be linked very easily into a mechanical braking system and, in the case of the motor car, the hand brake is a mechanical system operated by a lever inside the car.

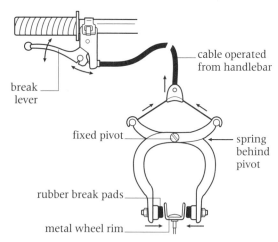

Figure 4.4.10 *Bicycle cantilever brake*

Bicycle brakes

Bicycle brakes are also mechanical, again operated by the pulling of a lever, the brake lever. The oscillating type of action from the lever is converted into a reciprocating motion that pulls on a cantilever-type arrangement as shown in Figure 4.4.10.

As the two separate wings are pulled in, the arms swing around the fixed pivot which also contains a spring. Once the brake lever has been released the brake pads are moved back away from the wheel rim. As can be seen from Table 4.4.3, the co-efficient of friction between metal and rubber is 0.4. Obviously, if it is wet, this figure, and the overall effectiveness of the braking system is less.

Tasks

1 Give two reasons why most cars have two different types of brakes.
2 Why should more time be given for braking in the wet, whether you are in a car or on a bicycle?

6. Clutches

The action of a clutch

A **clutch** is a type of shaft coupling device that allows a rotating shaft to be easily connected to or disconnected from a second shaft. It is critical, though, that the two shafts are in line. There are two main types of clutch:

- the positive clutch
- the friction clutch.

Positive clutch

A positive clutch can only be used if the driving shaft is brought to rest before trying to engage it. Each of the two ends of the shafts to be engaged have a number of claws fitted to them. As the claws on the driver and driven shafts are engaged they mesh together under pressure supplied by either springs or levers (see Figure 4.4.11a). The most common type of positive

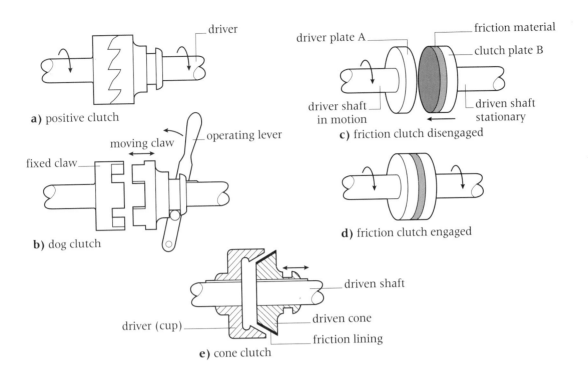

Figure 4.4.11 *Clutches*

clutch is the dog clutch or claw clutch and this is used on agricultural machinery and lathes (see Figure 4.4.11b). If you have ever tried to change the gears on a lathe before the driver shaft has come to rest you will have heard the chattering noise as a result.

A saw clutch is another type of positive clutch and the two clutch plates are saw-tooth in profile. This type of clutch can only give positive drive in one direction, since in the reverse direction the saw-tooth profile will try to separate the two plates.

Friction clutch

Friction clutches are used where it is necessary to engage or disengage the drive smoothly without having to bring any of the rotating shafts to a rest. These functions can be achieved with electric or hydraulic clutches but the friction method is regarded as one of the most effective systems.

To transmit the drive from one shaft to another as in Figure 4.4.11c–d, the system relies upon the friction between discs A and B. As the rotary one is brought into contact with the stationary one, the friction between the discs and the friction plate is increased until the clutch is fully engaged and both discs are rotating at the same speed. There are many variations on this but one of the most common is the cone clutch as shown in Figure 4.4.11e. A similar principle is used as the driven cone is

moved in and out laterally. The friction lining and the opposite bearing surface are in the shape of a cone and so when the driven cone is fully engaged there is minimal chance of any slipping. The torque capacity of a cone clutch is greater than a flat plate of the same diameter.

Single plate clutch

The single plate clutch is very common mainly because of its ability to produce a quick engagement or disengagement. The pressure to the friction plate is supplied by a number of coil springs placed around the pressure plate and held inside the clutch housing. Motion is transmitted from the driver shaft to the driven shaft when the friction plate is clamped firmly by the pressure plate. This is how the system would be configured and so the clutch would be permanently engaged. To disengage the clutch, the pedal is depressed and by a combination of levers and springs the clutch friction plate is withdrawn from the driven shaft (see Figure 4.4.12a).

Diaphragm spring clutch

The diaphragm spring clutch has one major advantage over the single plate clutch, it is much more compact, simpler and easier to use. It eliminates the need for the clutch springs and related casing because it uses a single diaphragm spring instead to provide the

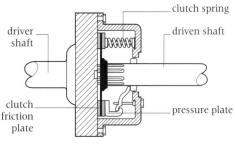

a) single plate clutch (engaged)

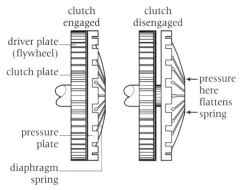

b) diaphragm spring clutch

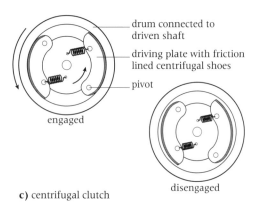

c) centrifugal clutch

Figure 4.4.12 *Clutches*

pressure. It is very slim and also requires fewer parts making it easier to service and maintain.

As the diaphragm is flattened, it relieves the pressure upon the clutch plate and, conversely, when the pressure is released the diaphragm returns to its original spring state and engages the clutch plate to the driven shaft (see Figure 4.4.12b).

Centrifugal clutch

A centrifugal clutch is another type and has a very different working action since it is semi-automatic in its operation. It consists of two shoes opposite one another. At one end they are pivoted and at the other end they are held under a little tension by a spring. The shoes are fixed via the pivot to the driver shaft and as the rotational speed is increased the shoes are thrown outwards until they end up pressing against the drum which is, in turn, fixed to the driven shaft. At this point the clutch is deemed to have engaged and it will continue to do so until the rotational speed of the input shaft is reduced (see Figure 4.4.12c).

This type of friction clutch is used on some motor lawn mowers and on small motor mopeds. An increase in the rotational speed of the driven shaft enables the lawn mower's blades to cut or the motor moped to engage a drive shaft allowing it to accelerate away as the revs increase.

> ### Tasks
> 1 What are the main differences between a positive clutch and a friction clutch?
> 2 Compare the action of a friction clutch with a positive clutch.

7. Screwthreads

Mechanical advantage

Inclined plane
An inclined plane is quite simply a sloping surface that can be used to gain a mechanical advantage when raising a load. It is thought that inclined planes were used to raise the huge stones used in the construction of the great pyramids in Egypt. The ramps were made from earth and soil and when the structure was completed the ramp was removed. Try to imagine the difference between lifting a heavy bucket in a straight lift vertically or by pulling it up a gentle slope.

Today, the inclined plane has many other uses. These include the ramps used for lifting a motor car off the ground enabling the motor engineer to work underneath and the gentle slopes on roads and motorways used to avoid making steep climbs. A key in a keyway is another inclined plane.

Wedges were also widely used by early humans and they are formed by placing two inclined planes back to back. Wedges can be used to raise heavy loads or to prise apart logs along the grains. Wedges have a cutting action whether it is in the form of an axe, a chisel edge or a lathe cutting tool.

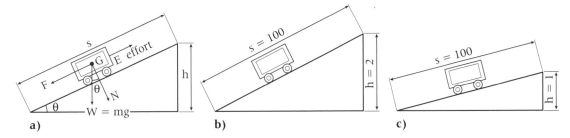

Figure 4.4.13 *The inclined plane*

Mechanical advantage can be gained when using an inclined plane to raise a heavy load. Consider the scenario illustrated in Figure 4.4.13a. The effort force can be calculated if the dimensions of the slope are known:

h = height of slope
m = mass of trolley
s = length of slope
g = acceleration due to gravity
u = angle of slope

where $\operatorname{Sin} u = \dfrac{h}{s}$

The mechanical advantage of an inclined plane can be calculated by:

$$MA = \frac{\text{Distance moved by effort}}{\text{Distance moved by load}}$$

$$= \frac{s}{h}$$

Example

Using the examples illustrated in Figure 4.4.13b and c, calculate the respective mechanical advantage for each example, given that s = 100 and h = 2 in Figure 4.4.13b and h = 1 in Figure 4.4.13c.

For example 1:
$$MA = \frac{\text{Distance moved by effort}}{\text{Distance moved by load}} = \frac{s}{h} = \frac{100}{2} = 50$$

For example 2:
$$MA = \frac{s}{h} = \frac{100}{1} = 100$$

It can be clearly seen that because of the steeper slope, Figure 4.4.13b has the greater mechanical advantage. However, it should be quite clear to see that the effort required to pull the trolley up the slope in Figure 4.4.13b will be twice that required to pull the trolley up the slope in Figure 4.4.13c.

Screwthreads

If an inclined plane were to be wrapped around a cylindrical shaft, a helix would be formed. If a spiral groove were to be cut along this path, a screwthread would be formed. Thus a screwthread can be regarded as an inclined plane. A screwthread can therefore be used to transmit motion and force with the same mechanical advantage as that of the inclined plane. A screwthread is shown in Figure 4.4.14a.

A screwthread made up from a single helix is known as a single start screwthread. It is possible to have more than one thread running around a shaft and these are known as multiple start threads.

Thread forms and uses

Screwthreads can be broken down into two basic forms:

• V-thread
• square thread.

The V-thread

The V-thread takes its name from the 'V'-shaped profile of the thread form (see Figure 4.4.14b). As a result of the large amount of friction that exists between the flanks and a nut, V-threads are used extensively for fasteners such as nuts and bolts, set screws and machine screws.

There are many different V-thread forms but by far the most commonly used type is the ISO metric thread, which was introduced in line with general metrification in the 1970s and where the major diameter and pitch of the thread is measured in millimetres.

Acme thread

When motion needs to be transmitted in conjunction with an engaging nut, as is the case on a centre lathe, an acme thread is used (see Figure 4.4.14c). The tapered sides allow the nut to become easily engaged with the screwthread.

Square thread

The square thread takes its name from the profile of the thread form (see Figure 4.4.14d).

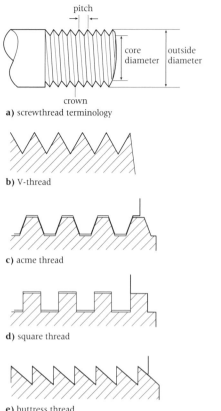

a) screwthread terminology

b) V-thread

c) acme thread

d) square thread

e) buttress thread

Figure 4.4.14 *Screwthreads*

As a thread type it is used mainly for moving parts of machines and lifting jacks. It is not as strong as the V-thread and the friction between the flanks is less.

Buttress thread

A buttress thread is used when a force has to act in one direction only, and so typically it is used in woodwork and other vices (see Figure 4.4.14e). It is generally fitted with a quick-acting release mechanism that allows it to be opened or closed rapidly.

Screw mechanisms allow heavy loads to be lifted and large forces to be exerted by using the mechanical advantage gained as a result of the inclined plane. Clamps and vices utilise square threads to tighten jaws which hold work while drilling or gluing. They are also used in engineering lifting devices such as screw jacks and scissor jacks.

> ## Task
> Construct a table of the four different thread forms and complete it with a cross-sectional view of the thread form and a list of its applications.

---

8. Transistors

You will have seen already that transistors can be used as electronic switches and current amplifiers by controlling the amount of voltage across the base and emitter junction. The point at which the transistor switches on, or is biased, is the threshold voltage and it is between 0.6 and 0.7 volts. At this point, the transistor allows a larger current to flow through the transistor from the collector to the emitter. The total current flowing through the transistor is given by the sum of I_{BE} and I_{CE}. The ratio between I_{BE} and I_{CE} is said to be the gain h_{FE} of the transistor and this factor varies between each type of transistor. Transistors are also rated according to the power that they can handle. It is a balance in terms of being able to find a transistor with a big enough gain that can handle large currents.

Darlington pairs

To obtain larger gains that are capable of handling larger currents, two transistors are connected together to form a **Darlington pair** (see Figure 4.4.15).

A Darlington pair also has increased sensitivity in terms of its use in a switching circuit. Since we now have two transistors connected, the voltage required at the base of TR1, shown in Figure 4.4.15a, has to be at least 1.4 volts before a current can flow in the collector. Conventionally, TR_1 is chosen with a high gain and TR_2 is chosen because of its current handling capacity. In school/college use, the transistors used to build a Darlington driver are normally a BC108 as TR_1 and a BFY51 as TR_2.

The overall current gain of a Darlington is the product of the respective gains of TR_1 and TR_2. If, therefore, TR_1 had a gain of 250 and TR_2 50, then the overall gain would be as follows:

Overall gain = $250 \times 50 = 12{,}500$

Where several Darlington drivers are required, instead of building them from discrete components, it is possible to buy them in an IC (integrated package) with up to eight Darlington pairs on a single chip.

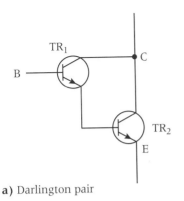

a) Darlington pair

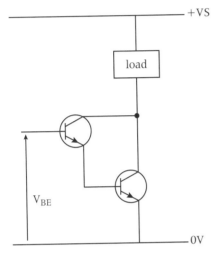

b) connected with a load

Figure 4.4.15 The transistor and Darlington pair

Transistors as transducer drivers

Output transducers are available in a wide range of forms and the different types will allow visual, audible or movement from motors as an indication that an event has taken place. All of these output devices can be described as a load and because they are being turned on by the switching action of the transistor, they are connected between the positive supply rail and the collector of the transistor (see Figure 4.4.15b).

When the threshold voltage is below 0.7, or 1.4 volts for a Darlington driver, no current flows across the collector emitter junction and therefore the output transducer is off. As the voltage on the base of the transistor rises above the threshold voltage, a larger current is allowed to flow across the collector emitter junction and the output transducer is turned on.

Field Effect Transistors (FETs)

Transistors have been shown to be excellent current amplifiers and electronic switches.

Field Effect Transistors (FETs) are voltage amplifiers rather than current amplifiers. A FET has three pins: source, gate and drain, and is available in two forms, a MOSFET and JFET.

The JFET

The JFET, as shown in Figure 4.4.16a, has a piece of p-type semiconductor as the gate and the channel, the central bar is an n-type semiconductor. This essentially creates a diode. If the voltage of the gate side is negative in comparison to the source no current will flow. This is where the JFET takes its name (junction type).

The MOSFET

The MOSFET (metal oxide) works in a similar way to the JFET (see Figure 4.4.16b). By making the gate more negative than the source no current can flow.

FETs can be switched on by a very small input voltage at the gate. This makes them very useful as amplifiers for low-powered processing circuits. This property also makes them an ideal choice for electronic switches that are controlled by high-resistance inputs such as touch switches, as indicated in Figure 4.4.16c.

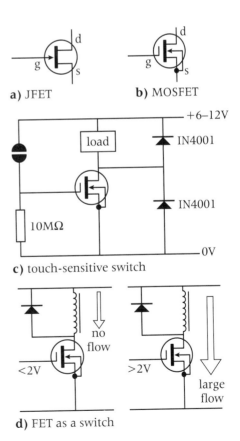

a) JFET   **b)** MOSFET

c) touch-sensitive switch

d) FET as a switch

Figure 4.4.16 Field Effect Transistors

The FET in this case makes a better switch than a conventional bi-polar transistor since it has a digital switching action unlike the analogue action of the bi-polar type. Once the switch has been touched, the FET is turned fully on and so allows a voltage to flow from drain to source, thus turning on the load connected between the positive supply rail and the drain (see Figure 4.4.16d).

In normal use the drain is connected to +VS via the load device, the source to zero volts and the gate to the input. A gate voltage of less than 2 volts results in the FET being fully off. Above 2 volts, the FET is fully on. Typically, solenoids and larger relays are connected as the loads since they require bigger voltages and currents to operate effectively. This also gives the opportunity to control a secondary circuit if a relay is used.

Key points

- FETs are used to drive high current devices.
- When the gate voltage is less than 2 volts, no current or voltage will be allowed to flow.
- Above 2 volts on the gate and voltage will be allowed to flow.
- FETs have a binary switching action.
- FETs are voltage amplifiers and are used in high impedance circuits.

Tasks

1 Make a list of the advantages of a Darlington pair over a conventional single transistor.
2 Why is the threshold voltage of a Darlington pair twice that of a single transistor?

9. Thyristors

A **thyristor** is another type of three-legged semi-conducting device that can be used as a special kind of switch (see Figure 4.4.17a). It is also known as a silicon controlled rectifier (SCR) since it is a rectifier which can control the power supplied to a load in a very efficient manner.

As with all of the semiconducting devices we have seen so far, they only conduct current when biased in a certain direction. The thyristor is no different to this and when forward biased it will not conduct until a positive voltage is applied to the gate.

The thyristor will continue to conduct even when the gate voltage has been removed.

It can only be switched off if:

- the supply voltage is turned off
- the supply voltage is reversed
- if the anode current falls below a certain level.

Using a thyristor to latch an output

Consider the circuit in Figure 4.4.17b as it fully demonstrates the switching action of the thyristor. When S_1 is closed, the bulb remains off since the current cannot flow through the thyristor. When S_2 is closed, current flows through the gate and turns the thyristor on or 'fires' it. The current now flowing through the thyristor from the anode to the cathode is sufficiently large enough to light the bulb even when S_2 is opened again. This action and behaviour is an example of how the thyristor can control DC power.

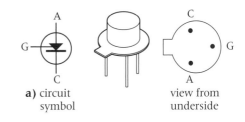

a) circuit symbol   view from underside

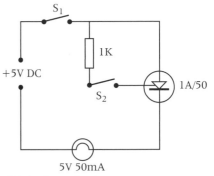

b) thyristor circuit

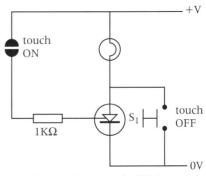

c) touch sensitive on and off light switch

Figure 4.4.17 The thyristor

Another way of describing this particular switching action is to say that the thyristor 'latches' the output. The output stays turned on even when the event that caused the output to turn on is removed. This switching action is very useful in alarm systems whereby a warning sound is triggered when someone breaks a light beam or treads on a pressure pad. The alarm will stay on until it has been reset by any of the methods identified above.

A very simple example of this latching ability is demonstrated in the circuit shown in Figure 4.4.17c. It has been configured as a touch sensitive on and off light switch.

Task

Analyse the circuit in Figure 4.4.17c and explain how it works by making particular reference to the actions at the anode, cathode and gate.

10. Logic

Logic gates

Electronic signals can essentially be broken down into two types: analogue and digital (see Figure 4.4.18a and b). The differences between these two types of signal are fundamental and both form major branches of electronics work.

Analogue signals have many different stages or levels. To say that it is dark or cold does not really give an accurate assessment of how dark or cold or indeed how dark and cold it is now compared to two hours ago. We tend to be a little more descriptive when making an assessment such as this to say 'It is very cold' or 'freezing cold'. The level can fluctuate between extremes of hot and cold and it can exist at any stated level in between.

A **digital system**, on the other hand, only has two states, on or off, 1 or 0, high or low. It cannot be warm; it is either hot or cold when measured or compared against a reference point or value.

Digital circuits are built from switches known as gates and they are available in different types on IC packages. The three most basic logic gate types are AND, NOT and OR. It is worth considering at this stage the fundamentals behind these three basic types of gate. From your knowledge of electronics you should be able to understand what will happen in each of the four circuits in Figure 4.4.18c–f.

In Figure 4.4.18c with S_1 open, the output is connected to 0v and therefore 0V appears at the output. Once S_1 is pressed the output is connected to both 0V and 9V rail and since there is no resistance 9V will appear at the output. The output can therefore exist in two states or conditions, high or low.

AND gate

In Figure 4.4.18f two switches are connected in series. The output will remain at 0V unless both S_1 AND S_2 are pressed simultaneously. This is the basic principle behind the AND gate.

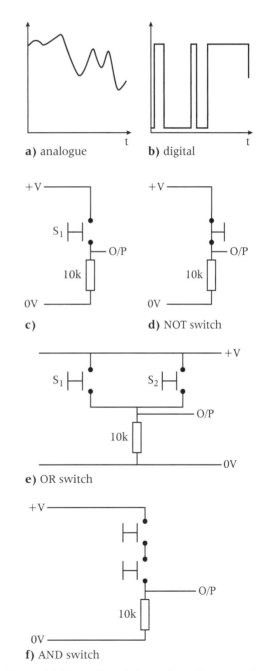

a) analogue   **b)** digital

c)   **d)** NOT switch

e) OR switch

f) AND switch

Figure 4.4.18 Logic switch configurations

Table 4.4.4 Logic gate summary (truth table)

Logic gate	Symbol	Input A	B	Output Z	TTL	CMOS
NOT (invertor)	A —▷o— Z	0 1		1 0	7404	4049B
AND	A, B — Z	0 1 0 1	0 0 1 1	0 0 0 1	7408	4081
NAND	A, B — Z	0 1 0 1	0 0 1 1	1 1 1 0	7400	4011B
OR	A, B — Z	0 1 0 1	0 0 1 1	0 1 1 1	7432	4071B
NOR	A, B — Z	0 1 0 1	0 0 1 1	1 0 0 0	7402	4011B
XOR (Exclusive OR)	A, B — Z	0 1 0 1	0 0 1 1	0 1 1 0	7484	4070B

OR gate

In Figure 4.4.18e two switches S_1 and S_2 are connected in parallel and therefore the output will go to 9V if either S_1 OR S_2 are pushed OR both simultaneously. This is the OR gate in its basic form.

NOT gate

The NOT gate is simulated in Figure 4.4.18d. A push to break switch has been used to hold the output high when the switch is in its closed position, and low at 0V in its open position. In this case, the output is in the opposite state or condition to that of the input.

Truth tables

The statements that have been used to describe the state and condition of the inputs and outputs are said to be logic statements.

1 If it is hot AND dry, then the plants must be watered.

2 If it is cold OR dark, then the heater must be switched on in the greenhouse.
3 If it is NOT dark, then turn off the light.

These three statements are all logical conditions and can be represented by switches. The possible inputs and output states are best recorded in a table and they are known as truth tables. By combining gates a whole range of additional functions can be generated. By connecting an AND and a NOT together, the result is a NAND, and an OR and a NOT make a NOR. The one other type of gate you need to consider is an XOR (exclusive OR).

The action of all these **logic gates** is shown in Table 4.4.4 which charts the particular patterns of inputs and outputs.

Two types of logic ICs are available, CMOS (Complementary Metal Oxide Semiconductor) and TTL (Transistor-Transistor Logic). Their working characteristics are summarised in the boxes below. They do have different voltage levels at which they change from being logic 0 to logic 1. Each type also has a range of voltage that is known as the open band. This region in terms of voltage levels should be avoided. Therefore, when switching from logic 1 to logic 0, it should be done as quickly as possible to avoid unpredictable behaviour in terms of the logic level.

Summary of CMOS chips

CMOS 4000
Voltage supply 3–15v
Negligible current drawn from supply
All unused inputs must be connected to 0v or to +v
Easily damaged by static
Output current just enough to drive an LED
Logic 0 < 0.3VS
Logic 1 > 0.7VS
0.3–0.7VS open band

Summary of TTL chips

TTL 7000
Needs stabilised supply
Draws a larger current than CMOS
Unused inputs will float to logic 1
Output current will drive an LED
ICs are electrically robust
Logic 0 < 0.8V
Logic 1 > +2.0V
0.8–2.0v open band

Tasks

Design some circuits that could be used to solve the following problems. For both solutions produce a full circuit diagram.

1 Design a light circuit which comes on below 0°C when it is dark.
2 Design a greenhouse watering system which will only water the dry plants at night.

Design problem

A system is required to warn the greenhouse keeper that the temperature fell below 0°C overnight.

The logic statement describes the circuit. When it is dark AND the temperature has fallen below 0°C, the LED should light and stay on.

When both the LDR and the thermistor are on, the LED is required to light up. This action is illustrated in the truth table (Table 4.4.5) and shows the action of an AND gate. The LDR and thermistor will be connected up to form a potential divider that will provide a changing voltage level from logic 0 to logic 1. Since the output trigger is required to stay on once triggered, a thyristor can be used to drive the LED via a protective resistor (see Figure 4.4.19).

Table 4.4.5 *Truth table*

LDR	Thermistor	LED
0	0	0
0	1	0
1	0	0
1	1	1

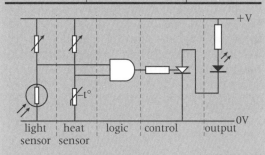

Figure 4.4.19 *Full circuit diagram*

Remember that all unused inputs have to be connected to either 0V or +V rail.

11. Circuit construction

Prior to following any design of an electronic circuit it is a good idea to model it before committing yourself to producing either a printed circuit board (PCB) or any other form of hard wired circuit.

Many software packages are now commercially available for use in schools/colleges such as 'Crocodile clips' and 'Electronics workbench'. These can be useful in modelling circuits and in simulating full working action. Signals can be generated in various waveforms, and oscilloscopes and meters can be used to see how the circuit behaves. The method of modelling used will obviously depend upon the availability of equipment and the degree of complexity of the circuit you have designed. A range of kits are available such as 'Locktronics' and 'Alpha boards' that can be used to build up some quite complicated circuitry. The boards used are similar to those that you would actually use as building blocks when designing a circuit using the systems approach; potential dividers, transistor combinations, latches, logic gates and various transducers.

Construction techniques

Matrix board
The board comes pre-drilled in a matrix formation. Pins are pushed through the holes where required and are connected together with wires. Components can also be soldered directly to the pins. The board is made from an insulating material.

Advantages
- Quick and easy to use.
- Circuit can be built in an identical layout to the circuit diagram.

Disadvantages
- Tend to be untidy.
- Very difficult to build in ICs.

Vero board
Vero board looks similar to matrix board with the same pin spacing, but underneath it has strips of copper running parallel in one direction. Components are inserted through the holes, but cuts in the tracks are necessary in certain places.

Advantages
- Cleaner method of production.
- Reasonably quick to prototype with.

Disadvantages
- Cuts in tracks needed.
- Final circuits will not always be in identical positions to those on the circuit diagram.

Bread board or prototype boards
Components are inserted into the board and the individual cells are connected in two separate vertical columns. Power rails are at the two extremes and run horizontally.

Electrical wires are used to make the connections between the cells.

Advantages
- Easy to build circuits rapidly.
- Easy to change and modify circuit.
- Can be used to build very complicated circuits.

Disadvantages
- Can become very muddled and may resemble a bird's nest.
- Circuits do not resemble circuit diagrams.

Printed circuit boards (PCBs)
Printed circuit board material is made from a material similar to that of vero board and matrix board or from a glass reinforced plastic (GRP).

The board is supplied copper clad on one or sometimes both sides with the latter type being used for very advanced and complicated circuits.

Once a circuit has been designed and tested either by using one of the systems boards or by computer simulation, a printed circuit board can be designed.

The components are generally fitted into a compacted area so as to minimise waste and production time. Modern CAD systems can produce PCB layouts from a circuit diagram but in an effort to minimise space, sometimes the tracks become too thin and are lost in the manufacturing processes that follow.

When designing a PCB mask you should first start by laying out the components on a planning sheet. You do need to allow sufficient space for the components to ensure clearance around the terminals. Once this has been done, the tracks can be added in to connect up all components and finally the power rails can be added.

It is worth giving some consideration to the size of tracks and pads in relation to the amount of power they may have running through them. It is also worth marking on to the board the polarity of the power rails and that of any other polarised components.

Producing a PCB

1 Produce a mask from the circuit diagram either with a pen on acetate or on a CAD system (see Figure 4.4.20).

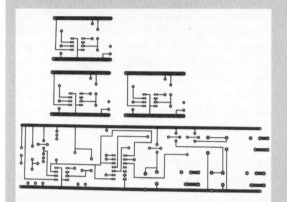

Figure 4.4.20 *PCB artwork*

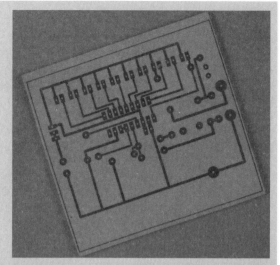

Figure 4.4.21 *Etched board*

2 The artwork can now be transferred to the board in one of two ways:
   a) direct on to the copper with an etch resistant pen
   b) phototransferred with photosensitive board.

The second method gives greater accuracy and quality and also allows for batch production. The mask should be placed top-side down on to the UV box and the material placed over the top. It should be exposed to the UV light for about two minutes.

3 The board should now be dipped into a solution of sodium hydroxide developer for about two minutes. The image will start to appear on the board as time passes. Once all the copper has been removed it should be washed in running water.

4 The board can now be etched in a solution of ferric chloride (see Figure 4.4.21). The solution should be agitated and the board checked at various stages. The processing time will vary as the concentrate of the solution becomes weaker.

Once all the copper has been removed the board can again be washed in running water.

It should be noted that when handling and transferring the boards from solution to solution and when washing them, gloves should be worn at all stages and tongs should be used.

5 The board now needs to be stripped of any resist material that is left over the copper surfaces on the etched board.

6 Finally, the board can be drilled with the correct-sized holes and the PCB can be cleaned with fine wire wool or carborundum paper.

All the components can then be inserted from the top side of the PCB and soldered in place.

ICs should be inserted into chip holders and a heat sink should be used when soldering in transistors and any diodes.

The completed circuit board is shown in Figure 4.4.22.

Figure 4.4.22 *Completed circuit*

Exam preparation

You will need to revise all the topics in this unit, so that you can apply your knowledge and understanding to the exam questions. In preparation for your exam, it is a good idea to make brief notes about different topics, such as 'Cams and followers'. Use subheadings, bullet point lists, sketches and diagrams where appropriate. A single side of A4 should be used for each of the headings from the Specification.

It is very important to learn exam skills. You should also have weekly practice in learning technical terms and formulae and in answering exam-type questions. When you need to answer any questions you should:

- read the question carefully and pick out the key points that need answering
- always show your working in calculations so you can gain marks for applying formulae, even if your final answer is incorrect
- match your answer to the marks available, e.g., for two marks you should give two good points that address the question
- always give examples and justify statements with reasons, saying how or why the statement is true.

Practice exam questions

1 A logic control circuit is needed to prevent the door of a washing machine from being opened if the machine is switched on and there is water in the machine.
   a) Produce a block diagram for a solution to the problem. (4)
   b) Generate a truth table and identify a suitable logic gate. (4)
   c) Draw a suitable circuit diagram and include all the components and sensors. (5)
   d) Explain how the use of logic circuits can be extended within the home for safety purposes. (2)

2 a) Compare the merits and limits of a belt pulley and a chain and sprocket for transferring rotary motion within a child's pedal go-cart. (8)
   b) Explain how the tension of the belt is maintained. (2)
   c) A driver pulley has a diameter of 250 mm and it is connected to a smaller pulley of 50 mm in diameter. Calculate the velocity ratio of the system. (5)

3 Two rotating shafts on the same centre line can be joined in several ways.
   a) Use annotated sketches and notes to describe two examples of how this can be achieved. (4)
   b) Make a sketch of Hooke's universal joint and describe how it works and give an example of where it can be used. (4)
   c) Describe three different methods of fixing a pulley to a shaft. (6)
   d) What are the advantages of using a splined shaft to hold a pulley? (1)

4 a) Using annotated sketches show the main differences between a positive clutch and a friction clutch. (9)
   b) Use examples to explain the suitability and applications of each type of clutch. (6)

5 a) Describe and illustrate how a pawl and ratchet can be used to arrest motion. (4)
   b) A rack has 120 teeth per metre and it meshes with a pinion having 40 teeth. How far does the rack travel in one and a half revolutions? (5)
   c) Use illustrated sketches to show two different methods of converting rotary to oscillating motion. Give an application for each method. (6)

5 Product development II (R5)

Summary of expectations

1. What to expect

You are required to submit one coursework project at A2. This project enables you to build on the knowledge, understanding and skills you gained during your AS coursework. The A2 project should, therefore, demonstrate a broader use of varying materials, a wider variety of skills and increasing knowledge of the technology associated with the A2 Specification.

At A2 level you will need to take a commercial approach to designing and manufacturing, working in a similar way to an industrial designer. This means working more independently, designing to meet the needs of others and taking responsibility for planning, organising and managing your own project work. This may involve the use of a wider range of people to support you in your work. For example, you could use the expertise of a visitor from business or make use of work-related resources. Do not forget to reference any help you get in your bibliography.

The A2 project should comprise a product and a coursework project folder. It is important to undertake a project that is appropriate and of a manageable size, so that you are able to finish it in the time available.

2. What is a resistant materials project?

An A2 Resistant Materials Technology project should:

- reflect a study of the 'technologies' involved in the A2 Resistant Materials Technology Specification
- be manufactured using materials listed in Unit 3A (Classification of materials)
- ensure that at least two thirds of the work focuses on resistant materials, both in the practical outcome and the coursework folder
- include a functioning product that matches its specification
- include increased emphasis on industrial applications and commercial working practices.

For example, an A2 Resistant Materials Technology project should be developed in collaboration with potential users or with a client (such as a local business or organisation).

This will enable the development of a designer-client relationship. Collaboration will need to include consultations with the client or users to develop a design brief and specification, together with input into the analysis and research. Discussions with the client or users will be expected to take place at critical stages throughout the project, enabling the use of feedback when making decisions. Remember to reference in your folder any changes made to the product design and/or manufacture as a result of feedback from the users or client.

3. How will it be assessed?

The AS project covers skills related to designing and manufacturing. It is assessed using the same assessment criteria as the AS project (see Table 5.1).

Table 5.1 AS coursework project assessment criteria

Assessment criteria	Marks
A Exploring problems and clarifying tasks	10
B Generating ideas	15
C Developing and communicating design proposals	15
D Planning manufacture	10
E Product manufacture	40
F Testing and evaluating	10
G Appropriate project	10
Total marks	110

You must attempt to cover all the assessment criteria A–G. The G criterion has been included to reflect that your project meets all the requirements of the Specification. You will need to undertake a project that has a level of complexity suitable for A2. It is very important, therefore, to check the appropriateness of your project with your teacher or tutor *at the start of the project*.

At A2 the assessment criteria demand a different level of response, requiring you to demonstrate a greater level of design thinking and more in-depth knowledge and understanding. You are also expected to take more responsibility for your own project management.

Your A2 project will be marked by your teacher and the coursework project folder will be sent to Edexcel for the Moderator to assess the level at which you are working. It may be that after moderation your marks will go up or down.

4. Choosing a suitable project

At A2 level you will need to design and manufacture a product that meets needs that are wider than your own. This will enable you to include a range of designing and manufacturing activities that are similar to those used in industry. You will need to design and manufacture one of the following:

- a one-off product for a specified user or client
- a product that could be batch or mass produced for users in a target market group.

The key to success is to identify a realistic user, client or target market need and solve this need through the design and manufacture of an appropriate product. Remember to evidence your understanding of industrial practices through the use of industrial type terminology and technical terms. You should make use of feedback from your user, client or target market group in order to access the full range of marks.

Planning considerations for the manufacture of your one-off, batch or mass produced product should include details of how one single product will be manufactured in your school or college workshop. You are not required to manufacture the product in quantity, although, depending on the type of product you develop, you may need to produce identical components for use in the product. Together with your production plan for one single product, you will need to include an explanation of how the product could be batch or mass produced. This will require you to highlight the changes that would be necessary to the manufacture of your one single product if it was to be made in quantity.

5. The coursework project folder

The coursework project folder should be concise and include only the information that is relevant to your project. It is essential to plan and analyse your research and be very selective about what to include in your folder. The ability to be selective is a high order skill which will enable you to access the full range of marks at A2.

Your coursework folder should demonstrate that you have achieved:

- a greater understanding of the design process (higher level design 'thinking')
- a higher ability to select and use relevant information (higher level research and evaluation skills)

- closer connections between relevant research and the development of ideas
- better understanding of the use of appropriate materials, processes and manufacturing techniques
- greater understanding of relevant technical terminology
- higher level communication and presentation skills
- appropriate use of ICT, including finding a balance between computer-generated images and those that are hand drawn.

Your coursework folder should include a contents page and a numbering system to help its organisation. The folder should comprise around 20–26 pages of A3/A2 paper. A title page, the contents page and a bibliography should be included as extra pages.

Table 5.2 gives an approximate guideline for the page breakdown of your coursework project folder. In the section on 'Product manufacture' it is essential to include clear photographs of the actual manufacture of your product. This should provide photographic evidence of modelling and prototyping, any specialist processes you have used including the use of CAD/CAM and show the stages of manufacture. Please note, however that the guideline for the page breakdown of your coursework folder is only a suggestion. You may find that your folder contents vary slightly from the guideline because of the type of project that you have chosen.

Table 5.2 Coursework project folder contents

Suggested contents	Suggested page breakdown
Title page with Specification name and number, candidate name, and number, centre name and number, title of project and date	extra page
Contents page	extra page
Exploring problems and clarifying tasks	4–5
Generating ideas	3–4
Developing and communicating design proposals	5–6
Planning manufacture	3–4
Product manufacture	2–3
Testing and evaluating	3–4
Bibliography	extra page
Total	20–26

6. How much is it worth?

The coursework project is worth 20 per cent of the full Advanced GCE.

Unit 6	Weighting
A2 level (full GCE)	20%

A Exploring problems and clarifying tasks (10 marks)

1. Identify, explore and analyse a wide range of problems and user needs

SIGNPOST
'Identify, explore and analyse a wide range of problems and user needs'
Unit 2 page 43

Look at Figure 5.1 and consider the questions.

Developing a project at A2
The A2 project enables you to draw together and apply all the knowledge, understanding and skills related to designing and making that you gained at AS level. This experience should provide you with a clear understanding of the assessment requirements and give you a solid basis for developing a new project at A2.

It may be helpful, at this stage, to read the AS and A2 exemplar projects in the Edexcel Coursework Guide, which demonstrate the standard at which you are required to work during the A2 project. You will be required to work more independently, which may involve using a wider range of people to support you in your work. Your most difficult decision now is to decide what to design and make that will enable you to demonstrate a higher level of 'design thinking'. New ideas or problems may have come to mind during your work on Unit 2, or when you discussed your project with others. In order to develop your A2 project, you will need to decide on a design context and a user, client or target market group.

Developing a commercial approach
At A2 you are expected to take a more commercial approach. This means designing and making a product that may have the potential to be batch or mass produced. In industry a prototype product is made prior to manufacture to test every aspect of the design before putting it into production. This commercial prototype product is as close as possible to the 'real' end product. Your product also needs to be as close as possible to the 'real' thing, so you should make it to the highest possible quality.

One way of developing a commercial approach to your project, is to collaborate with potential user(s) or with a 'client', which could be a local business or organisation. This will enable you to work in a similar way to a professional designer, who works to a client brief, meets the needs of others, makes use of feedback, works to a budget and to a deadline.

You will also need to make use of feedback from your user(s) or client, in order to access the full range of available marks. It is essential, therefore, to work out at the start of your project when and how you will consult with your user(s) or client so you can obtain their feedback about your product.

There are a number of ways to develop a commercial approach to project work and you could consider some of the following:

- Use work-related materials produced by a business, e.g. using a company information pack to help develop a product that could be marketed by that company or retailer. In this case you would need to research the needs and use feedback from an appropriate target market group.
- Use the expertise of a visitor from business, e.g. understanding a company's marketing strategies and the type of products they make. In this case, you could use the visitor as a client, consult with them throughout the project and use their feedback when making decisions.
- Make an off-site visit to identify a specific problem in the local community, e.g. visiting a community centre, primary school or a workplace, where different needs can be investigated.

Figure 5.1 *The Sinclair electric car was 'modern' in concept, but did not catch on with the public. Its failure may have originated from a lack of understanding of user needs. What was the target market for this product? What were the benefits of the car to users?*

- Use work experience as a context for designing and making a product, e.g. using a part-time job or work experience to spark off ideas about developing a product to meet specific needs.

Identifying and analysing a realistic need or problem and exploring the needs of users

SIGNPOST
'Identifying and analysing a realistic need or problem'
Unit 2 page 43

Once you have decided your approach for your A2 project, you can start the actual development process. It is always difficult at the start of a project to know exactly where and how to start, and what the end product will be – this is part of the excitement of product design. The best way forward is to undertake two tasks that are interrelated:

- identifying a realistic problem for specified user(s) that will lead to product development
- identifying the needs of potential user(s) and developing a product that will fulfil these needs.

Whichever approach you take, the key to success is to develop a designer/client relationship so that you can make use of feedback when making decisions.

You can explore the needs of potential users and look for product ideas by undertaking market research. In many industries market

Figure 5.2 Part of a student questionnaire

research is carried out to identify the taste, lifestyle and buying behaviour of potential customers. This establishes the profile of the target market group.

For manufacturers the 'customer' plays a key role in the product development process. Without customers there is no need to make products, so their views are vital if a product is to sell in the market place. Manufacturers need to ensure that their products meet customer requirements, at the right quality, at the right price and at the right time. For example, it is no good trying to sell a product that is made from purple plastic if the customers' concept is that purple is last year's colour! Feedback from customers is, therefore, crucially important if their requirements are to be met. Figure 5.2 shows how one student sought the views of potential customers.

Clarifying the task

SIGNPOST
'Clarifying the task'
Unit 2 page 44

Clarifying the task means deciding on the purpose for your product and how it will benefit users – and the image it may need to project in order to promote its market potential. Market research about buying behaviour may help here. You should also consider the factors that affect customer choice when buying products. These may include considerations of:

Task

Evidencing industrial practice: using market research techniques

Collect information from your user, client or target market group and investigate products using market research techniques:

a) Produce a product report through window shopping, going into stores, visiting galleries or museums. Identify product type, price ranges, market trends and new ideas.

b) Use questionnaires/surveys to identify user needs and values. Identify age groups, available spending money, favourite product types and brand loyalty.

c) Use product analysis to find a 'gap in the market'. Identify design styles, manufacturing processes, quality of design and manufacture and value for money.

- price and value for money
- **aesthetic factors**, like the product's finish or surface decoration
- **product performance**, such as reliability, ease of use, need for maintenance, safety in use.

> *To be successful you will:*
> - Clearly identify a realistic need or problem.
> - Focus the problem through analysis that covers relevant factors in depth.

2. Develop a design brief

> **SIGNPOST**
> 'Develop a design brief'
> Unit 2 page 44

Whichever approach you take in developing your A2 project, you should find that your early exploration of problems and user needs should help you develop a design brief. Take into account:

- the views of the potential users, client or target market group
- information about similar products
- the market potential of the product
- its benefit to the users.

Your brief should enable you to plan what, how and where you need to research, in order to develop a product that meets the needs of your potential users.

> *To be successful you will:*
> - Write a clear design brief.

3. Carry out imaginative research and demonstrate a high degree of selectivity of information

> **SIGNPOST**
> 'Carry out imaginative research and demonstrate a high degree of selectivity of information'
> Unit 2 page 45

At A2 level your coursework should demonstrate a greater understanding of the design process, higher level research and evaluation skills and increasing knowledge of the technology associated with the A2 Specification. Your coursework folder should demonstrate your ability to:

- undertake research that targets more closely the design brief. Don't waste time doing unnecessary research
- select and use relevant research information. Only include in your coursework folder information that is directly connected to your project. For example, don't include everything you know about hardwood if you are not using wood to make your product. Even if you are using wood, you still do not need to include everything you know about it, only information relating to its appropriateness for making your product
- make closer connections between your research, your product design specification and your design ideas. Making connections is what this unit is all about.

Collaborating with users or a client on your project will make it easier to target your research, because you will have specific requirements and users in mind. Include a range of primary and secondary research. This can include using questionnaires, analysing existing products, using statistical data and identifying market trends. At advanced level you should be thinking about a range of issues related to your product, such as the ease and cost of manufacture; the ease of maintenance; how to ensure the performance, quality and safety of your product; if there are any environmental issues related to your chosen materials or components.

In industry product design teams do not generally undertake market research themselves, but rely on information produced by the marketing department. Many manufacturers use **Product Data Management** (PDM) software to organise, manage and communicate accurate, up-to-date product information in a database. Everyone in the product design team has access to this information, making it easier and faster to get the product to market. Since you are not in this happy position, you have to do your own research, so bear in mind that you have to meet deadlines. If you have access to the Internet, you may be able to find useful information about existing products, e.g. about materials properties, product prices and styling. Many companies also provide information through company newsletters and case studies about their products. However, before you start any Internet research you need to know exactly what you are looking for and how to find it.

Find out web addresses before you start and try to avoid following interesting but useless leads.

All research that you undertake should enable you to write a product design specification. Review the criteria that are included in the AS specification because these basic criteria should be part of the A2 specification too. You should also refer to the further product design specification criteria required at A2 level to ensure that your research will enable you to address these criteria.

Stop and think!
Don't forget to reference all secondary sources of information in a bibliography at the end of your coursework project folder.

To be successful you will:
- Carry out a wide range of imaginative research, with a high degree of selectivity of information.

Develop a design specification, taking into account designing for manufacture

SIGNPOST
'Develop a design specification, taking into account designing for manufacture'
Unit 2 page 46

At A2 you may find that the development of your product design specification runs concurrently with writing your design brief, especially when you are working in collaboration with a client or users. Early exploration of the design context and discussions with the user(s) or client may provide enough information for you to develop the design brief and an *outline* product design specification at the same time. This can be very beneficial because it can help you to target more closely the research you need to do. As your research progresses you can amend and develop your design specification, until you reach your final product design specification. You could find that even this may need to be amended later on, after you have worked on and evaluated ideas for the product, or even after modelling and prototyping it.

Specification criteria
The A2 product design specification should take into account all the criteria that you worked with at AS level. At A2 you are expected to demonstrate a greater understanding of the design process. You can do this by developing a product design specification that takes into account more sophisticated specification criteria. The questions below should help you develop your A2 design specification

Questions about the design specification
- What influence will values issues, such as cultural, social, moral or environmental have on the purpose, function and aesthetics of your product?
- What influence will market trends and user requirements have on the market potential of your product? How would you develop an affordable product for image-conscious user(s)?
- What will be the life expectancy of your product? What maintenance will it require? What are the implications for the cost and quality of your product?
- What type of materials and components might be suitable? What are their properties and characteristics? How can you ensure availability at the right time and the right cost?
- What kind of processes, technology and scale of production might be suitable? Is the use of CAD/CAM to be specified in design and manufacture? What influence could the constraints of designing for mass production have on your product?
- What kind of quality assurance system can you put in place to ensure your product quality and reliability? Will this system make use of quality control, inspection and testing?
- What legal requirements and/or external standards (British Standards) related to performance, quality and safety do you need to take into account when developing your product?

Take into account scale of production
At A2 you should be developing a product for an individual user, a client or users in a target market group. Your identified scale of production will be one-off, batch or mass production, but you will be designing and manufacturing *one* product in your school or college workshop. You are not required to manufacture the product in quantity, although you may need to produce identical components for use in the product. When you

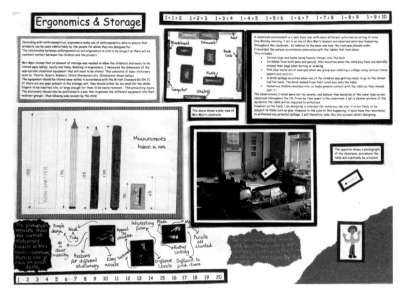

Figure 5.3 *Student research sheet*

plan the manufacture of your one single product, you will need to explain how it could be adapted for batch or mass production.

Your product design specification is the connection between research and ideas. It should guide all your design thinking and provide you with a basis for generating, testing and evaluating both your design ideas, your final design proposal and the end product. The design specification is, therefore, a control mechanism that sets up the criteria for the design and development of your product.

> **To be successful you will:**
> • Write a clear design specification.

B Generating ideas (15 marks)

1. Use a range of design strategies to generate a wide range of imaginative ideas that show evidence of ingenuity and flair

> **SIGNPOST**
> 'Generating ideas'
> Unit 2 page 47

You are expected to demonstrate a more mature approach to design when generating ideas at A2, which means making closer connections between your research, your product design specification and your ideas. In industry the product design specification forms the basis for developing ideas. Although your specification should provide inspiration both for aesthetic and functional considerations for design, it will probably be aesthetic considerations that provide the most freedom when generating exciting ideas. In your research you will have investigated user, client or target market needs relating to their preferences about products, investigated market trends relating to style and colour and investigated existing products that are similar to the one you intend to design and make. This kind of research information is vital if you are to generate imaginative ideas. Industrial designers rarely start developing ideas from scratch, mainly because they have to meet deadlines and because they have to design products that people will buy. They have to take shortcuts, which often involve using other product designs or the work of artists or designers as inspiration or as starting points for new ideas.

You can work in a similar way, using information about market trends and other aesthetic considerations to inspire ideas. You could:

- produce a '**moodboard**' of visual images to inspire ideas, e.g. make a collection of quirky images and products, a collection of colours, textures and cut-outs from magazines that suggest a mood or theme – these can be used to give your product an identity.
- make connections between old and new technology, e.g. adapt an 'old fashioned' car design to produce a new look for a modern domestic product
- use the work of a design movement to inspire the image of your product, e.g. reflect the Memphis style
- use an art movement or the work of an architect to inspire ideas, e.g. use the art movement Futurism or the work of the Spanish architect Gaudi to develop the form or styling of a product
- use the influence of technology to inspire ideas, e.g. use themes such as 'Technogames' or 'Miniaturisation'

- use themes built around values issues as a starting point for design, e.g. 'Eco-design'
- use the natural or built environment to inspire ideas, e.g. shells, fruit, grids, wrought iron work.

It is often a good idea to keep a notebook for jotting down ideas as **thumbnails** or quick sketches to help you develop design ideas. Thumbnails are small rough sketches showing the main parts of designs in the form of simple diagrams.

Sometimes it is helpful to try to put down as many initial ideas as possible in a set time, which is a bit like producing a brainstorm in image form. These initial ideas can be pasted or scanned and pasted into your coursework project folder rather than be redrawn – your project folder should show evidence of creative thinking rather than stilted copied-out work. At this stage, the examiner is looking for evidence of your design thinking. Quick sketches need to be produced fast, using pencils, pens, markers or the like. Use arrows and brief notes to explain your thinking and do not include too much detail at this stage.

To be successful you will:

Use a broad range of design strategies to generate and refine a wide range of imaginative ideas.

Think about this!
Many products in an industrial context are modifications, rather than original ideas. Inspiration for this type of designing can come through product analysis. In industry it may involve:

- adapting existing products to compete with successful 'branded' products
- developing existing products to appeal to a different target market group
- developing existing products through following new legal guidelines, i.e. related to environmental or safety issues
- adapting existing products through the use of new or different materials or processes.

2. Use knowledge and understanding gained through research to develop and refine alternative designs and/or design detail

As you become more involved with your ideas and start to think about them in greater depth you may need to produce larger, slightly more detailed sketches. These should still be produced quickly, but may start to show alternative ideas or some parts in more detail. Always add brief notes to explain your design thinking, so you provide evidence of how your research influences your ideas. An example of one student's work is shown in Figure 5.4.

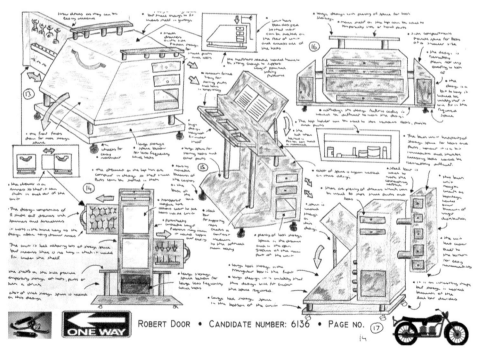

Figure 5.4 Generating ideas

SIGNPOST
'Use knowledge and understanding gained through research to develop and refine alternative designs ...'
Unit 2 page 48

At this stage, it may be helpful to use cut paper or simple 3D images to explore ideas. **One-point** or **two-point perspective** and the technique called '**crating**' are extensively used by designers to produce initial ideas. You may wish to add shading or texture, using pencil crayons or pale coloured markers to convey information about possible materials, e.g. to show if they are smooth and polished or matt. Knowledge and understanding about the materials or components you may use and about suitable processes or finishes can be evidenced by annotating your drawings.

Sometimes it is helpful to use 2D or 3D modelling in paper or card for developing initial ideas, especially if complicated shapes are involved. Simple modelling can give a real sense of the size and feel of a product, but if you work in this way be sure to provide evidence in your coursework folder. It is fairly easy to include 2D modelling, but you may have to photograph any 3D modelling work that you do.

Think about this!

Solving design problems is a complex activity because there are many conflicting constraints and possible solutions. For example, you must satisfy the brief, user or client needs, the constraints of manufacture, the limitations of materials and equipment and the demands of selling in the market place. As a designer-maker you have to respond to all these constraints and take on the many roles that in industry would be filled by design, marketing, planning and production teams. In industry the simultaneous design of a product and its manufacturing process, is called 'concurrent manufacturing'. As an individual taking on a range of design and manufacturing roles, you are also working 'concurrently'.

To be successful you will:
- Demonstrate effective use of appropriate research.

3. Evaluate and test the feasibility of ideas against specification criteria

SIGNPOST
'Evaluate and test the feasibility of ideas against the specification criteria'
Unit 2 page 49

As your ideas develop you should evaluate them against your design specification. You should also evaluate the feasibility and market potential of your ideas by getting the views of your client or user(s). It is always helpful to explain your ideas to others; always listen to their views as they can provide you with unexpected insights into your work. If you are using the expertise of a visitor from business or are working with people in the local community, they may be able to offer constructive criticism which will help you develop your design work further. Getting feedback is vitally important, not only because it will help you make decisions about your product, but it will enable you to access the full range of available marks. Remember to reference in your folder any changes you make to your design ideas as a result of feedback from your user(s) or client.

Testing the feasibility of ideas

In industry evaluation of ideas is sometimes done by constructing an evaluation matrix, which compares each idea against the specification criteria. Each idea is assessed using the following technique:

- + (plus), meaning better than, less than, easier than the specification criterion
- − (minus), meaning worse than, more expensive than, more difficult to develop than, more complex than, harder than the specification criterion
- S (same), meaning about the same as the specification criterion.

Each idea in turn is evaluated against the specification criteria. Each idea is given a score, either +, − or S. Scores for each idea are added up, to show the strengths and weaknesses of each one.

In industry a design team would look at the weaknesses of all ideas to see what could be done to improve them. Very weak ideas are then eliminated, resulting in the emergence of strong ideas, which can be developed individually or

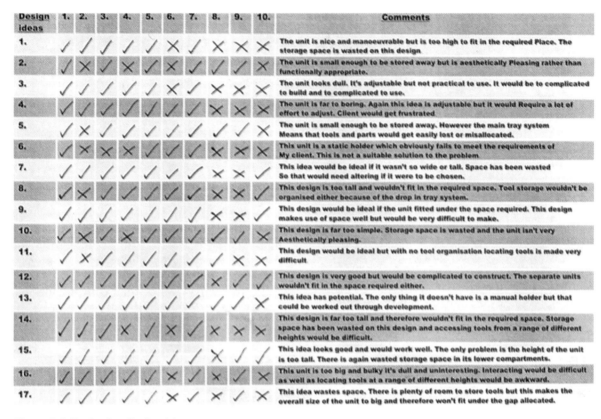

Design ideas	1.	2.	3.	4.	5.	6.	7.	8.	9.	10.	Comments
1.	✓	✓	✓	✓	✓	✗	✓	✗	✗	✗	The unit is nice and manoeuvrable but is too high to fit in the required Place. The storage space is wasted on this design.
2.	✓	✗	✓	✗	✓	✗	✓	✓	✓	✗	The unit is small enough to be stored away but is aesthetically Pleasing rather than functionally appropriate.
3.	✓	✓	✓	✓	✓	✗	✓	✗	✗	✗	The unit looks dull. It's adjustable but not practical to use. It would be to complicated to build and to complicated to use.
4.	✓	✓	✓	✓	✓	✓	✓	✗	✗	✗	The unit is far to boring. Again this idea is adjustable but it would Require a lot of effort to adjust. Client would get frustrated.
5.	✓	✗	✓	✓	✓	✓	✓	✓	✓	✗	The unit is small enough to be stored away. However the main tray system Means that tools and parts would get easily lost or misallocated.
6.	✓	✗	✗	✗	✓	✓	✓	✗	✗	✗	This unit is a static holder which obviously fails to meet the requirements of My client. This is not a suitable solution to the problem.
7.	✓	✓	✓	✓	✓	✓	✓	✗	✗	✓	This idea would be ideal if it wasn't so wide or tall. Space has been wasted So that would need altering if it were to be chosen.
8.	✓	✗	✓	✓	✓	✓	✓	✗	✗	✓	This design is too tall and wouldn't fit in the required space. Tool storage wouldn't be organised either because of the drop in tray system.
9.	✓	✓	✓	✓	✓	✓	✗	✗	✓		This design would be ideal if the unit fitted under the space required. This design makes use of space well but would be very difficult to make.
10.	✓	✗	✓	✗	✓	✓	✓	✓	✓	✗	This design is far too simple. Storage space is wasted and the unit isn't very Aesthetically pleasing.
11.	✓	✗	✓	✓	✓	✓	✓	✓	✗	✗	This design would be ideal but with no tool organisation locating tools is made very difficult
12.	✓	✓	✓	✓	✓	✓	✓	✗	✓	✓	This design is very good but would be complicated to construct. The separate units wouldn't fit in the space required either.
13.	✓	✓	✓	✓	✓	✓	✓	✓	✓	✗	This idea has potential. The only thing it doesn't have is a manual holder but that could be worked out through development.
14.	✓	✓	✓	✗	✓	✗	✓	✗	✗	✗	This design is far too tall and therefore wouldn't fit in the required space. Storage space has been wasted on this design and accessing tools from a range of different heights would be difficult.
15.	✓	✓	✓	✓	✓	✓	✓	✗	✓	✓	This idea looks good and would work well. The only problem is the height of the unit is too tall. There is again wasted storage space in its lower compartments.
16.	✓	✓	✓	✓	✓	✗	✗	✗	✓	✗	This unit is too big and bulky it's dull and uninteresting. Interacting would be difficult as well as locating tools at a range of different heights would be awkward.
17.	✓	✓	✓	✓	✓	✗	✓	✗	✓	✗	This idea wastes space. There is plenty of room to store tools but this makes the overall size of the unit to big and therefore won't fit under the gap allocated.

Figure 5.5 *Evaluating/testing ideas*

combined in some way. This kind of exercise gives the design team a greater understanding of design problems and potential solutions and a natural stimulus to produce design solutions.

Try using an evaluation matrix to evaluate your initial ideas. This should give you a clearer view about what is worth developing. Use written notes to explain this thinking.

You should also make a note of any further research you may need to do. After consulting with your user(s) or client, you may need to modify your design specification, to take into account any decisions made as a result of feedback from them. At A2 level you should be using a more refined approach to focus your ideas, so that they meet more closely the requirements of the specification.

> **To be successful you will:**
> - Objectively evaluate and test ideas against the specification criteria.

C Developing and communicating design proposals (15 marks)

1. Develop, model and refine design proposals, using feedback to help make decisions

SIGNPOST
'Develop, model and refine design proposals, using feedback to help make decisions'
Unit 2 page 50

Your aim is to develop and refine your chosen idea until you find the optimum solution – the best possible solution to your design problem. If you are developing a product that could be batch or mass produced for a client or users in a target market group, you will have to consider ease of manufacture. Even if you are developing a one-off product for an individual client, you will need to consider how easy your product will be to manufacture. In industry, planning the

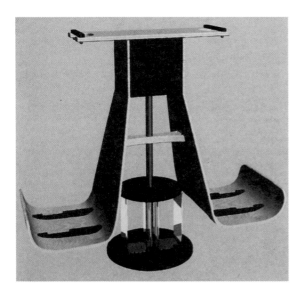

Figure 5.6 *2D CAD modelling of ideas*

manufacturing processes is a normal part of the design process.

Modelling and prototyping should play a key role in your production planning. You can use them to trial your design proposal, to explore materials and components, to work out manufacturing and assembly processes and for materials planning. Modelling and prototyping will enable you to consider every aspect of your design. They will enable you to make judgements about the visual elements, such as proportion, shape, styling details, colour, texture and the size and appropriateness of components. Many products, such as furniture or toys are modelled to ensure they are the correct size and easy to use. Figure 5.6 shows an example of 2D modelling.

To be successful you will:
- Develop, model and refine the design proposal, with effective use of feedback.

---

2. Demonstrate a wide variety of communication skills, including ICT for designing, modelling and communicating

SIGNPOST
'Demonstrate a wide variety of communication skills, including ICT for designing, modelling and communicating'
Unit 2 page 50

At A2 you are expected to demonstrate a higher level of communication and presentation skills to develop, model and refine your design proposals. This should include the use of relevant technical terminology when you are explaining technological or scientific concepts.

Task
Using ICT in industry
The increasing use of ICT by industry has had an enormous impact on design, through the use of CAD systems for computer modelling.

Every aspect of a product's development can be modelled using **Electronic Product Definition (EPD)**, in which all the data required to develop and manufacture a product is stored in a database. This means that even complex products, such as cars or aero-engines can be modelled electronically as **'virtual products'** and developed directly from the computer screen.

List the advantages to manufacturers of such a system.

You should use ICT if it is available to you, but you will not be penalised for non-use. ICT is useful for recording design decisions, data handling, identifying the properties of materials and for modelling ideas in 2D and 3D.

When using 2D modelling you can develop all the techniques you learned during your AS course. This may include modelling your product using:

- exploded views to show individual parts and how they fit together or to show hidden detail
- sections or cutaways to show the inside of the product
- CAD modelling – make sure you find a balance between computer-generated and hand-drawn images.

SIGNPOST
Factfile
Unit 2 page 51

When using 3D modelling you should also develop the techniques you learned in the AS course. Your modelling should ensure that your product will meet the performance and **ergonomic** requirements of your design specification.

Figure 5.7 *Working model of a glider*

Modelling to test performance requirements

Testing performance requirements may involve making more than one model to see how different parts of your design work. For example, the design of a car security system may need a model to test its structure and another model to test its clamping mechanism. When testing the performance of smaller models, you may need to use temporary methods of joining materials, such as sticky tape or paper clips. Larger models may need stronger fixings such as 'G' cramps.

SIGNPOST
'Anthropometrics and ergonomics'
Unit 3B1 page 118

Testing ergonomic requirements

Often when testing ergonomic requirements, designers work with 3D models to give a real impression of size and the relationship of the product with the user. Since there is no such thing as an 'average-sized' person, designers often use **anthropometric data** about measurements of the human body, such as height, weight, reach, leg and arm lengths and strength. If necessary, check out anthropometric data from standards organisations such as the British Standards Institute.

Another approach to dealing with ergonomic problems is to design for adjustability. For example, car manufacturers produce ranges of saloons, hatchbacks or estate cars to suit the needs of different consumers. Within each car there is adjustability, so that the controls, seats or mirrors can be changed to suit individuals.

Modelling techniques

You can use a variety of modelling techniques and a range of materials to make 3D working prototypes, '**lash-ups**' or mechanical models, for example:

- Sheet materials, such as paper, card and thin plastics, can be used for modelling ideas, as they are quick and easy to use and relatively inexpensive. Look out for useful modelling materials such as recycled packaging, or use flat sheets cut from drinks cans and odd bits of string or wire.
- Simple techniques like cutting, scoring and folding will enable you to explore curved and rectilinear forms. Product designers often model products in card and add details by drawing things like switches or dials on the surface. You could photocopy design details from magazines, cut them out and stick on, to give a realistic idea of your product.
- Clay or plasticine may be used for moulding solid models or polystyrene foam used for making block models.
- Frame models can be built to scale to explore and test structures, using anything that cuts easily, like drinking straws, strips of wood, uncooked spaghetti or wire.
- Construction kits can be used for testing mechanical or structural problems. Kits are useful for the testing of components, which can be quickly removed or replaced to test their usefulness.

Think about this!

A photocopier or scanner are useful for developing design details. Copy or scan mesh textures for detailing grills on speakers. Copy or scan your outline drawings so you can experiment with different colours and textures to create different surface finishes and materials.

Choosing a colour scheme

Colour is an essential characteristic of many products. It is a powerful marketing tool because when we look at a product it is usually the first thing we notice. Colour can convey strong messages about the product. For example, colour is often associated with specific products such as pastel blue or pink for baby products. Would these colours look 'right' used in the design of electrical equipment?

Some of our responses to colour are through association, e.g. red for danger, blues are cool, whereas browns and greens may suggest a natural quality. When choosing colours for your product, you need to be sure of the message that you wish to communicate. The creation of moodboards (see pages 299 and 338) can often be helpful in selecting colours that are appropriate to your product.

It is important to try out your product **colour scheme**. You could use photocopies or CAD software to try out different **colourways**. Experiment with different tones and try unusual combinations. Before colouring your final design it may be helpful to test your colours as near to full size as you can. Large areas of colour can look entirely different to a small colour swatch. You may, of course, decide not to colour your product and instead utilise the natural colours of the materials you are working with.

Using test models

You may need to use different types of **test models** to test different aspects of your design. For example, the design of a folding stool may need a full-sized model to test its structure and ergonomic characteristics. Other smaller models may need to be made to test the folding mechanism.

When developing your final design proposal you may need to test how your product might work. This is especially important if you are developing a product for use in a particular situation. As you refine your design proposal you will gradually arrive at the final prototype.

To be successful you will:
- Use high-level communication skills with appropriate use of ICT.

Think about this!

In industry, 3D prototypes are often made for products such as torches or telephones. Prototypes are made as accurately as possible to represent the appearance and function of the finished product.

When James Dyson was developing his cyclone-action vacuum cleaner, he made 5,127 prototypes!

Prototyping is a key process because it will enable you to test the product structure and to work out possible manufacturing processes. Modelling and prototyping will also enable you to test the suitability of a range of materials and components. Considerations about materials should include an understanding of the need for a well-finished product that is easy to maintain.

3. Demonstrate understanding of a range of materials/components/ systems, equipment, processes and commercial manufacturing requirements

SIGNPOST
'Selecting materials' Unit 2 page 52
'Testing materials' Unit 3A page 92
'Selection of materials' Unit 4A page 178

To be successful you will:
- Demonstrate a clear understanding of a wide range of resources, equipment, processes and commercial manufacturing requirements.

At A2 you are expected to draw on and use a higher level of understanding about materials, components and processes. You should make relevant and real connections between that understanding and your own design and manufacture. Modelling and prototyping should enable you to trial materials and components. It

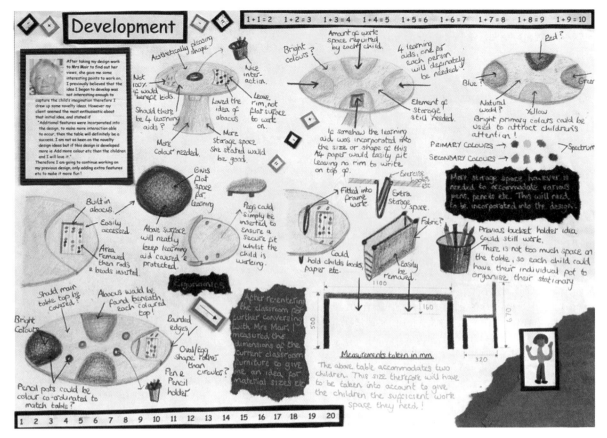

Figure 5.8 *Evaluation of the final design proposal against the specification*

may also give you the opportunity to explore a range of interesting materials and look for new ways of using them. Testing materials will enable you to select ones that are the most suitable for your product. Testing may include researching known properties and the use of **comparative testing**.

Do not forget to annotate your final design proposal, to explain how and why the materials and components meet the requirements of your product design specification. You should also consider the commercial manufacture of your product. An example of an evaluation of the final design proposal is shown in Figure 5.8.

4. Evaluate design proposals against specification criteria, testing for accuracy, quality, ease of manufacture and market potential

During the refinement of your final design proposal you will need to check its feasibility against your product design specification. You should also consult with your client or user(s) on the development of your product, as their views should provide you with feedback about its viability. You will need to explain:

- how your design proposal will meet the specification – will the product 'work'?
- how its aesthetic characteristics will meet the needs of your client or user(s)
- how the proposal will meet market trends and ergonomic requirements
- how the performance characteristics of your proposed materials, components and manufacturing processes will meet the quality and cost expectations of your client or user(s)
- how easy it will be to manufacture in the time available
- how you could manufacture the product in batch or high volume.

> **SIGNPOST**
> 'Evaluate design proposals'
> Unit 2 page 54

> *To be successful you will:*
> - Objectively evaluate and test design proposal against the specification criteria.

D Planning manufacture (10 marks)

1. Produce a clear production plan that details the manufacturing specification, quality and safety guidelines and realistic deadlines

SIGNPOST
'Planning manufacture'
Unit 2 page 54

You should produce and use a clear production plan that explains how to manufacture your product.

The work that you have already done during the research, design and development stages of your project should enable you to do this. During those developmental stages you had to take into account how easy your product will be to manufacture. In many industrial situations the planning of the production processes is a normal part of the design process. Your modelling and prototyping will have played a key role in your production planning. You used it to trial your ideas, to explore materials and components, to work out manufacturing and assembly processes and for materials planning.

Think about how long each different production process will take. Will you have enough time to make your product? Will you need to simplify anything? Do you need any special materials or tools? How soon do you need to order any materials or components so they are ready when you need them? At this stage, you need to estimate your production costs and a possible **selling price**.

Producing a production plan

Your production plan should include clear and detailed instructions for making your product. An example of production planning is shown in Figure 5.9. Although you will be making one product in your workshop, you will need to detail how identical products could be manufactured by batch or mass production. Planning quality into your work is therefore vitally important. Base your production plan on the one you used at AS level. You should also take into consideration the following:

a) Your manufacturing specification should include a fully dimensioned **working drawing** (see Figure 5.10). You could use **orthographic** 3rd angle drawings, or possibly use CAD software.

b) You should use quality control methods to ensure that identical products could be made. Plan your quality control at **critical control points** (**CCPs**) in the product manufacture. Use **quality indicators** to explain how to check for quality. Think about balancing the quality of your product against the cost of making it and the time available. What are the quality requirements of the client or users?

c) Use risk assessment procedures to check the safety of your manufacture. Are there any potential hazards? Does the design specification set out any safety standards that will help you assess risks? Are there any risks attached to the materials, processes and equipment you will use? Do you need to follow any safety regulations? Are there any risks in the use of your product? What about its disposal?

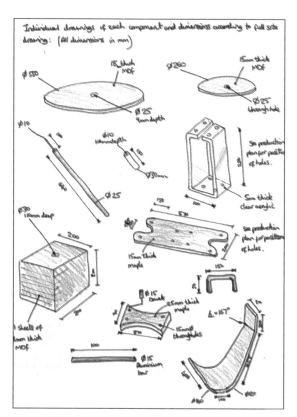

Figure 5.9 Production planning

Task
Evidencing industrial practice: quality control
Draw up a flow chart to show the CCPs in your product manufacture. For each CCP describe the quality indicators you could use to ensure the manufacture of identical products.

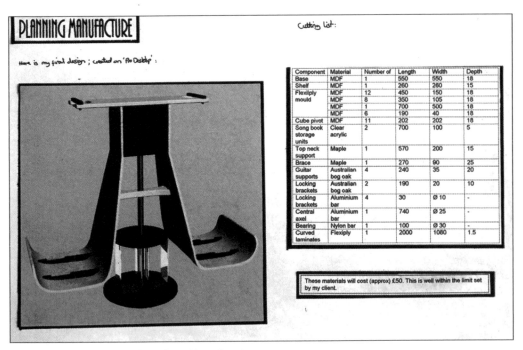

PLANNING MANUFACTURE

Here is my final design ; created on 'Pro Desktop' :

Cutting list :

Component	Material	Number of	Length	Width	Depth
Base	MDF	1	550	550	18
Shelf	MDF	1	260	260	15
Flexiply mould	MDF	12	450	150	18
	MDF	8	350	105	18
	MDF	1	700	500	18
	MDF	6	190	40	18
Cube pivot	MDF	11	202	202	18
Song book storage units	Clear acrylic	2	700	100	5
Top neck support	Maple	1	570	200	15
Brace	Maple	1	270	90	25
Guitar supports	Australian bog oak	4	240	35	20
Locking brackets	Australian bog oak	2	190	20	10
Locking brackets	Aluminium bar	4	30	Ø 10	-
Central axel	Aluminium bar	1	740	Ø 25	-
Bearing	Nylon bar	1	100	Ø 30	-
Curved laminates	Flexiply	1	2000	1080	1.5

These materials will cost (approx) £50. This is well within the limit set by my client.

Figure 5.10 *Fully dimensioned working drawing*

To be successful you will:
- Produce a clear and detailed production plan with achievable deadlines.

Factfile
Quality assurance (QA) and quality control (QC)

1 The aim of QA is to make identical products with zero faults. A QA system monitors every stage of design and manufacture. QA makes use of written documents such as:

- production plans
- detailed specifications
- production schedules
- costing sheets
- quality control and inspection sheets.

2 QC is used to test and monitor the production of products.

- QC means checking for accuracy at critical control points.
- Quality indicators are used to show how quality is checked using variables or attributes.
- QC makes use of standard sizes, dimensions and tolerances to enable quality to be checked.

2. Take account of time and resource management and scale of production when planning manufacture

SIGNPOST
'Take account of time and resource management and scale of production when planning manufacture' Unit 2 page 56

Many of the activities that you undertake during your A2 project will overlap. This is inevitable, because designing and making is a complex process. Planning a project is not easy because it involves estimating how long each activity will take. Use your AS experience of project planning to help you plan this one. Did you have to amend your time plan? Did some activities take longer than you expected? How did you overcome these problems? Did you find it helpful to use a Gantt chart to plan your project? Did you use one to plan your manufacture?

In industry project managers often use **critical path analysis** to plan the successful outcome of a project. This involves working out all the critical activities that must be undertaken and how one activity relates to another. Decisions have to be taken as to which activity needs to be done first; how long each activity will take; when each activity has to be done by; which activities can be done at the same time; which activities depend on the completion of other activities; and if any activities are more essential or critical than others.

The critical path is the one that takes the shortest time. It is often helpful to work backwards from the deadline, plotting when an activity has to start in order to finish on time. You could use a Gantt chart to plot the critical path of your product. Map each task against the time available, so you can prioritise the critical activities. Remember to use your Gantt chart or any other planning tool as a working document in which you record any subsequent changes you might make, if for example, delays occur. It is worth remembering that you will only be awarded marks for a production plan made before you manufacture your product.

> **To be successful you will:**
> * Demonstrate effective management of time and resources, appropriate to the scale of production.

> **SIGNPOST**
> 'Use ICT appropriately for planning and data handling' Unit 2 page 57

3. Use ICT appropriately for planning and data handling

The aim of using Information and Communications Technology (ICT) for planning and data handling is to enhance your design and technology capability. Although you will not be penalised for non-use of ICT, you should use it where appropriate and available. If you do have access to ICT you can use it for a variety of activities. For example:

* Find out costs of materials using e-mail or the Internet.
* Use spreadsheets to work out quantities and costs of materials and components.
* Plan the critical path of your product, using a colour-coded Gantt chart.

> **To be successful you will:**
> * Demonstrate good use of ICT.

E Product manufacture (40 marks)

1. Demonstrate understanding of a range of materials, components and processes appropriate to the specification and scale of production

> **SIGNPOST**
> 'Demonstrate understanding of a range of materials, components and processes appropriate to the specification and scale of production' Unit 2 page 58
> 'Working properties of materials and components' Unit 3A page 79
> 'Selection of materials' Unit 4A page 178

Your AS coursework experience should enable you to select and use materials and components with growing confidence. By this stage of your course, you should have developed a better knowledge of their working characteristics and a wider variety of skills. Your modelling, prototyping and testing of materials, components and processes, should also give you confidence in making your product. Most of the problems related to the product assembly should, hopefully, have been ironed out.

Your aim now should be to manufacture a well-made product. This may not necessarily be made to a very much higher quality than the product that you made at AS. However, your A2 product should 'work' in terms of meeting the design brief and specification. The product should function well and fulfil the design and manufacturing specifications more closely than your AS product did.

Scale of production

Your product will be made as a one-off, whichever scale of production you design it for. You should make and finish the product to the best of your ability and explain how it could be manufactured in high volume.

> **To be successful you will:**
> * Demonstrate clear understanding of a wide range of materials, components and processes.

2. Demonstrate imagination and flair in the use of materials, components and processes

> **SIGNPOST**
> 'Demonstrate imagination and flair in the use of materials, components and processes' Unit 2 page 59

You are expected to work creatively, innovatively and imaginatively with materials, components and processes. You can only do this if you have a good understanding of the materials and processes you use. During the modelling and prototyping stages you may have had the opportunity to explore a range of interesting materials and trial new ways of using them.

Task

Demonstrating imagination and flair
Creative solutions to design problems often come from exploring the characteristics of materials or from combining unusual ones. Experiment with the following finishes to see how you can improve the look of your product:

- sanding sealer/primer
- cellulose or emulsion paint
- acrylic varnish or wood stains
- metal or plastic polish.

Figure 5.11 *Evidence of high-level making skills shown through photographs*

Your ability to use materials, components and processes with flair should result in the production of a quality product that:

- meets the specification and is well finished.
- is well-designed and easy to use.

3. Demonstrate high-level making skills, precision and attention to detail in the manufacture of high-quality products

> ### SIGNPOST
> 'Demonstrate high-level making skills'
> Unit 2 page 59

At A2 you should place a greater emphasis on the prevention of **faults** through your use of quality assurance and quality control. This will involve using your production plan to monitor your product manufacture:

- Plan where you will check for quality during manufacture.
- Use tolerances and dimensions to check the accuracy of component parts of your product.
- Check the cutting action of tools.
- Check the accuracy of machines prior to cutting.
- Test components prior to assembly.

Your making skills should result in the production of a high-quality product. An example of this is shown in Figure 5.11. The product should be capable of being tested against the specification and used by the client or users for its intended job.

> **To be successful you will:**
> - Demonstrate demanding and high-level making skills that show precision and attention to detail.

4. Use ICT appropriately for communicating, modelling, control and manufacture

> ### SIGNPOST
> 'Uses of ICT in the manufacture of products'
> Unit 4B2 page 256
> 'Use ICT appropriately for planning and data handling' Unit 2 page 57

You should use Information and Communications Technology (ICT) to help your product manufacture, where it is appropriate and available, but you will not be penalised for its non-use. You are not expected to know how to use specific equipment or programs, but you should understand the benefits of using ICT to aid manufacture.

If your school/college has links with a remote manufacturing centre you may have the opportunity to create components using CAD/CAM software. This may involve using **video conferencing** to talk to a technician, downloading your CAM file and watching your design being produced on a CNC machine.

To be successful you will:
- Demonstrate good use of ICT.

---

5. Demonstrate high level of safety awareness in the working environment and beyond

SIGNPOST
'Demonstrate high level of safety awareness in the working environment and beyond' Unit 2 page 61

Safety should be a high priority in your work at all times. Safe production means identifying all possible risk and documenting safety procedures to manage and monitor the risk. This means that you should:

- identify hazards and use risk assessment procedures to ensure safe use of materials, tools, equipment and processes
- demonstrate awareness of safety in the workshop
- identify safety aspects relevant to the design, manufacture, use and disposal of your product.

Risk assessment

Risk assessment means identifying risks to the health and safety of people and to the environment. In practice, this means using safe designing and manufacturing processes and making products that are safe to use and safe to dispose of.

Manufacturers have a legal requirement to use risk assessment procedures to look for possible hazards in their products. They use British Standards to test and monitor production. All possible health hazards to employees must be eliminated and safety procedures have to be followed to ensure the safety of people at work. Some manufacturers use **Life Cycle Assessment** (**LCA**) to assess a product's impact from cradle (raw materials) to grave (disposal).

Tasks
Risk assessment
1 Research any appropriate British Standards related to your product type.
2 Draw up a chart to show the key stages in the design and manufacture of your product. For each stage list the risk assessment procedures required to make your product as safe as possible.

To be successful you will:
- Demonstrate good use of ICT.

F Testing and evaluating (10 marks)

1. Monitor the effectiveness of the work plan in achieving a quality outcome

SIGNPOST
'Monitor the effectiveness of the work plan in achieving a quality outcome' Unit 2 page 61

Your production plan is a key tool in monitoring the manufacture of your product because it enables you to control its quality. Use your production plan to record any modifications you make to your product or to the processes you use. Even the best-laid plans sometimes have to be changed through unexpected problems that arise!

Problems that do occur may be due to the availability of materials or equipment or due to time constraints. If, for whatever reason, you find that you are running out of time, you may have to take short cuts or simplify the design detailing on your product. This would obviously have an impact on the quality or 'look' of the product. Record any changes you make, before you forget, so another identical product could be made to the same standard.

To be successful you will:
- Make effective use of your work plan to achieve a high-quality outcome.

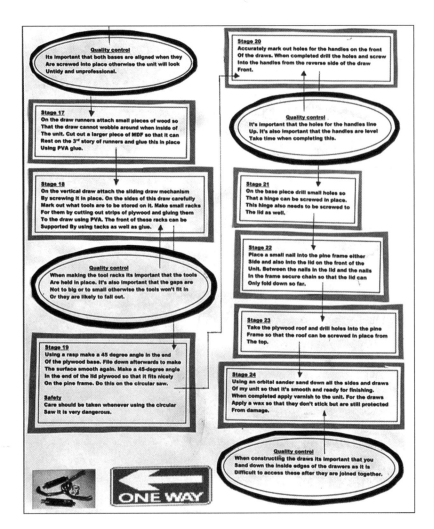

Figure 5.12 *Part of a manufacturing schedule*

2. Devise quality assurance procedures to monitor development and production

> **SIGNPOST**
> 'Devise quality assurance procedures to monitor development and production'
> Unit 2 page 62
> 'The cost of quality' Unit 4B1 page 208

Quality planning is a key process during product development and manufacture and you should use quality assurance processes and quality control checks to monitor quality. This includes using quality indicators at critical control points to check your product's manufacture.

Refer to the quality requirements that you set up in your product design specification. Did you take these into account when designing and developing your product ideas? Refer to the quality control checks that you put into place in your production plan. Use these to monitor the quality of your product.

The meaning of quality

In industry achieving quality means meeting standards. This makes it possible to make identical products that have a zero-fault rate. Quality can mean different things to different people:

- Quality for the consumer means a product's fitness-for-purpose. This can be evaluated through its performance, price and aesthetic appeal.
- Quality for a manufacturer means meeting the product manufacturing specification and finding a balance between the following:
  - profitable manufacture of identical products on time and to budget
  - meeting the needs and expectations of the consumer and the environment.

> *To be successful you will:*
> - Devise clear quality assurance procedures.

3. Use testing to ensure fitness-for-purpose

SIGNPOST
'Using testing to ensure fitness-for-purpose'
Unit 2 page 62

In industry testing of materials and components before manufacture is part of a quality assurance system. It requires the use of standard tests under controlled conditions. **Standard performance tests** can be set by the British Standards Institute and/or by individual manufacturers.

Tests on prototypes are made to test for performance, ease of manufacture, aftercare, maintenance and fitness-for-purpose. These tests ensure the production of quality products, avoid costly mistakes and protect the consumer against faulty or unsafe goods.

Testing to ensure fitness-for-purpose means testing the performance of the product so it meets the requirements of the specification and the users (see Figure 5.13). You should record the results of any testing that you do during and after manufacture. For example, you could test:

- the performance of the product against the design and manufacturing specifications
- that the quality of the product is suitable for users – this could mean using field trials to

Figure 5.13 Testing under working conditions

test the quality and ease of use of your product
- the product under working conditions or over extended periods, such as continuous running
- the product using external standards, such as British Standards, where appropriate
- use feedback from your testing to help you suggest how you could improve your product.

4. Objectively evaluate the outcome against specifications and suggest appropriate improvements

SIGNPOST
'Objectively evaluate the outcome against specifications and suggest appropriate improvements'
Unit 2 page 63

You should objectively evaluate and explain the success of your product in relation to the design brief and specifications. It can sometimes be hard to be objective about your own work. Your consultations with your client or user(s) throughout the design and manufacture of your product should give you unbiased opinions about your product's success.

Objective evaluation and feedback should help you decide how your product can be improved. As with your AS project, your suggestions for improvement should be based around the product's aesthetic and functional success, its quality of design and manufacture and its fitness for purpose. You should also suggest improvements in relation to the product's market potential. For example does it have potential for manufacture beyond one-off production? Could it be produced economically in batch or high volume? Could it be marketed to a wider target market? Could the product be made with consistently high quality and would it be reliable? Could it be sold at a price the client or user(s) could afford? Would the product provide them with an image they want the product to give them?

To be successful you will:
- Make effective use of testing to ensure fitness for purpose.

To be successful you will:
- Objectively evaluate the outcome and suggest appropriate improvements.

Student checklist

1. Project management

- Take responsibility for planning, organising, managing and evaluating your own project.
- Include photographic evidence to show hidden details or demonstrate the processes you used at each stage of manufacture.
- Include only the work related to the assessment requirements.

2. A successful A2 coursework project will:

- identify the needs of a specified user, client or users in a target market group
- develop a designer/client relationship that enables the use of feedback when making decisions
- select and use relevant research that targets more closely the brief and specification
- make closer connections between research, feedback and the development of ideas
- demonstrate high level communication and presentation skills and appropriate use of ICT
- be a manageable size so you can finish it on time
- focus on at least two thirds resistant materials listed
- include an increased emphasis on industrial practices, including the use of feedback
- include clear photographs of modelling, prototyping, testing and manufacture
- detail the manufacture of one product and show how it could be manufactured in quantity
- use a better understanding about materials, components and manufacturing processes
- demonstrate a wide variety of skills, a broad use of materials and increasing knowledge of A2 technologies
- manufacture a functioning product that matches specifications more closely than at AS level
- allow time to evaluate your work as it progresses and modify it if necessary
- be well planned so you can meet your deadlines.

3. Evidencing industrial practices in coursework

- Use industrial terminology and technical terms.
- Include a range of designing activities that are similar to those used in industry.
- Include a range of manufacturing activities that are similar to those used in industry.

4. Using ICT in coursework

- Develop the use of ICT for research, designing, modelling, communicating and testing.
- Develop the use of ICT for planning, data handling, control and manufacture.

5. Producing a bibliography

- Reference all secondary sources of information in a bibliography, e.g. from textbooks, newspapers, magazines, electronic media, CD-ROMs, the Internet, etc.
- Reference scanned, photocopied or digitised images. Do not use clip art at this level.
- Do not expect marks for any work copied directly from textbooks, the Internet, or from other students.

6. Submitting your coursework project folder

- Have your coursework ready for submission by mid-May in the year of your examination.
- Include a title page with the Specification name and number, candidate name and number, centre name and number, title of project and date.
- Include a contents page and numbering system to help organise your folder.
- Ensure that your work is clear and easy to understand, with titles for each section.

7. Using the Coursework Assessment Booklet (CAB)

- Complete the student summary in the CAB and *remember to sign it*. This should include your design brief and a short description of your coursework project.
- Ensure that the CAB contains a minimum of three clear photographs that show the whole product with alternative views and details.
- Write your candidate name and number, centre name and number and 6301/01 in the CAB by the product photographs and on the *back of each photograph*.

6 Design and technology capability (R6)

Summary of expectations

1. What to expect

Unit 6 brings together all the knowledge, understanding and skills that you have gained during your Advanced GCE course.

Although no new learning is expected during the Unit it is essential that you prepare fully for the Unit 6 exam.

2. How will it be assessed?

Unit 6 is assessed through a three hour Design Exam, in which you are asked to produce a solution to a given design problem and describe how the solution can be manufactured. Your solution should be developed through resistant materials. In this kind of exam you should demonstrate your ability to think on your feet, not to recall information.

The assessment criteria in Table 6.1 cover knowledge and understanding related to designing and manufacturing. You will be assessed on your ability to organise and present ideas and information clearly and logically. The style of assessment will remain the same each year, but there will be a different design problem each time the unit is assessed.

Table 6.1 *Design Exam assessment criteria*

Assessment criteria	Marks
a) Analyse the design problem and develop a product design specification, identifying appropriate constraints	15
b) Generate and evaluate a range of ideas	15
c) Develop, describe and justify a final solution, identifying appropriate materials and components	15
d) Represent and illustrate your final solution	20
e) Draw up a production plan for your final solution	15
f) Evaluate your final solution against the product design specification and suggest improvements	10
Total marks	**90**

3. The Design Exam

Your centre will be sent a Design Research Paper at least six weeks before the exam. This paper will give you a context for design, together with bullet points that give you direction about what to research.

The Design Paper will have one design problem that is based on the research context. In the assessment criteria a)–f) you are asked to:

- analyse the design problem, making connections between it and your research
- develop a product design specification in response to the problem and your research
- generate and evaluate a range of ideas based on your product design specification
- develop, describe and justify a final solution, identifying appropriate materials and components
- illustrate your final solution using dimensioned drawings and give details and quantities of materials and components
- draw up a production plan for your final solution, including manufacturing processes, the sequence of assembly and quality checks
- evaluate your final solution against your product design specification and suggest how it could be improved.

You may take *all* your research material into the exam and use it as reference throughout, but this is *not* submitted for assessment. The pasting of pre-prepared or photocopied sheets is *not* permitted. You will *not* be allowed to use ICT facilities during the examination.

You will be provided with answer sheets that will be all that you need to answer the Design Paper. More answer sheets may be used if absolutely necessary. You may separate the answer sheets, but must secure them with a treasury tag at the end of the exam. Suggested times for each section of the exam are given at the foot of each answer sheet.

4. How much is it worth?

The Design Paper is worth 15 per cent of the full Advanced GCE.

Unit 6	Weighting
A2 level (full GCE)	15%

Unit 6 requirements in detail

Synoptic assessment

This unit is called is called Design and Technology Capability, because it assesses the knowledge, understanding and skills you have learned throughout the course. Although no new learning takes place in Unit 6, you are expected to develop a 'synoptic understanding' of what you have already learned. In other words you are developing an overview of the knowledge and understanding related to your design and technology course, so that you can make *connections* between individual bits of learning.

This is how industrial designers work, making connections in order to develop their own creativity. For example they need to be aware of past, current and future trends, user and market requirements and keep up-to-date with events, films, exhibitions, current affairs, environmental and cultural issues. They must also develop, on a regular basis, a creative and technical understanding of materials and processes.

Unit 6 assessment

You are expected to apply your synoptic understanding of the whole course content to a given problem in the Design Exam. The exam has to take place at the end of the final year of the Advanced GCE course, so that it can assess all your learning. Unit 6 assesses the application of the following types of learning:

- knowledge and understanding of product development and manufacture
- knowledge and understanding of markets, users, materials, components, systems, processes, technology, scale of production, quality, health and safety, cultural, social, moral and environmental issues.

The unit also assesses quality of written communication. You should:

- use clear drawings and sketches
- answer clearly and coherently, using specialist terms where appropriate
- use accurate spelling, grammar and punctuation to make your meaning clear.

You are advised to practise exam skills to ensure that you are familiar with and understand the assessment requirements. This will enable you to fulfil your potential in the Design Exam.

Design Research Paper

The Design Research Paper will follow the same format each year. You will be given a context for design, together with bullet points that give you direction about what to research. This means that you will have a good idea of what to expect in the exam and can research appropriate areas. An example is given in the box below:

> Garden plants and trees have to be pruned regularly to keep them trim. Investigate the problem of pruning and cutting back garden plants, looking at the following specific areas:
>
> - the cutting mechanism
> - the handle and the activating mechanism at the bottom of the cutter
> - the system that links the two
> - the materials used.

The examiners do not want you to go into the Design Exam to find that you have researched the wrong information or to find the exam problem a complete surprise. As well as targeting your research around the specific areas indicated in the Design Research Paper, you should take into account the assessment criteria. For example the exam asks you to develop a product design specification, so make sure that you understand how to do this.

Design Paper

The Design Paper will have one design problem that is based on the context you have researched. An example is given in the box below:

> Your task is to design a method of cutting back the higher branches on tall trees.

Helpful hints

When you undertake an exam of this type you need to keep your eye on the time. Suggested times are printed at the bottom of each answer sheet. You also need to match your responses to the available marks; the more marks available the more work you need to do.

a) Analyse the design problem and develop a product design specification, identifying appropriate constraints (15 marks)

Research the context

SIGNPOST
'Aesthetics' section a) Unit 1 page 15
'Carry out imaginative research
'Product Appeal' section g) Unit 1 page 38
Unit 2 page 45, Unit 5 page 297

You should have access to the Design Research Paper at least six weeks before the exam. Read and analyse the design context, so you have a clear understanding of what you need to do. You should take responsibility for planning, organising, managing and analysing your own research.

The clear guidelines given in the Design Research Paper should enable you to target your research. This should include a variety of primary and secondary research, using a range of sources, such as the following:

- market research to identify trends and user requirements
- analysis of commercial products and the work of other designers
- research into materials, components, systems, processes and technologies
- research into legal requirements and external standards relating to quality and safety
- research into values issues, such as cultural, social, moral and environmental issues that may have an impact on the problem.

You will find it helpful to think of your research as being part of a design process that you will continue into the exam. Your research information may include notes, images, data, materials information, anthropometric and British Standards data. If, by chance, the question in the Design Exam should bring up something that you haven't researched in enough detail, you can refer to any other available material, since this is an 'open book' exam. However, this may have a drawback, in that looking up any more information at this stage could take up far too much of your valuable time, so you may be better off working with what you have.

You should analyse your research information before the exam, so you are familiar with it. Organise your research information under the same headings as the design specification criteria. Write a conclusion to each section of your research. This process will fully prepare you for the exam.

SIGNPOST
'Exploring problems and clarifying tasks'
Unit 2 page 43, Unit 5 page 295

Analyse the problem

In the exam you should read the Design Paper carefully so that you have a clear understanding of the design problem you have to solve. You will need to demonstrate this understanding through an analysis of the problem. An example of a design problem is given in the box below:

> Your task is to design a method of cutting back the higher branches on tall trees.

An analysis of the above task would be specific to the problem of cutting back the higher branches on tall trees. The analysis would need to:

- take account of the specific areas investigated, such as the cutting mechanism, handle, activating mechanism at the bottom of the cutter, the system that links the two and the materials used
- make reference to the research material that was collected.

Your analysis should be specific to the set design problem. A generic analysis will gain very few, if any marks. What is the specific need or problem? Where will the product be used? How will it be used? Who are the potential users? Your analysis should indicate the key points of the problem. This will show that you have a clear understanding about what is required. Analysis may be carried out in a variety of styles, with spider diagrams often being the most successful. Figure 6.1 shows how one student analysed a design problem.

Analyse the design problem (6)

Environmental issues:
• Use recycled materials
• Life-cycle analysis - what happens at end of life?

Quality:
• Should be well made and finished
• Quality checks within manufacture

User and target market:
• Home DIY enthusiasts - easy to use
• Suitable for men and women
• Suitable for right and left handed people
• Suitable for all drills
• (Average Ø43mm collar)
• Suitable price for home DIY
• Able to fit all sizes of workbench

Scale of production:
• High demand so mass production required
• Suitable materials for mass production

Performance:
• Should be durable - for home workshop environment
• Buttons for drill must be accessible
• Possible to dismantle!
• Easy storage
• Size - not too large

Processes:
• Mass production
• Material availability

CLAMPING A DRILL TO A BENCH TO MAKE A PILLAR DRILL

Legal requirements:
• Meets British and international safety standards:
• BS50144-2 - safety of handheld drills
• BS5750 - finish
• ISO 9000 - quality

Purpose:
• To allow safe drilling in a domestic environment
• To convert a handheld drill into a pillar drill

Cultural, social and moral issues:
• Incorporate different electrical systems
• Different sizes for different countries
• Does not offend anyone

Function:
• Hold the drill to the desk securely
• Allow for the drill to be lowered and raised
• Should be easy to operate - inexperienced user?

Figure 6.1 Analysis needs to ensure that six relevant aspects of the design problem are highlighted, together with at least three points of expansion/justification for each aspect highlighted

Making connections

Your analysis of the problem should be a short task. It should enable you to make clear connections between the design problem and what you have researched. This will make it easier to pinpoint relevant information that will help you develop a product design specification. In the exam you should *not* copy out any research materials. Your ability to research the context and to analyse your research material will be assessed through the quality of your analysis and product design specification.

Although you can use your research material in the exam you are *not* allowed to paste, stick or staple any pre-prepared or photocopied work onto your answer sheets. Although it may be appropriate to use ICT for research, you will not be allowed to use ICT facilities during the examination.

Develop a product design specification, identifying appropriate constraints

SIGNPOST
'Develop a design specification'
Unit 2 page 46, Unit 5 page 298

Your product design specification is important because it forms the basis for generating and evaluating your design ideas *and* for evaluating your final solution. The specification headings are printed at the top of your answer sheet and you should use them to provide a framework for your written product design specification.

Your specification criteria should be *specific* to the requirements of the set design problem and should demonstrate how your research and analysis have helped you make decisions about what your product will be like. Your specification criteria should be written as short, reasoned sentences that explain the requirements of the product that you will design in response to the design problem. (See the example of a design specification in Figure 6.2.)

Identify constraints and attributes to develop your product design specification (9)
SPECIFICATION
The holding system must:
• *Hold the handheld power drill securely*
• *Incorporate a mechanism so the drill can be lowered and raised*
• *Be securely attached to the workbench*
• *Be safe to use and comply with the relevant safety standards - see 'Legal requirements'*
• *Be relatively simple to operate*
• *Be comfortable for the user to use*
• *Be universal for all drills available (average 43mm Ø collar)*
• *Be a durable product able to withstand wear and tear of workshop*
• *Meet the DIY enthusiast market and be suitable for them to use*
• *Be easy to store*
• *Accommodate both cord and battery pack drills*
• *Be able to be mass produced to provide a low cost solution*
• *Be good aesthetically - to fit in with workshop environment but maybe to fit in with a brand image - colouring/style etc*
• *Be easily cleaned of sawdust, etc.*
• *Allow for all the relevant buttons to be accessible when in use*
• *Fit a variety of sizes of workbench*
• *Be a marketable, affordable product.*

Figure 6.2 *Identifying constraints and attributes to develop your product design specification*

The printed specification headings ask you to develop the following criteria:

- purpose: what the product is for
- function: what the product needs to do
- aesthetics: how the product should look, its style, form and aesthetic characteristics
- market and user requirements: market trends, user needs and preferences and ergonomic constraints
- performance requirements of the product, materials, components and systems: mechanical properties and working characteristics
- processes, technology and scale of production: manufacturing processes and technology required to make the product at an appropriate level of production; either batch or mass production
- quality control: the quality requirements of your product (and target market) and how you will achieve quality using quality control and quality standards
- legal requirements and external standards: how the product will meet safety requirements, referencing external standards where appropriate (British Standards are *not* to be copied out)
- cultural, social, moral and environmental issues that may influence your design ideas.

Helpful hints

There is a suggested time of 30 minutes available for section a) which is worth 15 marks. Check out how many marks are available for analysing the design problem and how many marks are available for developing the product design specification. Spend an appropriate amount of time on each activity so you have the opportunity to achieve the available marks.

b) Generate and evaluate a range of design ideas. Use appropriate communication techniques and justify decisions made (15 marks)

Generate a range of design ideas

SIGNPOST
'Generating ideas'
Unit 2 page 47, Unit 5 page 299

You are expected to generate a minimum of three feasible design ideas in response to the given design problem and your specification. Initial ideas should be in the form of good quality sketches, with annotation in sufficient detail to demonstrate your understanding of commercial methods of processing and fabrication. Make sure that your annotation is *specific* to your chosen materials and avoid the use of terms such as 'plastic' or 'metal'. You should instead be referencing specific materials such as acrylic, aluminium or plywood and specific processes such as injection moulding or casting. This is your opportunity to make use of your research information and to demonstrate what you have learned during your course.

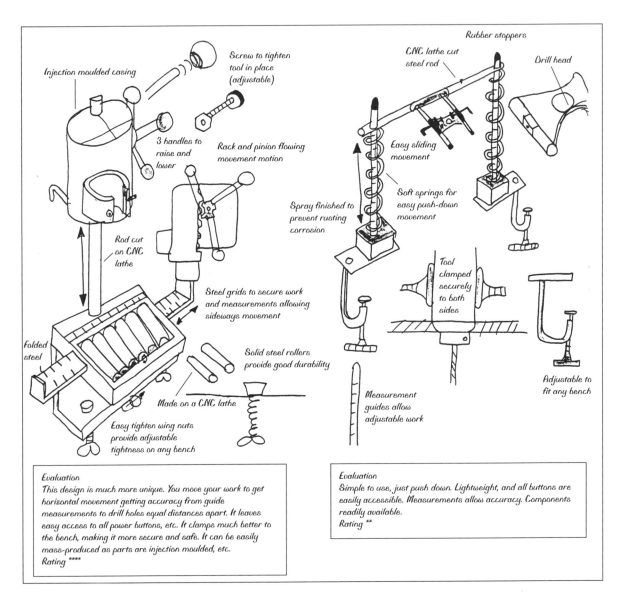

Figure 6.3 *Generating and evaluating ideas for a holding system for a handheld power drill*

SIGNPOST
'Use knowledge and understanding gained through research to develop and refine ideas'
Unit 2 page 48, Unit 5 page 300

You are expected to generate your own ideas; drawing and developing an existing product will not gain the available marks. Your choice of scale of production is also very important, because you need to evidence your under-standing of commercial methods of production. You should therefore be designing for batch or high volume production, not a one-off product.

Making use of the information you acquired during your research should enable you to develop a number of alternative design ideas and select one (or possibly two) that are the most promising. Figure 6.3 shows how one student generated ideas.

At this stage the examiner is looking for evidence of your design thinking in response to the requirements of your product design specification and your knowledge and understanding of materials and manufacturing processes. You will also gain marks for quality of communication, so make sure that you practice your drawing skills in advance of the examination.

Evaluate design ideas and justify decisions made

SIGNPOST
'Evaluate and test the feasibility of ideas against specification criteria'
Unit 2 page 49, Unit 5 page 301

All first ideas should be evaluated against the key points of your product design specification. The design or designs chosen for development should be explained and justified, using written notes. Refer back to your product design specification; how will your ideas meet the requirements you set out to achieve? Which are the best ideas and why?

You should, at the very least, provide a sensible justification of each of your ideas by explaining the pro's and con's of each.

Helpful hints

There is a suggested time of 30 minutes available for section b) which is worth 15 marks. Make sure you allow sufficient time to annotate your sketches and to justify which ideas are worth developing in section c).

c) Develop, describe and justify a final solution, identifying appropriate materials and components (15 marks)

Develop a final solution, identifying appropriate materials and components

SIGNPOST
'Developing and communicating design proposals'
Unit 2 page 50, Unit 5 page 302

In this section you are asked to produce 2D and/or 3D sketches that develop and refine your initial design idea(s). It is not appropriate to simply redraw your best idea from section b). The examiner is looking for clear evidence of how you have adapted and changed the characteristics of your initial ideas so the final solution will better meet the needs of your product design specification criteria. You should use a good graphic style to communicate the aesthetic and mechanical

SIGNPOST
'Demonstrate a wide variety of communication skills
Unit 2 page 50, Unit 5 page 302

aspects of your design. It is often helpful to use a backing sheet of isometric paper as a guide for 3D sketches.

You should annotate your 2D and/or 3D sketches to explain any hidden details, to evidence aspects of the product function and to explain the aesthetic, physical and mechanical properties of your chosen materials and components. Demonstrate your understanding of materials and commercial manufacturing processes through the use of appropriate technical terms. Your sketches should provide sufficient detail to explain how the product will work or function mechanically. Figure 6.4 shows how one student developed a final solution.

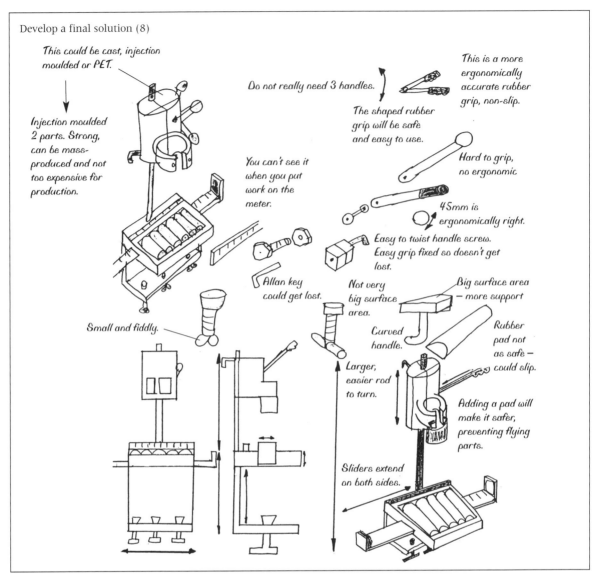

Develop a final solution (8)

This could be cast, injection moulded or PET.

Injection moulded 2 parts. Strong, can be mass-produced and not too expensive for production.

Do not really need 3 handles.

This is a more ergonomically accurate rubber grip, non-slip.

The shaped rubber grip will be safe and easy to use.

You can't see it when you put work on the meter.

Hard to grip, no ergonomic

45mm is ergonomically right.

Easy to twist handle screw. Easy grip fixed so doesn't get lost.

Allan key could get lost.

Not very big surface area.

Big surface area – more support

Small and fiddly.

Curved handle.

Larger, easier rod to turn.

Rubber pad not as safe – could slip.

Adding a pad will make it safer, preventing flying parts.

Sliders extend on both sides.

Figure 6.4 *Developing a final solution for a holding system for a handheld power drill*

SIGNPOST
'Justify the use of materials and components' Unit 1 page 17 'Demonstrate understanding of a range of materials and components' Unit 2 page 52, Unit 5 page 305 'Working properties of materials' Unit 3A page 79 'Selecting materials' Unit 4A page 178

Describe and justify your final solution

In the second part of section c) you are asked to describe and justify your final solution. This is *not* a re-run of your design specification, so you should not be describing what the product

should do, but explaining *why* and *how* the design you have developed is *the best solution* to the problem.

The most effective way to do this is to list and respond to the headings printed at the top of your answer sheet. You should use short reasoned sentences to describe and justify your design solution in relation to:

• function; how your product design meets the functional/mechanical aspects of your product design specification
• appearance; how the aesthetic characteristics of your product design meets the look, style, form and characteristics outlined in your specification
• performance; how your product design meets the quality and safety requirements

of the market and users outlined in your specification
- materials, components and systems; how the working characteristics of your chosen materials, components and/or systems meet the requirements of your specification
- processes; how suitable your chosen manufacturing processes are for the scale of production stated in your specification
- technological features; how modern technology such as the use of CAD/CAM and ICT could enable efficient manufacture of your final design solution.

Once again you will be making *connections* between what you set out to achieve (your product design specification) and how you hope to achieve it (your final design solution). It would be helpful to have your specification in front of you when you describe and justify your final solution, so that the points you make are relevant to the design problem. Figure 6.5 shows how one student described and justified a final solution.

Helpful hints

There is a suggested time of 30 minutes available for section c) which is worth 15 marks. Check out how many marks are available for your final design solution (you will lose marks if there is no development) and how many marks are available for its justification (you will gain more marks if you use accurate and appropriate technical terms). Spend an appropriate amount of time on each activity so you have the opportunity to achieve the available marks.

Describe and justify your final solution, referring where appropriate to:
- Function
- Appearance
- Processes
- Performance
- Technological features
- Components/Systems
- Materials

I have designed a solution like this with adjustable height for the tool so that any thickness of material can be used. The material I have used is mild steel mainly because it is durable and strong. The rollers allow horizontal movement, which I chose because it is simple but very effective in moving work sideways for efficient use. I chose to use a spray finish on all steel surfaces to make it fit in with others and give the look of quality. I designed the handle with ergonomics in mind, making it easy to use and grip for efficient use. The clamping bolts are large and made from steel so this will ensure that the unit fits to the workbench safely and securely as specified. The casing is injection moulded because it will be hardwearing and easy to batch/mass produce. The base is made from steel that has been folded. I chose this because it means there are fewer joints, making the solution stronger with less chance of flaws. There are movements on the vertical and horizontal rulers to make the solution easy to use to get work accurate to the nearest mm. The rack and pinion movement method was chosen as it allows for steady flowing movement providing a good mechanical system.

Figure 6.5 *Describe and justify your final solution*

SIGNPOST
'Evaluate design proposals against specification criteria'
Unit 2 page 54, Unit 5 page 306

d) Represent and illustrate your final solution (20 marks)

Represent and illustrate your final solution

SIGNPOST
'Demonstrate a wide variety of communication skills' Unit 2 page 50, Unit 5 page 302

This section asks for you to 'represent and illustrate' your final design solution, using:
- clear construction/making details
- dimensions/sizes
- details and quantity of materials/components

- clear and appropriate communication techniques.

Do not be confused about this, as it is *not* a repeat of the previous section c) or a catalogue-style illustration in full colour! You should instead produce good quality dimensioned drawings of your final design solution using clear and appropriate drawing techniques that show how to manufacture the product, together with details and quantity of your chosen materials and components.

Orthographic 3rd angle drawings are not required in the Design Exam. Your ability to produce fully dimensioned working drawings is

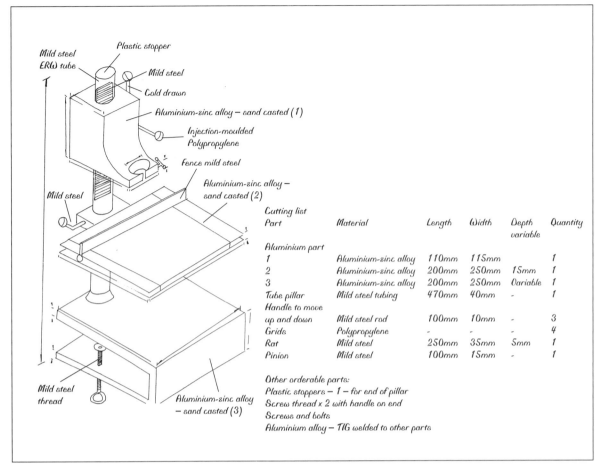

Mild steel
ERW tube

Plastic stopper

Mild steel

Cold drawn

Aluminium-zinc alloy – sand casted (1)

Injection-moulded
Polypropylene

Fence mild steel

Aluminium-zinc alloy –
sand casted (2)

Mild steel

Mild steel
thread

Aluminium-zinc alloy
– sand casted (3)

Cutting list					
Part	Material	Length	Width	Depth variable	Quantity
Aluminium part					
1	Aluminium-zinc alloy	110mm	115mm		1
2	Aluminium-zinc alloy	200mm	250mm	15mm	1
3	Aluminium-zinc alloy	200mm	250mm	Variable	1
Tube pillar	Mild steel tubing	470mm	40mm	-	1
Handle to move up and down	Mild steel rod	100mm	10mm	-	3
Grids	Polypropylene	-	-	-	4
Rat	Mild steel	250mm	35mm	5mm	1
Pinion	Mild steel	100mm	15mm	-	1

Other orderable parts:
Plastic stoppers – 1 – for end of pillar
Screw thread x 2 with handle on end
Screws and bolts
Aluminium alloy – TIG welded to other parts

Figure 6.6 *Representing and illustrating the final solution*

tested in your coursework. However, in the exam your drawings should provide sufficient detail for the examiner to understand how your final design solution is to be manufactured in an appropriate scale of production.

Appropriate graphic techniques could include dimensioned drawings that show different views of the product and exploded drawings that show any hidden details. Make sure that your dimensions conform to British Standards. You should also include a conventional style cutting list that shows details and quantities of the materials and components required to manufacture your final design solution.

Remember that marks are available in this section for the use of clear and appropriate communication techniques and for good use of technical terms that demonstrate your understanding of industrial manufacture. Figure 6.6 shows how one student represented and illustrated the final design solution.

Helpful hints

There is a suggested time of 40 minutes available for section d) which is worth 20 marks, making this the highest scoring section in the Design Exam. Check out how many marks are available in this section for:

- clear construction/making details
- dimensioned drawings of your final design solution
- a cutting list with details and quantities of the materials and components required
- clear and appropriate communication techniques.

Spend an appropriate amount of time on your drawings and cutting list so you have the opportunity to achieve the available marks.

e) Draw up a production plan for your final solution (15 marks)

SIGNPOST
'Produce a clear production plan' Unit 2 page 54, Unit 5 page 307

Draw up a production plan

This section of the Design Paper asks you to draw up a production plan that describes the production requirements of the solution to include:

* assembly processes/unit operations
* sequence of assembly/work order
* quality checks

In your coursework units you produced very detailed plans for the manufacture of your product. In the Design Paper however, you should produce a simple production plan to show:

* the main industrial/commercial manufacturing processes you intend to use to produce the elements of your assembly
* clear sequencing of your proposed assembly with specific commercial assembly techniques
* quality checks performed at specific stages of manufacture and assembly.

The type of processes and assembly required will depend on your chosen materials *and* the scale of production identified in your product design specification. For example, a high volume product with thermoplastic component parts may require the use of injection or blow moulding and limited finish.

On the other hand a batch-produced child's wooden toy with a number of identical component parts may require the use of simplified fabrication and assembly methods and a high quality finish.

It is not advisable to combine one-off and mass production methods in your production plan, because it will signal to the examiner your lack of manufacturing understanding. Instead you should concentrate your efforts on the use of batch or high volume production techniques and the use of appropriate technical terms. These may include references to technological features, for example, how the use of CAD/CAM could enable efficient manufacture of your final design solution.

Your production plan should be clearly organised if you are to demonstrate your manufacturing understanding to the examiner. You are more likely to achieve higher marks in section e) if you use a flow diagram to show the sequencing of your proposed assembly, with details of specific materials, commercial manufacturing processes and quality control checks.

Quality control

SIGNPOST
'Quality control' Unit 1 section d) page 35
'Devise quality assurance procedures'
Unit 2 page 62, Unit 5 page 312

Quality control is an important aspect of your production planning. Refer back to the quality control criteria in your specification. It may help to remember an industry saying that 'quality cannot be manufactured into a product, it has to be designed into it'. Make sure that any comments you make about quality control refer to your specific product manufacture, rather than being generalised comments about how 'checks should be made at certain stages'. You need to state exactly where and how you will check for quality by identifying:

* the critical control points (CCPs) *where* you will check for quality and accuracy
* quality indicators that describe *how* you will check for quality. For example, will you use dimensions and tolerances to check the accuracy or fit of joints or mechanisms? Will you check quality against specific aspects of the product design specification? Will you use sensory checks of touch and vision to check the finish?

Figure 6.7 shows how one student drew up a production plan.

Helpful hints
There is a suggested time of 30 minutes available for section e) which is worth 15 marks. In order to achieve the available marks you must address all the headings printed at the top of your answer sheet, including the manufacturing processes used to produce the elements of your assembly, sequence of assembly and quality checks.

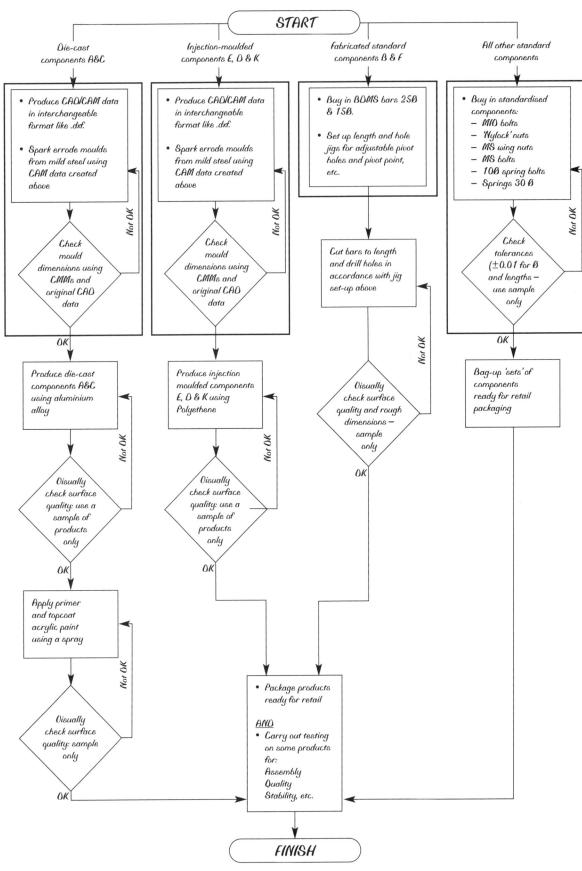

Figure 6.7 A production plan

f) Evaluate your final solution against the product design specification and suggest improvements (10 marks)

Evaluate your final solution against the product design specification

SIGNPOST
'Objectively evaluate the outcome against specifications and suggest improvements'
Unit 2 page 63   Unit 5 page 313

The last section of the Design Exam asks you to evaluate your final solution against your product design specification and suggest improvements. Efficient time management throughout the exam will ensure that you have sufficient time to complete this section.

Your evaluative comments should be objective and justified in order to achieve the available marks. If you evaluate your final solution against your product design specification you will have something to measure your product design against. How could you test the product to ensure it performs in use? What kind of tests would be appropriate? How well will any mechanisms function? How safe will it be to use? Are your chosen materials sufficiently durable to enable the product to meet its quality requirements? Could you make identical products? How and why? What are the product's best features in relation to the design specification? In what way is it a marketable product? Figure 6.8 shows how one student evaluated the final design solution.

Suggest improvements

SIGNPOST
'Product appeal' Unit 1, section g) page 38
'Developing a commercial approach'
Unit 5 page 295

You should suggest realistic improvements that would enable your product to better meet the needs of your product design specification. This

---

Evaluation: The final and completed drill holder has had to fulfil the specifications of the project.

Purpose and function: Firstly, it functions perfectly as an item that houses a standard handheld drill, and has the ability to provide vertical movement at 90°.

Market and user requirements: The design of the product accommodates the different sizes of drill - it does this by using the adjustable clamp. It covers the 5-95% of human sizes, so complies with anthropometrics. The lever is comfy and provides accuracy. The handle has also had the sharp edges removed, reducing risks to health and safety.

Quality control: The production of the device incorporated many quality checks to enable a high-quality finished product. This will help increase user expectations.

Performance requirements: The structure itself is very sturdy and still stable when bearing lots of weight. It also has the option of being attached to a workbench. The drill holder has a form of mechanical advantage that holds and moves the drill out at 90° and is still accurate. This is done by a lever system. Due to the drill holder being produced in many parts it is quick and easy to set up.

Environmental issues: The components of my design can be separated, thus enabling each part to be recycled.

Legal requirements: If the drill holder was going into production, then it would qualify for external standards.

Modifications: If the product was to enter the market at mass production level, then a few changes would have to be made.

Firstly I would incorporate many different-sized pins. This would enable a maximum range of movement for a large number of different drills.

Secondly, I would change metal clamps to plastic ones – this would keep the price of production down as well as weight.

Another modification is a device that leaves everything locked when the drill is not in use. This would reduce the danger aspect of the drill and keep things together when they are not being used.

Another modification is to enclose the springs in metal tubing. This would be done for two reasons, the first being to keep the springs protected from damage, and the second is to prevent the users' fingers getting trapped.

A final modification would be to allow for bigger uprights, depending on the size of the component you are drilling.

Figure 6.8 *Part of an evaluation of the final solution*

may include improvements in response to the performance, quality, safety, market and user needs that you identified. How could any of these aspects be improved? What changes could you make to your product design to make its manufacture more efficient in relation to your chosen scale of production? How could you make use of modern materials and/or modern technology, including the use of CAD/CAM, automation or robotics to enable more efficient manufacture of your product?

Helpful hints

There is a suggested time of 20 minutes available for section f), which is worth 10 marks. Check how many marks are available for evaluating the final solution and how many marks are available for suggesting improvements. Spend an appropriate amount of time on each activity so you have the opportunity to achieve the available marks.

Exam practice

Revise what you have learned

Revising and reviewing what you have learned during your advanced level course will help you prepare for the Unit 6 exam. In Unit 6 you will find 'Signposts' that refer you back to other AS and A2 units. It would also be helpful to re-read your Unit 1 notes about industrial practices, such as specification development, scale of production, manufacturing processes, quality, health and safety.

Practice doing timed design tasks

You should be familiar with all of the design processes that you will follow during the exam. They are similar to those that you used in your coursework.

Read the whole of Unit 6, so you are absolutely clear about the exam requirements. Practice doing timed design tasks that correspond to the design processes you will follow in the Design Exam.

a. Analyse
- Analyse a design problem set by your teacher or tutor.
- Analyse a body of research information related to the design problem; perhaps downloaded from the Internet, from CD-ROMs or from textbooks.
- Develop a product design specification based on the design problem and your research.

Exam tip
Analyse your own research before the exam, so you are familiar with it. Make a list of the product design specification criteria and organise your research information under the same headings. Write a conclusion to each section of your research. This process will fully prepare you for the exam. Practise developing product design specifications.

b. Generate ideas
- Generate a range of design ideas based on your product design specification and research.
- Evaluate the feasibility of each idea against your product design specification.
- Justify the design you have selected for development.

Exam tip
Practice producing quick design ideas in a set time. Always annotate your drawings and give reasons for your design decisions. Always make use of your product design specification when evaluating design ideas.

c. Develop ideas
- Develop a chosen idea into a workable solution.
- Describe and justify the solution in terms of its purpose, function, appearance, performance, quality, safety, the materials, components, systems, processes and technological features to be used.

Exam tip
Show how your ideas develop by annotating your drawings. Explain your thoughts about your chosen idea. How does it meet the specification requirements? How might it be made? Will it be easy and practical to make? Are the manufacturing processes appropriate to the scale of production? Are any parts or components the same size or shape? Can their manufacture be easily repeated? Can you use any bought-in parts or components?

d. Represent and illustrate the solution
- Illustrate and annotate the solution using 2D or 3D drawings.
- Use exploded drawings to show hidden details.
- Include dimensions and sizes of component parts.
- Provide details and quantities of materials and components.

Exam tip
Annotate your drawings so an examiner can understand how you intend the product to be made. You are *not* required to produce a full working drawing in the exam.

e. Production plan
Describe how to make the product. Include the following:
- commercial manufacturing processes
- the sequence of assembly
- quality checks.

Exam tip
Produce a flow diagram to show the sequence of assembly for the product. Describe the manufacturing processes and show where and how you would check for quality.

f. Evaluate
Evaluate your solution against your product design specification, suggest how your product could be tested after manufacture and suggest realistic improvements.

Exam tip
Suggest improvements to the design and manufacture of your product so it better meets the needs of your specification.

Practice doing a complete timed exam

Practice a complete exam, working to the same time and under the same conditions as the Unit 6 Design Exam. Choose from the following four Design Research Papers and corresponding Design Papers. Use the assessment criteria and marks below to help you.

Table 6.2 Assessment criteria

Assessment criteria	Marks
a) Analyse the design problem and develop a product design specification, identifying appropriate constraints	15
b) Generate and evaluate a range of ideas	15
c) Develop, describe and justify a final solution, identifying appropriate materials and components	15
d) Represent and illustrate your final solution	20
e) Draw up a production plan for your final solution	15
f) Evaluate your final solution against the product design specification and suggest improvements	10
Total marks	90

Design Research Paper 1

Some people say that interior design follows the colour and styling influences of high street fashion. Investigate the following specific areas:

- colour and style trends in the interiors market
- domestic knock down seating
- aesthetic and functional requirements of new home owners.

Design Paper 1

Your task is to design inexpensive seating that can be used in a modern kitchen area.

Design Research Paper 2

A clock manufacturer wants to promote sales by developing a new range of modern wall clocks. Investigate the following specific areas:

- wall clocks currently on the market for young children
- technologies and materials used in wall clocks
- the use of clocks as a teaching aid.

Design Paper 2

Your task is to design a wall clock that is suitable for teaching young children to tell the time.

Design Research Paper 3

Home DIY enthusiasts often need a means of securing handheld power tools to the workbench. Investigate:

- ergonomics associated with a range of power tools
- mechanisms that enable vertical and horizontal movements in workshop machines
- methods of securing equipment to work benches
- locking power tools to workbenches.

Design Paper 3

Your task is to design a holding system for a handheld power drill that will convert it into a bench mounted pillar drill.

Design Research Paper 4

A torch manufacturer needs to update the design and manufacture of torches required by young people undertaking outdoor pursuits. Investigate the following specific areas:

- design styles of existing torches
- technologies and materials used in torches
- the promotion of torches and batteries.

Design Paper 4

Your task is to design a torch suitable for use by young people who undertake outdoor pursuits. The torch will be marketed to promote the sale of the manufacturer's own brand of batteries.

Student checklist

1. Understanding the research context

- Make sure that you read the Design Research Paper carefully so you have a clear understanding of what you need to research.
- Take responsibility for planning, organising, managing and analysing your own research.
- Make sure that you analyse your research *before* the exam.

2. Preparing for the design exam

- Review what you have learned about designing and making products.
- Practise doing timed design tasks that correspond to the different sections of the exam paper.
- Practise doing a complete timed exam.
- Make sure that you understand the assessment requirements, so you will know how much time to spend on each section of the exam paper.

3. Evidencing your capability in the design exam

- Produce a short analysis of the problem you are asked to solve.
- Show the influence of your research in your product design specification.
- Show clearly how your ideas unfold. Annotate your drawings.
- Demonstrate a variety of communication skills, including graphics, diagrams, flowcharts and written work.
- Allow enough time to evaluate your work as it progresses.
- Use industrial terminology and technical terms to demonstrate your understanding of commercial manufacture.

4. Exam hints

- Collect together all drawing and writing materials and practise any drawing techniques you may need to use.
- Prepare a backing sheet with heavy lines as a guide for written work.
- Prepare a backing sheet of isometric paper as a guide for 3D sketches.

- Collect together all your sketch books, folios, notebooks and technical data compiled as part of your exam research. You may also refer to any relevant British Standards. Be sure to analyse your research *before* the exam.
- During the exam you will be provided with headed answer sheets. Extra sheets may be used if *absolutely* necessary. Be sure to write your name and number and centre name and number on any extra sheets you use. Remember to fasten together all your answer sheets *in the correct sequence* with a treasury tag at the end of the examination.

5. Exam day

- Arrive half an hour before the exam to get yourself organised.
- Read the exam question carefully and identify key points in the question. Do not copy out the design problem.
- Use a pencil or pen for writing and sketching. Try not to rub bits out, as it is better if the examiner can see your thinking. Take a pencil sharpener with you.
- Only use colour after you have completed a section, or spend the last ten minutes adding colour.
- If you make a mistake or go completely wrong, state it and attempt to get back on the right track. Do not throw away any work as it will be helpful for the examiner to see your 'design thinking'.
- You will be assessed on your ability to organise and present information, ideas, descriptions and arguments clearly and logically. You will get marks for quality of communication.

Help! What if my project goes wrong?

- If your Unit 6 design exam doesn't meet your expectations, don't worry! Your teacher or tutor will be able to advise you on the best way forward.

Glossary

A

Adjustable sensing inputs – transducers configured in potential dividers to sense changes in the surrounding environment and produce an electrical signal accordingly.

Advertising – any type of paid-for media that is designed to inform and influence existing or potential customers.

Advertising Standards Authority (ASA) – regulates all British advertising in non-broadcast media.

Aerobic – an oxygenated environment. Aerobic biological processes use micro-organisms that need oxygen to degrade organic industrial waste to carbon dioxide and biomass.

Age hardening – a material may become harder as heat is applied.

American National Standards Institute (ANSI) – administrator and coordinator of the United States voluntary standardisation system founded in 1918.

Anaerobic – an oxygen-free environment. Anaerobic biological processes use micro-organisms and biofilters to degrade industrial waste to methane, carbon dioxide and biomass.

Analogue signals – type of electronic signal that can exist at any level between the two extreme points of high and low

Annealing – the process that relieves internal stresses within a material as a result of cold working.

Artificial intelligence (AI) – a branch of computer science concerned with developing computers that think/act like humans.

B

Bandwidth – the amount of HYPERLINK 'data.html' data that can be transmitted or received in a fixed amount of time; expressed in bits per second (bps) for digital devices. The higher the bandwidth the faster the rate of data transfer. See 'ISDN'.

Bar code (data communication tag) – machine-readable pattern of stripes printed on a component part or a finished product to identify it for production processes, stock control, pricing or retail sales.

Binary signal – a digital signal with only two values: high ('on' or '1') or low ('off' or '0').

Bioremediation – a biological process, where naturally occurring microbes or additional micro-organisms are used to clean up land that is contaminated with potentially degradable organic material.

Biotechnology – uses naturally occurring proteins called enzymes to produce environmentally friendly waste treatment processes and to develop new products. The use of yeast in bread is an early example of biotechnology.

Blow moulding – the process of using air, under pressure, to give form to products by 'blowing' plasticised material into moulds.

Braking systems – mechanical systems that make use of brakes to arrest motion.

Brand – a product or process with a marketing identity that belongs to one producer.

Brand loyalty – involves buying a chosen brand of product, because it provides a perceived level of reliability or quality.

Brand name – (also trade-mark or trade name) protects and promotes the identity of a product or process, so that it can't be copied by a competitor. A branded product usually has additional features or added value over other generic products – making it 'special' in the eyes of consumers.

Break-even point – point at which products sold at a certain price will equal in value the cost of their manufacture.

British Standards Institution (BSI) – an independent, non-profit-making and impartial body that serves both the private and public sectors. BSI works with manufacturing and service industries to develop British, European and International standards.

Buy in – components or sub-assemblies that are purchased from another manufacturer for use within a product, e.g. a gearbox may be bought in by a car manufacturer.

Buying behaviour – establishes how people make buying decisions and factors that influence these decisions.

C

CAD modelling – involves a number of representation techniques such as vector or raster graphics. Models are used for variety of purposes ranging from a simple record of a design with critical manufacturing dimensions through to a fully interactive simulated product or system model that can be viewed in operation.

Capacitor – an electronic device that is capable of storing an electronic charge.

CEN – the European Committee for Standardisation. It implements the voluntary technical harmonisation of standards in Europe, in conjunction with world-wide bodies and European partners.

CENELEC – the European Committee for Electro-technical Standardisation.

Cleaner design – aimed at reducing the overall environmental impact of a product from 'cradle to grave'.

Cleaner technology – the use of equipment or techniques that produce less waste or emissions than conventional methods. It reduces the consumption of raw materials, water and energy and lowers costs for waste treatment and disposal.

Closed question – provides a limited number of possible answers to choose from.

Closed-loop system – a system that has a degree of feedback built into it that enables a degree of checking to see whether actions or processes have been carried out.

Clutch – type of shaft coupling that allows a rotating shaft to be easily connected or disconnected from a second shaft.

Cold forming – processes that do not use heat to soften or plasticise material.

Compatibility – hardware and software applications capable of being used in combination without any technical problems. If systems are compatible, computers can 'talk' to other computers and to equipment such as CNC machines.

Competitive edge – the reason why a customer might choose a certain product rather than its competitors.

Components – the parts of a product that go to make up the whole.

Compound gear train – a series of gears connected together, some on common shafts, which allow rotational speeds to be increased or decreased.

Computer Integrated Manufacture (CIM) – a system of manufacturing that uses computers to integrate the processing of production, business and manufacturing information in order to create more efficient production lines.

Computer simulation – method of modelling manufacturing processes, designs or other product characteristics using computer software.

Computer-aided engineering (CAE) – use of computer systems to analyse and simulate engineering designs under a variety of conditions to see if they will work.

Conductivity – the measure of a material's ability to have heat or electricity passed through it.

Consumer demand – the potential for the demand to 'pull' products through the distribution system; often stimulated by marketing and promotion.

Consumer goods – products purchased by consumers for their own consumption.

Consumer society – a social culture in which consumers are encouraged by advertising to buy consumer goods.

Continuous Improvement (CI) – (Kaizen) involves companies systematically looking for opportunities to make manufacturing operations leaner and more cost effective whilst also getting the most from their workforce by involving employees in all aspects of their operation. It aims to develop a culture where all employees are communicating better, working proactively to meet the company's business objectives and where implementing improvements is a matter of course.

Conversion – in timber production, the process in which a felled tree is turned into a useable source of timber.

Co-polymerisation – process in which two or more monomers combine to form a new material.

Coupling – joint that allows a rotating shaft to be easily connected or disconnected from a second shaft.

Crating – way of drawing a product by imagining it being made up of a number of boxes joined together.

Critical control points (CCPs) – points during the production cycle at which a product is monitored, to ensure that it is successfully manufactured to specification; ensures that any faulty components are rejected before they are processed further or built into the final assembly.

Critical path analysis – the breakdown of the whole manufacturing process into an ordered sequence of simple activities.

Critical technologies – technologies that need to be in place for a product to develop, e.g. the availability of well-established sensor technologies is critical in the development of industrial robots.

Cupping – a fault in timber where the board is hollowed along its length.

Current – the flow of an electric charge through a conductor.

Customer profile – profile of potential customers, such as gender, age, family group, income, education, beliefs and attitudes, taste, lifestyle and perception of products.

D

Darlington pair – two smaller transistors connected together, increasing the overall gain and sensitivity.

Data storage devices – such as CD-ROMs that are used for storing digital electronic information known as data.

Demographics – patterns and trends of population and society, such as age, gender or income bracket.

Dendrites – a crystal that has branched during its growth and has a tree-like look.

Design management – the planning of a product to include organisational, economic, legal and marketing considerations, as well as decisions about form and function.

Design specification – sets out the criteria that the product aims to achieve.

Designing for manufacture (DFM) – aims to minimise costs of components, assembly and product development cycles and to enable higher quality products to be made.

Desktop Video Conferencing (DTVC) – video conferencing applications that use video cameras mounted on standard desktop computer system such as an Intel-based PC, Apple Macintosh, or Unix workstation.

Digital signal – a signal that can only take fixed values between two points.

Digital system – electronic system that can exist in one of only two states: on or off.

Diode – an electrical component that will only allow a current to pass through it in one direction.

Direct costs – see 'variable costs'.

Down time – unproductive period when a computer system or machine is not operational usually because of technical problems, maintenance or in the case of machines, setting up new tools or reprogramming tools on a CNC machine.

Download – to get electronic information, software, files and documents from the Internet on to a computer system.

Ductility – the ability of a material to be drawn into a longer, thinner cross-section.

E

Economies of scale – occur when the cost of producing each product falls as the total volume of products produced increases.

Efficiency – a measure of what you get out in relation to what you put in.

Elastic deformation – when a material returns to its original shape and length once a deforming force has been removed, it is said to have been elastically deformed.

Electromotive force (emf) – a source of energy that can cause a current to flow in an electrical circuit or device.

Electronic Data Interchange/Exchange (EDI or EDE) – the electronic transfer of commercial or organisational information from one computer application to another. It is also known as paperless trading.

Electronic Product Definition (EPD) – makes use of CAD/CAM systems in which all of the product and processing data is generated and stored electronically in a database. The whole production team has access to the database, which evolves as the new product is developed. EPD enables the use of Computer Integrated Manufacture.

Enabling technologies – provide the useful technologies, for example drive motors and power control systems that make critical technologies effective.

Environmentally friendly plastics – plastics capable of bio-degrading naturally.

Enzymes – naturally-occurring proteins, used to create industrial products and processes. These enzymes are the same kind that help us digest food, compost garden rubbish and clean clothes.

ETSI – the European Telecommunications Standards Institute.

European Standards Organisation – joint standards organisation called CEN/CENELEC/ETSI.

Evaluation matrix – used to compare and evaluate a number of ideas against specification criteria. Each idea is given a score showing its strengths and weaknesses. Very weak ideas are eliminated, resulting in the emergence of strong ideas, which can be developed individually or combined in some way.

Expert systems – part of a general category of computer applications known as artificial intelligence (AI). They either perform a task that would normally be done by a human expert or they support the less expert to complete a task.

Exploded drawing – shows a product or component pulled apart, laid out in an ordered and linear form.

External failure costs – occur when products fail to reach the designed quality standards and are not detected until after being sold to the customer.

Extranet – an intranet that is partially accessible to authorised outsiders.

F

Fabrication – the joining and fixing together of various materials and components to form a new product.

Feedback – information generated within a system or process to enable modifications to be made to maintain the operation of a system or to ensure a consistent level of production.

Field effect transistors (FET) – electronic voltage amplifier.

Figure – the natural decorative pattern of the timbers grain.

File Server – a computer with data that can be accessed by other computers.

File Transfer Protocol (FTP) – method of transferring information files from Internet libraries directly to a computer.

Finite resources – see 'non-renewable resources'.

Firewall – a hardware or software system designed to prevent unauthorised access to or from a private computer network (see 'intranet').

Fitness-for-purpose – a product's fitness-for-purpose can be evaluated through its performance, price and aesthetic appeal.

Fixed costs – (indirect or overhead costs) fixed costs remain the same for one product or hundreds as they are not directly related to the number of products made. They include design and marketing, administration, maintenance, management, rent and rates, storage, lighting and heating, transport costs.

Foamants – bulking agents used as additives or fillers in the production of plastics.

Force field analysis – maps the forces for and against an idea or concept and the forces for and against changing it.

Form – created when a 'shape' becomes three dimensional, e.g. a circle becomes a sphere or cylinder.

Function – the means by which a product fulfils its purpose.

Fusibility – the ability of a material to join or fuse to itself or other materials.

G

Gantt chart – a simple chart that maps each task against the time available, together with an order of priority.

Geometric modelling – using computer programs for representing or modelling the shapes of three-dimensional components and assemblies. Geometric models are the basis of all CAD/CAM systems.

Glass Reinforced Plastic (GRP) – a matting of glass strands held rigid in a polyester resin; also called fibreglass.

Global manufacturing – the manufacture, by multinational companies, of products that may be designed in one country and manufactured in another.

Global market place – the marketing of products such as washing machines and cars, across the world. To be successful in this global market place, a company has to have a product that appeals to people in different countries and cultures.

Gravity die casting – the process by which molten metal is poured into metal or graphite moulds.

H

Hard sell – a hard sell advertisement has a simple and direct message, which projects a product's Unique Selling Points (USPs).

Hazard – source of or situation with potential harm or damage. Hazard control incorporates the manufacture of a product and its safe use by the consumer.

Heat treatment – the changing of a material's properties and characteristics due to the application of an external heat source.

High-technology production – the production of 'high tech' products, which emphasise technological appearance and modern industrial materials.

HTML (Hyper Text Mark Up Language) – text-based coding system and scripting language used when writing web pages.

HTTP (Hyper Text Transfer Protocol) – a transport protocol used when transmitting hypertext documents across the Internet.

Hyperlink – an electronic connection that allows links between different web pages to be made, usually shown in a different colour and/or underlined.

I

Indirect costs – see 'fixed costs'.

Industrial terminology – includes the use of technical terms, such as critical control point or production plan to demonstrate your understanding of industrial practices.

Injection moulding – highly automated manufacturing process in which a plasticised material is injected into a mould cavity under high pressure

Interface – device that will allow electrical signals into and out of a computer.

Internal failure costs – occur when products fail to reach the designed quality standards and are detected before being sold to the consumer.

Intranet – a network based on the Internet belonging to an organisation that is accessible only by authorised users with user names and passwords.

Inventory – a company's merchandise, raw materials, finished and unfinished products that have not yet been sold.

IOS (International Organisation for Standardisation) – world-wide federation of national standards bodies from some 130 countries, one from each country. IOS is a non-governmental organisation established in 1947.

ISDN (Integrated Systems Digital Network) – a high-speed, wide-bandwidth electronic communications service to carry digital data, digitised voice or video across digital phone lines.

ISO 9000 – a set of management processes and quality standards to ensure that a product meets the customer's requirements.

Isometric paper – has vertical lines, with all other lines drawn at 30° to the horizontal; useful as a backing for sketching an isometric view, in which the product is drawn at an angle with one corner nearest to view. In this type of drawing all vertical lines on a product remain as vertical, while all horizontal lines are drawn at 30° to the horizontal on the paper. No vanishing points are used and the height, width and length are shown as parallel sets of lines.

Isotope – one or two or more atoms having the same atomic number which contain different numbers of neutrons.

ISP (Internet Service Provider) – a company providing a connection to the Internet.

J

Jidoka – (autonomation) Japanese term for the automatic control of defects, a machine finds a problem, finds a solution, implements it without outside assistance and then carries on.

K

Kaizen – See 'continuous improvement'.

Kanban – Japanese term for a card signal or visual record, 'Kan' meaning card, 'Ban' meaning signal.

Kite Mark – a seal of approval by the British Standards Institute, awarded to any product that meets a British Standard, as long as the manufacturer has quality systems in place to ensure that every product is made to the same standard.

L

Laminating – process of sticking sheets of laminate or veneers together in either flat sheets or over curved formers.

Lash-ups – quick, rough models used to work out and test the relationship between different parts of a design.

Lattice structure – the pattern adopted when the atoms of a liquid solidify.

Level/scale of production – the size of production, e.g. a one-off such as a bridge or thousands such as chocolate bars.

Lever – a rigid rod that pivots about a fixed fulcrum.

Life-cycle assessment (LCA) – evaluates the materials, energy and waste used in a product through design, manufacture, distribution, use and end-of-life, which could be disposal, re-use or recycling.

Lifestyle marketing – the targeting of potential market groups and matching their needs with products.

Light-dependent resistor – a semiconductor whose resistance changes as the amount of light falling upon it changes.

Linkages – a series of levers connected together to change the direction of motion.

Liquid crystal display (LCD) – numerical and alphanumerical display system used in calculators, digital watches, etc.

Local Area Network (LAN) – collection of computers connected together to share information and other computer resources such as a printer.

Logic – a structured way of thinking or a set of operating principles applied to a manufacturing system or product to allow it to perform a specified task.

Logic gate – series of electronic switches that give a known output when a certain configuration on the input pins exists.

Logistics – the detailed organisation and implementation of a plan or operation such as supplying and moving parts, components and finished products within and from a manufacturing system.

M

Malleability – the ability of a material to be beaten or pressed into a shape without breaking or fracturing when cold.

Market driven – the concept that promotional activity and marketing pushes products through the market group to pull products through the distribution system.

Market led – the concept that promotional activity and marketing stimulates demand in customers in a distribution system.

Market potential – the potential for a product to sell into a specific target market group.

Market research – identifies the buying behaviour, taste and lifestyle of potential customers and establishes the amount of money they have to spend, their age group and the types of products they like to buy.

Market segment – a group of people with similar needs who wish to buy a certain type of product or service.

Market segmentation – a marketing technique that targets a group of customers with specific characteristics.

Market timing – attempting to predict future market directions, usually by examining recent price and volume data or economic data, and investing based on those predictions.

Marketing – anticipating and satisfying consumer needs while ensuring a company remains profitable.

Marketing plan – a set of marketing activities developed to match a company's products to selling opportunities; involves developing a competitive edge by providing reliable, high quality products at a price customers can afford, combined with the image they want the product to give them.

Mechanical Advantage (MA) – a mathematical relationship which exists between the load and effort in relationship to levers. The greater the MA, the easier it becomes to move the object.

Mechanical systems – a system that relies on a mechanical action to convert an input into an output motion.

Media – agencies such as the press, television or posters that carry advertising.

Metal crystals – basic unit cells which make up the lattice structure of a metal.

Metal grains – small crystals that form between dendrites on cooling.

Micro-structure – the structure of material as observed under a microscope.

Milestone planning – project management process involving identification of key points or milestones that needed to be reached in a production process if a product is to be successfully completed on time and to budget.

Miniaturisation – came about through developments in microchip technology, resulting in ever smaller products.

Modelling – visualising design ideas using hand or computer techniques in two dimensions (2D) or three dimensions (3D).

Modem (MOdulator/DEModulator) – an electronic device that connects a computer to a phone line allowing the transfer of data to and from other computers when connecting to the Internet.

Monomers – a compound whose molecules can join together to form a polymer.

Moodboard – used by a professional designer to explore moods or themes and to give a product an identity. Moodboards communicate ideas on design, illustrating themes, trends, form, colours, texture and styling details. These product 'stories' are inspiration for generating design ideas.

Multimeter – measuring device used to measure current, voltage, resistance, and also used as a continuity tester.

Multinational companies – operate in more than one country and used to be mainly associated with mineral exploitation or plantations, such as cotton or food.

N

Niche markets – target market groups for whom products are designed and marketed.

Noise – unwanted electrical signals, e.g. fuzzy TV pictures caused by electrical interference.

Non-renewable resources – finite resources, such as oil or coal, which will eventually be exhausted unless action is taken.

Normalising – process applying only to steel and used to refine the grain after it has become coarse grained as a result of forging or work hardening.

O

One-point perspective – the simplest form of perspective drawing in which the front view is drawn as a flat two-dimensional image. All receding lines are then taken back to a single vanishing point, to give a three-dimensional view.

Open-loop system – a control system that incorporates no feedback, being a pure linear progression from the input to the output.

Orthographic drawing – see 'working drawing'.

Output transducers – devices such as bulbs, motors and alarms.

Overhead costs – see 'fixed costs'.

P

Parametric designing – involves establishing the mathematical relationships between the various parts that make up a shape or a product. Once the parameters are determined a designer can model exactly what would happen if particular sizes were redefined because if one measurement is changed all the others are changed in the correct proportion.

Patents – issued by government authority, these documents grant the sole right to make, use or sell a design, making it both unique and protected.

Performance modelling – working prototypes that enable the designer to test the function of a design against the design specification.

PEST – part of the basic structure of a marketing plan. It involves analysing values, such as political, economic, social and technological issues related to marketing a product.

Photochromic glass – type of glass that darkens when exposed to light and returns to its original state in the dark.

Photovoltaic cell – a semiconductor that generates a small voltage when exposed to bright light.

Pictorial view – shows the most realistic view of a product, sometimes called an 'artistic impression'.

Piezo-electric actuators/transducers – electronic device capable of generating a small voltage when pressure is applied, or a small movement if voltage is applied to it

Planning horizon – how far to plan forward, determined by how far ahead demand is known and by the times to pass through the manufacturing operation.

Plastic deformation – when a material has been extended beyond its elastic limit it will not return to its original shape and can then be said to have been plastically deformed.

Plasticity – the ability of a material to be moulded.

Poka-yoke – Japanese term meaning a device or procedure to prevent a defect during order-taking or manufacture (also called baka-yoke). The nearest translation is 'foolproofing' or 'mistake-proofing'.

Polluter pays – the concept that those generating, handling and treating wastes should pay large fines if they allow potentially harmful materials to enter the environment.

Polymerisation – chemical reaction that occurs when a polymer is formed.

Potential divider – two resistors connected in series, set up to divide the potential in the ratio of resistor one to resistor two.

Potentiometer – three-legged device that can be configured to work either as a potential divider or rheostat.

Prevention costs – costs of 'making it right first time'. Prevention costs include those relating to the creation of and conformance to a quality assurance system and the management of quality.

Primary processing – the conversion of raw materials into usable stock for production, e.g. steel making.

Primary research – facts and figures that are collected specifically to provide information and help achieve the research objectives.

Primary sector – concerned with the extraction of natural resources such as mining and quarrying.

Product Data Management (PDM) software – integrates the use of computer systems, including CAD/CAM and computer integrated manufacturing (CIM). PDM software enables the design and development of virtual products on screen. The software organises and communicates accurate, up-to-date information in a database, monitors production and enables fast, efficient and cost-effective manufacturing on a global scale.

Product design cycle – process leading to the design and manufacture of a product involving design, make, redesign and remake, which starts with a perception of need and includes many influences throughout the process such as government policy, manufacturers, advertisers, retailers and consumers.

Product viability – essential to the existence of a manufacturing company and to the employment of its workforce; relates to the cost of manufacture, the product's market potential and the potential profit from manufacturing the product.

Production capacity – the maximum number of products that can be made in a specified time.

Production chain – the sequence of activities required to turn raw materials into finished products for the consumer.

Production plan – shows how to manufacture a product, based on the breakdown of the whole process into an ordered sequence of simple activities; includes all specifications, the stages of production, resource requirements, and the production schedule.

Production schedule – an ordered sequence of processes that are required to manufacture a product.

Production team – flexible, organised, skilled, versatile people, who work collectively, make joint decisions and share the responsibility for the design and manufacture of products.

Productivity – a measurement of the efficiency with which raw materials (production inputs) are turned into products (manufactured outputs). High productivity results in lower labour costs per unit of production and a higher potential profit.

Profit – the amount left of the selling price of a product, after all costs of manufacture have been paid.

Programmable logic controller (PLC) – small but complex systems containing timers, counters and many other special functions capable of almost any type of control application, including motion control, data manipulation and advanced computing functions such as manufacturing plant management.

Protocol – an agreed standard or set of rules. See 'File Transfer Protocol' and 'HTTP'.

Pulley – a circular disc normally with a V-shaped groove cut around its circumference.

Q

Qualitative research – an investigation to find out how people think and feel about issues and why they behave as they do.

Quality control (QC) – checking at critical control points against specifications for accuracy and safety, so that a product meets consumer and environmental expectations.

Quality indicators – quality control techniques, such as inspection, testing and sampling, that are applied at critical control points during manufacture to ensure the product meets specifications. Quality indicators may be attributes that can only be right or wrong, such as using the correct type of wood or variables that can vary between specified limits, such as meeting a tolerance of +/–1.0mm.

Quality Management System (QMS) – uses structured procedures to manage the quality of the designing and making process.

Quality of design – a product that is well-designed and attractive to the target market; meets specifications; uses suitable materials; is easy to manufacture and maintain; and is safe for the user and the environment.

Quality of manufacture – refers to a well-made product, that uses suitable materials; meets specifications and performance requirements; is manufactured by a suitable, safe method; is made within budget limits to sell at an attractive selling price; and is manufactured for safe use and disposal.

Quantitative research – an investigation to find out how many people hold similar views or display particular characteristics.

Questionnaire – a standardised set of questions designed to collect data that is relevant to the research objectives.

Quick Response Manufacturing (QRM) – a manufacturing system able to respond quickly at all levels of business or production processes in response to market trends and changing demand patterns.

R

Rapid Prototyping (RPT) – a CNC application that creates 3D objects using laser technology to solidify liquid polymers in a process called stereo-lithography.

Raster graphics – (bit map graphics) images of a surface or solid model produced by an intensity of points called picture elements or pixels.

Rectification – the process of converting an alternating current into a direct current.

Recycling waste materials – form of waste management in which waste materials from the production process are used in a different manufacturing process.

Relay – device used to interface two separate circuits that operate at two different supply voltages.

Renewable resources – flow naturally in nature or are living things which can be regrown and used again. They include wind, tides, waves, water power, solar energy, geothermal, biomass, ocean thermal energy and forests.

Resistance welding – welding processes that use a material's resistance to the flow of electrical current in order to generate sufficient heat to provide localised melting and fusing of the material.

Resistors – electronic component used to control the current flowing in an electrical circuit.

Re-using waste materials – see 'recycling waste materials'.

Right first time – the aim of quality assurance, to make sure the product is right first time, every time. It involves making products that meet the specification, on time and to budget.

Risk assessment – identifying risks to the health and safety of people and the environment.

S

Seasoning – the process of reducing the moisture content in timber.

Secondary processing – the working of a material using engineering processes such as turning or milling.

Secondary research – facts and figures that are already available, having been collected for another purpose by a range of organisations.

Secondary sector – concerned with the processing of primary raw materials and the manufacture of products.

Selling price – price at which a product can be sold in order to make a profit. It generally includes variable costs, fixed costs and a realistic profit.

Semiconductor transducers – semi-conductors whose resistance changes depending on the surrounding environment.

Server – a host computer that distributes and stores data on a network.

Shaft – rod that rotates and normally has fixed to it pulleys, sprocket wheels or gears.

Shape memory alloys – alloys which can be plastically deformed at pre-determined temperatures.

Shape memory polymers – plastics that revert to their original form when heated.

Smart materials – the properties of smart materials can change in response to an input, such as Piezo-electric actuators; provide opportunities for the development of new types of sensors, actuators and structural components, which can reduce the overall size and complexity of a device.

Soft sell – promotes a product's image, with which consumers can identify and is often associated with brand advertising.

Solar panels – these panels normally have water pumped through them that gets heated by the sun's energy.

Specialised components – components that are manufactured specifically for a particular product application.

Sprocket – thin wheel that has tiny teeth around its edge, normally used with a chain to transmit rotary motion, as on a bicycle.

Standard components – components such as nuts and bolts that are supplied ready to use.

Standards – documented agreements with technical specifications or other precise criteria to be used consistently as rules, guidelines, or definitions of characteristics, to ensure that materials, products, processes and services are fit-for-purpose.

Statutory rights – what consumers should reasonably expect when buying or hiring products and services. Statutory rights are enforced and regulated by a wide range of legislation relating to consumer protection and fair trading.

Strategic technologies – ways of thinking and operating, e.g. artificial intelligence.

Sub-assemblies – component parts of a product that are already made up of smaller components.

Supply chain – companies and organisations that collaborate to produce raw materials, components and end-products for specific end-uses aimed at specific target market groups.

Survey – way of collecting quantitative data, often about behaviour, attitudes and opinions of a sample in a target market group.

Sustainable development – a concept that puts forward the idea that the environment should be seen as an asset, a stock of available wealth. If each generation spends this wealth without investing in the future, then the world will one day run out of resources.

SWOT – part of the basic structure of a marketing plan. It involves analysing a product's strengths, weaknesses, opportunities and the threats from competition.

Synoptic assessment – the drawing together of skills, knowledge and understanding acquired in different parts of the whole A level course.

T

Target market group – all the customers of all the companies supplying a specific product.

Target marketing – the process of identifying market groups and developing products for it.

Technical drawing – contains factual information relating to appearance and dimension and is based on British Standard BS7308. See 'working drawing'.

Telematics – a new technology that allows a product to be managed electronically from receipt of the customer order through development, manufacturing, delivery and after-sales support.

Tempering – process of removing the brittleness caused as a result of hardening.

Tertiary sector – concerned with industries that provide a service; employs the most people in developed countries and includes education, retailing, advertising, marketing, banking and finance.

Test marketing – involves introducing a product in a small sector of a target market to test its viability before incurring the expense of a full-scale product launch.

Test models – used to test different parts of a design and are often built from kits to test mechanical, structural or control problems.

Thermistor – a semiconductor whose resistance can change depending on the temperature around it.

Thermo-ceramics – ceramic materials capable of withstanding exceptionally high temperatures.

3D CAD systems – a computer aided design system that can produce virtual images in three dimensions to present more realistic representations of products and assemblies.

Thumbnail – a small rough sketch showing the main parts of a design in the form of simple diagrams.

Thyristor – three-legged electronic semi-conductive switch that can be used as a latch.

Time bucket – the unit of time on which a production schedule is constructed and is typically daily or weekly.

Time delay circuit – a capacitor/resistor network that is capable of producing an electronic time delay.

Tolerance – the degree by which a component's dimensions may vary from the norm and still be able to fulfil its function.

Total design concept – design using multimedia 'toolkits' to access an integrated on-screen design modelling environment that includes systems linked to production databases to analyse and plan for manufacture.

Total Quality Control (TQC) – the system that Japan has developed to implement Kaizen for the complete life cycle of a product.

Transducer – device for converting physical signals into electrical signals. An input transducer responds to a physical change by producing an electrical signal to represent the change. An output transducer takes an electrical signal from a system and produces a physical change as an output.

Transistor – a semiconductor device that can exist as an insulator or conductor. It can be used as an electronic switch and amplifier.

Transmission systems – mechanical device for transmitting motion to another part of a system, such as two shafts beside each other.

Turning – the process of machining resistant materials using a lathe.

2D CAD drawings – have length and width but no depth; they are two-dimensional.

Two-point perspective – most common form of perspective drawing in which the vertical lines stay vertical, while all other lines recede to two vanishing points. These points are placed on a horizontal line called the eye level. If a product is drawn below eye level, the top will be visible. If it is above eye level, the underside is visible.

U

Unique selling proposition (USP) – a product's unique features and advantages over a competitor's products.

Unix – a computer operating system that was developed by AT&T in the 1960s. The system was used extensively during the establishment of the Internet.

Upload – to send electronic information from your computer to another location via the Internet or other types of network (the opposite of download).

URL (Uniform Resource Locator) – convention used when naming pages on the World Wide Web.

V

Vacuum forming – a plastic processing method in which a softened plastic sheet is pushed down on to a mould, to make products such as baths.

Value analysis – the process of close study of a product in order to reduce manufacturing costs and/or increase the product's perceived value.

Variable costs – (direct costs) variable costs increase with the number of products made. They include depreciation of plant and equipment.

Vector graphics – (object-oriented graphics) are images comprised of a collection of lines rather than dots as in raster graphics.

Velocity Ratio (VR) – the relationship between the input and output speeds of the driven and driver shafts.

Videoconferencing – a conference conducted between two or more participants at different sites using computer networks to transmit audio and video data.

Virtual Reality Modelling Language (VRML) – a specification for displaying and interracting with 3D objects on the World Wide Web.

Volatile organic compounds (VOC) – solvent emissions produced by manufacturing processes. VOCs are involved in the formation of photochemical oxidants, such as ozone, which is a major cause of smog and poor air quality. VOC emissions can be treated using biotechnology.

Voltage – a difference in potential between two points in a circuit.

W

Waste minimisation – involves reducing, re-using or recycling materials used in manufacture.

Web browser – software such as Netscape Navigator or Microsoft Internet Explorer that provides the interface between a computer and the Internet; for example, it allows the capture and display of Web pages.

Work hardening – the process of making a material harder by working it, e.g. pulling it through a die to make it smaller in cross-section.

Work order – see 'production schedule'.

Working drawing – drawn full size or to scale and contains factual information relating to appearance and dimension. An orthographic drawing is produced to BS7308, which forms the basis of the international standard to which all technical drawings are made. It should include all the necessary information for you or anyone else to make the product.

Work schedule – see 'production schedule'.

World Wide Web (WWW) – part of the Internet consisting of millions of pages of electronically stored information and graphics, complete with hyperlinks. The Web has now become a gigantic global marketplace for products, services and self-promotion.

Index